NATIONS [illegible] ORLD

ARGENTINA — H. S. Ferns
Professor of Political Science, University of Birmingham

AUSTRALIA — O. H. K. Spate
Director, Research School of Pacific Studies, Australian National University, Canberra

AUSTRIA — Karl R. Stadler
Professor of Modern and Contemporary History, University of Linz

BELGIUM — Vernon Mallinson
Professor of Comparative Education, University of Reading

BURMA — F. S. V. Donnison, C.B.E.
Formerly Chief Secretary to the Government of Burma Historian, Cabinet Office, Historical Section 1949-66

CHINA — Victor Purcell, C.M.G.
Late Lecturer in Far Eastern History, Cambridge

CZECHOSLOVAKIA — William V. Wallace
Professor of History, New University of Ulster

DENMARK — W. Glyn Jones
Professor of Scandinavian Studies, University of Newcastle-upon-Tyne

MODERN EGYPT — Tom Little, M.B.E.
Former Managing Director and General Manager of Regional News Services (Middle East), Ltd, London

EL SALVADOR — Alastair White
Lecturer in Sociology, University of Stirling

EAST GERMANY — David Childs
Senior Lecturer in Politics, University of Nottingham

MODERN GREECE

John Campbell
Fellow of St Antony's College, Oxford

Philip Sherrard
Lecturer in History of the Orthodox Church,
King's College, London

HUNGARY

Paul Ignotus
Formerly Hungarian Press Counsellor, London, 1947-49,
and Member, Presidential Board, Hungarian Writers' Associati

INDONESIA

Donald W. Fryer
Professor of Geography
University of Hawaii

James C. Jackson
Professor of Modern Asian Studies
Griffith University, Brisbane

ITALY

Muriel Grindrod, O.B.E.
Formerly Editor of International Affairs *and*
The World Today
Assistant Editor The Annual Register

MEXICO

Peter Calvert
Senior Lecturer in Politics,
University of Southampton

NORWAY

Ronald G. Popperwell
Fellow of Clare Hall, and Lecturer in Norwegian,
Cambridge

PAKISTAN

Ian Stephens, C.I.E.
Formerly Editor of The Statesman,
Calcutta and Delhi, 1942-51
Fellow, King's College, Cambridge, 1952-58

PERU

Sir Robert Marett, K.C.M.G., O.B.E.
H.M. Ambassador in Lima, 1963-67

THE PHILIPPINES

Keith Lightfoot
Naval, Military, and Air Attaché, British Embassy,
Manila, 1964-67

POLAND

Václav L. Beneš
Late Professor of Political Science,
Indiana University

Norman J. G. Pounds
Professor of History and Geography,
Indiana University

PORTUGAL	J. B. Trend *Late Fellow, Christ's College, and Emeritus Professor of Spanish, Cambridge*
SOUTH AFRICA	John Cope *Formerly Editor-in-Chief of* The Forum *and South Africa Correspondent of* The Guardian
THE SOVIET UNION	Elisabeth Koutaissoff *Formerly Professor of Russian, Victoria University, Wellington*
SPAIN	George Hills *Formerly Correspondent and Spanish Programme Organizer, British Broadcasting Corporation*
SWEDEN	Irene Scobbie *Senior Lecturer in Swedish, University of Aberdeen*
SWITZERLAND	Christopher Hughes *Professor of Politics, University of Leicester*
SYRIA	Tabitha Petran
MODERN TURKEY	Geoffrey Lewis *Senior Lecturer in Islamic Studies, Oxford*
YUGOSLAVIA	Stevan K. Pavlowitch *Lecturer in Balkan History, University of Southampton*

NATIONS OF THE MODERN WORLD

CZECHOSLOVAKIA

The Author

William V. Wallace graduated in History at the University of Glasgow and in Czechoslovak Regional Studies at the University of London. He has visited Czechoslovakia several times since 1949 and has researched in its archives. He has also travelled and studied in the Soviet Union. In 1953-54 he lectured at the University of Pittsburgh and studied the history of Slavonic immigration into the United States. He has held lecturing appointments in the Universities of London, Aberdeen, and Durham, and is now Professor of History in the New University of Ulster, Coleraine. He has contributed to *International Affairs, Slavonic Review, Journal of American Studies*, etc.

CZECHOSLOVAKIA

By WILLIAM V. WALLACE

Routledge
Taylor & Francis Group
LONDON AND NEW YORK

First published 1976 by Westview Press

Published 2018 by Routledge
52 Vanderbilt Avenue, New York, NY 10017
2 Park Square, Milton Park, Abingdon, Oxon OX14 4RN

Routledge is an imprint of the Taylor & Francis Group, an informa business

Library of Congress Cataloging in Publication Data

Wallace, William V
Czechoslovakia.

(Nations of the modern world)

Includes index.
1. Czechoslovak Republic—History. I. Title.
II. Series.
DB196.W28 1976 943.7 76-4494
ISBN 0-89158-027-1

ISBN 13: 978-0-367-02068-2 (hbk)
ISBN 13: 978-0-367-17055-4 (pbk)

Note on the Pronunciation of Czech and Slovak Names

THE STRESS IS ALWAYS on the first syllable. An accent (e.g., á or ů) lengthens the vowel.

c is pronounced like the ts in tsar
č is pronounced like the ch in church
d' is pronounced like the d in duty
ě is pronounced like the ye in yes
ch is pronounced like the ch in loch
j is pronounced like the y in yawn
ň is pronounced like the n in new
š is pronounced like the sh in shall
t' is pronounced like the t in tune
u is pronounced like the oo in soot
ý is pronounced like the ee in meet
ž is pronounced like the s in usual

ř is a composite sound like rr and ž spoken at the same time. It occurs, for example, in the name of the composer, Dvořák.

Contents

List of Illustrations

(All are inserted between pages 192 *and* 193)

List of Maps

Acknowledgements

ACKNOWLEDGEMENTS are due to the following copyright-holders for permission to reproduce the illustrations:

Čestmír Amort, *Heydrichiáda* (Prague, Naše Vojsko, 1965): 13
B. Bílek, *Fifth Column at Work* (London, Trinity House and Lindsay Drummond, 1945): 12
M. Bouček, *Praha v Únoru 1948* (Prague, Státní nakladatelství, 1963): 20
Camera Press Limited: 7, 9, 11, 18, 26, 27, 28, 31, 32
Czechoslovak News Agency: 22
E. B. Hitchcock, *Beneš* (London, Hamish Hamilton, 1940): 6
V. Hlavsa, *Praha očima staletí* (Prague, Orbis, 1967): 1
Jaroslav Kladiva, *Kultura a politika 1945-1948* (Prague, Svoboda, 1968): 19
B. Laštovička, *V Londýně za války* (Prague, Státní nakladatelství, 1961): 15, 17, 29
Compton Mackenzie, *Dr Beneš* (London, Harrap, 1946): 16
F. Němec, *Social Security in Czechoslovakia* (London, Czechoslovak Ministry of Foreign Affairs Information Service, 1943): 10
Karel Pichlík, *Zahraniční odboj 1914-1918* (Prague, Svoboda, 1969): 3, 4
Paul Popper Limited: 2, 8, 14, 21
VHÚ, Prague: 5

Numbers 23, 24, and 25 are from the author's own collection

Introduction

CZECHOSLOVAKIA ONLY CAME INTO EXISTENCE IN 1918. But the history of the Czechs and Slovaks and the lands they inhabit goes back a long way. It is a history that is important for its own sake as well as for the legacy it gave the modern state and the understanding it brings to a study of present-day Czechoslovakia. It is also a history so rich in material and so closely linked with the fortunes of other peoples that its earlier centuries deserve detailed treatment, impossible within this book. Enough must be said, however, to indicate where the Czechs and Slovaks came from and what they looked back to.

The new state came out of the national movement, which could be placed quite far back in time. However, to appreciate the circumstances in which Czechoslovakia emerged and the driving-forces behind it, it is best to start in the aftermath of the 1848 revolution. It was then that the Czechs and Slovaks joined those peoples known, and knowing themselves, to be searching for their identity and ultimately their independence. It was then that economic, social, cultural, and political forces came together in sufficient measure and with sufficient strength to transform provincial politicking and academic curiosity into a national movement of European dimensions.

* * * * *

The Slav tribes, from whom the modern Czechs and Slovaks are descended, moved into the area that Czechoslovakia now comprises between the fifth and seventh centuries. They displaced existing Celtic settlements, of which many interesting remains have been found. But the first important state to emerge was Great Moravia. In the course of the ninth century its frontiers extended into the Hungarian plain and provided the first and one of the few instances of Czech and Slovak groups living under one rule. Initially it derived its Christianity from Byzantium through the missionaries Saints Cyril and Methodius. Their names were subsequently much revered; and the tradition of looking to the East for occasional guidance or support was firmly established. However, the Germans were already too well established as neighbours for it to be possible for Moravia to resist the blandishments of the Western Church. The Czechs and Slovaks, therefore, spent the next thousand years or so in the Western orbit, at times pleased to co-operate with Rome, at others in conflict with Rome's representatives. The inroad of the Magyars to the Hungarian plain at the end of the ninth century not only destroyed Great Moravia but also confirmed the separation of the Czechs and Slovaks from purposeful contact with Byzantium. It had the further long-term effect of splitting the Czech and Slovak tribes. The Czechs passed the next ten centuries or thereabouts in conflict with the Germans, and the Slovaks the same time under Magyar rule.

The Czechs were remarkably fortunate in their geographical location. Bohemia and Moravia are surrounded by mountains, lower in the south-east than elsewhere, but a fair barrier against the incursion of enemies. The country is rich and wooded and a natural centre of communication. The Vltava runs north to the Elbe and the Morava south to the Danube, and there are passes enough for a good series of roads. The Slovaks were less happy. Pushed back into the foothills of the Carpathians, they learned to be stalwart, but they lacked prosperity. It was therefore the Czechs, under the Přemyslid dynasty which saw them through to the start of the fourteenth century, who were able to resist their neighbours, clear their woods, open their silver mines, build their towns, and lay their roads. By the time the ambitious, successful, German Luxemburg family acquired the Czech throne in 1310, Prague was already a commercial centre of importance. But Bohemia and Moravia were not completely defensible, and their very strategic and economic value made them a natural object of German ambition. Over four centuries, German interference in the affairs of the Czech Lands left its mark. One prince became a feudatory of the Holy Roman Emperor; another gladly received a crown; another got the office of Imperial Cupbearer; yet another won recognition of the Přemyslids' hereditary rights. In one sense the Czechs profited; but in another they did not, since they became increasingly involved in Imperial wrangles. In a time of Imperial weakness in the thirteenth century the Czechs became temporary masters of the Austrian Lands and made an enemy of the rising house of Habsburg. Finally, during the twelfth and thirteenth centuries there was a steady acceleration of German immigration to the mines along the frontier and to towns throughout the country.

Economically this was advantageous; but it added an internal dimension to Czech-German competition, so that by 1310 the relationship of the Czechs with Germany and with their own Germans had established itself as a continuing issue in their history.

The accession of John of Luxemburg was of great importance to the Czech Lands. He involved his new subjects in the affairs of all Europe, he won them Silesia, and he secured his son's election as Emperor. From the time of Charles IV, who was king of Bohemia-Moravia from 1346 to 1378, dates much that is best in the Czech past. Prague became the hub of the Holy Roman Empire and the Czech Lands its centre. The economy prospered and the capital flourished. Charles added to the style and culture of Prague by importing architects from all over Europe and building much of the Gothic that has given it character and brought it admirers ever since, and by establishing the university that bears his name. The intellectual ferment that followed put the Czechs at the forefront of reformist ideas and, along with the rapidly changing social situation, turned the Czech Lands into the seat of perhaps the first Christian reformation.

In an age of mounting criticism of the Church for its blatant materialism and involvement in politics Czech scholars and theologians drew some of their inspiration from abroad, but for the most part the reform movement was native. Jan Hus was only one among several outstanding critics who questioned the yawning gap between teaching and practice and who went so far as to advocate that laymen should partake of the chalice. But he was the most famous because of the actions he took and the results to which they led. In the opening decade of the fifteenth century his doctrines were well publicized and won many converts; it was a direct challenge to Rome. He also appealed to the artisans and the urban poor and to the peasants in the countryside, all of whom had grievances against better-off German immigrants. As dean of the faculty of arts in the university, where the Czech majority among the students were subordinate to the non-Czech minority, he found himself advocating the expulsion of the Germans. It was a challenge to the Empire and to Rome's political involvement in its affairs. In 1412 he was excommunicated. In 1414 he was summoned to the council of Constance to answer a charge of heresy—and given a promise of safe conduct by the Emperor; but in 1415 he was burned at the stake. A confrontation between the Czechs and the Imperial forces, backed by Rome, was virtually inevitable and came, on a question of the succession, in 1420. The first reformation was followed by the first of the religious wars, called at the time a crusade.

Jan Hus had international standing; but most Czechs saw him as a national martyr. The war that lasted until 1434 produced its heroes and its legends too. The era of Hus and the Husite wars is one that has frequently served the Czechs for inspiration. Yet the wars further embittered Czech-German relations; and practically exhausted the Czech Lands. The Czechs were not beaten; they were allowed at the end to give the laity communion in both kinds. However, they had frequently been split among themselves on religious and social grounds; and it finally took a pitched battle between the two main groups to get agreement to peace-making. War had proved very costly, and the peasantry in particular were impoverished. By contrast, the landowners, especially the German, were more firmly entrenched and even the towns began to feel their pressure. The Czech Lands started on that slow decline which led to their total submersion in the Empire in the seventeenth century.

There were still moments of glory. One such was during the reign of Jiří of Poděbrad, a noble elected king by the estates. His proposal in 1464 for a league of Christian kings to maintain the peace of Europe and to protect it against the Turks was one of the earliest models for an international order to do what Pope and Emperor together could or would not do. Unfortunately, however, his suggestion reflected not only the manifest disintegration of medieval Christendom and the growing threat to it after the Ottoman capture of Constantinople in 1453, but also the weakness of the Czech Lands in a Europe of great powers. It was also significant that, in order to preserve his own position among the nobles and to shield his kingdom against further Papal and Imperial intervention, he had to persecute the so-called Czech Brethren, a pacifist but radical and reformist group, and so weaken further the ideological core of Czech independence. It was virtually inevitable that, when a Czech army was defeated and the Czech king slain by the Turks in 1526, the Czech nobles who now dominated the estates should choose as their king a future Emperor, the Habsburg Ferdinand I.

The history of the Czechs was now interlocked with that of the Austrian Habsburgs and their domination over what still passed for the Holy Roman Empire. Theoretically the Czechs were still independent. They had their own estates and they elected their own monarch; their thought was reinvigorated by the ideas of Luther and Calvin; and during the reign of Rudolf II, who conducted the Imperial court in Prague from 1583 to 1612, the Czech Lands again became a centre of learning and culture, housing some of the great names in European astronomy and painting. But the basis for their independence was fast disappearing. Intermittent Turkish ravages gave the Czechs little taste for isolation and the Habsburgs every excuse for intervention. The Turkish stranglehold on the Balkans terminated the once lucrative trade through the Czech Lands to the Middle East. The discovery of the new sea routes to the Orient moved commerce and banking to the north-west of Europe and further undermined the prosperity of central Europe. The precious metals unloaded from the New World drastically reduced the value of Czech silver. The Czech economy lost its viability, and the burghers lost in power to the nobles. The nobles in turn improved their wealth and standing by increasing their holdings at the expense of the gentry and by exploiting the peasants through the imposition of feudal-type dues. Service to the Habsburgs as kings of the Czech, Austrian, or Hungarian Lands, or as Emperors, was rewarded by grants of land in Bohemia, Moravia, and Silesia, so that more and more alien families were introduced. By the beginning of the seventeenth century both the possibility and the likelihood of Czech resistance to total subservience to the Habsburgs seemed slight at the very time that Habsburg ambition was reaching its zenith.

There was more than one revolt against Habsburg rule in the course of the sixteenth century. But their suppression was invariably used as an opportunity for strengthening the hand of the nobles against the other estates. The very success of the Czechs in retaining some semblance of independence and persisting in their mainly Protestant ways also incited one of the Habsburgs to settle both accounts with them. While still heir apparent, Ferdinand II helped to organize a vain attack on Czech liberties. All he succeeded in doing was spreading Czech hostility to the ranks of the nobility and ensuring that, when the estates met in 1618 to elect a new king, they did not choose him but opted instead for his enemy the Elector Palatine Frederick IV. It was, however, the last gallant gesture of the old and declining Czech Lands. Frederick was not merely a poor revolutionary. As a Calvinist, he was anathema to the Jesuit-trained Ferdinand; and as a leader of the Protestant Union in the Empire and an Imperial elector, he was already enough of a political danger. The Czech revolt escalated into the so-called Thirty Years War. The Czech rebels were comparatively few; they could not call on a thriving citizenry and they could get little help from an enserfed peasantry; they had few independent institutions and little wealth. They were too slow to get allies and found none to uphold their cause to the end. The supposedly religious wars of the sixteenth century became the naked political struggles of the seventeenth and eighteenth. After their defeat at the battle of the White Mountain in 1620 the Czechs lost their independent place in history for two centuries. The Habsburg Emperors became hereditary kings of the Czech Lands; they eliminated the Czech nobility and gentry and replaced them with German-speaking foreign adventurers; they took away the few privileges of such Czech burghers as were left, and let the landowners heap burdens on the peasantry; and they forced the entire population back into Catholicism.

After 1620 many of the leaders of the revolt went abroad to carry on the struggle in all the armies of Europe. Religious persecution forced thousands of other Czechs to flee, the most famous of them perhaps the Czech Brethren pastor Jan Amos Komenský, or Comenius, renowned for his advocacy of enlightenment and humanity in education. But the Peace of Westphalia which ended the Thirty Years War in 1648 and the treaties which ended the plethora of struggles right down to the Revolutionary and Napoleonic wars left the Czech Lands securely in the Emperor's hands. Even Napoleon's final destruction of the Holy Roman Empire in 1804 did not affect the Habsburgs' hold on them. They were an integral part of the new Austria, of the Habsburg Empire.

The period after the White Mountain was not all darkness. Admirers of Baroque in architecture might even think of it as a period of light. The Czech language was kept alive by the peasantry; and there were Catholic priests who imbibed the spirit of the past and kept it living, if hidden, in their manuscripts. The fierce peasant risings against the conditions in which the nobility made them live, work, and die were savagely repressed well into the eighteenth century. But the atmosphere of the European Enlightenment spread slowly even to the Habsburg Empire, and both Maria Theresa and Joseph II introduced some reforms to their dominions. Thus in 1781, six years after the most violent rising yet in Bohemia, Joseph published a decree which restored to the peasants their freedom of movement. They were still obliged to give labour service, or make payment in lieu; and they had other burdens. But the first step had been taken towards emancipation and towards large-scale migration to the towns, both of which would in the end stimulate social and national revolution. The eighteenth century also saw the first signs of an industrial revolution in the Czech Lands. Most of the great estates had long milled their own flour or brewed their own beer, but some of the more aware now turned to manufacturing textiles in modern factories. However ill-gotten, there was agricultural wealth for industrial development, some of which materialized in the towns at the turn of the century. Yet, of more immediate importance than the changing circumstances of country and town was the changing attitude of the nobles. Another by-product of the European Enlightenment was the steady strengthening of central government. Although this had much to commend it, the effect on the nobles in the Czech Lands—of foreign extraction and German speaking though they were—was to encourage in them a kind of Czech provincialism. They had their rights, and some of them now had wealth; they were not going to be pushed around by people in Vienna. In 1784 a group of them established what was allowed in 1790 to assume the privileged title of the Royal Bohemian Society of Sciences and became the centre of the Czech cultural revival.

Although some of the fighting of the years 1792-1815 took place on Czech soil, there was no direct impact from the ideas of the French Revolution. Subsequently, so long as Prince Metternich was the major influence on Habsburg policy, the whole atmosphere was inimical to change. Yet the situation in Europe was different. An almost legendary European empire had been beaten; France itself had roughed out a nationalist theory, had practised it, and produced a nationalist reaction; the future lay not with the old empires, but with the new nations—though the change might take time. Isolation or not, Metternich or not, the Czechs could not for long continue outside the European mainstream. Existing trends took on a new significance. The peasantry were increasingly disgruntled with the battery of obligations expected of them and with the high-handed behaviour of the landowners' officials. The number of urban workers was growing, and the distress of depression and unemployment was becoming more common. The cautious cultural revival gathered speed; and more and more Czechs in the countryside and the towns began to realise that they really were Czechs.

It was again under the patronage of a noble family that the Bohemian Museum was set up in Prague in 1818 to house important scientific collections. Its German journal failed in 1831; by contrast, the circulation of the Czech version grew rapidly. The German provincial nobility also gave essential support to a number of outstanding scholars whose writings facilitated and shaped the cultural revival. Josef Dobrovský made Czech a literary language once more by reforming the orthography, producing the first grammar, and writing a history of the language and its literature. Josef Jungmann translated foreign classics to demonstrate the capabilities of Czech and put together the first large dictionary. Pavel Šafařík, Slovak by birth, dissected the early history of the Slav peoples and made the Czechs justifiably proud of their ethnic origins. And most outstanding and influential of all, František

Palacký set to work on his great history of the Czech nation which not only reconstructed the past but effectively created a national philosophy out of it. It was also Palacký who made a success of the Museum journal in Czech by transforming it into an outlet for nationalist thought and who used the Museum as a base for developing the *Matice česká*, or Czech Foundation, which collected money for publishing in Czech. Though patronised by the nobility, Palacký soon outdistanced them. By the 1840s they were petitioning for a restoration of the rights of the Czech estates, which meant German rights, but Palacký was feeling his way towards Czech national claims within or even against the Empire. The *Matice česká*, numbering only a handful when it was founded in 1831, was over two thousand strong by 1848. And in the meantime the small but growing Czech middle class in Prague had begun to penetrate various hitherto German organisations and to establish political clubs of their own.

The backbone of this Czech movement was provided by intellectuals. Some were writers, others merely graduates. The school reforms of Joseph II had made it possible for numbers of young Czechs to show their abilities and even get to university. Intellectuals gave the lead when the call for revolution spread outwards from Paris in 1848. But they were not alone. The nobles made demands, though they began to retreat when the revolt became more radical and more obviously Czech. With the intellectuals were the small businessmen, who looked to liberal reforms to improve their commercial standing. To the left were the students and a smaller group of workers who fought the Austrians on the June barricades. In the background were the peasants, hopefully awaiting emancipation. There were thus many streams in the revolt, but the rebels were neither numerous nor united. The intellectuals and the middle class stood aloof from the June uprising; the peasants did not come to its aid. No more than 1,500 fought the troops, about 800 of them students and 400 of them workers, the remainder officials, shopkeepers, and such like. And after June, leadership once more devolved on the intellectuals. The Czech national movement was baptised in the years 1848-49, but it was a tiny and unco-ordinated infant.

Like most other revolts in central Europe in 1848-49, the Czech revolt was in part subdued and in part collapsed. It was nonetheless highly significant. It was first and foremost a national phenomenon. It quickly frightened off the local Germans and it came to verbal blows with those trying to set up an independent, united Germany. It showed its preparedness to accept a compromise by proposing the establishment of an Austro-Slav state on federal lines, but it also organised a Slavonic congress in Prague. Second, the social elements behind it were quite clear. The peasantry did not revolt; but the very fact that emancipation was given to them by the new Emperor, Franz Joseph, showed that he recognized them as a latent force. Whatever their numbers, the middle and working classes played their part and their ambitions were stirred. There was a considerable number of youthful revolutionaries, and some women died at the barricades. Above all, the intellectuals coined the phrases that nurtured future revolt. When Palacký wrote that he was a Czech of Slavonic blood, he was addressing himself to the German nation; but his words gave notice to his own people as well as to others that the Czech nation had come back to life. The Czechs produced their first important newspaper and hammered out their first modern political programme. The Habsburgs yielded the use of Czech for limited purposes in university and secondary education. And the Czechs began to co-operate with the Slovaks.

This last factor was of enormous importance. The history of the Slovaks from the tenth century was largely the history of Hungary, but they did have links with the Czechs. In the fifteenth century Husite soldiers were recruited in Slovakia and occasionally sought refuge or settled there. Between 1434 and 1526 four of the kings of the Czech Lands were also kings of Hungary, and from 1526 the Habsburgs were usually kings of both. Lutheranism spread as widely in Slovakia as in the Czech Lands in the sixteenth century; yet it did not entirely succumb to Catholicism in the seventeenth. Here Slovakia was more fortunate. But the reforms of Maria Theresa and Joseph II made less impact on Slovakia because the Hungarian nobility were determined to extend their own independence of the Habsburgs. In this respect the Slovaks were worse off. From 1526 to well into the eighteenth century they had to support the greater part of the Hungarian nobility, refugees from Turkish rule in the rest of Hungary. And they lacked the agricultural wealth of the Czechs. Unlike the Czechs, they were therefore unable to boast a glorious past and their circumstances at the beginning of the nineteenth century made the prospects of a national awakening less likely.

Yet even before 1800 there was important pioneering activity. In 1792 Anton Bernolák, linguistic scholar and Catholic priest, established a Slovak Learned Society in Trnava to publish and distribute books in the western Slovak dialect. In 1803 the Lutheran high school in Bratislava set up a centre for the study of Czechoslovak literature. There were other organisations; but these two already represented fundamentally different themes in the Slovak revival, the one seeking to re-create something genuinely Slovak, the other with a strong leaning towards a close alignment with the Czech revival. Other Slovaks, like Šafařík, and Jan Kollár, whose poetry and pamphlets were dedicated to promoting the unity of all the Slavs, went to the Czech Lands and wrote in Czech. In underdeveloped Slovakia this kind of division was probably inevitable. However, the policy of magyarisation, which gained increasing momentum in the 1830s and 1840s, made the question of the literary language and its political consequences absolutely crucial. Against this background, in 1843, L'udovít Štúr, now the leading light in the Bratislava school, got together with some writer friends and decided to develop the central Slovak dialect as probably the most likely to unite all Slovaks. In 1845 he began to publish the *Slovenskie národnie noviny* (*Slovak National News*), and he very soon achieved his purpose. With some modifications his choice was accepted, at least among the Slovaks. From most of the Czech writers it received little but abuse.

Magyar policies and Slovak aspirations were inevitably on a collision course. The outward spread of revolution in 1848 produced the first encounter. Slovak writers, students, pastors, priests, teachers, and officials published their petitions. There were some scattered risings among miners and peasants. With official Habsburg encouragement several hastily armed Slovak detachments attacked the Magyar rebels. Štúr and one or two others went to Vienna and later to Prague to join forces with other Slavs; Štúr was particularly active in the Slavonic congress. None of the Slovaks submitted excessive demands. As their first-ever programme, *The Demands of the Slovak Nation*, showed, they were concerned to protect themselves through some measure of autonomy, not to destroy Hungary, still less the Empire. But they suffered grievously at the time from Magyar excesses; and despite the military support and basic loyalty they rendered to the Emperor they received no recognition in return.

Yet, like the Czechs, the Slovaks made some profit from 1848-49. They established an image of themselves as revolutionaries, as at least incipient nationalists. They won the respect and concern of many Czechs. Štúr made an enormous impression in Prague; for a time he won the wholehearted support of Palacký and particularly of Karel Havlíček, the leading journalist who had previously attacked him. He was also himself impressed by the Czechs; and he began seriously to discuss a Czech-Slovak union. So, too, did Havlíček and Palacký and many Czechs. In that sense, 1848-49 was an important beginning. There were many vicissitudes ahead for the Czechs and the Slovaks separately, and for their mooted union.

But the idea of an independent and united state of Czechoslovaks was now a historical possibility.

* * * * *

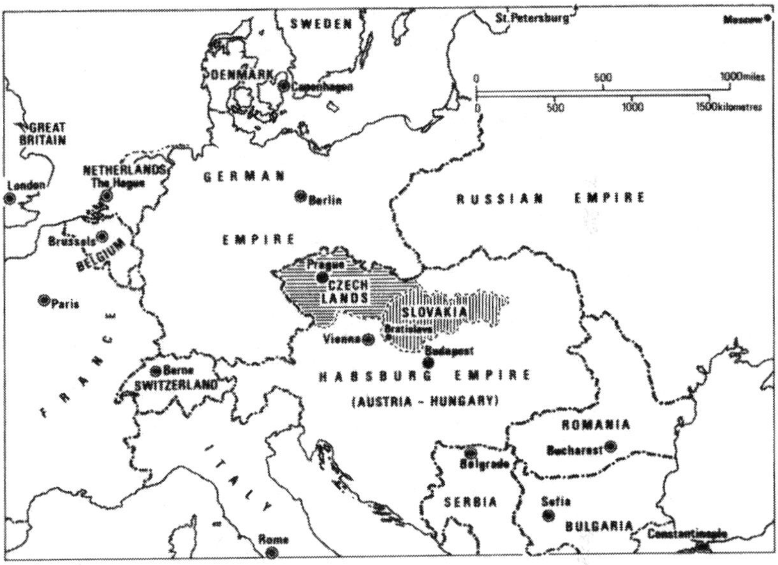

1 The Frontiers of Czechoslovakia before the First World War

However it was as yet neither a defined aim nor a certainty. In 1848-49 the Habsburg Empire proved its staying power. On the other hand, the Czechs and Slovaks sensed themselves to be part of a movement that was to change the entire face of Europe. The whole of Belgium and the southern part of Greece had achieved national independence before 1848-49. In due course, a tiny Serbia edged nearer independence in 1856, and a sizeable Rumania achieved it in 1859-61. Italy followed suit in 1860, Germany in 1870, both of them defeating Austria in the process. Bulgaria achieved independence in two stages in 1878 and 1885. And in 1912-13, the Balkan states carved up the remnants of the Turkish Empire in Europe. Indeed, long before 1914 the disruptive force of nationalism had already spread to Asia, and the chance of its leaving the Habsburg Empire unchanged was almost nil. But in the aftermath of the 1848 rebellions the road ahead for the Czechs and Slovaks was a long one. It took the First World War to get them to the end of it.

BOOK ONE

CHAPTER I

The Czech Lands 1849-1878

The Demographic Background

In discussing the history of the Czech Lands after 1848-49 it is possible to distinguish a number of periods, the first of them running down to 1878. However, fundamental to their history throughout the nineteenth and early twentieth centuries was their growth in population and its rapidly changing distribution. Between 1800 and 1850 the growth was from under 5 to more than 7 million, an increase of about 45 percent in fifty years. In the next sixty years the population rose to more than 10 million, an increase of about the same in the slightly longer timespan. Between 1850 and 1910, too, more than a quarter of a million Czechs emigrated to the United States alone, so that the rate of increase may really have been as rapid as before. Throughout the nineteenth and early twentieth centuries, therefore, mounting population pressure in the Czech Lands demanded change for survival's sake, if for nothing else. The growth in numbers was not steady; and so neither was the demand. The accelerated growth of the 1820s contributed to the unrest of the 1840s; that of the 1850s to the unrest of the 1870s. But it was the century-long trend that was important. Overpopulation in the countryside more than anything else made emancipation inevitable in 1848-49. Urban population growth after 1848 both created a new source of demand for change and made it more effective by concentrating it. In 1843 some 18 percent of the population lived in towns with more than 2,000 inhabitants; by 1910 the figure had risen to 45 percent. Between 1828 and 1910 the population of Prague grew from 89,000 to 617,000, that of Brno from 34,000 to 207,000, and, most strikingly of all, that of Ostrava from a thousand to 167,000 and of Plzeň from 8,000 to 109,000.

The ethnic composition of the population also changed. Just before the revolts of 1848-49 people of Czech nationality accounted for 60 percent of the population of Bohemia and 70 percent of that of Moravia; the rest were mainly German. In Silesia the picture was different, since 32 percent of the population there was Polish-speaking and the Czechs, with 20 percent, were outnumbered by the Germans with 48 percent. Thereafter, in a period of overall population growth throughout the Czech Lands, the Czechs multiplied faster than the Germans. By 1880 they accounted for 63 percent of the population of Bohemia, and continued to increase their numbers in Moravia and Silesia until in 1910 they could claim respectively 72 percent and 24 percent as against 70 percent and 20 percent. Since the 1910 statistics were collected by the Austro-Hungarian government at a time of rising national tension, it is possible that the percentages it was allowed to show were biased against the Czechs. But they are sufficient to indicate why the Czechs were pressing for change and why the Germans were afraid of it.

Of equal importance was the ethnic redistribution of the population. The Czechs migrated to the towns and multiplied. There were not only more of them, absolutely and relatively in the country as a whole, but they were challenging the Germans in what had hitherto been a German preserve. This comes out clearly in figures for Prague. In 1848-49 the capital was essentially a German-speaking town. But as it grew, it became more and more Czech. Already by 1880 the 42,000 people who still spoke German as their first language represented only 14 percent of its population; by 1910 37,000 represented a mere 6 percent. The Czechs obviously dominated Prague. On the other hand, and crucially, they did not yet hold a proportionate share of the top positions. In the public services and other professions in 1900 there were to be found about 42,000 Czechs and some 8,000 Germans; yet these absolute figures represented only 23 percent of gainfully employed Czechs but almost 56 percent of Germans. By contrast, about 52 percent of gainfully employed Czechs worked in industry compared with about 19 percent of Germans; but only about one-twenty-fifth of this Czech percentage held administrative or technical positions compared to about one-third of the German percentage. These occupational imbalances were reflected in differences in social positions. In 1900 there were two-thirds as many Czech as German families with two or more domestic servants; but whereas this represented little more than 3 percent of Czech households, it represented 13 percent of German. In short, the Germans held more than their proper share of the best jobs and enjoyed more than their fair share of the easy life. They were therefore bound to be the envy of the Czechs. Of course, the experience of Prague was average rather than typical. The process of Czechisation went much more rapidly in many of the towns of central Bohemia; Plzeň, in 1868, was one of the last to win its own predominantly Czech administration. In Moravia, on the other hand, the process was slower; as late as 1918, Brno, Olomouc, and Ostrava still had exclusively German administrations. The fact remains, however, that the ethnic redistribution of the population made the towns inevitable centres of national conflict in the six or seven decades down to the First World War.

Economic and Social Change

Demographic change in the Czech Lands was interlaced with steady economic and social development. The thirty years after 1848-49 were characterised in particular by the first real momentum in industrialisation. The exigencies of the Napoleonic wars had added cotton thread to the list of textile products and had given a fillip to the production of sugar from local beet. But at the time of the revolt, machines in factories were still comparatively rare. There was too much labour tied to the land and anxious to work at home for a pittance, and too many feudal proprietors with an obvious vested interest in marketing the sugar extracted on their estates. Similar factors operated elsewhere in the economy. The first coke-fired iron furnace was established in 1836; the first rolling-mills were also built about the same time. But charcoal-burning iron foundries, long established on large estates, were reluctant to yield the day. The output of iron and the demand for coal were, therefore, rather low. To gain significant impetus, the industrial revolution needed peasant emancipation. Thus the basis of cottage industry would be destroyed, the para-industrial position of landowners would be undermined—and an urban labour force and an urban demand for industrial goods created.

The abolition of labour service on the land freed the peasants to migrate to the towns. The movement was neither sudden nor complete. An expanding urban population made industrial development possible, but it also took a sizeable increase in factory production to attract the peasants into the towns. The more peasants who abandoned the countryside, the more rewarding and attractive it became for those who remained. But the movement was enough to switch a turgid industrial revolution into top gear. Between the early 1850s and the late 1860s almost the entire production of cotton and woollen cloth moved into factories; the production of linen cloth followed soon afterwards. Between the early 1850s and the early 1870s sugar output increased tenfold, the bulk of it from factories without any landed connection. The 1860s also saw the turning-point in flour-milling and brewing as steam turned off the diminutive village water-mills and concentration destroyed the smaller breweries.

The movement of population was not the sole factor in accelerating the industrial revolution. The side-effects of absolutist policies were important. Thus the Habsburg Emperor's decision to abolish internal tariffs in 1850 was meant to reinforce his control over his dominions, but it also created an expanded market for Czech goods. Moreover, when the stimulus came, the Czech Lands formed an obvious centre for growth. They had an abundance of convenient coal, particularly in Ostrava and Kladno, to provide steam-power for the new factories. When a demand built up in the period 1867-73, for example, the output of lignite was more than doubled and the output of bituminous increased by half without difficulty. Iron was in a less favourable position. There were sizeable deposits of ore at Nučice, but these had a high phosphorus content, not much use for the manufacture of steel until the Gilchrist-Thomas process was perfected in 1878. The new process was first applied in the Kladno works in 1879; and only then could the Nučice deposits be exploited intensively. But steel had been produced before this, partly from imported ore and partly through the exercise of technical ingenuity. In the 1860s sulphuric and hydrochloric acid were already being used to reduce the phosphorus content of the local ore; and the production of pig-iron of good quality had been rising since the 1850s. Local industrial skill was in fact a further stimulus to growth. In mining it went back to the silver of the Middle Ages, in industrial processes in general to the glass and porcelain manufactures of the intervening years. Much of the new factory machinery, particularly for textiles, was imported from Germany or Britain. But between the early 1850s and the early 1870s there was a remarkable expansion in the engineering industry. Everything from machine tools to farm machinery was turned out. By the end of the period there was even an export trade in engineering goods. There was also an export trade in sugar and beer, other areas where the Czechs showed inventive talent both in devising sophisticated equipment and in improving chemical processes.

Manufacturing industries developed on a broad front, paper and fertiliser, for instance, adding to the variety of products. There were workers and consumers; raw materials and talents. But there was at least one further requirement—capital. Here, too emancipation played a significant role. In due course industrial development generated capital of its own. But it was the removal of surplus labour from the countryside that made possible large-scale beet cultivation by the big landowners in the 1850s and greater output from the smaller owners in the 1860s. Supplying the raw materials for expanding industry was profitable business and produced an entirely new lending class. The Czech Lands were as generously provided with agricultural endowments as with mineral deposits. Potatoes for distilling did well in southern Bohemia, just as barley for the malt industry prospered in the Haná or hops for the brewing industry in the Žatec area. Successful farming produced surplus capital for investment in industry—not to mention demand for industrial products. Only a part of this surplus took the direct route into industrial concerns. After 1848-49 banks began to appear as agents for agricultural credit and as middlemen between the prosperous farmers and the rising industrialists. Founded in 1868, the Živnostenská Bank in particular played a crucial role in the provision of fresh capital for Czech industry. What agricultural prosperity initiated, industrial expansion continued.

However, some capital emanated from Germany and France; and much more was German-Austrian, stemming from private banking ventures or government guarantees. The Czech Lands were very attractive for their agricultural prosperity, their natural resources, and their industrial promise. They lay between Austria proper and Germany, objects of economic interest to both. But they had particular value to the Habsburg government. They were an important base in the developing struggle with Prussia for control of central Europe. The events of 1848-49 proved that they were more secure than the Italian or Hungarian provinces of the Empire; and Italian independence in 1860 and Hungarian autonomy in 1867 made the Czech Lands almost Hobson's choice for German-Austrian capital. Indeed, many factors combined to produce the peculiar situation that the greater part of Austrian industry was sited in the Czech Lands.

Another impelling factor in the steady economic development of the Czech Lands was transport. The strategic requirements of the eighteenth and early nineteenth centuries had made the system of roads in the Czech Lands better than in any other part of the Habsburg Empire. The links were good not only with Vienna but also with important cities across the frontiers, such as Nuremberg, Dresden, Breslau, and Warsaw. Internally there were good alternative roads between Prague and Cheb, and Prague and Brno. Labour, agricultural produce, industrial goods, enterprise, and capital could move with ease both across and around the Czech Lands. Growing prosperity along the main routes encouraged the building of secondary roads. There was no shortage of stone; basalt, granite, and gneiss supplied most of the needs. Water transport also played its part. The establishment of the so-called Saxon-Bohemian Steamship Company in 1851 was significant. Czech trade could pass to and from Hamburg along the Vltava and Elbe rivers. But a topography rich in roads and rivers was also attractive for railway development.

The first horse-drawn vehicles running on wooden rails began to shuttle between Mauthausen and České Budějovice in 1823, but they were essentially a curiosity. It took British equipment and government finance to launch the proper railway era. The line from Vienna reached Břeclav in Moravia in 1839 and Přerov two years later. From there it branched north-west to reach Prague in 1845 and north-east to arrive in Krakow in 1848. Prague was linked with Dresden by 1851 and with Nuremberg by 1861; internal links were formed with Brno in 1849 and with many other lesser towns in the 1850s and 1860s. There was certainly enough track operating or under construction to stimulate economic development in the post-1848 period. State capital for railway-building became more difficult to find and state policy more uncertain in the late 1850s and 1860s as the conflict with Prussia came to a head. But private capital built a number of important local links, and after 1867 state construction recommenced on a large scale. Everything came together to develop the economy of the Czech Lands.

The process of industrialisation was inevitably long. But within two decades of the 1848-49 revolt it had gone far enough for it to be possible to describe the economy as no longer mainly agricultural. Of the working population the percentage engaged in agriculture had already dropped to 52 percent by 1869. Some 29 percent were engaged in industry, some 3 percent in trade and transport, and the remaining 16 percent in the liberal professions and miscellaneous occupations. This had important, although unquantifiable, social consequences. The Czech population was producing a small middle class of industrialists and businessmen, a larger lower-middle class of shopkeepers and officials, and a mushrooming working class, as well as a not easily assigned miscellany of teachers and lawyers. In the countryside social stratification went hand in hand with the distribution of land. Privately owned properties of 50 hectares and over made up about a quarter of one percent of all the holdings and about 20 percent of all the land. For properties of 5 to 50 hectares the figures were approximately 25 and 47 percent, and of less than 5 hectares 73 and 8 percent. The fairly exclusive group of largish landowners was mainly German. However, what was significant from the Czech point of view at this stage was the growing and mainly Czech middle group who could provide the capital for a developing industry and the leadership for an underprovided peasantry. Economic change altered the structure of society in the Czech lands and this in turn gradually transformed politics.

Political Developments

In practice, economic and social changes were haphazard, and their implications were not immediately clear to contemporaries. What was obvious at the time was the political situation, and it was not encouraging. Indeed, throughout the Habsburg Empire the decade after 1849 was later characterised as the period of neo-absolutism. But it was a little while before the absolutism was complete. In Czech eyes the great figure of the revolt was František Palacký who had denounced pan-Germanism and chaired the Slavonic congress. He had played a leading role in the Empire-wide constituent assembly as a staunch champion of Austro-Slavism. As a historian and man of action, he was the embodiment of nascent Czech nationalism, and, just over fifty, he was still in the prime of life. He was not immediately arrested (nor subsequently court-martialled); and for over a year he was able to protest. But in 1851 he found it expedient to retire to his estate in Lobkovice to continue writing his mammoth history, and in 1852 he felt compelled to retire from his various nationalist activities in the Museum and elsewhere. František Ladislav Rieger, Palacký's son-in-law and his junior by twenty years, was another of the great figures of 1848-49. A lawyer by training, he too had been a member of the constituent assembly and a prime mover in the drafting of a doomed bill of rights. But where Palacký had been patronised by the nobles and had married the daughter of a landed family, Rieger had turned against them in 1848 and behaved like the typical middle-class liberal his birth had made him. It was not very long before he thought it wisest to go abroad. More radical than either Palacký or Rieger, and yet more of a realist, was Havlíček. Only in his late twenties, he had edited *Národní noviny* (*National News*), the first great Czech nationalist newspaper that was started up in the first days of the revolt, as a means of promoting the revolution and educating the revolutionaries. He had little time for romantic notions of the Slavs (he had visited Russia); he was very ready to give a reformed Empire a chance. But after the failure of the revolt, he condemned the restoration of autocracy and saw the closure of *Národní noviny*. In January 1850 he established a new paper, *Slovan* (*The Slav*), in Kutná Hora, and then came into conflict with *Videňský denník* (*The Vienna Daily*), a government propaganda newspaper. He survived trials in Kutná Hora and warnings from the magistrates of Prague; but in August 1851 he read the signs and ceased to publish. Nevertheless, in December he was arrested and sent to the remote township of Brixen in the Austrian Tirol. When he was released in April 1855, suffering from tuberculosis, he returned home only to find his wife dead and to die himself a year later at the age of thirty-five. By that time the power of the Emperor Franz Joseph and his ministers was complete.

During most of the 1850s there was no free Czech press. The trials of students and writers began in 1850 and led to many imprisonments. A student republican club, the Brothers of the Red Banner, was exposed in 1853 and proscribed. What remained after 1848-49 of the so-called Czech Party retained a tiny voice on the Prague city council, but weighted votes gave control to the German Centre Party. Opposition, even criticism, became impossible. As the fifties wore on, a number of the convicted were amnestied, but police surveillance of the politically minded continued on a substantial scale. In these circumstances it fell to men and women of letters to maintain and strengthen the sense of Czech identity. In 1855 Božena Němcová published *Babička* (*The Grandmother*), a tale eulogising all that was most memorable and distinctive in the Czech countryside. In the later fifties Jan Neruda published his first sentimental poems. Czech political development had been stopped, but the cultural revival went on its way. And the Imperial government assisted, not just by virtually proscribing politics, but by putting through a series of administrative, economic, and commercial reforms whose centralising aspects made the Empire more German and therefore less likeable than before. Perversely, it eventually contributed to a Czech political revival by suffering a defeat at the hands of France and Piedmont in 1859.

Defeat by a foreign power would of itself have been a serious blow to the Habsburgs. But it was even more serious to go down to what claimed to be a national movement and to see a new nation created, the more so since it involved surrendering Habsburg territory. Neo-absolutism was undermined; and the aspirations of the other nationalities were revived. For many reasons the revival was strongest in Hungary, but signs soon began to appear in the Czech Lands too. As Franz Joseph started a series of constitutional experiments to retrieve his position—the October Diploma in 1860 followed by the February Patent in 1861—the Czechs re-entered the political arena. On 1 January 1861 Rieger published a manifesto in the very first number of a new Czech newspaper, *Národní listy* (*The National Gazette*). He went back to what might be termed the conservative programme of the pre-1848 era, state rights or the restoration of autonomy to the historic lands of Bohemia, Moravia, and Silesia. This evoked sympathy from the local nobility. On 6 January Rieger met their spokesman, Count Clam-Martinic, and reached agreement with him on a state rights policy. Clam-Martinic became president of the Museum and Prince Schwarzenberg vice-president; and Rieger put aside his dislike for their class. On the basis of an alliance with the aristocracy and a programme of state rights what came to be called the Old Czech Party stood ready for the next twenty or thirty years.

But the situation was not the same as that of pre-1848. Although the local diets were restored, the February Patent made it quite clear that power was not to reside with them but with the Imperial diet—insofar, that is, as it resided with anyone other than the Emperor and chosen ministers. The system of election was also so organised as to ensure that the Czech population could return no more than one-third of the members to either the Bohemian or the Moravian diet. These local bodies then elected members to the Imperial diet. Unfairness was inevitable. Of the 54 Bohemian members only 20 were Czechs; of the 22 Moravian members only 4 were Czechs, even including the aristocratic allies of the Old Czechs as Czechs (which at this stage, of course, was reasonable enough). Germans of various political leanings but of mostly centralist views therefore dominated the Imperial diet. The Hungarians, desirous of something more than mere provincial recognition, stayed away; but the constitution recognised the uniqueness of Hungary's position by authorising separate sessions of the diet to handle essentially Austrian matters. This left only minor groups like the Poles to whom the Czechs could look for co-operation in pursuit of federalisation, and the Poles were afraid to upset Vienna when they were anxious for its help against St Petersburg and Berlin. The outlook was neither as good nor as hopeful as it had been before 1848.

The old politicians were in a dilemma; whether to work inside or outside the constitution imposed on them by the Habsburg Emperor. Locally the dilemma was solved by regularly introducing resolutions condemning the electoral system, though they were always defeated. Vienna presented the greater problem. There one could make the widest appeal, but it was a frustrating experience to be almost completely ignored. From the start, Palacký, who was a member of both the Bohemian and the Imperial diets, and Rieger wished to boycott Vienna. But they bowed to the will of some of their colleagues, particularly from the Moravian diet, who had less previous experience and fewer preconceptions. In September 1861, however, Palacký left Vienna and never resumed his seat; and in February 1862 Rieger compromised by simply lapsing into silence. Both were honest men, anxious to do their best. Palacký opted out and found himself powerless. Rieger hung on, but with the same result. There was no easy answer. Meantime, both became conscious of new forces at work in Czech society and politics.

The achievement of Italian unity and independence in 1860 was in part the work of a mature national movement. Palacký and Rieger appreciated this very well. They also appreciated that the

Czech national movement was as yet nothing like so mature: one reason why they stuck to the programme of state rights. But they sensed a new spirit among the Czechs. In the opening decades of the nineteenth century the Czech literary renaissance and political revival had gone hand in hand. In the 1850s literature eventually carried the torch for politics. Subscriptions were invited to build a national theatre. A provisional one was opened in 1862 and the foundation stone for its permanent successor laid in 1868. In the 1860s music also entered the field. In 1861 Bedřich Smetana was among a number of founders of Hlahol, a Prague choral society whose motto read 'through song to the heart, through the heart to the homeland'. In 1848 he had written a 'Song to Freedom'; now returned from exile in Sweden, he wrote some of his most nationally orientated work. He finished his opera *The Brandenburgers in Bohemia* in 1863 and performed both it and his new *The Bartered Bride* in 1866. He gave the first performance of *Dalibor* in 1868 on the occasion of the stone-laying ceremony for the national theatre. Literature and music came together as an emotional expression of national sentiment. Physical culture contributed too. In 1862 the first *Sokol* was founded: a gymnastic organisation whose declared purpose was 'by the education of the body and the spirit, by physical energy, by art and science, by all moral means, to revive the homeland'. Six years later, in 1868, there were sixty *Sokol* organisations. Although not directly political, they still had a profound political effect. Ultimately they became a quasi-military body. Meanwhile they were a forcing-house for Czech nationalism. One of the co-founders, Dr Miroslav Tyrš, looked upon them as fulfilling a Darwinian function in respect of the national movement . Certainly they gave expression to a much wider range of views than had been heard before. Of the Prague members in 1868 it has been calculated that approximately 40 percent were tradesmen and merchants, 30 percent shopkeepers, 10 percent factory-owners, 14 percent members of the professions, officials, and teachers, 3 percent students, and 3 percent well-to-do farmers. Of the provincial members in the same year there was a lower percentage of tradesmen, merchants, shopkeepers, and factory-owners, but a higher of the others; some 8 percent were classed as peasants. But inside and outside Prague the *Sokol* embraced a wide social spectrum. They dipped lower in the social scale than the Old Czechs had yet contemplated politically, though they did not yet include workers. The base of the national revival was widening significantly, and older politicians could not remain insensitive.

These, however, were early days. There already existed working-class groups that might be regarded as early examples of socialist or trade union activity. But they were few, small and politically unimportant. Nationalist activities were occasionally coincidental. Authors and composers wrote for enjoyment and profit as well as for the future of the Czech nation. Physical exercise was pleasurable and health-giving, the company satisfying. For some there were artistic directorships and university professorships to be won. The politicians who had been at the helm in 1848-49 could be excused for not putting too much credence in new forces calling for more urgent action in the 1860s. Alongside the old guard, however, there was already a young guard. Karel Sladkovský, a left-wing radical, and Prince Rudolf Thurn-Taxis, an impatient noble, were both to be found in the latter group. So were the brothers Edvard and Julius Grégr, who soon got control of *Národní listy*. Differences between the two groups ranged from matters affecting the national theatre to views about education. In 1863 disagreement over the Polish rebellion—the Old Czechs did not wish to attack the Russians whom they regarded as the leaders of Slavdom, but those soon to be called the Young Czechs thought it more important to support a nationalist cause—almost destroyed what little unity remained. Differences of social outlook also became more obvious. In the long run the split was to prove too fundamental to overcome.

At this stage the net effect was simply to push the older politicians into tougher attitudes. On 4 June 1863, Palacký and Rieger persuaded the majority of their Czech colleagues in the Bohemian diet to boycott the Imperial diet. But they could not secure unanimity, or any support from the Moravian diet. The declaration introduced into the Imperial diet on 25 June was sharp in its condemnation of the February Patent and complained bitterly of the discrimination being exercised against Czechs. It marked the beginning of a period of passive resistance to Habsburg government and in that particular was a response to the growing sense of nationalism in the Czech Lands. But it was signed by only eleven out of the twenty delegates from the Bohemian diet and by none of the four from the Moravian. The older politicians had failed to find unanimity and so to take effective action.

This partial boycott contrasted with the total Hungarian boycott that had been in force since 1861. It therefore made no impact at all. If the young politicians were disappointed and even scornful, they could themselves claim no greater success in giving a lead to the Czech people. On 8 January 1864 Thurn-Taxis suggested to a meeting, which included Sladkovský and the Grégrs, that they should set up a liberal party dedicated to the work of widening the franchise and attacking privilege. But those present would not agree among themselves and the new party was stillborn. Shortly afterwards, Thurn-Taxis ran into financial difficulties and did considerable harm to his radical friends by withdrawing from active politics and informing the Emperor about some of his earlier activities. The young had done no better than their elders. Indeed by 1865 when at last all the Czechs did withdraw from the Imperial diet, the old hands might be said to have resumed leadership of the national movement.

The year 1865 was an important landmark. For some time the Magyars had been campaigning for their independence. As Franz Joseph reeled under his defeats by Bismarck in the struggle for supremacy in Germany, they began to step up their campaign. In April and May 1865 Count Deak, their acknowledged leader, published a series of newspaper articles, putting the case for a dualist settlement under which the Austrian and Hungarian states would enjoy equal rights. The February Patent and the Hungarian boycott had already foreshadowed this and considerably irritated the Czechs. So in the same two months Palacký published a series of newspaper articles in which he analysed the 'Idea of the Austrian State'. In his view the Imperial government could assume three possible forms, centralist, dualist, or federalist. The first he rejected as allowing the Germans to dominate the Magyars and the Slavs, the second as allowing the Germans and the Magyars to dominate the Slavs. The only form of government the Czechs would accept was the federal. Anticipating the triumph of dualism, he then went on to issue the stern warning: 'We existed before Austria, and we will continue to exist after Austria disappears'. Palacký was a historian; but he was not just a historian being prophetic. He was still the pre-eminent Czech politician. He had worked all his life for some form of federalism and he would continue to do so. But he recognised the reality of an accelerating Czech nationalism and he foresaw the anti-Slav character of dualism; he knew that, if the Magyars got their way, there would be no holding the Czechs. With their independent past and their thirst for recognition, they would settle for nothing short of equality in the Empire or for its destruction. Even if he could, he would not try to gainsay them. He might have fallen behind the wishes of his younger brethren but he now pointed the way ahead.

In December 1867 dualism came to pass, the end of a fairly complicated process beginning with Franz Joseph's defeat in the Austro-Prussian war of 1866. The new dual monarchy of Austria-Hungary had as almost its only shared features the monarchy itself, the army, central finance, and foreign policy. But while the Magyars got all they wanted, the Czechs got nothing. The decisive battle was fought on their soil at Sadová near Hradec Králové (in German, Königgrätz). Prague was occupied by Prussian troops and gave its name to the treaty that ended the war. But battle-grounds seldom profit from the battles. At the height of the war the Prussian high command issued a proclamation to the Czechs, implying that it would support their claims to independence. In Prague a remarkable degree of freedom was immediately allowed to the press and to the theatre. But the Prussian actions were purely tactical. With the conclusion of peace, promises were forgotten. Of course, not even the future Young Czechs were keen to exchange Austrian rule for Prussian support. Indeed, at the outbreak of the war, many Czechs declared their loyalty to the Emperor and offered help. Rieger went in person to Vienna to express the feelings of the citizens of Prague. Historically the Czechs had no love for Germany. But good faith brought no reward either. The Magyars, who if anything had been disloyal, got the dualism they wanted; the Czechs got nothing. Franz Joseph was not interested in change for change's sake. He simply made concessions where he felt he had to retrieve his position. The Magyars represented the greatest internal threat and they might, if conciliated, produce the most telling reinforcement. The Czechs were no threat at all and had neither leadership nor fighting tradition to offer him in his moment of need.

It has been argued that with a little skill the Czechs could have won something. The *Ausgleich* that was legalised in December 1867 was first announced in February. From then on the Czechs made no secret of their dislike for it. When a fresh Bohemian diet met in April, Rieger at once condemned dualism. He moved a resolution that representatives should not attend the Imperial diet, but inevitably his resolution was defeated. He then read a protest against dualism as a violation of state rights and in company with all his Czech colleagues walked out of the Bohemian diet. The Czechs in the Moravian diet did the same, and passive resistance became unanimous. This was an act hardly calculated to win Franz Joseph's sympathy and it finally crystallised the Czechs' negative policy. But they could be excused for failing to see any sign of concession to their demands. After all, fresh Bohemian and Moravian diets were assembled with the sole purpose of white-washing dualism, and they were again elected on a rigged franchise that returned a false German majority.

At any rate, in the course of 1867 Czech annoyance rose to considerable heights. Ever since 1789 every radical in Europe had looked to France at one time or another. More recently, dissatisfied ethnic groups had turned to Napoleon III as nationalist champion.

It was now the turn of the Czechs. In May 1867 Palacký and Rieger went publicly to see him. They received no immediate diplomatic or other help, but they were advised to make their case more widely known in France. In other words, they took the first step towards recognising that they led a national movement, that they might have to take their nation outside the Habsburg Empire, and that to do so they would need foreign support, not least that of France. A month later, in company with other Czech politicians, they paid a visit to Russia. Ostensibly they were attending an ethnographic exhibition in Moscow. But this in itself was a demonstration of their anger, since the exhibition was Panslavist. They went on to make Panslavist speeches at various banquets, and they were also received by the Tsar. They got even less support from him than from Napoleon; Alexander II had never been a partisan of Panslavism and was now anxious, for conservative and foreign policy reasons, to sustain the power of Austria. They also earned the disapproval of the Panslavs for their attitude to the Polish question. But the whole expedition was evidence of the new mood among the Czechs and of their leaders' awareness of the value of outside assistance.

To some extent Palacký and Rieger had been pushed into intransigence by pressure from below. What provoked them into international action was the folly of dualism from above. Dualism also intensified the pressure from below. During the war the crown jewels had been removed to Vienna for safety. Their return on 28 August 1867 was made the occasion of a great demonstration in Prague. This condemned dualism and declared support for a policy of restoring state rights. The actual implementation of dualism provoked more public protests. Opportunities were readily found when the foundation stones of the national theatre were at last laid on 15 May 1868 and again when Palacký celebrated his seventieth birthday on 14 June. The stone-laying ceremony in particular was an elaborate demonstration of discontent. There were patriotic concerts and fireworks, banquets and fiery speeches. In all, nineteen stones from different historic sites were laid, the most significant perhaps from Mount Řip, the legendary birthplace of the Czech nation. The importance of the date was not forgotten; it was twenty years after the revolt of 1848. To emphasise that the Czechs were not alone, the organisers went on to promote a Slavonic congress attended by some fifty representatives of other Slav peoples. In the end, the whole series of events turned into a spontaneous exhibition of mass national sentiment.

At the same time there appeared a wider and more systematic movement. Large-scale open-air meetings were held throughout the Czech Lands, taking the name *Tabor* from the period of the Husite wars. In less than four years, it has been calculated, well over a million people attended well over a hundred such meetings. The younger members of the Czech Party did most of the organising, but it was Rieger who laid down the political line, state rights. He even commissioned a legal historian, Josef Kalousek, to write articles and pamphlets and eventually a book on the subject. But the social composition of the movement and its political objectives were wider and more varied than this suggests. Artisans and shopkeepers called for more high schools to use the Czech language; peasants demanded reduced land-taxes; workers protested against bad labour conditions and social discrimination. Yet there was a genuine sense of unity. National bitterness following the *Ausgleich* was widespread; the anniversary of Jan Hus's martyrdom was a favourite day for demonstrations. The institution of Czech-dominated assemblies in Bohemia and Moravia emerged as a universal demand. Strains developed between the older and younger politicians as to whether abstention from the provincial diets was wise, but abstention triumphed and unity persisted. The aim of the Czech people as a whole was still national parity, not national independence, but in an unprecedented way they were acting as a people.

The Austrian government resorted to timeworn repressive measures. Martial law was introduced in Prague in 1868; and in the same year more than 700 Czechs were sentenced to imprisonment on political grounds. Some *Tabory* were forbidden, while others were broken up by the police or the army. But the deputies' political boycott continued, and in 1869 twice as many people as in 1868 took part in meetings. The boldness of the leaders also increased. In the summer of 1869 Rieger again went to Paris and personally submitted to Napoleon III an almost treasonable memorandum advocating French support for the federalisation of Austria as one possible means of winning Austrian help against Prussia. It was certainly a far-reaching step that Rieger would not have taken but for his increasing awareness of national solidarity. The attitude of the Emperor and his ministers to this was not entirely negative. At best, they were genuinely anxious to meet moderate demands; at worst, they simply wanted peace. In particular, of course, they were determined to restore Habsburg power in Europe by continuing to put their house in order. This meant compensating the Czechs to some extent for not getting as much as the Magyars and up to a point balancing them against the Magyars. Whatever the motives, a policy that had been embarked upon after the débâcle of 1866 could only be speeded up with Prussia's victory over France in 1870 and the establishment of the new Germany. If the Habsburg Empire was to regain its position or even just retain its independence, it would have to quieten the Czech provinces that formed the bulk of its frontier with Germany. In February 1871 Franz Joseph appointed Count Hohenwart, a conservative Catholic of Viennese family, to be his Austrian prime minister and to settle the Czech question.

This seemed to vindicate the policy of opposition the Czech leaders had followed since the *Ausgleich*. The new government contained two Czechs, though neither was a political figure. Josef Jireček, the historian son-in-law of Pavel Šafařík, became minister of education and Karel Habětínek, a professor at the university of Vienna, became minister of justice. Hohenwart did not wish to go all the way to meet Czech demands, but he genuinely wanted a workable compromise, as did Franz Joseph, provided his rights were not contravened. But the road to dissolution was paved with good intentions. The Fundamental Articles that were finally hammered out with the Bohemian diet in September-October 1871 as the basis for a settlement went part way to concede what Palacký and Rieger wanted. The rights of the kingdom of Bohemia were to extend to a variety of functions from taxation and police to the control of education. Within Bohemia itself there were to be separate Czech and German administrative enclaves and electoral *curiae*. There was to be a Bohemian chancellery and, in place of the Imperial diet, a congress of delegations, primarily for economic questions, to which the Bohemian diet, in common with the other crown-land diets, would henceforth send its chosen representatives. The changes were to be put before a general diet of Bohemian, Moravian, and Silesian representatives. All in all, the Fundamental Articles represented far-reaching concessions. They had their faults: they were constitutionally complicated and socially conservative. They were negotiated with the Bohemians, not the Moravians; the former felt they did not go far enough towards state rights for the whole kingdom, the latter felt slighted and even threatened. As it happened, however, shortcomings did not matter. The Emperor dropped the entire scheme.

The proposals were fiercely opposed by Count Andrassy, the Hungarian prime minister. Hungary had not won equality with Austria to share it with Bohemia. Still less were the Magyars willing to agree to federalisation in Austria since it might lead to federalisation in Hungary, which would raise all their subject peoples to the same level as themselves. But the fiercest opposition came from German politicians. The Germans in Bohemia would not accept the reduction in their privileges. More important, Germans throughout Austria had been unexpectedly affected by Bismarck's success. From resenting his triumph they had begun to admire his creation of a mighty German nation and to view their own future as best safeguarded in alliance with, not against, him. They caught the nationalist infection and saw the Hohenwart proposals as an attack on their German rights. The fact that the Czechs had aligned themselves with France and championed Russia rebounded against them. The Austro-German politicians made it clear that, if they were pushed too far, they might seek the intervention of Bismarck; and Austria-Hungary would be no more. That was enough for Franz Joseph. By the end of October Hohenwart and his more enlightened colleagues were put in the position where they had no option but to resign and watch their solution of the Czech problem consigned to the scrap-heap.

In a way, the Czechs had no right to expect the good fortune that befell them when Franz Joseph first selected Hohenwart. On the other hand, they did have a right to feel aggrieved when he disavowed Hohenwart and abandoned the Fundamental Articles. In the circumstances their resort to a boycott was natural. However, the wisdom of continuing it was soon questioned. It could be argued that without it there would have been no Hohenwart overture in the first place. Clam-Martinic and the provincial nobles, and Palacký, Rieger, and several more of the old leaders, were firmly inclined to this view. But as early as April 1872 it took all their influence and powers of persuasion to reverse a majority decision of the Czech deputies to return to the Bohemian diet. For it could be argued the other way round that, had Czech representatives taken their seats in the Imperial diet, say, in 1870, they could have turned a federalist minority into a majority and have won concessions from Franz Joseph before Bismarck's triumph altered the situation. Certainly, once Franz Joseph had plumped for the line of least resistance and begun to follow the policy favoured by his German and Magyar subjects, he had no need of Czech support and could laugh at a Czech boycott. The Czechs' absence from Vienna in particular made no impact; their presence might at least promote special interests. All the more reason to make a start by going back to the local diets. With France defeated and Russia distracted, there could be no appeal for outside assistance. The Czechs had a right to feel aggrieved; but to sulk in a corner was not the best way of achieving recompense.

The break with the past took time. There was a natural sense of loyalty to the old policy. The electoral system at Land and Imperial levels was weighted against the Czechs, and the paucity of Czech representation made participation look an unfruitful field. The aristocratic-middle-class alliance was still the basis of the Czech

Party. But a breach came in 1873-74. The last to join the boycott had been Alois Pražák and the other Czech deputies in Moravia; in November 1873 they were the first to abandon it by returning to the diet in Brno. The following January they also returned to the Imperial diet. They did so with protestations and resolutions; but they had broken the boycott. Their reasons were simple. The Germans were in an altogether more powerful position in Moravia than in Bohemia, particularly in the towns, and in the view of the Moravian Czechs it was more important to win concessions, however small, by parliamentary attrition than to make grand but fruitless gestures. The Czechs in Bohemia, many of them diehards, had a greater sense of importance. The aristocracy were already an anachronism, but powerful. Palacký and Rieger, still dominant in the national movement, were convinced abstentionists. Even Palacký's death in 1876 did not break Rieger's determination. In the last few years of his life Palacký had been too preoccupied with completing his *History of Bohemia* for his death to undermine Rieger's position. And Rieger himself had been inclining gradually towards a more ossified, conservative approach from the moment in 1861 when he first came to terms with the nobles. But the break with the old policy had to come in Bohemia too.

In fact it began in 1874. In December of that year several of the so-called Young Czechs founded a new party. To distinguish it from the existing organisation they called it the National Free-Thinkers, though the two groups were still referred to as Old and Young Czechs. The leaders were Rieger's critics of former days, Sladkovský and the Grégr brothers. Their differences with him were not new; but they were much sharper. By this time the Young Czechs were in fact so opposed to the boycott that seven of their number returned to the diet in Prague (though they still rejected the idea of participating in the Imperial diet). The boycott had gained nothing; the Moravian deputies had already abandoned it. And the whole policy was redolent of the increasingly unpopular and unproductive alliance with the Bohemian aristocracy. The attitude of the Young Czechs stemmed from their radical views. But there were other reasons. The seven who returned to the diet—and who were elected on the specific pledge that they would—came from wealthy rural districts. The farmers there were not anti-nationalist; but they had interests they wished to see furthered. The price of their crops was more important to them than the niceties of state rights. Noble landowners could happily boycott the diets and know that their economic interests would be looked after by influential friends in Vienna. But ordinary farmers had no means of pressing their grievances other than through the diet.

Now, however, there were new and serious grievances. The Czech Lands, like the whole of Austria-Hungary, had just entered a period of economic crisis. In May 1873 there had been a crash on the Vienna exchange; prices on the Prague exchange had been falling for a year before that. By 1874 industry throughout the Czech Lands was badly affected. For the next four or five years the annual output of iron and heavy machinery, for example, was down by a third. Textile production, already feeling the effect of foreign competition, was no more able to maintain its previous level. The glass industry, geared for export, suffered from a depression that was almost world-wide. Sugar refining, linked with the banks, was equally hard-hit. Distilleries had as much difficulty as coal-mines in finding a market—and more than one brewery went bankrupt in the period. Thus what began with industry spread to agriculture. Industry demanded less in the way of beet, potatoes, and hops. Further, with perhaps a third of the industrial labour force unemployed and wage-levels dropping, there was less demand for farm produce and prices declined. There was soon a depression in agriculture too. Everyone in the Czech Lands suffered in one way or another. The very well-to-do were everywhere cushioned and wanted to do little, while the unemployed and destitute were ill-organised and could do nothing. But those in the middle both needed and had a channel of protest. It was the larger but now not so prosperous farmers who gave their votes to deputies who would sit in the diet in Prague and speak on their behalf. They had backed the Old Czechs in the past; now in different circumstances they backed the Young Czechs. The agricultural depression was slow to lift; increasing competition from American grain prolonged the agony. The farmers continued to support the Young Czech policy of participation. Where farmers led, shopkeepers and artisans soon followed. The Hohenwart fiasco and the economic depression of the mid-seventies together drove the radical wing of the national movement to abandon the discredited tactics of passive resistance. And Rieger or no Rieger, the Old Czechs could not hold out against the tide for ever.

In the background, other forces were at work. Ten Czechs helped to establish the All-Austrian Workers Party at Neudörfl in April 1874. Exactly four years later fourteen Czechs at a meeting in Prague established their own Social Democratic Workers' Party. But although these events have a retrospective importance, at the time it was international events that had the greater influence. In 1875 the South Slav provinces of Bosnia and Hercegovina rose in revolt against the Turks and soon much of the Balkans was aflame. Over the winter of 1877-78 Russia beat Turkey to her knees. The sympathies of the Czechs were wholeheartedly with the South Slavs and their Russian supporters. Funds were raised, meetings were held, letters were sent. Rieger went twice to Paris in pre-1870 fashion to seek help for the South Slav and Czech national causes. He appealed indirectly for Russian backing for the Czech cause. He saw Russia's triumph in 1878 as comparable to Prussia's in 1866 for its possible effect on Austria. The boycott was still the only way to make Vienna yield. But France was cautious, and Russia's triumph was short-lived. With the Treaty of Berlin marking Russia's failure and passing both Bosnia and Hercegovina to Austria to occupy and administer, Rieger finally changed tack. There were now more Slavs in the Habsburg Empire; the time had come to end the boycott and make Slav weight felt in Vienna. Fresh elections in Bohemia in September 1878 gave the Old Czechs 68 seats and the Young Czechs a mere thirteen. But on a vote, only five deputies held out for a continuation of the boycott. One of them was Rieger; he could not actually vote for such a basic change. Equally, however, he could not oppose it and he accepted the verdict of the majority. The boycott was over at last.

By 1878 passive resistance had become discredited and the whole idea was later much maligned. It deserves better repute. It was based on the assumption that the Emperor could surrender to Czech non-co-operation as he had done to Magyar. But the Czechs did not have a native aristocracy; they had to look to provincial Germans. Unlike the Magyars they were not the superior social and economic ethnic group within their own kingdom. They were also a Slav island in a German sea, which made the Emperor and his German subjects view them differently from a Magyar island in a Slav sea. As yet, too, they lacked the social and cultural cohesion and power of national movements that had been successful elsewhere in Europe. From this point of view the boycott was a mistake. Nonetheless, it probably lent cohesion to the national movement at an important time. Austrian repression and exclusiveness might have done that anyway; and the boycott was to some extent simply a means of nursing a grievance. But particularly in the period of the *Tabor* movement, it strengthened the general sense of solidarity both between provinces and among social groups and gave urgency to the development of Czech political life. It also prevented individuals or groups from splintering steadily away to the other side and it almost won what would have been a great victory in 1871. That the Hohenwart affair encountered defeat conceivably proves that co-operation with Vienna was no more rewarding, or alternatively that the boycott was a poor course but the only one. When it was abandoned, the Czechs won concessions but no enormous triumph. That they won anything at all was in part due to circumstances quite outside their control. But it was also the result of the strength that the national movement had built up in the boycott period. In short, whatever passive resistance may have failed to achieve, it certainly left the movement much stronger than it had found it. At a stage when the Emperor was unwilling to grant autonomy to the Czech Lands, passive resistance was a necessary part of the nation's education, though perhaps it lasted too long.

The Czech deputies were back in the Bohemian diet by the end of September 1878. Just over a year later their representatives returned to the Imperial diet. That they could take the second step was the result of the Emperor's change of attitude to the Austro-German deputies who had lorded Viennese politics for almost a decade. He was particularly incensed at their unwillingness to accept the extension of Austrian hegemony to Bosnia and Hercegovina for fear it might tip the balance inside Austria-Hungary towards the Slavs. It was not that he held a brief for the Slavs; but he thought he saw a future for his Empire in the Balkans. So he dismissed his so-called Liberal cabinet and replaced it with middle-of-the-road ministers whose function was to govern, if necessary with Slav support. Count Taaffe, whom Franz Joseph charged to form the new government, entered into negotiations with the Czechs and, to show his goodwill, appointed Pražák minister without portfolio. For his part, Rieger has been criticised for demanding much and getting little. Among other things, he wanted the Emperor to be crowned king of Bohemia, a reform of the electoral law, Czech professorships at the University of Prague, and a separate school board for Bohemia. Taaffe promised nothing except the chance to argue for these things in the diet; a memorandum on state rights was merely noted. Perhaps Rieger was a little inept. Certainly he was past the peak of his leadership. Yet he did secure the return of the Czechs with their basic position reserved; and some of the demands he put forward were soon granted in the diet. Yet his very achievement signalled the end of his major political service.

State rights might come in time. Even the Young Czech Edvard Grégr did not oppose them; he merely thought that, if granted at this stage, they would not transfer power from Vienna and would represent a hollow gesture. In the meantime the struggle for autonomy could proceed on different lines. There were lesser citadels for an ambitious people to storm. There were many areas of what a later generation would call civil rights where the struggle could centre. This was really what participation was about.

Within a month of their return to the Imperial diet the Czech members submitted a fresh memorandum to the Emperor in which they called for equal rights for the Czech language in government offices and courts, in the University of Prague and secondary schools, and in tradesmen's institutes. There was no mention of state rights. But this was a fundamental civil right which struck at the heart of Austro-German superiority. The German representatives from the Czech Lands reacted quickly and submitted a memorandum of their own. In April 1880 the Czechs secured a partial victory. Under the new language ordinances Czech took its place alongside German in the 'outer' work of government in Bohemia and Moravia and won minor recognition along with Polish in Silesia. A year later an Imperial decree divided the University of Prague into separate Czech and German institutions. And just over a year later still, in October 1882, the franchise was lowered for elections to the Imperial diet. The new policy was reaping rich dividends.

Nor is the description 'rich' entirely an exaggeration. Many of the demands of 1879 had not been met. The 'inner' offices remained sacrosanct. But ordinary Czech citizens could now opt for their native language in dealing with minor officials. This was a considerable convenience; and it also conveyed a sense of impending victory. More important, it obliged these officials to be competent in both languages. Most Czechs already knew German and most Germans were unwilling to learn Czech. This disseminated status and aroused ambition. Czechs began to look with envy on the whole range of bureaucratic positions. The change also held out the prospect that one day the Czechs would more or less govern themselves through their own civil service. The effect of the foundation of a separate Czech university was more far-reaching still: there was more to it than the convenience of education in Czech at the highest level; the new university provided many important cultural posts for Czechs. Tomáš Masaryk became the first professor of philosophy. The university also trained generations of Czechs ambitious for employment in Czech-speaking institutions, be they governmental or educational. But the fact of a Czech university was even more important: it was a symbol of the successful revival of Czech culture. The grammars and dictionaries had produced the literature. Now the literature had produced the university. From the university would come a more sophisticated Czech thought, in line with modern developments elsewhere in the Empire and in Europe. From it would come political ideas and leadership, too, as Masaryk was to show. Above all the university was a symbol of the independence of the Czech Lands. The glories of the Husite period had been founded on the original university of 1348; but with the end of Czech independence after 1620 it had become in effect a German institution. Now a Czech university had been created and Czech independence could not be far off. The electoral concessions of 1882, however minimal, were all the further proof that was needed.

CHAPTER 2

The Czech Lands 1878-1900

Economic and Social Change

WHATEVER ITS ULTIMATE AIM, the Czech national movement still had a long way to go, but it now began to quicken its pace. The fate of the national theatre was symbolic. It took from 1868 until 1881 to complete, and it was scarcely open when it was burned down. However, new subscriptions were immediately raised and within two years it was open again. Having once sampled progress, the Czechs speeded up. What really increased the tempo was the acceleration of economic and social change. In particular, there was a new stage in the industrialisation of the Czech Lands, part of a wider European movement: a reaction to the depression of the 1870s, a result of scientific discoveries and technological improvements, a response to outside pressures from Germany and the United States and to local tariffs. The Czech Lands were as well-endowed and as well-situated to profit from these circumstances as they had been in earlier decades. By 1900 more than a third of the railway track in the Empire was to be found there, a remarkable proportion considering the long distances involved in other provinces. The Czech Lands also boasted the most complete network of roads. In the twenty years between 1880 and 1900 the production of anthracite almost doubled and of lignite almost trebled; the output of pig-iron increased fivefold. The machine-tool industry developed rapidly to meet the growing demands of new factories and enterprises at home, the locomotive and coach-building industry to meet the needs of impatient railway-builders in the Balkans as well as at home. The output of processed sugar-beet increased by two-thirds; indeed, all the processing industries based on farm produce made very quick strides. New enterprises also emerged rapidly; steel-making took immediate advantage of the Gilchrist-Thomas process; electro-technical and chemical factories sprang up to diversify industry and resuscitate agriculture; in 1886 the Škoda works produced their first armaments. Cotton found a new lease of life in the export trade to south-east Europe and Asia Minor, though it was in this period that textiles lost their predominance in the Czech economy to processed foods and heavy industrial goods. Czech industry grew immensely in size and variety, and consequently in the number of persons it employed and the range of skills they had to learn. The population in these two decades grew twice as fast as in the previous two, and yet the proportion that lived in towns still managed to rise at a slightly faster rate. It was a period of very rapid urban growth indeed, particularly in newer centres such as Kladno, Plzeň, and Ostrava. Within the towns there was also a trend towards bigger workshops. At the end of the century, factories employing more than a hundred workers represented about a third of one percent of all factories but accounted for about 30 percent of all workers. The size of many individual businesses also grew in a period when the rapid introduction of technical improvements and the steady expansion of the market made sense of amalgamations and takeovers. Much of the share capital for these industries was held by the great Vienna banks, but already by 1900 Prague banks had managed to acquire 15 percent of it. There was an upsurge of big business in the Czech Lands and Prague was bidding to be its financial centre.

By the end of the nineteenth century Czech society was much more sophisticated than it had been half or even three-quarters of the way through. For one thing, there was a recognisable and significant middle class. Statistics are elusive, but some figures for Prague in 1900 are helpful. Of adults in recognisable occupations the self-employed and the administrative and technical staffs together accounted for 47 percent. Not all of these, of course, were middle class in the generally accepted sense. A breakdown according to domestics employed shows that about 33 percent of the families in Prague had one servant, and 8 percent two or more. Prague was certainly not typical of the whole of the Czech Lands; as a highly industrialised capital city, it had more than its fair share of businessmen and officials. But these figures give some indication of middle-class weight at a crucial point. About 49 percent worked in industry, but, understandably, no more than about one percent in agriculture. The percentage in trade and transport was 24, in various other occupations, including public service, about 26. These figures reveal just how untypical was the Prague situation. Comparable statistics for Bohemia and Moravia as a whole show that just over 38 percent of the employed worked in industry and the same in agriculture, that only about 8 percent worked in trade and transport, and 15 percent in the various other occupations, the implication being that inevitably the middle class outside Prague was smaller than inside. The class was nevertheless both numerous and important. Other occupational and social groups were also becoming more distinct. If the percentage of the employed engaged in industry in 1900 was about 38, in 1869 it had only been 29. In the closing three decades of the nineteenth century the percentage engaged in agriculture dropped from 52 to 38, whereas the percentage engaged in trade and transport jumped from 3 to about 8. Although the proportion of those occupied in other ways hardly altered, there was a clear trend away from the traditional occupations to more modern ones. More particularly, a strong class of industrial employees was emerging with its own specific attitudes to Czech society and politics. As a class it was not altogether homogeneous; for one thing, there was considerable wage-differentiation. Workers in the building industry, for example, earned 40 percent more than textile-workers; workers in the steel-mills 75 percent more. There were other differences. The percentage recorded as being engaged in industry included the self-employed as well as employees; in Prague the proportion of self-employed to employees in 1900 was about one to five. Then again, although the rapid advance of industrialisation and urbanisation made the countryside more self-conscious, there was no close-knit homogeneity among those who worked the soil. Holdings of less than 2 hectares accounted for just a fraction more than 48 percent of the total holdings; those of 2-5 hectares accounted for almost 25 percent; those of 5-10 hectares accounted for almost 13 percent; and so on up the line to holdings of more than 100 hectares, which accounted for less than a third of one percent of the total number but in fact farmed more than a third of the soil. And whereas the small holdings were worked almost exclusively by family labour, the large ones were run by officials using wage-labour. In sum, social differentiation in the Czech Lands was as rapid and as marked as economic development.

Economic and social changes of this far-reaching kind would have produced tensions in any European country. It took Britain long enough to come to terms with its working class; Russia failed. It required the most famous revolution in history to expedite the rise of the middle class in France; in Germany it took all the profits of business and all the attractions of war to keep the middle class out of its proper place in politics. But in the Czech Lands every social problem was complicated beyond belief by the additional factor of ethnic division. There were German workers as well as Czech, and Czech businessmen and bankers as well as German. There were confrontations where Czechs were on top as well as the other way round, and confrontations where only Czechs or Germans were involved. But for the most part it was Czechs who were the rising or the aggrieved group, whether factory hands, shopkeepers, officials, or factory owners. And this was true whether the ambition or disgruntlement was between or within social groups. The better-paid German artisan or the more highly privileged German bureaucrat was as much the target of his Czech fellows as the German industrialist was of his Czech employees or the German aristocrat was of the Czech *nouveaux riches*. Complicating every question was also the inevitable feeling among the Czechs that the government, at whatever level, Imperial or provincial, was of the other nationality and therefore alien. Social issues, however small, became national issues at the drop of a syllable. The converse was also true. From the Austro-German point of view disputes took on an extra significance when it seemed that the German people or the Habsburg Empire was at stake. The surprising thing is that tension did not explode more often or more immediately.

Political Developments

The social condition of the Czech Lands in these years was not unrelievedly gloomy. Industrialisation and urbanisation produced poor factory and housing conditions. In particular, working hours were long and wages relatively low. There were harsh periods of unemployment and poverty. These were the circumstances attendant on industrial revolution. But the Imperial government was not totally insensitive. By its financial and tariff policies it maintained the momentum of industrialisation, and it introduced some social legislation. In the period 1883-88 a number of laws were passed regulating hours of work and forbidding the employment of juveniles in factories. Laws on accident and sickness insurance were also introduced. This legislation was general throughout Austria and was based largely on Bismarck's policy of killing socialism by kindness. But it was also a result of the new policy of participation; Czech deputies helped to make the laws. There were concessions at other levels too. In 1884 the ministry of commerce in Vienna drew up new regulations for election to chambers of commerce in the Czech Lands; it lowered the rating qualification and widened their social representation to include shopkeepers and better-off tradesmen. Yet all these concessions were minimal and palliative. And as early as 1886 they were enough, along with the earlier political concessions, to drive the Germans into the same kind of boycott of the Prague diet as the Czechs had just given up.

In the course of the 1880s serious agitation on the Czech side came not in industry but in agriculture. The socialist movement throughout Austria was distracted by a controversy between its radical and moderate factions, and much of the attention of the diminutive Czech Social Democratic Party was taken up with trying to unite the two as well as with trying to avoid an ethnic split. From 1848-49 the prosperity of Czech agriculture had built up steadily. There had been hard times and individual or group misfortunes. Some of the best labour had left for the factories in disgust at the lack of opportunity, and some of what remained existed at subsistence level. But the overall picture was one of economic success. In the eighties and nineties there was a continued rise in yield and production. One of the peculiarities of agriculture was its close connection with industry; a new link, for example, was the habit that had grown up among poorer peasants of earning part-time wages in the towns. So as industry recovered from the depression, agriculture did the same. Nevertheless, these were hard years in the countryside for some. In the period 1884-89 there was a sugar crisis. Supply outran demand, and the effect was felt among both refiners and beet-growers. This sometimes meant that it was felt twice by the same people. A second and more serious misfortune was the grain crisis. It began with the industrial depression in the 1870s, and, because of competition from the cheap grains of North America, the Ukraine, and Hungary, it continued well into the eighties. The sugar crisis was eventually overcome by restricting the cultivation and processing of beet. But a measurable relaxation in the grain crisis had to await a rise in American export prices in the late 1890s—something outside Austrian control. Before either crisis passed there were fierce outcries from those hardest hit. Some farmers and peasants suffered scarcely at all. Cattle-raisers profited from cheap cereals (refrigeration was only beginning to cut import prices, and the downward trend was partly combated by a rising demand); and potato-growers had no foreign competition. Peasants with tiny plots grew no grain, fed their animals a little more economically, and continued to live off their vegetables. But the larger-scale farmers and the better-off peasants with their fields of beet and corn lost both capital and income and called on the politicians for action.

Only a few years before, they had exerted their influence on the Young Czechs to found their own party and break with the boycott. They now led them on to destroy the Old Czechs. Relations between the two foremost political groups had been strained for some time, but for deep-felt national reasons they had grouped themselves together in the Imperial diet to form a Czech Club. When the 1885 elections (under the extended franchise) returned 57 Czech members, there were still excellent reasons for sticking together. There were many manifestations of Austro-German opposition to further concessions. For example, the originators of the so-called Linz Programme of 1882 advocated the transfer to Hungary or to an autonomous Galicia of all Slavs other than the Czechs and Slovenes to make Austria a more German state. By 1885 one of their number, Georg von Schönerer, had broken away to form a wholly anti-semitic, anti-Slav German National Union whose violent Pangermanism proved immensely popular. But, in the event, the Czech Club fell apart. Rieger became the prisoner of a policy of co-operation with the Emperor. In 1883 he told a public meeting that the destiny of the Czech nation was linked with the Habsburgs; but there were very few Czechs who did not remember the tragedy of 1871. In 1885 he lent his parliamentary support to the Triple Alliance, which drew Austria-Hungary, Germany, and Italy together against Russia and France; and yet he had built his reputation on his advocacy of Panslavism and good relations with the French. Conversely, the Grégr brothers became more sensitive to public disquiet. They were particularly conscious of discontent in the countryside. Some of the Young Czechs represented rural constituencies and were kept constantly posted on the well-to-do farmers' needs. In 1884 there appeared in Moravia the so-called Bohemian-Moravian Peasant Association and, within four years, a similar group in Bohemia styling itself the Regional Politico-Economic Association for Small Farmers. Initially, the Moravian group made more of a mark. In 1886 it began to publish a twice-weekly newspaper which, in September of the same year, set out a long list of desiderata. Some of these were directly concerned with immediate problems—assistance for beet-growing and sugar-refining, the regulation of grain prices, a reduction in rail-charges, and a tariff policy in the farming interest. Others affected farming generally—a reduction in taxes and the regulation of credit. And some raised old problems—a reform of the game laws and peasant exemption from military service. The list was extensive, detailed, and very demanding. What the Moravians pioneered, the Bohemians continued. In 1888 they were in touch with Edvard Grégr about the desirability of putting up farmers as candidates for the next provincial diet elections. It was under this pressure and against a background of their previous differences that the Young Czechs finally quarrelled with the Old. In May 1887 Grégr and three others walked out of the Czech Club. In January 1888 they were joined by three more to form an Independent Czech Club. The effect of the new alliance between Young Czechs and farmers was immediate and overwhelming. In the provincial diet elections of 1889, particularly in the beet and grain-producing areas, Young Czech candidates swept the board and left the Old Czechs a pitifully reduced minority.

This was merely the start. Franz Joseph was annoyed at their victory, but his annoyance increased their popularity further. He was also worried by escalating Austro-German chauvinism. To pull the rug from under both sets of rebels he got Taaffe in 1890 to produce a compromise between the Old Czechs and the German Liberals. This proposed the duplication of a number of institutions in the Czech Lands; henceforth, for example, there would be separate Czech and German school and agriculture boards. There would also be distinct *curiae* in the local diets. Negotiated with the up-and-coming groups, this policy might have stood a chance. Excluding them inevitably killed it. But it probably stood little chance, particularly with the Young Czechs. Sensing their power, they were in no mood to see the Czech Lands partitioned; and they obviously represented the popular view. In the Imperial elections of 1891, not one Old Czech was returned from a rural district; only twelve survived at all. The eighteen provincial nobles who had hitherto allied themselves with the Old Czechs quickly deserted. Altogether thirty-seven Young Czechs were elected to the Imperial diet. It was the end of the Old Czechs and the downfall of Rieger. Once champion of Czech autonomy, he was now to be found appealing to the Emperor for funds to fight the Young Czechs, complaining about the dangers of universal suffrage and socialism and finally accepting an Imperial barony. Czech nationalism had become more widespread and radical, and poor Rieger more isolated and conservative. Yet, as the farmers swept on and the others caught up, the Young Czechs were themselves to suffer the same fate. They taught their compatriots professional politics, and ultimately they had to face the consequences.

The electoral triumph of the Young Czechs put an end to Taaffe's compromise. Within two years it put an end to his government. A minister who could not come to terms with one of the minorities and yet was increasingly unpopular with the Austro-Germans was of little use to Franz Joseph. There followed several governments designed to keep the peace, that is, to satisfy the subject peoples, but, above all, to retain the support of the Austro-Germans. Reforms did emerge. There were already four *curiae* in the Imperial diet, representing the great estates, trade, the towns, and the country. A law of 1896 added a fifth, a general *curia,* and this expanded the electorate considerably. Officially, like the Old Czechs before them, the Young Czechs were still wedded to state rights as their ultimate aim. In the interim, however, their tactics were to press, again like the Old Czechs, for maximum concessions from the Imperial government. But they sought economic reforms as well as political changes. Their popularity was correspondingly high, and in the Imperial elections of 1897 (under the 1896 franchise) they won 62 of the 63 seats that went to Czechs. Since the Austro-German deputies carried the labels of various political parties and since only the Galician deputies outnumbered them, the Young Czechs were a force to be reckoned with in Vienna. They therefore made overtures to Count Badeni, then prime minister, and agreed to enter his government on condition that he immediately made crucial concessions on the language question. In retrospect these may seem trivial, but in fact they carried political and economic consequences. Badeni's Language Ordinances of April 1897 gave Czech the same standing in much of the 'inner' civil service as had been conceded to it in 1880 in all of the 'outer'. They also accepted the principle that proceedings begun in Czech should be continued in it. The same rules were to be applied to Bohemia and Moravia (though not Silesia), thus conceding, if only by implication, the administrative non-divisibility of the two provinces. Finally, by 1901 all officials in Bohemia and Moravia were required to prove their competence in both languages. The whole arrangement would greatly have increased the autonomy of the Czech Lands, and would have provided a growing number of official posts for bilingual Czechs. It would have represented a considerable achievement for the emerging Young Czech leader, Josef Kaizl. But despite fairly careful preparation, there was a furious outcry among Austro-Germans of all shades of opinion and from all walks of life. Initially the reaction came mainly from Pangermans and Liberals, but as Badeni resorted to unparliamentary tactics, he brought the Christian Socialists and the Social Democrats down on his head as well. There were even fisticuffs in the Imperial diet. Again this was too much for Franz Joseph. Opposition from his German subjects was bad; a looming revolt was unthinkable. In November Badeni was dropped; and with him went his Language Ordinances.

This was probably the last opportunity of satisfying the Czechs short of independence. The Young Czechs, like the Old, had tried a gradualist policy with a limited objective. There was no doubt about their rebuff; and anger was widespread. Ordinary Czechs lived a long way from Vienna, but throughout the Czech Lands they lived cheek by jowl with Germans. Feelings had run high before. In 1893, for instance, there was an outburst among the young people of Prague. Fired by their new education, of all parties and of none, impatient of their elders, and infuriated by the persistent superiority and repressive authority of the Austro-Germans, they demonstrated against the person of the Emperor himself, on his birthday. With typical insensitivity, the Imperial government saw to it that almost seventy of them were sentenced to long terms in jail; and subsequent leaders in the national movement did not easily forget. This time feelings ran higher still. Czech-German clashes on the Badeni issue reached such proportions in Prague and its environs that in December 1897 the Imperial government imposed martial law. There was then peace for a time. But the damage was incalculable; the Austro-Germans had twice destroyed a reasonable basis for the Czechs remaining subjects of the Emperor—once in Hohenwart's time and now in Badeni's. Barring the unexpected, the only road for the Czechs after 1897 was one leading out of the Habsburg Empire.

Many circumstances combined to make this a long road and not immediately obvious. One was the proliferation of Czech parties, or what might be called the social differentiation of the Czech national movement. The Old Czechs with their strong aristocratic connection had virtually faded, displaced by middle-class Young Czechs from the towns who had political feeling enough to respect the needs of the workers and to recruit some of the farmers. But although the Young Czechs denounced the Austro-Germans for torpedoing the Language Ordinances, their own prestige suffered. They had also been elected on a franchise which favoured the well-to-do, and disgruntlement against the Germans was spreading rapidly down the social scale. In the last analysis the Young Czechs were urban middle-class. In the early 1890s they had fought on farming issues, but when it came to the crunch in 1897, they staked everything on a political issue whose economic aspect was in the interest of an aspiring urban bureaucracy. And in 1898 Kaizl did not find it out of place to join the new government in Vienna as minister of finance. This he deemed to be consistent with a policy of realism, but it was the realism of the businessman, the industrialist, and the shopkeeper. The Young Czechs had ceased to represent more than one section of a much broader national movement.

In the circumstances, the farmers inevitably sought other means of remedying their grievances and discovered interests they held and could promote in common. Forming new political parties also became fashionable. For the election of 1891 the Young Czechs had adopted an agricultural programme drawn up by a south Bohemian farmer, Alfons Šťastný, who was already active in farming associations. After the elections, Šťastný set up an autonomous section of the party, the Bohemian-Moravian Economic Group, to handle agricultural matters. It soon began to act independently, particularly in the interest of the middle farmers. Over the winter of 1896-97 a further organisation appeared, the so-called

Association of Czech Agriculturalists, founded by Stanislav Kubr and working separately on matters concerning farmers in the upper-middle range. So the beginnings of a political split with the Young Czechs were in evidence before the tragic happening of 1897. Thereafter, it was only a matter of time. In 1899 the wholly separate Agrarian Party was founded out of Kubr's group, to be joined by Šťastný's a year later. In the course of the depression the Czech farming community had discovered itself through its association with the Young Czechs, but by 1900 it had publicly established its independent, united political existence.

At least for a spell, the Young Czechs had courted the farmers. They had been neither for nor against the workers, but in any case things had been quiet in the 1880s. By the time excitement grew in the nineties, it was too late for them to do anything to win the workers to their side. The first sign that the socialist movement had recovered from its decade of internal wrangling had come in 1890 when it organised a series of successful May Day demonstrations throughout Austria. The one on Střelecký Island in Prague mustered about 40,000 people and made quite an impression, not least on the election-minded Young Czechs. But the latter's attempt to divert Czech nationals away from their fellow socialists met with little success. For some time, in fact, multinational socialism seemed the one great hope for the Habsburg Empire's survival. At its congress in 1897 the All-Austrian Social Democratic Party accepted that it should alter its organisation to become a federation of parties; and at its congress two years later it pinned its flag to the mast of a federation of nationalities for the governance of the Empire. At a time when Czechs and Germans were otherwise at each others' throats, federalism as a party's practice and declared aim offered some chance of peace. In the Imperial elections of 1897 the Social Democrats won altogether 15 seats, eleven of which were located in the Czech Lands. If Franz Joseph had been prepared to cultivate socialism, or if other Austrian parties had been willing to co-operate with or copy the All-Austrian Social Democrats, then there might have been a happier ending to the Habsburg story. But there was little chance of this. And weaknesses began to appear within the socialist movement. When it adopted its federal structure in 1897, it was partly a defensive gesture; in the midst of the Badeni imbroglio, Czech-German tensions at all social levels were too much for a centralised structure to survive. So by the end of the century the Czech Social Democratic Party had an existence of its own, though still within the All-Austrian movement. The five Czech Social Democratic deputies maintained their opposition to state rights, but they nevertheless faced the dilemma of how to be federalist without being attacked by the other Czech parties and at the same time to be nationalist without being attacked by their German colleagues. It was to cost them some support, but not their position as the new party of the Czech working class.

The 1890s saw the Young Czechs displace the Old, the appearance of the Agrarians, and the Social Democrats coming into their own. At bottom the new political parties were as nationalist as the Old Czechs had been, but in a more sophisticated society they represented different groups first and the general interest of the nation second. In the same spirit the nineties produced other new parties. The Catholic National Party and the Christian Social Party were both founded in 1896. Their outlook was less nationalistic than the Young Czechs' and less materialistic than the Social Democrats'. Their own differences were mainly social, the first representing the upper stratum of consciously Catholic society in town and country, the second the lower; but in general they tended to co-operate. Foremost among their leaders was Jan Šrámek, a priest destined to play an important role in subsequent politics in Czechoslovakia. Among other parties to develop were a Radical Progressive Party in 1897 and a Radical State Rights Party in 1899, both more outspoken and more broadly based than the Young Czechs, one putting its emphasis on social change, the other on national. Their leading figures—Alois Hajn and Antonín Čížek; Alois Rašín and Karel Sokol—had been prominent in the youth demonstrations in Prague in 1893. The young poet Stanislav Kostka Neumann had in fact been imprisoned. In 1897 he began to publish a journal, *Nový kult (New Culture),* as an outlet for his anarchist writings, and to gather a smallish group of like-minded people around him. Most of these splinter politicians were educated middle class, some even intellectuals. They were dissatisfied with the entrenched position of the Young Czechs and the dogmatic attitude of the Social Democrats; they were neither rural enough to join the Agrarians nor devout enough to join the Clericals; so they founded their own parties. Yet another reaction to the political frustration of the day was the establishment in 1897 of the so-called National Socialist Party. This had no link, ideological or otherwise, with Hitler's later party of the same name. On one side, its origins lay in an objection to the non-national attitudes of the Social Democrats and the anti-socialist propaganda this led to. On the other, they lay in the faith that many middle- and lower-class people put in some of the tenets of socialism, without subscribing to its lofty international idealism; they wanted to be socialists, but they were nationalists. In Bohemia (though not Moravia) the

National Socialists proceeded virtually to sweep the Social Democrats from the scene. And the man who presided was another of the youths of 1893, Václav Klofáč. The economic and social development of the Czech Lands and the unyielding attitude of the Emperor and his Austro-German subjects combined to make the nineties politically a most productive period for the Czechs.

Tomáš Masaryk

In 1900 there were some still predominantly German areas in the Czech Lands. But over the country as a whole, it was the Czechs who made up the great bulk of peasants and workers, of farmers and traders. Their hold on the middle class was growing all the time. But in every social group, at every level, they seemed to find their chances of improvement or advancement blocked by Germans. In the Bohemian diet, and in the Moravian after 1905, they were the majority; in the Imperial diet they formed an important minority. In Prague and Brno they could discuss and occasionally influence decisions on local hospitals, roads, and other *minutiae:* but they did not govern themselves, although control of the municipal administration in Prague was of considerable importance. In Vienna they could criticise or contribute, but not decide. In short, they lacked power. On the other hand, they had built up umpteen organisations designed to give their numbers political effect in due course. Yet for that very reason there was now a serious danger that the national movement would remain divided or even collapse. There was, of course, no historical law that demanded that it must carry on to the summit of national independence. But if the Czechs were to remedy more of their grievances, they knew they would have to produce a more united effort from their political parties. It was understanding of this that led in 1900 to the establishment of the so-called National Council in Prague. It was a body representative of political and other organisations; it claimed to be above party and to stand for the entire nation; and in fact it did some useful co-ordinating work in a time of uncertain purpose. Yet it was not totally representative, for it excluded the Social Democrats. Even without them, it had some wide differences of opinion to overcome. Like the whole national movement at this stage, it lacked a definite sense of direction.

Up to the time of his death, Palacký had been the dominant figure in the national movement. He had provided its ideology and leadership. There had been other writers and public figures; but none had contributed so much. With his death, someone was required to fill a similar but different role. Even had he lived, it would not have been enough to write of a once glorious Czech past and to work for state rights as a means of resurrecting it. It is significant that no one could be found to continue his mammoth work on Czech history into the modern period, and that soon after his death the Old Czech Party broke up. The new age was one of proliferating ideas and multiplying parties. In Europe at large Marx and Darwin came into their own and Freud and Nietzsche began to write. European nations flourished, it seemed, not on a unified nationalist party but on a multiplicity of sectional groups, conservative, liberal, socialist. The talents demanded of a new philosopher-statesman were therefore far greater than those demanded of Palacký. He had to meet the challenge both of new ideas and of new parties. Equally, of course, the very multiplicity of concepts and groups demanded a commanding personality if the national movement was not to disintegrate. The man who met the challenge and ultimately made the nation was Masaryk.

Literary and musical figures continued to contribute to the enrichment of Czech cultural life. Svatopluk Čech, the poet, Alois Jirásek, the novelist, Jakub Arbes, the journalist and belle-lettrist, were among a number who reached European stature in the final quarter of the nineteenth century. Antonín Dvořák reached international stature; he spent three years composing in the United States. All of these men were artists before they were Czechs, but the national element in their work was almost overpowering. They provided atmosphere and continuing inspiration for the national movement, although the time was past when its very existence depended on them. Alongside was a whole generation of lesser-known poets and journalists spreading the gospel of reform. The radical nationalist thinkers even included Catholic priests. However, more important in both sustaining and directing the national movement was the new generation of university professors. They lived in an exciting period and had excited students to teach. It was hard for them not to comment on contemporary Czech politics, to support the national movement, and to criticise Austria. Outstanding professors included the Czech philologist Jan Gebauer and the Czech historian Jaroslav Goll. Numbered among their students were the Prague rioters of 1893. But towering above them all was Tomáš Masaryk.

Masaryk was born in Hodonín, a small town in Moravia. This circumstance was important. He grew up in the countryside and understood it; he enjoyed but was never mesmerised by town life, whether in Brno, Vienna, or Prague. His father was born a serf and virtually continued to live as one after 1849, first on Imperial estates and later in service to private landowners; his mother, too, was in service. It was wholly natural, therefore, that he grew up with great sympathy for the underdog and a strong dislike for the idle rich. He owed his education first to his mother, next to good fortune, and in the last analysis to his own efforts both in studying and in earning his keep. He could not but believe in the gospel of hard work, while at the same time accepting that opportunity was essential. His mother was a good Catholic, but had little time to go to church; his father went occasionally, but only in fear of hell. It was a domestic atmosphere conducive to a lessening of faith and a growth in tolerance. The idle rich he learned to dislike were Germans; he had scuffles with his German school-fellows in Brno and disputes with his German fellow students in Vienna. But neither scuffles nor disputes were very serious; and he made many good German friends even in Leipzig, where he went to study for a year. His attitude to Czech-German relations was broadminded. Hodonín was situated on the frontier with Slovakia and Masaryk's father was Slovak-born, another set of circumstances that considerably influenced him. He was naturally inclined to think in terms of links with his Slovak co-nationals. He married an American, Charlotte Garrigue, a young New Yorker whose father came from Copenhagen and whose mother came from Chicago; and he never thought entirely in terms of Austria-Hungary. By inclination he was a philosopher; the title of his doctoral dissertation was 'Plato on Immortality'. But he read avidly and soon found himself out of the philosophical field; his acceptance thesis for his Vienna lectureship was on 'Suicide' and was in essence a work of sociology. His philosophy, being social and political, was highly relevant to the problems of the day. When he became a professor in Prague in 1882, he was already equipped for his eventual philosopher-statesman role.

He was not yet a public figure, even as a teacher or a writer. He was a mere thirty-two and he had been in Prague only twice before. But he was not long in acquiring fame even outside his academic role. He began in a modest way in 1883 by editing the critical monthly review *Atheneum*. This soon carried him into political controversy. Some fifty years before, Václav Hanka, the then director of the Museum library, had let his nationalist enthusiasm run away with him in forging a series of medieval manuscripts intended to prove that Czech literature had its origins in the ninth century. The forgeries had deceived a number of outstanding men of letters, including Palacký, despite occasional authoritative attacks on their authenticity, and they had become part of the national myth. In 1886 Masaryk published an article in *Atheneum*, written by Gebauer, calling for a re-examination of the manuscripts. It was the beginning of a controversy that lasted several years and that won him many enemies, but that in the end vindicated his belief in establishing the truth as a means of supporting, not harming, the national cause. In 1887 he joined in the publication of *Čas* (*Time*), a new periodical with a wider public appeal, and in the same year he made his first tentative venture into politics. He joined with Kaizl and the young Karel Kramář to form the so-called Realist group. In the then fluid state of politics their main purpose was to press for reform in general rather than to advocate a particular policy, though they had firm ideas about improving the press. Despite the fact that Rieger stood by the Hanka manuscripts, they initially badgered the Old Czechs. But with the Young Czech success of 1889, the Realists became ginger-group to the new party. Masaryk still did not regard himself as a politician, but he was being increasingly drawn towards politics. In both the Bohemian and the Imperial elections of 1891 he stood successfully as a member of the Young Czech Party. Yet two years later he fell out with it and laid down both mandates. The Young Czechs were not radical or honest enough for Masaryk. He did not wish to be a politician in the pejorative sense of the word.

So whereas Kaizl and Kramář remained in the Young Czech Party, Masaryk pursued an independent and individual line. From 1893 onwards he edited the influential journal *Naše doba (Our Age)*, publishing a series of critical articles of his own. He also completed several important studies. In 1895 he published *The Czech Question,* in which he set out his view of Czech history and the ethical principles that directed its course; and in the same year he published *Our Present Crisis,* which strictured the Young Czechs. Three years later it was the turn of the Social Democrats to feel the force of his criticism when, in his *Social Question,* he attacked Marxism for its materialist approach. He therefore built up a reputation for perspicacity and independence and attracted a following of young people in particular. He also strengthened his reputation for having the courage of his convictions. In 1899 he became involved in the public defence of Leopold Hilsner, a young Jew falsely convicted of ritual murder. He was impelled to do so by his humanity and rationality, both of which were grossly hurt by evidence of anti-semitism. As a result of his intervention he was subjected to great abuse and even forced temporarily to abandon his lectures. But he also became more widely known and committed to reforms. Finally, in 1900 he could resist no longer and he helped to establish the Czech People's Party, or Realist Party, which set him on the road to be in fact philosopher-statesman to his people.

CHAPTER 3

The Czech Lands 1900-1914

Economic and Social Change

BY THE TURN OF THE CENTURY the Czech Lands were, in the words of a Czech historian, a nation without a state. Fifty years of rapid growth had seen many economic and social changes, and in the course of these the national movement had finally become what its name implied. Among the Czechs there was a very strong sense of common heritage and culture, common complaints and ambitions. Admittedly, there were great differences in economic interest and social attitude, which were clearly advertised in the range of political parties. But on specific issues, or at particular moments of tension, these differences were forgotten. Wide social stratification and party differentiation were in any case the rule rather than the exception in the earlier twentieth century; and the Czech political map did not alter fundamentally till the start of the Second World War. What was specially significant was that the many parties were all Czech. Some were so in the double sense that they did not extend beyond the Czech Lands and that they did not embrace Germans. Others like the Social Democrats were Czech only in the single sense that they were autonomous structures within a wider all-Austrian organisation. In the pre-1914 period there also appeared a similar array of German parties confined to the Czech Lands: the Progressive, the Popular, the Pangerman, the Radical, the Christian Socialist, and the Agrarian. In short, although the Czech Lands were not even autonomous, let alone independent, there was enough activity centred in them for both Czechs and Germans to act in some things as if they were. This was a view that outsiders were also beginning to adopt. There had been an American consulate in Prague for some time. In 1897 the French established one, and they were soon imitated by the British, the Germans, and the Swiss, whose consuls began to speculate about the political future of the Czech Lands. In the Olympic Games of 1908 and 1912 the Czechs participated as a separate delegation from 'Bohemia'. It might be said that the Czech nation had arrived.

The question that remained was whether the nation would rest content or go on to seek statehood and, if it did, whether at federal level or independently. Factors external to the Czech and Habsburg situations were to play a crucial role in deciding the issue; but these apart, it was highly unlikely that things could remain exactly as they were, particularly given the continuing demographic and economic pressures. In the decade 1900-10 the population of the Czech Lands grew by 7½ percent. The ½ percent reduction on the previous decade was illusory since the number of Czechs emigrating to the United States alone more than doubled. The population of Prague increased by only 21 percent compared with 29 percent in the previous ten years, and there was an equivalent slowing-up in the rate of country-to-town migration; but in 1910, 2 percent more of the population lived in towns than in 1900. Industry outpaced the growth in urban population. The most significant advance was in the production and use of electrical power. Many new stations were built to run machines inside the factories and tramcars outside. Oil came into increasing use for firing generators and for motor transport. All this raised the efficiency and output of industry. In some instances there were remarkable jumps in productivity; in the Ostrava coal-mining region, for example, output increased by some 33 percent in the decade 1900-10, whereas the labour force increased by only 0.1 percent. A more highly sophisticated technology boosted the production of machine-tools and chemicals. Industrial expansion necessitated more canals and railways and a rise in the production of steamboats and locomotives. A motor-car industry emerged, and the Czechs turned out their first aeroplanes shortly before the war. International tension gave a fillip to the armaments industry of Plzeň, which in turn stimulated improvements in the making of steel. Austria-Hungary might lag in the world industrial league-table; but in 1913 the Czech Lands claimed about 85 percent of Austria's coal production, for example, and about 95 percent of its sugar output. Between 1900 and the outbreak of war there was also an agricultural boom based on a rising demand for food and a series of good harvests, and the Czech share in Austria's production of cereals increased—from 44 to 53 percent of its rye, for instance, and from 47 to 53 percent of its oats.

Inevitably there were far-reaching social and political repercussions. Rapid population-growth generated demand for a wide range of consumer goods which could not be provided when light industry was neglected. Migration into the towns generated a particular demand for housing which was also in short supply. There was a marked industrial recession in the years 1901-03, affecting heavy industry in particular. Austro-Hungarian reaction to the Russo-Japanese war of 1904-05 helped to restore production to full pitch. But there were further slight recessions associated with the annexation of Bosnia-Hercegovina in 1908 and the Balkan wars of 1912-13, and it was only the prospect of a more general war which put the economy back on its feet again. Shortages were a constant source of discontent to all. While the recessions lasted, they hurt the urban population; and periodic unemployment produced spasmodic but serious outbursts of working-class agitation. Wage-levels also tended to be generally lower among Czech workers than among German, and this added to their mounting sense of grievance. So as far as the working population was concerned, attachment to Austria appeared to confer fewer and fewer benefits. At the same time, other Czechs carved out comfortable niches for themselves within the existing structure. There was a disproportionate growth in the numbers employed in the professions, in public service, and in trade. By and large the first two groups felt themselves aggrieved, unable to rise to the top. But the third group profited greatly from the size of the Austro-Hungarian market and from the export possibilities offered by influence in the Balkans and the Ottoman Empire. Some textile families made considerable profits and acquired positions of great economic and social importance. Bankers prospered; the Živnostenská rose from eighth to fifth place in the hierarchy. So there were some Czechs to whom the continuance of the Habsburg Empire was not anathema. The agricultural boom also produced more contentment in the countryside than for several years. The middle farmers fared particularly well. Apart from higher crop prices, they were able to take advantage of co-operatives and use chemicals and machinery. On the other hand, poorer peasants became much poorer. Rents rose, and there was an increase in the number hiring themselves out for labour. Behind the prosperity there was a degree of poverty that gave renewed impetus to the national movement.

Political Developments

The pressures that built up in the 1890s continued into the next decade. Some Czechs were barely affected; some even profited. But discontent outweighed contentment. Even so, economic hardship and social frustration were not enough to drive the nation into open revolt. What it really wanted was not clear. The Young Czechs and some other parties clamoured for state rights; but this would inevitably have involved the subjection of a German minority to a Czech government and was fiercely resisted. The Czechs just as fiercely opposed partition into separate Czech and German regions. This was an approach much favoured and several times attempted by the Emperor; but the Czechs would go no further than the Moravian Compromise of 1905, under which elections to the Moravian diet were held in separate Czech and German *curiae*, but the diet itself met and did business as a single body. Masaryk adopted a middle-of-the-road policy. He rejected both state rights and partition. Instead, he advocated a system of federalisation in Austria based on autonomous nationality groups, Czech, German, Slovene, and Polish. Given the complexities of the nationality situation and the bitterness of Czech-German animosity his idea was a little unrealistic and impractical. But he rather put the Habsburg Empire on trial. He did not seek an unfair position for the Czechs over the Germans; and he did claim for other nationalities the same justice as for Czechs and Germans. Yet what he and all the others really wanted was a place among the nations of Europe, which by this stage virtually meant independence.

For half a century the Czech national movement had been enabled to give greater effect to its growing strength by real if minor extensions to the franchise. Yet Masaryk opposed a further extension. His view of democracy was qualitative, not quantitative. Against the Social Democrats he argued that universal suffrage would bring no greater benefit than had aristocratic privilege. By contrast, the Social Democrats held to universal suffrage as an article of faith: the electoral means of giving force to the numerical strength of the working class. But even they did not put it in the forefront of their active programme; in the economic hardship of the early 1900s they put their main emphasis on supporting strikes, campaigning about wages, and complaining about prices. The impetus came from above.

With the onset of the twentieth century the Habsburg Empire could hardly resist a universal suffrage that had been accepted by so many others in the late nineteenth. When in 1905 Tsarist Russia accepted it, however reluctantly and with whatever restrictions, the singularity of the Habsburg Empire became still less defensible. The rise to political maturity of the peasant class and the gradual emergence of the working class impressed a small knot of enlightened men whom Franz Joseph called on to be prime ministers in the opening years of the century. He himself had other motives. Universal suffrage did not necessarily mean popular control of the government. On the other hand, its application to Hungary could break the power of the fractious Magyar nobility. In the event, it was not introduced in Hungary as the threat proved enough. However, once mooted, it could not be avoided in Austria since there the political parties immediately awoke to its possibilities. In the

Czech Lands the Young Czechs, most Agrarians, Masaryk and his Realists, and ultimately the National Council supported it. But the most active campaigners on its behalf were the Social Democrats who, partly in co-operation with their colleagues in Vienna, worked up to strikes and meetings from September through November 1905. The campaign was fierce and widespread and was brought to an end only in December when the Austrian government indicated its firm intention of extending the franchise the following spring. It took until December 1906 to get proposals agreed, but universal adult male suffrage had finally arrived.

Masaryk was a pragmatist. In the end he backed universal suffrage for practical reasons; it would increase the number of Czech votes in the Imperial and provincial elections. For practical reasons he also counselled the Social Democrats not to press their political demands too far; Tsarist Russia might be ripe for social revolution, but not yet Austria-Hungary. They heeded his advice and identified themselves more closely with the idea of national revolution. Most other politicians took the same course for similar reasons. Despite their very real differences on social issues the Czech parties now came together in the national movement. The Emperor lent them his assistance. In introducing universal suffrage he also hoped it would turn his subjects' minds to social questions and alleviate the national problem. Up to a point he was successful; in the elections of 1907 the Czech Social Democrats, for example, won almost 40 percent of the Czech votes and seventeen out of the 74 seats. But in distributing seats he gave a disproportionate weight to Austro-German voters everywhere. Whereas he assigned one seat to every 40,000 Germans, he fixed the number of Czech votes required at 55,000. Thus the Germans who comprised some 36 percent of the Austrian population ended up with 45 percent of the diet seats, whereas the Czechs who comprised some 23 percent ended up with only 21 percent. Universal suffrage left the Czechs still underprivileged in comparison with Germans, and, even more important, it left the Czech Social Democrats at a disadvantage in comparison with their German co-believers. Franz Joseph strengthened the Czech national movement and made the Czech Social Democrats a firm part of it.

By this stage it was probably too late to find a means of governing Austria-Hungary, or even just Austria, reasonably acceptable to all its national groups. The disintegrating force of nationalism was too strong elsewhere in and out of Europe. Of course, without the war of 1914, things might have been different for everyone. It is sometimes argued that the Moravian Compromise of 1905 could have been the prototype of an acceptable form of government: all the provincial diets could have been elected on national lines but have conducted business as single units. There is a touch of truth in this, and many of the Czech politicians accepted it in that spirit. But it was accompanied by the same kind of gerrymandering as was franchise reform. The Czechs had a majority in the Moravian diet; but whereas according to population they would have had 35 seats to the Germans' fourteen, they were in fact granted 30 seats to the Germans' nineteen. In one way it was unimportant; they had their majority. But it cast doubts on the Emperor's intentions and confirmed the Czechs' long-standing feeling that they were meant to remain for all time second-class citizens. If war intervened to prevent the extension of the Moravian principle, the war itself was in part the product of Franz Joseph's failure to deal equitably with all the nationality groups in the Habsburg Empire.

On a broader front he was also following a foreign policy that ran counter to the interests and sympathies of his Slav subjects, the Czechs among them. By 1907 Austria-Hungary was in appearance as well as reality the junior partner in the Dual Alliance with Germany. This in itself would have been enough to disturb the Czechs, whose contacts with Pangermanism had been unhappy. But since 1894 the French and the Russians, whom the Czechs had long regarded as their natural friends, had been in alliance against the two central powers. This meant that, if there were a war, the Czechs would find themselves on the wrong side. By its recent anti-British moves, Germany had made things more difficult; Britain now had an *entente* with France and Russia. In a war, therefore, the Czechs would find themselves doubly on the wrong side, obliged to fight against a people whose practices were so much closer to their own ideals than were those of the Germans. In 1908 Austria-Hungary annexed Bosnia-Hercegovina outright. In terms of foreign policy this was an anti-Russian move; it also had the effect of committing Austria-Hungary much more firmly to Germany's aggressive attitude. Almost everything Austria-Hungary did in subsequent international crises had the self-same effect. Internally, this had two consequences. The ruling Austro-German and Magyar peoples showed less willingness to grant equality to the Slavs, and the Slavs in turn became less inclined to see their future lying within Austria-Hungary. No group felt this more than the Czechs, who were particularly affected by the annexation of Bosnia-Hercegovina. They had a soft spot for the southern Slavs, many of whose leaders had studied in Prague, and they quickly realised that a move directed against them was a danger to the future of the Czech Lands.

Two national leaders in particular found themselves increasingly in opposition to the policy of the Emperor. Kaizl and Kramář had been partners with Masaryk in founding the original Realist group in 1889. In 1890 all three reached a temporary accommodation with the Young Czechs, but whereas Masaryk struck out on his own again in 1893, the others went on to make their connection lasting. After Kaizl's death in 1903 the field was wide open to Kramář, and by 1908 he was the leading figure in the Young Czech Party. At forty-eight he was already a seasoned politician both in Prague and in Vienna. A lawyer by training and reasonably well-to-do, he had studied in Berlin, Strasbourg, and Paris as well as at home. He had travelled to Russia and married there. Altogether he was a man of wide experience. A Czech nationalist, he did not necessarily wish to destroy the Habsburg Empire. Essentially his aim was to give the Slav majority in Austria-Hungary a decisive voice in its government. As a corollary, he was anxious to see an end of the Austro-German alliance and its replacement by an Austro-Russian understanding. This policy of Neoslavism was asking a lot of the Emperor even in his few more enlightened moods. But the events of 1908 provided an incentive to seek mass support for it. There was another incentive. In the Imperial elections of 1907 the Young Czechs won only fourth place among the Czech parties, and Kramář now saw himself as a fading figure. He needed a rousing cause; and there seemed to be none with more potential than Neoslavism.

In fairness it must be said that he ran his first Slav Congress in 1908 before the annexation. It must also be said that it required courage to pursue a Neoslav policy. For at least ten years the Austrian secret police had been watching anyone with Panslav sympathies. He organised congresses in St Petersburg in 1909 and in Sofia in 1910, and a Slavonic exhibition in Prague in 1911. He even tried to organise a press bureau. This project came to nothing, and the congresses tended to demonstrate Slav disunity outside the Habsburg Empire. But there remained a basic Czech hostility to the Emperor for soundly Slav reasons, and Kramář found himself more and more at loggerheads with the government and under attack by the Pangermans. By 1914 he was sure that Austria-Hungary must be reorganised on Neoslav lines, or something more drastic would happen.

Kramář was pro-Russian. Personal factors apart, he considered Russia, backward and all as it was, likely to be of much more help to the Czechs than, say, Serbia. He also reckoned on the reform of Russia itself. Others of its supporters saw Neoslavism in a different light, as a means of promoting the Czechs within Austria-Hungary or of protecting it against a possible Reich German takeover. There were others who simply sought to exploit the tension between Austria-Hungary and the Balkan Slavs to their party political advantage. Klofáč, leader of the National Socialists who had gained a mere nine seats in the Imperial elections of 1907, engaged in various doubtful negotiations with Russian and Serbian politicians. But the man who found himself most genuinely and popularly in opposition to Vienna on the whole Slav question was Masaryk.

He was not easily moved by vague sentiments, and he had no specific political ambition. His attitude to the annexation of Bosnia-Hercegovina was determined neither by emotion nor by thought of possible political advantage. His view of Russia was different from Kramář's. As his *Spirit of Russia* showed, he had a very shrewd understanding of the country and particularly of its people; but he was not blind to its faults, especially those of its government. He therefore never evinced an automatic pro-Russian or even Panslav attitude. Among the South Slavs he had many friends, some of them former students. Yet not even these links inclined him to unthinking Panslavism. To him the annexation was evidence that Austria-Hungary had passed the point where reasonable co-operation was possible. In its wake, too, he became involved in the legal defence of the South Slavs. Here again his motives were in no sense Panslav. He clashed with the Vienna government in a characteristic pursuit of equity and commonsense. In the spring of 1909, fifty-three Croats were condemned in Zagreb on charges of treason. The evidence was clearly false, but it took courage to force the government to admit it. Masaryk attended the trial and raised the affair in the Imperial diet. His case was devastating, and eventually the convictions were quashed. In 1910 he again became involved in exposing falsehood. Official documents, published by the Austro-German historian Friedjung, tried to show that Serbo-Croat politicians within Austria-Hungary took both orders and money from the Serbian government outside, and they became the subject of a libel case. Masaryk proved that they had in fact been concocted in the Austro-Hungarian legation in Belgrade and passed back to Friedjung through the foreign ministry itself. Deception at the very heart of government was something Masaryk could not abide. He did not spare his words. In the Imperial diet he reduced the foreign minister to silence and won a great victory. In so doing he gained wide popularity among the South Slavs and among his fellow countrymen. He also earned the hatred of the Emperor's ministers. Like it or not, he became the main symbol of nationalist, anti-Habsburg sympathies.

However, before the outbreak of war in 1914, he had not yet reached the point where he felt that Austria-Hungary must be destroyed. The Czechs were already a nation; they need not yet assert their independence and acquire statehood. His policy was essentially one of federalisation, of autonomy on an ethnic basis for all the Habsburg peoples. In this he differed from Kramář and the Young Czechs. Like him, they did not yet advocate the break-up of Austria-Hungary. But their federal programme was based on provincial units such as the Czech Lands, a mild form of state rights. Masaryk was also at variance with the Social Democrats. In their view, a federal reorganisation would have to be based on personal autonomy. This he considered simply impractical. But like almost all other political parties they too agreed that talk of independence was premature. There was growing social, economic, and political frustration throughout the Czech Lands. There was a particular mood of discontent that arose from the annexation and the general sense of tension in Europe as a whole. But until 1914 there was no group except the small Radical State Rights Party that advocated an end to Austria-Hungary and the establishment of Czech independence. It was the war, and Masaryk, that transformed the situation.

CHAPTER 4

Slovakia 1849-1875

The Demographic Background

THE SLOVAK REVOLT OF 1848-49 was both more and less of a success than the Czech. The Slovaks' aim was low—limited provincial autonomy—and so their failure was less of a blow. At the heart of all their demands was the desire to curb Magyar power, and they achieved something of this. The whole of Hungary was now ruled from Vienna; and if Imperial absolutism after 1848-49 was fairly tough, it was more bearable than Hungarian chauvinism before. In the long run, unfortunately, the story was different. The curb on Hungary did not last. When eventually the Magyars regained and extended their autonomy, the Slovaks found themselves in worse plight than before. The revolt bore a bitter harvest.

In one important respect, population growth, the development of Slovakia after 1848-49 was remarkably similar to that of the Czech Lands, and yet significantly different. Between 1800 and 1850 the population of Slovakia grew from just over 2 million to just under 2½ million, an increase of about 14 percent in the first half of the century. In the next sixty years it rose to almost 3 million, an increase of about 16 percent. But apart from the obvious fact that the Czech Lands started from the higher base, the percentage rise in Slovakia was less than a third of that in the Czech Lands in the first period and little more in the second. The figures for emigration from Slovakia were higher. The peak of Slovak movement to the United States was reached after the end of the century in the years 1901-10. Whereas then something like 100,000 Czechs crossed the Atlantic not to return, possibly some 200,000 Slovaks made the same trip. There also appears to have been much more local movement from Slovakia to Budapest than from the Czech Lands to Vienna. Even so, the population growth-rate in Slovakia was still short of that in the Czech Lands. It could therefore not make the same impact on Hungary as Czech growth on Austria. In 1910 the Czechs made up about 23 percent of the population of Austria, the Germans almost 36 percent. By contrast, the Slovaks made up just over 9 percent of the population of Hungary, the Magyars about 48 percent. In overall Austro-Hungarian terms, too, the Slovaks represented 4 percent of the total population and so had less nuisance value than the Czechs with 13 percent. And all the time the Czechs were improving their position while the Slovaks were losing ground.

This divergence stemmed from the difference between Czech and Slovak mortality rates. In the Czech Lands in the years 1851-57 the number of live births per thousand of the population was on average 38, the number of deaths 29. The corresponding rates for Slovakia were 38 and 36. In the years 1891-1900, the Czech figures were 36 and 26, the Slovak 41 and 29. The Czech birth-rate dropped a little, the Slovak rose; but the significant fact is that it was only towards the end of the century that the Slovak death-rate fell to the level the Czech had been in mid-century (and as it fell further towards 1910, so also did the birth-rate). A further difference between Slovakia and the Czech Lands was in the extent and rate of urban growth. The proportion of the Czech population that lived in towns of 2,000 or more rose from 18 percent in 1843 to 45 percent in 1910. The earliest figure available for Slovakia shows the proportion there as 19 percent in 1869; and the rise by 1910 was to no more than 23 percent. A number of Slovak towns did grow in size; Bratislava expanded from 32,000 inhabitants in 1828 to 93,000 in 1910, and Košice from 12,000 to 44,000, the one trebling its size, the other more or less quadrupling it. Yet in the same period, Prague grew seven times as large and Brno six; and at the end of the period, Bratislava and Košice were hardly bigger than Prague and Brno respectively had been at the beginning. There can be no questioning the fact of population growth in Slovakia; but as its momentum was less than in the Czech Lands, so was its effective concentration.

Economic and Social Change

The area in which the Slovaks were settled was not only much smaller than the Czech Lands but, relative to its size, it was much poorer. It had less agricultural soil and much of what it had was of an inferior kind. There were rich patches in the south and west, and there was a wide range of pursuits, from the cultivation of beet to the growing of hemp, and from the raising of sheep to bee-keeping. Industrially, there was little activity. Gold, silver, and copper had been mined since the Middle Ages, but there was little sign of factory production. Domestic industries—all of them attractive, if primitive—made the economy self-sufficient. But the area was backward, and life, at least for the peasants, was very hard.

The revolt of 1848-49 did introduce some changes to agriculture.

For one thing, there was a rise in activity and an increase in productivity on the estates of the great Hungarian landowners. These developments were most marked on the Hungarian plain, but they were not insignificant in Slovakia. The abolition of the customs frontier between Austria and Hungary in 1850 exposed Hungarian farming to the demands of the growing Austrian market in foodstuffs. Compensation paid to the landowners for their loss of feudal services enabled at least the more extensively propertied among them to capitalise their production. Some machinery was introduced, and more modern methods of farming employed. The actual implementation of emancipation also benefited the former feudatories. The so-called Urbarial Patent of 1853 allotted between a half and two-thirds of all the arable and grazing land in Slovakia to the great landowners. Over the next decade, too, they increased their share through a long run of legal actions before special commissions, also set up in 1853. They received four-fifths of the woodland, and the best four-fifths at that. In addition, the Urbarial Patent left them their lesser seigneurial rights, extending from distilling and quarrying to hunting and fishing. The landowners also found themselves relatively free to impose semi-feudal levies on the peasants, from contributions in kind to periods of labour. In a slowly emerging new age the landowners prospered.

Not so the Slovak peasants. Unlike some of their Czech fellows, none of them had been in the least well-to-do before emancipation, and the Urbarial Patent gave them little opportunity to better themselves. Those who did receive land found it too scant or too poor to enable them to accumulate capital; alternatively they found themselves subject to new exactions. Many of them still used the wooden plough; they left strips fallow in rotation and denuded the forests. Other peasants were wholly without land. Some found seasonal labour in Austria or central Hungary. Others worked on local estates for low wages, often paid partly in kind. In marked contrast to the Czech Lands after 1848, peasant agriculture struggled along at subsistence level. A poorly endowed Slovakia, badly treated at the emancipation, produced prosperity for a minority of landowners and poverty for the great mass of the people. And again in contrast with the Czech Lands, there was no compensation to be found in industry.

The industrial revolution in the Czech Lands did not begin with the events of 1848-49. It had been under way for decades. In Slovakia there certainly had been industrial enterprises of a kind before 1848-49; but even after that, there appeared no more than the beginnings of a revolution. That the new age was now so slow in coming was in part because it had not started up before; there was little tradition and less capital. It was also the result of the incomplete nature of the changes introduced in Slovakia in the period 1848-53. The peasantry were not entirely freed of obligations to the landowners, so that they were not as able as their Czech contemporaries to drift towards towns and industry. They were certainly not granted the conditions in which many of them might have accumulated capital to develop industry. The great Hungarian landowners were put in a privileged position, but everything contrived to press them into agriculture or, at best, the industries connected with it. For its part, Imperial policy was aimed at making the best of a unified economy, so that both state and private industrial capital gravitated towards the western half of the Empire. For this reason, railways were stretched out rather slowly in Slovakia, as in Hungary as a whole. Consequently, the internal market in these regions was very laggardly in its growth, and the little industrial development there was crowded towards Budapest, or, to a much lesser extent, Bratislava. Yet even Slovakia was not quite without development.

In the 1850s and 1860s some 2,000 miles of railway-line were constructed in Hungary as a whole; but only 250 of these were in Slovakia, mainly in the south where the line from Vienna to Budapest passed through Bratislava. At first they were financed by the Imperial government, anxious to bring Hungarian cereals to the Austrian market. Later it was Hungarians who financed them to open the entire Danubian plain to the export possibilities in grain. None of this profited Slovakia, or was meant to. The post-roads built in the eighteenth century also ran east to Košice and south-east to Budapest. In the fifties and sixties poor minor roads wandering through Slovakia were still badly maintained by forced peasant labour. The Danube was almost irrelevant to the Slovaks for transport purposes, and most of its tributaries were only suitable for rafting. Indirectly, however, railway construction did contribute to the industrial development of Slovakia. The production of iron-ore there more than doubled in the fifties, while the production of pig-iron grew about fivefold; in the sixties the rise continued at a slower rate. By 1867, Slovakia produced almost three-quarters of Hungary's iron-ore and two-thirds of its pig-iron. The mines and foundries were in Magyar hands, most of them the property of great landowners. But many of the workers were Slovaks, and the gradual if slow improvement in technical efficiency introduced a generation of them to the industrial revolution. The outer ripples of the revolution also affected some other traditional Slovak manufactures. Factories and steam-power spread to textiles, leather, paper, and wood, though on nothing like the scale to be observed in the Czech Lands. Perhaps most progress in the technological sense was to be found in food-processing. By the sixties, Slovak flour-mills prided themselves on employing more steam-power than Czech, but milling, like distilling and other such activities, was only semi-industrial, being located mostly on the great estates and run by their owners. One significant exception was a sugar-refinery employing 700 workers in the town of Šurany and another employing three hundred in the town of Gabčikovo, both owned and run by Czechs with the most up-to-date equipment.

However, all this was still the pre-history of the industrial revolution. Between 1846 and 1869 the population of Bratislava grew from 37,000 to 46,000, but the number of those who actually worked in industry at the end of that time was less than 5,000. On average, the number of workers per enterprise was just over two, though there were some fairly large individual enterprises. For Slovakia as a whole the percentage of the employed population working as labourers in industry in 1867 was about 5, whereas in the Czech Lands it was already more than 18. On the other hand, however slow and small the industrial growth, the evils of industrialisation had also arrived; wages were low and hours of work long. If there was little industry for the peasants to go to, there was also little incentive for them to go to what there was. In country or in town the Slovaks were a poor people.

Political Developments

The limits imposed on emancipation, the slow change in agriculture, and the slow growth in industry all combined to retard the Slovak national movement in contrast to the Czech. This did not mean that the movement was dead or that it failed to draw strength from the mass of the Slovak people. Their rebellious days of 1848-49 were not forgotten. Throughout the 1850s and 1860s, too, there were constant demonstrations of social and economic unrest. At scattered points throughout the country there were minor peasant risings. Particularly in 1852 and in the period 1859-64 there were violent protests against expropriations and semi-feudal impositions. Naturally the most turbulent of the workers were the miners; they had both a tradition of independence and growing numbers. There were troubles in Banská Štiavnice in 1852 and 1854 and in Spiš and other mining centres in 1851 and 1859-63. But the force the peasants could exert was crude and was easily dealt with by the military. In any case, there were disagreements among the different peasant groups, between the landed and the landless, and between those with larger plots and those with smaller. The workers were best organised in the mining-towns where they had the numbers; but they also were divided from artisans and from people in service of various kinds.

The grievances of ordinary people in this period mainly concerned everyday things, but they were largely directed against Magyars. In another way, too, their grievances were linked with the national movement. A natural spokesman for the miners of Banská Štiavnice in 1852 was Samuel Ormis, a twenty-eight-year-old teacher in the local Lutheran school, a man of great human compassion and strong national feeling. Men such as he kept popular discontent and nationalist politicians in close touch. The local intelligentsia—teachers, priests, and writers of various sorts—were perhaps as numerous in proportion to the population of Slovakia as in the Czech Lands; and many were like Samuel Ormis, prepared to publish their views and go to prison for them. They kept the Slovak national movement alive.

At a higher level the movement went through a trying time. The fifties saw division and heartbreak. The new government in Vienna was not at all anxious to assist the Slovaks' cause, however much they had helped to defeat the Magyars. It refused to entertain the appeals made by Štúr and other radical Slovak politicians and put them under continuous police surveillance. In addition, it established in Vienna an advisory group of conservative Slovaks, presided over by Kollár, now very much opposed to Štúr. According to its lights, this group did try to help Slovakia; in 1850 Kollár even tried to set up a cultural association. The government also established a newspaper, the *Slovenské noviny* (Slovak News), and allowed Kollár to influence its policy. Once again, the conservatives who produced it tried in their own way to mirror Slovak views. But within six months of its first number, Kollár changed it from a Slovak to a Czech-language paper, pursuant to his own ideas about Slavdom. This merely gave credence to the government and the Magyar view that the Slovaks lacked the prerequisite for autonomy, their own language. Kollár's political co-operation with the government was just as damaging. In the crucial period after 1849, he gave it an air of respectability and split the opposition. By the time he died in 1852 the national movement had used up much of its steam in internal wranglings, and the *Slovenské noviny* could be allowed to degenerate into a government mouthpiece. For Štúr these were sad times. He outlived Kollár by four years, dying in 1856. But he first had to watch Kollár and his group abet the Habsburg government in its anti-Slovak actions and then pass his remaining years powerless to resist the government or arouse his countrymen. In 1853 he was able to publish a book on folklore in Prague and a book of songs in Bratislava. He was able to keep in touch with a number of leading Czechs, including Palacký. Politically, however, he could do nothing, and he took to writing *Slavdom and the World of the Future*, which was really a testament of despair. For the Slovaks he saw no prospects within the Habsburg Empire and their only hope in an ultimate link with Russia. The old leaders were finished.

The period of absolutism in Slovakia was politically tough. To Magyar economic exploitation was added Habsburg political direction. The whole of Hungary was divided into regions and sub-regions for the purpose of administration from Vienna. Slovakia was split into two main regions. Some Slovak figureheads were used and some minor officials were brought in from the Czech Lands. Essentially, however, Slovakia was ruled by the Habsburg bureaucracy, backed up, as required, by the Imperial army. There was not the slightest suggestion of Slovak autonomy. The status of the Catholic Church was enhanced; but the independence of the Lutheran Church, which had done most to nurture the spirit of revolt, was very severely curtailed. Moreover, there seemed to be a threat of cultural oppression; it looked for a while as if magyarisation would simply be replaced by germanisation. Yet in contrast to Magyar rule, the despotism of Vienna was enlightened. The law was more impartially administered. The use of Slovak was allowed in lower courts and in subordinate government offices. Education in the mother tongue was authorised in local schools, though in practice most secondary schools used German. There was no self-government; but neither was there really bad government.

This, in fact, helped to keep the Slovak spirit alive. The place accorded to the Slovak language was important. The presence of Czech officials acted as a constant reminder of the Slovaks' links with their neighbours; and many of the Czechs set out deliberately to cultivate the relationship. Beneath the level of Kollár and Štúr, the political pressure from Vienna tended to bring different groups together. Privileged Catholics like Ján Palárik, a young priest and publicist, drew close to Lutheran colleagues like Jozef Hurban, a heroic figure from 1848-49, above all in defence of the language. It was an important association. It kept the national movement in being and ready for the next possible move forward. The moment came in 1860-61.

The October Diploma and the February Patent were born of Austrian discomfiture at the rise of the Italian nation-state. Though they still preserved Habsburg power, they marked the end of unbridled absolutism. The Magyars, however, regarded them as only the first stage in the winning of an improved constitutional position for Hungary and began the campaign that eventually won them equality with the Austro-Germans in the Habsburg Empire. The Slovak nationalists also sprang to life. Their motives were twofold. On the one hand, they saw Magyar intransigence towards Vienna as an opportunity for them, too, to seize the initiative. On the other, they feared lest a Magyar triumph would spell doom for themselves. But divisions reappeared. Matters came to a head in the spring of 1861 with the calling of elections for the diet in Budapest. Palárik quickly threw in his lot with the Magyar politicians to found the so-called 'new school' of Slovak thought. On 19 March the rising leaders of the 'old school', Ján Francisci and Štefan Marko Daxner, both veterans of 1848-49, published the first number of a new nationalist newspaper, the *Pešťbudínske vedomosti* (*Budapest Information*), with one as the editor and the other as the director. However, although a number of Slovak candidates did stand for election on 2 April, none were successful. The franchise was against them. Most of the 'old school' politicians, therefore, began to talk of summoning a separate Slovak Assembly. After suitable preparation in the columns of the *Pešťbudínske vedomosti* it met on 6 June in the town of Turčianský Sv. Martin. The following day, a widely representative crowd of Slovaks, estimated to number as many as 5,000, unanimously approved a *Memorandum of the Slovak Nation.*

It was a remarkable document. Its main draftsmen were Francisci and Daxner, but it was hotly discussed for two days and agreed among an assemblage which included Lutheran and Catholic priests, teachers and lawyers, traders and peasants, and even survivors of the Slovak nobility. Palárik and others of the 'new school' also came and supported it. In the circumstances, it was inevitably a compromise document, and it did not go to the lengths of that other document, the *Demands of the Slovak Nation* of 1848. It sought Slovak autonomy, but not a separate diet. However, it called for wider use of Slovak in schools and administration. It advocated the establishment of a law academy in Slovakia and of a chair of Slovak language and literature in the University of Budapest, and it requested permission for the establishment of literary and cultural societies with their own funds. Finally, in its moderation, it renounced the idea of separating Slovakia from Hungary or of jeopardising Hungarian unity, but called for reciprocal language rights for Magyars domiciled in the Slovak region and Slovaks domiciled outside it.

High hopes were entertained of the *Memorandum.* Its very existence was a sign of strength, its moderation even more so. Within the Empire, the prevailing political mood appeared to be one of concession; Budapest was almost bound to be accommodating.

The outcome, however, was rather different. The Assembly at Turčianský Sv. Martin had established a National Committee. Its leaders, Francisci and Daxner, negotiated with the new Hungarian diet, but they found little sympathy and won no concessions. Indeed, the Slovaks became targets for a campaign of political defamation. The Magyars were in a mood, not to yield points, but to win them for themselves. So the Slovak National Committee appealed to Vienna. In December 1861 they persuaded Štefan Moyses, the sympathetic Croat bishop of Banská Bystrica, to lead a deputation to see the Emperor. For this purpose they prepared a fresh memorandum that reverted to the 'old school' attitude in requesting separate political institutions for Slovakia. A compromise with the less radical 'new school' point of view had won them nothing from the Magyars. To resume a tougher line appeared to make sense, not least at a time when the attitude of the Czechs, too, was hardening. The Emperor listened graciously and later agreed to some of the Slovak demands. He authorised the foundation of a Slovak society, the *Matica slovenská*, and the extended use of Slovak in some secondary schools. He decreed that the language of official business should be that used by the local population, or by the majority according to available statistics. He appointed a number of Slovaks to positions in his Hungarian administration. However, he did not yield on the fundamental point, a separate political identity. What he would not concede the Czechs, he could scarcely be expected to hand to the politically much less advanced Slovaks. If it was necessary for him to bargain with anyone, it was with the Magyars. They were one of the ruling peoples; their leading politicians could be shown the Slovak memorandum as a sign of the Emperor's confidence in them. In a deteriorating international situation, they were also potentially the greatest troublemakers; they could therefore be threatened by the Emperor making accommodating signs to the Slovaks, but they could not be provoked by anything so rash as a promise of autonomy to one of their own subject peoples. Another Slovak delegation to Franz Joseph in September 1863 also failed to win fundamental political concessions.

The leaders of the 1860s could claim their successes. The Assembly, the Committee, the two memoranda, the delegations, were all notable achievements after the frustrations of the fifties. Nevertheless, the Slovak politicians were outwitted by their Magyar counterparts. They could not win a single seat in the Hungarian diet elected in 1865, and they were simply ignored in the talks leading up to the *Ausgleich* in 1867. Earlier differences reappeared. The 'old school' continued to pin its hopes on Vienna; the 'new school' put its faith in the younger Magyar leaders. Nonetheless, these were formative years for the Slovak national movement. The *Matica slovenská* played a particularly important role. It became a centre not only of literary revival, but of political education. Poetry could hardly avoid the issues of the day. Research into the past was bound to touch on the biggest issue of them all. The business of preparing material in Slovak for teaching in secondary schools was itself a nationalist act. Housed in Turčianský Sv. Martin and supported by voluntary subscriptions, the institution itself became a national symbol. With Moyses and Francisci as its first president and vice-president, it inevitably acted as a Slovak political club. To some extent, it softened the politicians' differences. It also raised Turčianský Sv. Martin to the status of Slovakia's quasi-capital and made it in 1870 the natural home for the *Národnie noviny* (*National News*), a newspaper founded by Slovak nationalists to replace the *Pěsťbudínske vedomosti.* Without the *Matica slovenská,* the national movement might easily have collapsed of disappointment.

As things turned out, it remained fairly active into the mid-seventies. But its unity and effectiveness were greatly reduced. The reason was partly its lack of widespread popular support. The national movement was still an affair primarily of the educated: the priests and the ministers, the lawyers and the teachers. The more immediate reason, however, was the *Ausgleich*. If the Czechs felt frustrated, the Slovaks felt abandoned. A saving feature of 1849 had been direct rule from Vienna. At a stroke, the *Ausgleich* removed that protection and substituted the authority of Budapest. What hurt was not isolation from the Czechs—the links had been tenuous for some time—but subjection to the Magyars. Everything was not immediately black. The nationalist mood in Europe was strong; from Russia there were echoes of militant Panslavism; in the Czech Lands the *Tabor* movement was in full flood. The 'old school' politicians still felt able to press their former demand for a special status for the Slovak region. But by contrast, the men of the 'new school' were more than ever convinced of the need to come to terms with the Magyars. They established their own newspaper in Budapest, the *Slovenské noviny* (*Slovak News*). For a time there was almost as much warring between the two Slovak 'schools' as between all the Slovaks and the Magyars. It was a division similar to that which frequently split the Czech national movement, just as inevitable, and just as unfortunate. It played into Magyar hands. Budapest adopted the old Imperial policy of enhancing the authority of the government by exploiting the difference among subject nationalities. In 1868 it granted the Croats a measure of autonomy, but firmly refused it to all other groups. Even though the two Slovak 'schools' came together for a brief spell in November of that year, their differences remained deep and easily exploited. The Nationality Law of December made some concessions. It guaranteed certain nationality rights in church, school, and local government matters. Fundamentally, however, it was based on the concept of a Hungarian nationality to which all the peoples belonged and which gave the Slovaks no theoretical right to exist.

In practice, too, the position of the Slovaks grew worse. Within a year, the ageing Jozef Hurban was sent to prison for daring to publish a series of articles criticising the new law. Even in these circumstances, the two 'schools' could not resolve their differences. The 'new' continued to seek co-operation with the Hungarian government as a means of alleviating the situation. The 'old' founded a league of women and a league of youth, and proceeded to re-establish their newspaper and intensify their activities in Turčianský Sv. Martin. For a short spell it seemed as if their efforts might be rewarded with some success. Moyses died in 1869. Francisci became president of the *Matica slovenská*, and Viliám Pauliny-Tóth, a publicist of long experience, became vice-president. The same year, Pauliny-Tóth was elected to the Hungarian diet for the mixed Slovak-Serb region of Nový Sad and at once began to use his dual position to press for changes in line with 'old school' demands. As in the case of the Czechs, the circumstances of the Franco-Prussian war seemed to offer the Slovaks an opportunity to wring concessions from their government. At this point the 'old school' even found themselves backed by the 'new'. But the Slovaks were more of a failure than the Czechs. Vienna conceded nothing; Budapest counter-attacked. In the elections of 1872 the Hungarian government applied every conceivable pressure to oust Pauliny-Tóth. He lost his seat, and there were no compensating gains. In 1873 the government established a Hungarian Union to foster the idea of Hungarian nationality and refused to sanction a similarly inspired Slovak Union organised by Francisci. It then resorted to a full-scale campaign of magyarisation. In 1874 the three existing Slovak secondary schools were closed and their property confiscated. Two Lutheran and one Catholic, they were accused of educating their pupils in an unpatriotic way—which meant in a non-Magyar way. A year later, the *Matica slovenská* was itself closed on the grounds that it was an unpatriotic institution promoting Panslavism. Protests proved of no avail. Under its statutes, its property was supposed to revert to the nation that had raised the greater part of it. It was confiscated, however, on the pretext that the Slovak nation did not exist. With the destruction of the *Matica slovenská*, the national movement lost its inspiration and support and came on very hard times.

CHAPTER 5

Slovakia 1875-1900

Economic and Social Change

THE *AUSGLEICH* REPRESENTED a major turning-point in Slovak national fortunes in two ways. The Hungarian government resorted to a policy of magyarisation that virtually crippled the old national movement, but also embarked on a programme of economic development that eventually gave it new life. Agricultural change since emancipation had not improved the lot of the peasants, but it had certainly added to the wealth of the Magyar landowners who increasingly found themselves with capital to invest. Austrian capital was also available for industrial development. A main stimulus to growth, however, was the attitude of the government, that the new Hungary must not remain an agricultural country inferior in status to Austria, an attitude only hardened in the 1870s and 1880s by falling grain prices and rising tariff barriers.

The role of the government and the effect of its policy on Slovakia is well illustrated in the case of railway-building. Most lines before 1867 had been financed by private investors, with official encouragement, to transport cereals from the central Danubian plain to the Austrian market. Slovakia had been affected only marginally. After 1867, most of the new lines radiated outwards from Budapest and were constructed with government finance. Hungary's raw materials were located in its mountainous periphery, including Slovakia. To get at them meant building railways. To get at them in Hungary's interest, it turned out, meant the state building railways. The main privately financed line constructed after 1867 (it was finished in 1872) was that between Košice and Bohumín, but it carried almost half of Slovakia's iron-ore off to be worked in Austrian Silesia. A government anxious to develop Hungarian industry could hardly tolerate this; by 1900, either through construction or purchase, it owned more than 90 percent of the railway system. And incidentally, Slovakia benefited. Of the 9,000 miles of track in Hungary as a whole 1,500 lay in Slovakia. It was no longer a wholly backward province.

This was also true industrially. By the end of the century the Slovak share in the production of iron-ore in Hungary was down from almost three-quarters to just over half, and of pig-iron from over to under two-thirds; but in each case production increased absolutely more than threefold. There were also important changes in the structure of industry; the number of firms dropped and their size increased, so that one ironworks at Podbrezová employed as many as 2,000 men. Budapest became the main centre of machine production. In the last three decades of the century, however, Slovakia raised its output of lignite thirteen times over, so that it produced practically a fifth of the Hungarian total. There were also developments in manufactures depending on local materials such as wood, sand, and stone; paper-mills, glass-works, and cement factories all became fairly common. Finally, there was growth in industries linked with agriculture: flour-milling, sugar-refining, distilling, and even textiles. Here, however, progress compared unfavourably with that on the richer Hungarian lowlands.

Some of the new factories were owned by the government, particularly for iron and steel. Much of the capital was Magyar, some Austrian, some foreign. But there were also elements of Slovak capital. Credit associations and savings banks first appeared in Slovakia during the 1860s and 1870s, encouraged by the nationalist leaders who appreciated their political as well as their economic and social value. The first proper bank to be founded was the Tatra in Turčianský Sv. Martin in 1884. Others followed, and by the end of the century it was estimated that the stock capital of the Slovak banks equalled a fifteenth of those in Budapest. In social terms this meant that there were signs of an emerging middle class. Certainly, the pattern of society was changing. The percentage of the employed population working as labourers in industry in 1857 had been about 5; by 1900 it was about 12. The percentage engaged in industrial pursuits at all levels was 17, in transport 2; the corresponding figures at the end of the previous decade had been 15 and 1. The 1900 figures for the Czech Lands were higher—38 percent of the employed population engaged in industry, 3 percent in transport. Yet Slovakia could already boast 3 percent in commerce and banking, and the same percentage shared between the public services and the professions. Cities and towns were growing. The population of Bratislava increased by a third between 1869 and 1900, from 46,000 to 61,000, the population of Košice by two-thirds, from 22,000 to 35,000. The little town of Zvolen more than trebled in size, from a population of 2,000 to one of more than 7,000. In all, over 21 percent of the total population now lived in towns of more than 2,000 inhabitants, compared with

19 percent in 1869. Here again, the Czech figure of 43 percent was much higher. Yet, even if it was behind in the race, Slovakia was nonetheless on the move.

All that was happening in Slovakia, however, was not necessarily happening to Slovaks. Those who declared themselves to be of Slovak nationality in 1880 numbered about 63 percent of the entire population. By 1900 the percentage was down to 61, though the drop may have resulted from tampering with the statistics. At any rate, only two-thirds of the people going through these changes were really Slovak. In the towns, where most of the changes were taking place, the situation was even worse. In those numbering 2-10,000 inhabitants the Slovaks made up little more than half; and in the handful numbering more than 10,000 they accounted for only a fifth. It was in this sense in particular that the Slovak situation was less advanced than the Czech; by 1900, for example, nine-tenths of the citizens of Prague claimed Czech nationality. It was little compensation that a quarter of a million Slovaks lived in central Hungary, or that one in every eight of the citizens of Budapest was a Slovak. On the contrary, this was itself evidence of the depressed state of those Slovaks who had had to go south to find jobs which, menial though most of them were, were still better than they could find at home. Some Slovaks did make a success of their lives in Budapest; and rather more were successful in Slovak towns. Even here, however, they had nothing like their proportionate share of the better-paid or more prestigious jobs, particularly in the public services and the professions. Yet the real sign of continuing backwardness was the fact that such a large proportion of the population of Slovakia, the vast majority of them Slovaks, still lived in the countryside and tried to make a living out of some form of agriculture. In 1900 the percentage in the Czech Lands was 38; in Slovakia it was still as high as 66.

It had been higher ten years before when it stood at more than 68. At the time of the *Ausgleich* it must have been higher still. To some extent the drop, although slow, was the result of the attractions offered by industrial growth. It also reflected changes in the countryside. Emancipation had not freed the peasants from all their old obligations, and here and there a number of new ones had been imposed. Labour obligations were particularly common. What destroyed them gradually was partly the climate of opinion, but rather more the growing capitalisation of large-scale agriculture that made forced labour much less profitable than wage payments, and made both less profitable than possession of the land. Legal actions were also used to reduce the size of peasant holdings, or to appropriate them altogether. Not all holdings were dwarf-sized, but the larger were mostly rented from great estate-owners or their middlemen. In theory, a law of 1896 enabled tenants to buy up their holdings; but they had to prove that they or their families had tilled the land in question for at least fifty years and they also had to pay an almost impossible purchase price. This militated against the growth of a well-to-do peasantry, as well as driving more peasants off the land. Between 1870 and 1896 the number of individual holdings in Slovakia decreased from about 500,000 to just over 400,000. The vast majority of those that disappeared were under 5 acres. The number of medium-sized, of from 5 to 50 acres, increased fractionally, but the number of larger also dropped. The same amount of land was owned in bigger lots by fewer people. Comparative figures are not available, but in 1896 the distribution was very uneven. Holdings of up to 5 acres comprised about 52 percent of the number, but accounted for less than 6 percent of the available land. Those between 5 and 50 acres comprised only about 2 percent of the number, and yet they accounted for practically 58 percent of the land. Indeed, the disparity was really more marked. About 800 people, owning over 1,000 acres each, held among them about 36 percent of the region's agriculturally usable territory.

For a single peasant family a plot of 5 acres meant little more than subsistence farming. Two-fifths of the smallholdings were in fact less than one acre. Peasants working them could only survive by hiring themselves out for labour elsewhere. At the time of the emancipation, too, a large minority of the peasants had received no land at all. So the number of those hiring themselves out had always been in excess of those living wholly on the returns from their own land. The decline in the number of smallholdings simply added to the body of peasants in search of full-time wages. The peasants were not simply attracted to industries and other alternatives; they were driven to them.

Among the peasantry there was, indeed, a grim process of pauperisation. Industrial growth was not fast enough to absorb the entire surplus from the countryside. There were wages to be earned on the big estates, where wheat and barley production increased spasmodically in the last quarter of the century. However, it was also the big estates that introduced most new farm machinery, thus reducing the demand for labour, and for a while they too felt the effect of the agricultural depression in Europe. In addition, those in the north and east were less prosperous than the rest. In fact, the number of wage-earners in agriculture dropped slightly in the years 1869-1900, a period of population growth. Even for those fortunate enough to find employment, wages were not high, being on average some 20-30 percent poorer than those pertaining in central Hungary, which were themselves relatively low. Some could find relief by going south, or even south-west into Austria. But for the many who had neither land nor jobs in the country and who were unable to find work in the towns, the only answer other than starvation was emigration, particularly to the United States. The statistics are unsatisfactory, but the numbers involved were large. The movement got under way in the 1870s, primed by American needs, but it developed a full head of steam only in the eighties and nineties as the hardships of the Slovak population increased. It is estimated that by the end of the century some 400,000 people had emigrated from Slovakia to the United States. This represented an annual loss of almost six in every thousand of the population of median age, twice the corresponding loss in the Czech Lands and five times that in Germany. It represented a total loss equal to approximately one-seventh of the population figure for Slovakia in 1900. Some of the emigrants were enticed by the promise of the heaven that awaited them across the sea—whether or not it did. Others went simply because their passage was paid by relatives who had preceded them. Villagers followed successful neighbours. Yet the real driving-force was poverty. About 90 percent of those who made the journey were from poor or unemployed peasant families, and of the remainder, many were from mining families or from the unskilled workers in the towns. The greater number hailed geographically from the north and east of Slovakia. In contrast to Ireland, Slovakia did not suffer a potato famine; but as with Ireland, emigration was the only escape from a terrible backwardness.

It was not only Slovaks who emigrated from Slovakia. There were Magyar peasants in Slovakia as well as on the Hungarian plain. However, at the bottom of the social scale in the countryside it was Slovaks who predominated. At the other end, the reverse was true. Of the nearly 800 people owning holdings of over 1,000 acres in 1900, only ten had Slovak as their mother-tongue. The Magyar owners of holdings between 100 and 1,000 acres outnumbered their Slovak counterparts by three to one. Nevertheless, what must not be forgotten in all these figures is that there were Slovaks who owned large or even very large parcels of land, just as there were Slovaks who were rising in industry, state service, and the professions. The real trouble was the disproportionate number of successful Magyars. The position in teaching is illustrative. Slovaks comprised about 10 percent of the population of Hungary in 1900, but less than 7 percent of the teachers in technical schools and less than 2 percent of those in colleges were Slovaks. In a sensitive area the Slovaks had achieved nothing like the positions their numbers warranted.

Political Developments

From 1849 to 1875 the Slovak national movement had lived in what might reasonably be termed a fool's paradise. During those years Magyar power was either curbed or appeared capable of being curbed. The proscription of the *Matica slovenská* in 1875, however, was a clear sign that the Magyars had not only shaken off all the restraints imposed on them by Vienna, but that they were able and anxious to impose even greater restraints upon the Slovaks. Magyarisation had not been defeated in 1849; it had only suffered a temporary setback. What the Slovak movement had to face after 1875, therefore, was not a campaign for greater rights, but a struggle for survival. In 1874 all three Slovak secondary schools had been closed; in the years up to 1900 more than half the Slovak primary schools were also closed. A law of 1879 made Magyar compulsory in secondary schools. In 1883 an Educational Society for Upper Hungary was founded in Nitra to spread knowledge of the language and feeling for the Hungarian idea; and a further law of 1891 made Magyar compulsory even in primary schools. A knowledge of Magyar was already mandatory for entry to state service, and it was increasingly obvious that only genuine Magyars got in. A law of 1874 had so rigged the franchise that continuing Magyar hegemony was assured. Thereafter, influence on the open ballot or simple military interference on election days guaranteed the rest.

Slovak nationalism clearly had a tough fight on its hands. There was a sense in which the policy of magyarisation helped it. Many of the grievances of the last quarter of the century were economic or social. Low wages, land scarcity, and barriers to promotion would in other circumstances have produced interest groups cutting across the different national lines; and there were traces of this in later years. Magyarisation, however, healed the interest divisions and gave Slovak nationalism a certain unity. On the other hand, magyarisation brought more problems than advantages. It was very difficult to produce a nationalist élite where there was no national system of higher education, and almost as difficult to maintain wide popular support where primary schooling was also under siege. There was also the tendency for the talented or the ambitious to go over to the other side.

If the task confronting the Slovak nationalist movement was new, so in time was the nature of the movement. The changing composition of Slovak society was bound to affect it. Economic grievances and social aspirations had to give it a new character, even a greater urgency. Yet the pace of change was not quick enough; the growth of the middle class in particular was too slow to give the movement real force by the end of the century. The very fact of emigration sapped its potential strength by drawing off many of the most discontented or the most able. On the other hand, by a curious twist of fate, the emigrants became part of the nationalist movement.

For some time it was the old leaders and the old tendencies that persisted in the movement. Moyses had died in 1869 and Palárik a year later; Pauliny-Tóth died in 1877, but Hurban not till 1888. In the year the *Matica slovenská* was closed down, Francisci was only fifty-three, Daxner a year younger. Daxner died in 1892, but Francisci saw the new century in. There were enough old politicians around to continue the previous policy. Indeed, the only party of any size was the Slovak National Party that had emerged from the Slovak Assembly with the original *Memorandum,* and in the altered circumstances it simply adhered to it without much notion of how to give effect to it. Hurban resurrected the idea of linguistic fusion with Czech and went off to consult Rieger in 1877; but he got no active support. He also petitioned Franz Joseph in 1878 to revive the *Matica slovenská,* but again without success. Pavol Mudroň, a Martin lawyer who became leader of the party in 1877, was only forty-two, but he was also wedded to the ideas of the 1860s, during which he had grown to political maturity. In 1877 Hurban's son, Svetozár Hurban Vajanský, the emerging party ideologist, was younger still, only thirty. Yet he, too, was full of past ideas. In particular, he was a Slavophil. He believed in cooperation with the Czechs, whom he saw both as close kin and as the leading Slav nation in the Austro-Hungarian Empire. This was to be significant for the future, though uncomfortable for the present. However, Hurban Vajanský saw the main hope for the Slovaks in the rise to supremacy of all the Slav peoples, led by Russia. This was largely a pipe-dream, and it was even more unfortunate for the present. It confirmed the Magyars in their belief that Slovaks like Hurban Vajanský and his colleagues in the National Party were traitors; and it also won them support for their belief from the Austro-Germans and from the Emperor. The period following 1875, one of Russian intervention in the Balkans on the grand scale, was hardly the best time for Slovak nationalists to propound Slavophil views. That they should have done so is perfectly understandable. They might have lost one battle, but, with the help of big brother, they would win the next, or the next again. But their attitude was unfortunate in another way. Hurban Vajanský's views were almost messianic. The Slovaks should simply await the coming; all they need do in the meantime was preserve the faith.

In fairness to Hurban Vajanský, it must be admitted that it was difficult enough to preserve the faith, and that he and his like contributed magnificently to the task. Perhaps more than anything else, he was a poet; and in periods of trial poets keep the spirit alive. He was still writing at the time of his death in 1916, and more than once he went to prison for his views. Yet the same attitude of passivity was responsible for an unwise decision on the part of the National Party. In 1884 its leaders declared their loyalty to the Imperial crown and Hungarian state, but also announced that they would not participate in the elections of that year. The reasons they gave were wholly sound. The Hungarian government was abusing the law against the Slovak people and terrorising the Slovak electorate; no political party in the Hungarian diet so much as recognised the existence of a Slovak nation. Their decision was also quite understandable. Why participate in an election when they were bound to lose? Why not abstain in protest? On the other hand, it stemmed from their belief that all they could and should do at this stage was withstand the Magyar onslaught and await some outside miracle. And it had unfortunate consequences, particularly when it was repeated for the elections of 1887 and 1892. The Hungarian government was allowed to act as if there was indeed no Slovak opposition, only pro-Magyar voters; as if there was one Hungarian nation. Such Slovak voters as there were, were at best disenfranchised, at worst disorientated. The national movement lost political leadership and political experience. And the party itself lost impetus, some degree of credibility, and contact with reality.

This in no way meant that the National Party ceased to function politically. In 1886 it was forbidden to proceed with a congress to celebrate the twenty-fifth anniversary of the *Memorandum*, but it was successful in establishing a National House in Turčianský Sv. Martin in 1889. To some extent this was a substitute, if a not very grand one, for the *Matica slovenská*. In addition, the National Party continued to publish its newspapers and periodicals in Martin and to spread its various politico-cultural activities elsewhere. Yet even its base in Martin was now a mistake. The town was little and barely growing; it was not the best centre for keeping in touch with a gradually changing Slovak society. By the 1890s, however, the National Party seemed almost to have given up the fight.

In the early 1890s its spirit revived a little. From the start, much of its support had come from what might loosely be called professional people and intellectuals, from lawyers, priests, teachers, writers, and students. For the most part it continued to receive their loyalty, though relative to the population their numbers seem to have declined. It had also enjoyed the backing of Slovak merchants in the towns. At first there had not been many of them, but more appeared with the gradual economic growth of the 1870s and 1880s. The establishment of the Tatra Bank was significant. By 1884 there were bank officials and small investors—be they business proprietors or well-to-do peasants—to lend a touch of middle-class support to the National Party. This infusion of new strength, however slight, was one element in its revival. Another was the rumbling of working-class discontent.

The National Party was not unaware of the grievances felt by factory workers in the new and expanding industries. Neither was it unsympathetic. It simply had no policy. Or rather, it saw workers' grievances in mainly national terms. Slovak factory-hands were being exploited by Magyar factory-owners, just as the Slovak middle classes were being kept out of the public services by the Magyar gentry and their puppet government. The solution in both cases was a nationalist one. To some extent this was right, and the workers knew it. Yet nationalist slogans brought no immediate relief—and occasionally the owners of factories were Slovaks. Here and there, workers began to look for other answers, in strikes and in political organisations of their own. There had been strikes in the sixties; there were more in the seventies. Many groups were involved, from railway workers on isolated tracks to printing workers in several towns at once. Though benefit societies were set up, trade union organisation was weak. The workers were too few and too scattered. Successful strikes were also few; the employers could usually rely on support from the government, local or central. For a while in the eighties strikes were fewer; the pace of industrialisation was increasing, and so was the practice of emigrating as an alternative to going on strike. Yet enough occurred to upset even the Slovak middle classes, small as were its industrial interests. For some years strikes were probably fewer for another reason. Various forms of working-class political organisation had appeared in Hungary in the late sixties in the wake of the First International. A society called Forward had been founded in Bratislava in 1869. As elsewhere in Europe, the seventies were a period of dispute, of rival organisations feuding for the loyalty of a smallish factory labour force. In 1880, however, a unified organisation was established, the so-called Universal Hungarian Workers' Party. In the best Marxist tradition it fought on behalf of the Slovak working class as well as the Magyar and included Slovak as well as Magyar functionaries. In the best Marxist tradition its programme was also relevant to the needs of the time, particularly demands for a ten-hour working-day and social security benefits. Partly as a result of its pressure, a law of 1884 put a sixteen-hour limit on the working-day, although this was not always observed.

Its existence was another factor reducing the incidence of strikes for a time. Yet as the eighties rolled on, they returned. Bratislava was particularly prone to them. The National Party was no happier about these strikes. Nor could it draw comfort from the state of working-class political organisation. The Universal Workers' Party continued on its way despite harassment by a hostile government. It lost some of its influence as local groups reappeared and ideological disputes were vigorously renewed. It was too strongly orientated towards Budapest. New benefit societies were not necessarily socialist and paid scant attention to it; trade unions reappeared to lead the strike actions that it obviously could or would not organise. Yet it survived as one of the bases on which was founded the Hungarian Social Democratic Party in 1890. And it was this as much as anything that made the Slovak National Party look to its laurels.

The emergence of the Hungarian Social Democrats was inevitably a shock for the older established party. It could see a long-term rival. What was conceivably of more consequence was the fact that the new organisation envisaged a Hungarian solution to Slovakia's problems, whereas the National Party advocated a local Slovak one. Or put another way, the new party thought not of a national, but of a class, conflict. This was not only contrary to the policy of the National Party; it also threatened to undermine its wider support. Some working men had been members of the *Matica slovenská,* and some of the new factory workers read the party's newspapers. The National Party liked to think of itself representing the entire nation, and it could not therefore disregard the threat now presented by the Socialists. This was another reason why it tried to pull itself together.

A further factor was its sudden awareness of what was going on in the world outside Slovakia. The traffic to the United States, for example, was not one-way. Some migrants returned, and news of American happenings percolated back. Small fraternal societies had been appearing among the American Slovaks for some time. In 1890, however, Peter Rovnianek, a twenty-three-year-old Slovak journalist just two years landed, succeeded in establishing a National Slovak Society based in the city of Pittsburgh. Admittedly its major function, thousands of miles distant from Slovakia, was to care for the interests of American Slovaks. Nonetheless, its motto was political—'Liberty, Equality, Fraternity'—and one of its declared objects was to assist kinsmen 'across the Atlantic in their efforts to make and keep their homeland, in the heart of Europe, a land of free men with free institutions'. This kind of news, and the material and literary help that came with it, were natural stimuli to some kind of political revival, as were developments nearer Slovakia.

There was the lesson of what was happening in the Czech Lands: about 1890 the Young Czechs supplanted the Old. Politically nearer, inside Hungary, there was the example of an upsurge of nationalism among the Rumanians, whose situation was very similar to that of the Slovaks. Their National Party had been founded in 1881 and was now in the midst of a struggle to resist magyarisation. In 1891 it received some encouragement from the setting-up in Bucarest of a Rumanian Cultural League, and the following year it submitted a memorandum to the Emperor in which it not only set out all its complaints but demanded autonomy for the Rumanians and the other suppressed peoples of Hungary. When its memorandum was rejected both by the Emperor and by the government in Budapest, it was published for the entire world to see. For the Slovak National Party this was the tilting factor, an occasion for solidarity. A Slovak journalist, Gustav Augustiny, already edited the Rumanian National Party's newspaper, *Tribuna*. Now was the time to do more. Three Slovak delegates attended a conference of the Rumanian National Party in Sibiu in July 1892 and agreed to full inter-party co-operation. The following January there was another conference, which was also attended by several Serbian representatives from southern Hungary, and it was agreed to prepare a congress of all the suppressed peoples of Hungary. The Slovak National Party had found a new lease of life. When seventeen Rumanians were put on trial in May 1894 for their 'treasonable' activities, three Slovak lawyers undertook their defence before the Hungarian court.

The trial was a judicial farce, and thirteen of the seventeen were sent to prison and fined. The whole incident only intensified the magyarisation policy of the Hungarian government. But co-operation between the suppressed nationalities did not end. In August 1895 a congress of Slovaks, Rumanians, and Serbs was held in Budapest itself. It condemned the Magyar view of a single Hungarian nation and demanded autonomy for each of the suppressed peoples in matters of administration and justice; it called for universal suffrage and secret balloting, and for freedom of assembly and of speech; it sought non-interference in church affairs and self-administration for local schools. It marked the high-point of co-operation between the nationalities and the zenith of their success. They had the Hungarian government worried, and even secured attention in the world press. But success brought its own problems. The Hungarian government retaliated by applying pressure to the appropriate bodies to remove from office those priests and teachers who had participated in the congress and by restricting still further the freedom of assembly and speech. No concessions whatever were made to the nationalities' demands. In 1896, a joint protest by the three groups against the celebration of a thousand years of the Hungarian state were simply drowned in repression and propaganda.

However, the period from 1890 to 1896 was one of revival and reorientation for the Slovak National Party. Its representatives at the congress of 1895 included some of the lawyers who had come forward for the 1894 trial as well as old hands like Pavol Mudroň and Hurban Vajanský. In working with their colleagues from Transylvania and Slavonia, they refurbished old policies and devised new lines of action for themselves and their party. A campaign was begun for the opening of new Slovak schools and the reestablishment of the *Matica slovenská*. The Slovak scene was as lively as it had been in the 1870s. Yet both the combined nationalities body and the Slovak National Party made the same mistake. At the 1895 congress all the nationalities together decided to stand aloof from elections to the Hungarian diet and in 1896 the Slovak National Party decided specifically not to participate in the election of that year. Passivity, however understandable, lost the nationalities the advantages they would have gained from operating actively as a single political propagandist group. Passivity also demoted the Slovak National Party from its position of leadership and began to fragment the Slovak national movement a little.

For the 1896 election the National Party actually advised such electors as it had to vote for the newly-founded Hungarian People's Party. In the prevailing circumstances of Magyar terror this was reasonably intelligent. A Magyar-dominated group, that for religious and social reasons was opposing the ruling Liberals, could be expected to suffer less during the election from the attention of Magyar police and bully-boys than any Slovak group. The People's Party also claimed to represent the religious interests of moderate Catholics and the social interests of small proprietors, and it therefore appealed to many among the Slovak voters. It was anti-socialist; but it certainly acquired more votes than it lost that way. It was also noticeably anti-semitic; but for that very reason it won widespread support at a time when Jewish refugees from Tsarist persecution were allegedly carving out lucrative careers for themselves throughout the towns and countryside of Hungary. Finally, partly on principle, partly for electoral advantage, the People's Party came out in support of implementing the Nationality Law of 1868. This was enough to commend it to a Slovak National Party that was anxious to secure at least basic rights for the Slovak people. In the event, the People's Party secured only a handful of seats in an election marred by more than the usual amount of police brutality, and was thus in no position to help the Slovaks, even if it had really wanted to. All the National Party had therefore succeeded in doing was damaging its image and squandering its support.

In the last few years of the nineteenth century it was thus a much-reduced body. Even when pushed along by new forces and strengthened by fresh recruits, it was unable to give a lead to the national movement. The responsibility was not entirely its own. Following the election of 1896, the policy of magyarisation was carried further by the so-called Liberal government of Baron Bánffy. When meetings were prohibited and strikers shot down, it was difficult for anyone to do anything. Economic progress also further divided the Slovak people without producing a dominant social group. In the long run, fragmentation of the national movement was doubtless inevitable. In the late 1890s, however, it was incomplete and not wholly damaging. Support for the Hungarian People's Party, for example, had driven several Slovaks to take a new look at the national movement, among them a young priest named Andrej Hlinka. He had been brought up in the atmosphere of the Slovak National Party, but in 1895, while in the little town of Liptov, he joined the People's Party. He did not sever his connection with the National Party, but what attracted him about the other organisation was its interest in the peasantry. Although only thirty-one, he was already greatly concerned to promote practical, self-help organisations among the people at large. In 1898 he even became a candidate for the People's Party in a by-election. However, that date also marked the beginning of his estrangement from it when he saw its interest in implementing the Nationality Law declining and when he became aware of how few Magyars voted for him. He had not yet decided to found a Slovak People's Party or to break completely with the National Party; but he had certainly tested a new dimension of the national movement.

The late 1890s also witnessed the continued strengthening of another dimension. The Hungarian Social Democratic Party still distracted the attention of many Slovak workers from what nationalists considered the proper purpose of political agitation. The contribution made by Slovaks to the party was certainly of some importance, perhaps greater than that of any other nationality. Bratislava workers were particularly active. Improved connections also developed between the party and trade unions in many parts of Hungary, so that working-class organisations as a whole became more united, and to that extent more distinct. The strikes of the period affected many towns and trades, and extended their objectives to prices as well as wages, to housing conditions as well as hours of work, and to universal suffrage as well as union rights and privileges. In short, working-class organisation became more political, which attracted it away from nationalism. On the other hand, the Hungarian Social Democratic Party was weakened by a dispute about the tactics to be followed where the working class was comparatively small. It mirrored European quarrels. It also faced a powerful government that drove many of its more radical leaders into impotence in the countryside. In a rural society it had no policy on the peasant question. National issues also kept impinging themselves upon what in other countries were social matters. The official attitude to the national question was very inadequately thought out. It strongly supported the right of every ethnic group to use its own mother-tongue, but otherwise it acceded to the idea of a single Hungarian nation, regarding anything else as inimical to the unity of the working class. This ultimately annoyed the Slovak working class. By the end of the century, Slovak Socialists were much more active in promoting their beliefs in Bratislava than in contributing to party debates in Budapest. In any case, the Slovak working class was not large enough to remain aloof from the national questions agitating Slovakia as a whole. A Slovak workers' journal had already flourished for a few years in Budapest itself, and it was clearly just a matter of time before Bratislava would be able to boast its own socialist party.

Hlinka and the Socialists had one thing in common, an inclination to look to the Czechs for inspiration and assistance. In the tradition of Kollár, Hlinka believed firmly in Panslavism as the key to a happy future. In *Katolické noviny* (Catholic News), of which he became a co-editor in 1897, he regularly advocated Czech-Slovak reciprocity on the Kollár model. In the case of the Socialists the idea was something of an accident. There had been Czech workers in Budapest for many years; but it was the growing persecution of the late 1890s that brought Czechs and Slovaks together there. It was a Czech suggestion, for example, that there should be a distinct Slovak workers' journal to cater for them both. In any case, these were the years in which Socialists in the Czech Lands were being called on to face up to nationalism as a key political issue; so it was natural enough for their Slovak brethren to look across the frontier for advice. By 1900 the Czechoslovak ideas of Hlinka and the Socialists were only beginning to form. But at least they were a bond between themselves and also between them and some figures emerging in the National Party.

The failure of the latter to capitalise on its earlier successes and take a positive attitude in the election of 1896 inevitably produced an internal reaction, from the very young, from the students. Elsewhere in Europe, it was normal enough for graduates to travel abroad to complete their studies. In the case of Slovakia, intending students had to go away to get any university education at all. Some went to Budapest, some to Vienna. With the reinstatement of the Czech University in Prague, most went there. The majority of them came from families with some means, or from families that might be classed as intellectual. They were already biased towards nationalism, and being young they were also ripe for absorption of new ideas. Contact with the lively Czech national movement was an exciting experience in itself, but in the 1890s in particular the young Slovaks in Prague came under the influence of Masaryk and the Realists, who were conscious of the importance of Slovakia for their own national movement. In 1896 they established the Czechoslovak Union, dedicated to promoting both the cultural and economic development of Slovakia and Czechoslovak unity. They even interested Hurban Vajanský in their organisation and its objectives. A group of them then set about trying to establish some kind of youth movement in Slovakia on Czech lines. The leading figure was Vavro Šrobár, a medical student, who finally managed in 1898 to found a journal to give Slovak youth its say. Edited by Pavol Blaho, a former medical student from Vienna, published monthly in the Slovak border town of Skalica where Blaho now practised, and printing articles from Slovak students at home and abroad, *Hlas* (*The Voice*) became the focal point for young supporters of the National Party anxious to push it in the direction of a positive Czechoslovak policy. On Masaryk's advice, *Hlas* initially adopted a cautious approach. It called for Slovak secondary schools and a Slovak university; supported language rights and administrative reforms; and advocated universal suffrage. It also preached Czechoslovak co-operation, but accepted the existing Hungarian state; and endeavoured to educate Slovak youth away from anti-semitism and religious excess. In place of Hurban Vajanský's passive messianism, it offered a policy of practical and detailed work within defined limits. Above all, it accepted an educative role for itself. Unfortunately, *Hlas* did not persist long in this policy. It began to attack old-fashioned views within the National Party and the influential politicians who held them and to alienate rather than educate those who held different views outside the party. It became a propagandist rather than a practical journal and although it influenced a variety of young Slovaks, it did not succeed in establishing a youth movement. It produced its own disputes between Šrobár and Blaho, and it roused some opposition to the Czechoslovak idea as an anti-clerical one. Nevertheless, within the National Party, it entrenched the Czechoslovak idea more firmly than ever Hurban Vajanský's Panslav notions could have; and outside, it certainly implanted it as one of the possible alternatives for the future. A combined Czechoslovak approach to the problems of the day now featured in the thoughts of the several political groupings that went to make up the Slovak national movement of 1900.

In the history of the movement there is no magic attaching to the end of the nineteenth century. Yet it was much more broadly based, if more loosely linked, in 1900 than it had been at the time of the *Demands* of 1848, or of the *Memorandum* of 1861, or even in the days of the *Matica slovenská*. Despite a fierce policy of magyarisation since the *Ausgleich,* it had survived as a living force, however weak and divided. Yet it was neither impossibly weak nor wholly divided. It lacked telling economic and social power; but here and there it was beginning to speak of a policy as well as to think of survival. The *Memorandum* had represented a retreat from the *Demands,* and ever since the *Ausgleich* it had been let slide into the background. Yet there was now talk of specific policies within the framework of a Czechoslovak national movement. That this was so was partly the outcome of social change, partly the result of the faith and courage of leaders of differing opinions and varying abilities, from ageing conservatives to youthful radicals. Slovakia lacked a large élite, but it had one of quality. These were difficult days for priests and ministers to stand up for nationalism; the Lutheran Church was even more wedded to the establishment in Hungary than the Catholic. Yet there were many who spoke out for the Slovak cause. These were also difficult days to come by a Slovak education. Yet letters flourished and kept the language alive, and writers infused patriotic spirit into the minds of old and young. With the exception perhaps of Pavol Országh-Hviezdoslav, few of the poets were known abroad, but their contribution to the national movement in a difficult period was no less substantial. The contribution of the Slovaks in the United States was also quite remarkable. In the case of a more highly developed movement it might not have meant so much. Slovaks writing home, however, were frequently more nationalistic than Slovaks living at home. The National Slovak Society not only sent funds to individuals in need, but also kept in regular contact with emerging leaders such as Blaho. The *American Slovak News* also penetrated to Slovakia and was important in spreading nationalist ideas in just those most backward areas from which so many emigrants had come.

The Hungarian government testified to its influence by trying unsuccessfully to have it closed down by the Pittsburgh chief of police in 1896. There were other newspapers as well, and innumerable pamphlets. Some emigrants returned to take part in the national movement. Indeed, the importance of the emigrant contribution to the strengthening of the national movement was attested by the trouble the Hungarian authorities took both to spy on emigrant activities in the United States and to ban the import of their papers and books. Finally, the new life in the Slovak national movement owed more than a little to Masaryk. In this, as in so many other things, he was already well in advance of his compatriots.

CHAPTER 6

Slovakia 1900-1914

Economic and Social Change

AT THE TURN OF THE CENTURY, Slovakia, in contrast with the Czech Lands, could not be described as a nation without a state. There was a national movement; behind that there was a genuine Slovak consciousness which was becoming more intense and certainly more widespread. But too large a section of the population of Slovakia was still Magyar and wanted to remain so, and too many of the rest did not yet feel strongly. No foreign state appointed a consul in Bratislava as in Prague, and foreign observers like Henry Wickham Steed and R. W. Seton-Watson were still to discover the existence of Slovakia. For its part, the national movement was uncertain about its aims. There was no talk of federalisation, but there had been talk of autonomy. Interest in Czechoslovak co-operation had nothing to do with the possibility of independence. Certainly, there were vague ideas about a glorious future. For the moment, however, the real aim of the national movement was to survive and make gradual gains. Continuing economic and social development in Slovakia pushed in the same direction.

The population continued to grow. In 1910 it was almost 5 percent higher than in 1900. This was only two-thirds of the increase in the previous decade. But it was the ten years from 1901 to 1910 that saw the highest-ever rate of emigration from Slovakia to the United States; half as many made the trip and did not return as in the previous thirty years. The true increase in population in the first decade of the twentieth century was probably over 10 percent. The fact that numbers equalling more than half the absolute increase went abroad shows just how strong the pressure was. In the same decade there was a slight rise to 23 in the percentage of the population that lived in towns and a rise in the numbers in particular towns, such as Bratislava and Košice. Yet in absolute terms, there were rather more people living in the countryside in 1910 than in 1900. If there was a larger urban population, there was greater rural overpopulation. On the other hand, the nature of employment continued to change. In 1910 nearly 20 percent of the population was engaged in industry as against 17 percent in 1900; for transport the figure was 3 against 2 percent. In absolute as well as relative terms there were fewer people engaged in agriculture in 1910 than in 1900, though it was still the main form of employment. Clearly, more industry found its way into the countryside, or into the very small towns, and more peasants were driven to take it up. Significantly, there was little change in the percentage of the population employed in trade, the public services, and the liberal professions. Even more significantly, the percentage of the population that could actually claim Slovak as their mother-tongue dropped by at least a percentage point; and the proportion of them who held good positions or sizeable properties remained infinitesimal. Two examples will suffice. Of more than 6,000 public officials working in Slovakia in 1910, only about 150 could be classified as Slovaks, a mere 2.5 percent. Of the industrial capital invested in Slovakia in 1910 only 1 percent was Slovak-owned.

All this had important consequences. There were more Slovaks looking for more work. Those who went abroad eased the pressure. They also sent money home; in fact, there seem to have been links between the National Slovak Society and the Tatra Bank. Some thousands of Slovaks found their way to Budapest, fast becoming a large industrial and population centre; but their contribution to solving the work problem in Slovakia was slight. Industry, of course, provided much new employment. There were two economic crises in the pre-war period, one running from 1900 to 1903 which hit heavy industry particularly hard, and the other from 1913 to 1914 which was more generally damaging. In the interval, however, there was considerable development, much of it supported by government funds. In heavy industry, the biggest expansion was in the output of iron-ore, but in the intermediate range of industries there was expansion in textiles and even in chemicals. By 1913 Slovakia accounted for close on 20 percent of the industrial production of Hungary; this included some 70 percent of its iron-ore, 55 of its paper, 35 of its textiles, and 20 percent of its chemicals, though less than 5 percent of its machinery. Indeed, compared with certain other parts of Hungary, Slovakia was industrially fortunate. On the other hand, when considered as a unit, it was over-weighted in the direction of the provisioning industries, which together accounted for almost one-fifth of its total output, and the metal-working industries, which together accounted for over one-third. The really sad fact, however, was that all the new industry was still unable to provide enough employment for Slovakia's surplus labour. Even those who found factory jobs had their problems. Though there were some genuine improvements in working conditions, it was still true in 1910 that two-thirds of the male labour force worked more than ten hours a day. For Hungary as a whole it has been calculated that the real value of wages declined by over 10 percent in the period 1900-13; and for Slovakia, that wages among Slovak workers were 30 percent lower than those for Magyars.

In agriculture in general, there was now a marked recovery from the effects of the depression. On the bigger estates, the gradual process of improvement continued. However, this simply accelerated the pauperisation of the poorer peasantry. Emigration was only a partial and irregular cure, for it left many peasants behind and sometimes returned others. There was a mammoth outflow in 1905; but the American depression of 1908-09 sent practically the same number back. Emigration was also an unnatural cure. It took the able-bodied men in particular, and left the least fit at home to scrape a living from tiny plots. For their part, agricultural labourers had sometimes to spend eighteen hours a day in the fields, but they were lucky to find a hundred days work in the year. Agricultural wages were generally lower than industrial; the labour supply saw to that. Health conditions in the countryside were poor, and epidemics not uncommon. And it was the Slovak peasantry that seemed to come off worst in almost everything. In arguing with local officials, for example, Magyar peasants had the advantage of knowing the language and therefore of being able to exercise their guile. Man for man, Slovak peasants paid more in taxation than Magyar; it was a crude form of magyarisation, if nothing else.

Political Developments

Out-of-work labourers and underemployed peasants were bound to nurture discontent. So were underpaid workers and land-starved farmers. When so many of the bosses and estate-owners were Magyars, complaints were almost forced to assume a national character. When other workers and other peasants, who just happened to be Magyar, got much higher wages and paid much lower taxes, the trend towards nationalisation of economic grievances was inevitably accelerated. When a small but fairly ambitious middle class was stopped in its tracks by Magyar restrictions, it could not help but become more nationalistic than ever, which is precisely what happened in the years after 1900. University graduates with diminishing prospects in the public services were natural recruits to a more active national movement. So were small businessmen, forbidden to accept Czech financial assistance. It was hardly surprising when in 1901 the National Party changed its policy and participated actively in the election of that year.

Quite sensibly, its candidates took as their main electoral plank the Nationality Law of 1868. For good measure, they also called for universal suffrage and the much overdue redrawing of electoral boundaries. They won four seats. With so small a number they could not even begin to make an impact on the Hungarian diet, particularly since the Rumanians and Serbs had again abstained in the election. Nevertheless, four deputies gave the National Party a political presence. Their electoral programme also represented a direct challenge to the Hungarian government. To call for the implementation of the Nationality Law and to demand electoral reform was to ask it to step down from its entrenched position of racial dominance. At one stage, it appeared as if this might not be too much to expect. In 1905-06 there was a fierce tussle between a now extremist Hungarian government and Franz Joseph. What the Magyars particularly wanted was their own tariff and their own army. The point Franz Joseph was least willing to concede was the army, and, to dish the Magyars, he got ready to introduce universal suffrage in Hungary as he was already introducing it in Austria. This was the moment of greatest hope for the Slovak national movement. Universal suffrage would have conveyed many Slovak members to the Hungarian diet. Sadly, the moment passed. The Magyars were too astute to fall into a trap. They conceded defeat on the army issue and emerged from the crisis clutching their still restricted franchise. They also embarked on their fiercest magyarisation campaign yet to create a single Hungarian nation while there was still time. It was against this background that the Slovak national movement had to play out the period until the First World War.

If the franchise had been democratic and the elections fair, the Slovaks might have returned as many as forty of their own people as deputies in Budapest. As it was, they were able to elect four in 1901, one in 1905, seven in 1906, and three in 1910. It was some consolation to be able to co-operate with the Rumanian National Party when it also abandoned abstention; but its numbers were low too: fourteen in 1906 and only five in 1910. There was nothing the Slovaks could do but keep a tiny flag flying. They could not promote political reform. They could not even temper further acts of magyarisation, such as the Education Acts of 1907 which extended state control to denominational schools. Indeed, some of them lost their freedom. Ferdiš Juriga, a Catholic priest elected in 1906, was imprisoned for two years for 'incitement'; his lay colleague Milan Hodža received an only slightly shorter sentence on the same charge. All hope of a parliamentary solution of the Slovak problem was gradually extinguished in the last years of peace.

In fact, all sanity seemed to disappear. This was shown in the treatment meted out to Hlinka, who in 1905 went as priest to Ružomberok, a little town near Turčiansky Sv. Martin, and at the end of the year founded the Slovak People's Party. It was a logical step in his own development, and he was being no more politically active than many of his Magyar colleagues. In the election of 1906, however, his party was nothing like strong enough to put forward its own candidates, and so he lent his assistance to Šrobár, campaigning as one of the ginger-group of the National Party. Magyar priests supported Šrobár's opponent. Šrobár almost won, and immediately found himself on trial for 'incitement'. Although no action was taken against the Magyar priests, Hlinka was suspended from his care for taking part in politics and put on trial on the same empty charge. Both were found guilty and sent to prison, Šrobár for one year, Hlinka for two. In 1907 Hlinka was brought from prison to face another charge of 'incitement', this time in his farewell letter to his parishioners, and sentenced to a further year and a half. The Hungarian government turned a reasonable critic into a really bitter opponent, as well as making him a martyr. To increase his hostility and strengthen his following, it created a few more martyrs. Hlinka had collected funds to build a new church in his home village of Černova. In October 1907 the villagers protested at the insensitive appointment of a pro-Magyar priest, but they were fired upon, fifteen of them were killed, and others wounded. The following March, fifty-nine of them were sent to join Hlinka in prison. It was increasingly difficult to think of a peaceful solution to the Slovak problem, never mind a normal parliamentary one. It was rather surprising, then, when Hlinka re-established his Slovak People's Party in 1912 to work for a solution within Hungary. It was also inevitable, given that there was as yet no genuinely viable alternative. But both Hlinka, as leader of the party, and Juriga, as its secretary, had spent sufficient time in Magyar prisons to hate Hungary and eventually to cast it off.

In comparative Slovak terms, Hlinka was a considerable figure by 1914. So was Hodža, who had also suffered imprisonment, but did not wholly abandon hope of bettering the Slovaks' position within Hungary. He was a Realist in the Masaryk sense, and although only twenty, was made a member of the editorial board of *Hlas* when the periodical was founded in 1898. He stayed with it until its demise in 1904. But in 1903 he also began to edit *Slovenský týždenník* (*Slovak Weekly*) and in 1910 *Slovenský denník* (*Slovak*

Daily), both aimed at a wider readership than *Hlas*, particularly among the neglected peasantry. First elected to the diet in 1905, he was still a deputy at the outbreak of war. As a Realist, he was simultaneously more radical and more positive than many Nationalist Party supporters, anxious to get through to the peasants and also willing to make the most of the tiny political opportunity allowed to the Slovaks. His imprisonment did not sway him from this policy. He continued to cultivate the peasantry and to exploit his position in the diet for propaganda. From 1910 onwards, however, he looked increasingly towards an Austro-Hungarian solution to Slovakia's misfortune. He was already attuned to this, as was Hlinka, by his steady advocacy of Czechoslovak co-operation. As the situation deteriorated in Hungary, however, he found himself more and more attracted to the ideas of the Archduke Franz Ferdinand who, in his dislike for the Magyars, was now associated with proposals to put the various Slav peoples on a par with the Germans and the Magyars. How serious the archduke was in his intentions is beside the point. Hodža was in contact with him and genuinely believed that some new political structure would emerge for Slovakia upon his accession to the throne. Should this not come about, however, Hodža was too far committed to the nationalist cause and too embittered by his experience of the Magyars to want to stay docilely within Hungary. There could be separate autonomous Czech and Slovak provinces within a reformed Habsburg Empire, or a single Czechoslovak province. There could be an autonomous Slovak province within Hungary. But the existing trend could not continue. Slovakia could not be permitted to disappear from history.

Behind Hodža, as behind Hlinka, there was growing peasant support. Though the one was Lutheran, the other Catholic, they co-operated closely at one stage. In the election of 1906, Hodža worked in collaboration with the People's Party. Personal circumstances separated them in the years before the war; so did their own and their supporters' religious views. Hlinka went on to resurrect his People's Party, in which the interest of the Catholic Church was strong, Hodža to magnify his influence within the National Party. Politically, however, both continued to receive backing from the peasantry. In the end, Hodža had perhaps more support than Hlinka. He was the more independent personality as well as the superior publicist; the circulation of his *Slovenský denník* exceeded that of Hlinka's *L'udové noviny* (*People's News*). Both, however, realised the political value of the Slovak peasantry and gave a rural flavour to the national movement. It was too soon to set up a Slovak agrarian party as such, but in their separate ways the two men did what was possibly the next best thing. What this meant was that the peasantry had begun to make their weight felt and were strengthening the separatist tendencies of the national movement. Within the Social Democratic Party, too, separatist tendencies increased as the workers made their influence felt.

By the end of the century Slovak members of the Hungarian Social Democratic Party were already somewhat restive. As time wore on, they also became conscious of the changing mood of the Slovak people and the hardening attitude of the Hungarian government. Slovak workers were particularly hard-hit by the early depression in heavy industry and were especially aware of the revolutionary events in Tsarist Russia. Slovak Socialists could not remain unresponsive. What was important now was not primarily that there were strikes, but that they pulled the Slovak Socialists towards nationalist rather than class-conscious attitudes. In October 1904 a group in Bratislava published the first monthly edition of *Slovenské robotnícké noviny* (*Slovak Workers' News*), which five years later became a weekly. In June 1905 a Slovak Social Democratic Party was established independently in Bratislava under the leadership of Emanuel Lehocký, a tailor's assistant. Nine months later it rejoined the Hungarian party to become simply its Slovak committee; but the separation process could not be reversed indefinitely. The Hungarian party persisted in its pro-Magyar attitudes, and the Slovak committee loosened its bonds year by year until in April 1914 it became effectively an independent organ. The last few years of hardship before the war strengthened the dislike of most Slovak workers for the Magyar politicians and factory-owners who seemed to be the source of all their troubles. The Social Democrats could accordingly go with the nationalist tide, or sink. In principle they were federalists, but in face of intransigence from the Hungarian government and lack of sympathy from the Hungarian Socialists, they had no option but to swim with the tide. They even began to talk of supporting the Slovak bourgeoisie in promoting the national revolution.

Pressure from below drove the National Party to abandon its passive attitude to Hungarian politics. It reaped only persecution and heightened magyarisation. Consequently, its supporters and allies were driven to consider the possibility of more extreme solutions to Slovakia's problems. Further pressure from below—in response to Magyar pressure from above—pushed the newly emerging political parties in the same nationalist direction. The vicious circle continued. The strikes that immediately preceded the war, for example, met with very severe repression. The Magyars succeeded in producing the opposite result to the one they intended; pushing the Slovaks into the arms of outsiders, prominent among them the American Slovaks. The National Slovak Society sent money to Hurban Vajanský to assist the National Party, it brought across Blaho and others to maintain interest in the United States, and it paid Tomáš Čapek to visit Slovakia and publish an absorbing study in English, *The Slovaks of Hungary*. In 1907 it also helped to found the Slovak League, an association of Slovak societies in the United States dedicated to work for Slovak independence. Formed in the wake of the Černova shootings, it lent particular support to Hlinka. In 1911 a Slovak Socialist Party was established in Cleveland, and it was undoubtedly a factor in the decision to organise the separate Slovak Social Democratic Party in Bratislava. The Slovaks in America, more nationalist than the Slovaks at home, were enabled, with the restrictions the Magyars imposed on Slovakia, to influence their brethren towards more radical views than might otherwise have been the case.

However, the most important group of outsiders to whom the Slovaks were driven for succour were the Czechs. The Slovak Socialists found it easy to seek advice from Czech Socialists across the border very much at odds with their German colleagues. It was on Czech advice that *Slovenské robotnícké noviny* was published. Czech delegates attended conferences of Slovak Socialists and, what was more important, supplied them with occasional financial help. Hlinka also looked across the border to the Moravian People's Party, which provided a Catholic tradition different from that of the Hungarian hierarchy. Hodža had belonged to the *Hlas* group and later, in the columns of *Slovenský denník*, was a regular advocate of Czechoslovak co-operation; but both he and Blaho became more and more interested in the policies and activities of the Czech Agrarians and accepted financial help from them to set up agricultural associations in Slovakia. In August 1908 the Czechoslovak Union in Prague sponsored a meeting between Czech and Slovak representatives in the Moravian border town of Luhačovice to discuss questions of cultural and economic co-operation, and similar meetings followed annually. In August 1909 a group of Slovak youth met in Turčianský Sv. Martin and decided to publish a new review, *Prúdy* (*Currents*), under the editorship of Bohdan Pavlů. In the tradition of *Hlas*, it made the very young as convinced of the need for co-operation as their elders. Even the old men within the National Party responded to the attractions of practical economic co-operation with well-to-do Czechs. There had long been sound reasons for the Slovaks to work with the Czechs, but it took Magyar intransigence to make them wholly overriding.

Mounting pressure from all quarters eventually drove the National Party to take some demonstrative public action. In June 1911 the ageing Mudroň led a deputation to the Hungarian prime minister with a memorandum that sought an end to the wrongs done to the Slovaks contrary to the letter and spirit of the Nationality Law of 1868. A legitimate request, it was simply pigeonholed. Resubmitted in 1913, it was again ignored. So the National Party took a further initiative. In May 1914 it gave the lead in forming, on the Czech model, a Slovak National Council. This was to represent the interests of all Slovaks and to co-ordinate the activities of all parties. Its chairmanship rested with the president of the National Party, now Matúš Dula, but its membership included, for example, the Socialist Lehocký. Dula was also getting on in years; but the Council was remarkably representative of Slovak views and drew up a programme stressing the need for close co-operation with the Czechs to secure federalisation throughout Austria-Hungary. It is significant that, just before it was formed, a meeting of Czech politicians in Prague, sponsored by the Czechoslovak Union, protested against the persecution of the Slovaks and called for federalisation. The national movement in Slovakia was not yet seeking independence, and certainly did not see Slovakia as part of a Czechoslovak state. But it was proceeding in harness with the Czech movement for autonomy of some kind for both the Czech Lands and Slovakia.

CHAPTER 7

The Creation of the Czechoslovak State

1914

THE SLOVAK NATIONAL MOVEMENT was not as powerful or sophisticated as the Czech. Yet in 1914 even the Czech movement did not really think in terms of national independence. Certainly, the story of the last century was crowded with successful national revolutions. However, the Czech Lands were physically small in comparison with Italy or Germany and geopolitically at a disadvantage in comparison with Greece and Bulgaria. Conceivably 1914 changed things; all the new nation-states had been born in war. On the other hand, the wars had been caused, directly or indirectly, by the emerging nations. The war that broke out in 1914 had only a little to do with the Czechs; in this they contrasted particularly with the Serbs. Previous wars had penetrated to Czech soil, but had made little difference to Czech history. No one could foresee that this war would be different, that it would continue for four years, that it would shatter Austria-Hungary itself and cripple its imperial neighbours, Germany and Russia, and that it would promote national and social revolution. Czech politicians did not immediately see the war as their long-awaited opportunity.

It does not follow that, but for the war, there would have been no independent Czech, Slovak, or Czechoslovak state, that what emerged in 1918 was an artificial creation. Those who say so do not seek to understand history, but to change it. The Czech and Slovak national movements, separately or together, were bound at some point in an era of nation-states to secure an improvement in their political position. Being economic and social pressure-groups in an age of economic and social revolution, they were equally bound to better their standing in the community at large. The First World War altered the time-scale. The two national movements gradually reacted to it and gained both independence and unity. The war also altered the framework within which they had to operate. Up to 1914 it had been the Habsburg Empire, modified in 1867 to become Austria-Hungary, but during the war that crumbled and then collapsed. Thereafter, the framework was international, with at one time a political vacuum to be filled, with at others domination by Germany or Russia to be faced. These frameworks affected the character of the economic and social pressure-groups, adding international stimuli and restrictions. Successive acts had different backcloths; but they remained consecutive parts of the same history.

The Czechs, the Slovaks, and the Outbreak of War

As was to be expected, reaction to the situation created by the war came first from the Czechs. Among the public at large, feelings were rather mixed. Total war was still unknown. To begin with, the closure of the Imperial diet and the instant suspension of all civil rights, even the closure of the local diets, had little effect on most ordinary citizens. The only ones immediately affected were young men subject to general mobilisation. Many of them were angered particularly at the prospect of fighting Russia. Of the politicians, the majority were caught a little off guard. The clerical parties automatically declared loyalty to the monarchy. The Social Democratic Party doggedly denounced the war as capitalist and imperialist. Kramář, the Young Czech leader, wrote in obscure terms about alternative outcomes to the war. Klofáč, leader of the National Socialist Party, was rather more outspoken in his criticism of the alliance with Berlin and found himself unceremoniously imprisoned. There was no organised, uniform reaction.

It was not easy to know how to react to the war. Masaryk was not caught off guard because he had been half expecting it. He was also quite clear what it implied. It finally proved the barrenness of Franz Joseph's policies and the unfitness of Austria-Hungary to continue as a political entity. However, it was less easy to decide how to topple Austria, and not until December was he finally convinced that he must go abroad and fight for his country there. Partly this was his natural caution, and partly his wish to make all the necessary preparations. Yet even he waited for events to convince him. In the autumn and winter of 1914 others besides Klofáč were imprisoned. Several newspapers and journals were closed down; and several people were executed for distributing anti-Austrian literature. There were also anti-Austrian demonstrations among Czech units in the army. By the end of the year it was clear that, though the spirit of opposition was growing, the idea of open opposition to governmental policies had become impossible at home.

Masaryk was the most important Czech figure to go abroad, but he was not the first. That honour belonged to Lev Sychrava, a radical young lawyer and journalist who was active in the State

Rights Party and had close contacts with Masaryk and Klofáč. He went to Switzerland in September 1914 to begin the long task of informing Western opinion about the Czech cause and making contacts with Czechs living abroad. In fact, the wartime movement to establish an independent state really began abroad. As early as August 1914 Czech units were set up within the French and Russian armies, and Czech colonies in various parts of western Europe began to organise pro-independence propaganda. In September, a Czech National Association was constituted in Chicago to unite Czech organisations in the United States to work for Czech independence at the peace conference that would follow the war. Yet, whoever initiated the revolutionary movement, and wherever lay its support, what it required for victory was someone to see the way ahead and then give positive leadership. That was where Masaryk's genius lay.

Kramář had talent and prestige. All along, his ambition had been to win support from Russia, and he now began to negotiate through intermediaries in Sofia. With the success of its army in Galicia, Russia's stock among the Czech public rose towards the end of the year, and there were even hopes of a Russian liberation. Kramář, however, was content to await developments; in December he was still in the midst of slow negotiations. He also failed to take the other parties into his confidence; and he negotiated for a settlement that would have been unlikely to win wide approval. What he proposed to Russia in the event of victory was an autonomous kingdom or principality under the Tsar. He was careful to advise the Russians against entering Czech territory except for strategic reasons, but he nonetheless argued for something less than complete independence and contemplated the exchange of a near-autocrat for a total one. Masaryk's views were quite different. He was anxious to have Russian support, but not to submit to Tsarist control, and made it his business to carry the other parties with him. Although he conducted lengthy negotiations before committing himself to the struggle for independence, once the die was cast, he bent all his energy to the task.

In some ways it was strange that Masaryk should emerge as the man who liberated his nation in war. For one thing, at sixty-four he was already an old man. For another, as a philosopher he was better attuned to the arts of peace than to fighting battles. On the other hand, with his years came his prestige. He enjoyed an immense reputation within the Czech Lands; he had many protégés among the Slovaks and the other Slavs of the Empire. He had important friends in intellectual circles in Paris and London, men such as Ernest Denis and R. W. Seton-Watson. He had visited

Russia more than once and was on good terms with several influential figures. He had twice lectured in the United States, and he was well known in Czech immigrant circles there. Moreover, as his career had shown, he was no recluse, but a believer in the Platonic concept of the philosopher-statesman. In a cultured era he went down well with public figures, while as a man of scholarly humility he was at home with ordinary men and women. There was also a small element of the accidental in his success: he was warned in good time to go abroad quickly and avoid arrest. In another sense, too, Masaryk was a success because the task demanded a man of his particular type. Geographically, the Czech Lands were no place for an armed uprising. In any case, the public mood was one of disillusionment and discontent, not desperation. What the situation required was not a guerilla fighter, but a political strategist and diplomatic negotiator who could harness internal and international forces to create a new state for the old nation. For all that, Masaryk was a remarkable man and he did not simply fulfil a need. He made the state when perhaps no one else could; and he gave it much of its distinguishing character.

By the accident of his birth, Masaryk could not help but be interested in the fate of Slovakia. His political philosophy reinforced his natural sympathies, and by the time war broke out in 1914 he had been promoting Czech-Slovak co-operation for over twenty years. As early as October, in a discreet approach to the Entente powers, he indicated that any new state established after the war would have to include Slovakia, and this remained his stand throughout the war. In this way, Masaryk was as happy a discovery for the Slovak as for the Czech national movement. The first reaction of the Slovak National Council to the outbreak of the war was to declare its loyalty to the Emperor and suspend its political activities. There were many reasons. The Slovak national movement had nothing like the dimensions of the Czech, which was itself not particularly tough at this stage. In addition, the police were more active in Slovakia than in the Czech Lands. Hodža, for example, was sent to join an official press bureau in Vienna, and his *Slovenský denník* was banned. There was disgruntlement among Slovak soldiers called to the eastern and southern fronts; but there was also a widespread inclination to await the arrival of freedom with the Russian army. Hurban Vajanský's messianic beliefs had spread wide and sunk deep. As the Russian advance slowed down, disillusionment and indecision spread among citizens and politicians alike. Freedom from Hungary seemed more unlikely than ever. If it had been difficult to preach disaffection at the outbreak of war, it became impossible as the Hungarian government's security grip inevitably tightened. Co-operation with the Czechs was unattractive when they themselves seemed to be doing little. Someone was needed to rescue the Slovak national movement by giving it leadership and direction and also to harness outside forces calling for Slovak freedom.

The kingdom that Kramář proposed embraced the Slovaks. The army companies recruited in France and Russia included Slovaks. The new Czech National Association in Chicago began to make overtures to the existing Slovak League, which in turn began to look for allies. Russia offered to annex Slovakia in the interest of its autonomy. There were all sorts of forces at work and plans afoot. Masaryk proved the man to use them for the benefit of Slovakia. Admittedly there was more than a suggestion of *realpolitik* in his policy for Slovakia. Its union with the Czech Lands would create a single state large enough to survive between Germany and Russia. Yet there was much to recommend this policy for its own sake. There was even more to recommend it when the alternatives were no independence at all, or incorporation in the empire of the Tsars. Masaryk gave Slovakia its chance.

Masaryk, the Czechoslovaks, and the Beginnings of Recognition

One of the things that persuaded Masaryk to make a fight of it was his belief, shared by no more than a few others, that the war would last for at least three years. He knew that success for the Czechs and Slovaks would depend on more than the defeat of Germany and Austria-Hungary. Time was required to prepare the Entente powers to support the idea of yet another small independent state. When he finally stopped abroad in January 1915, more than three years in fact lay ahead of him—and several unexpected bonuses. Perhaps he may have anticipated the exigencies of the Entente as the war rolled on, and therefore their need for all sorts of allies. However, he certainly did not foresee the entry of the United States into the war. Nor did he envisage that Russia would both spread revolution and collapse as a result of it. These were strokes of fortune that he quickly put to good use. However, at the beginning of 1915, he had an objective and an organisation, and the main thing was to get down to work.

The organisation Masaryk built up in the Czech Lands was later to be called the Mafia. There were no vendettas, but there was much cloak-and-dagger. In talks with other political leaders, Masaryk began to consolidate it before his departure. Despite the inconvenience of having to flee too soon, he managed to form at home an inner group, comprising two Realists, two Young Czechs

(Kramář and Rašín), and the *Sokol* president. He also began to establish connections with other parties, in particular with the Social Democrats and the Agrarians, to form a line of communication between those abroad and domestic opinion. Once out of the country, he adapted and extended the propaganda network Sychrava had constructed in Switzerland to spread his ideas among the Czech colonies in Europe and America and to influence foreign public opinion. He used the remarkable talents of Emanuel Voska, a Czech who had made a modest fortune in Kansas marble, to organise a secret courier service throughout Europe and raise subscriptions from Czech immigrants in the United States. But although he had managed to persuade Kramář to join his group in Prague, he could not enjoin him to come abroad. Kramář preferred to await the advent of the Russian army. Others found it hard to plump for the Entente. Bohumír Šmeral, the Social Democratic leader, would not believe that Austria-Hungary could really be destroyed, while Antonín Švehla, leader of the Agrarians, preferred to keep his options open. Unfortunately, the Russian army suffered reverses and simultaneously the Vienna government became suspicious of Masaryk's activities. In May 1915 Kramář, Rašín, and several other important figures were arrested, among them Masaryk's daughter, Alice. This was a heavy blow to the Prague end of the Mafia. A few months later, Edvard Beneš also had to flee. Yet, in an odd way, it was all a blessing in disguise.

If it lost Masaryk the active assistance of Kramář, it also relieved him of a Russian embarrassment. If Russia had swept into Slovakia and the Czech Lands, the change in Czechoslovak fortunes would most probably have been less radical and acceptable than in the end it was. Again if, in Beneš, Masaryk lost a key organiser at home, he gained a superb diplomat abroad. When the war began, Beneš was only thirty. By international standards, this was comparatively young for serious politics, and but for the war he might have taken much longer to rise to fame. He was well prepared, however, for the challenges facing him. The tenth child of a prosperous small farmer, but educated in Prague, he knew the people and the problems of both country and town. By the age of twenty-five he had travelled and studied in Germany, Britain, and France and had acquired a doctorate in law from the University of Dijon as well as one in philosophy from the Charles University in Prague. His travels had given him a liking for the West and had fortified his dislike of Pangermanism; and his studies had brought him firmly to the conclusion that the minimum concession Austria-Hungary could possibly grant the nationalities and survive was autonomy. As a young intellectual in the years before the war, he could hardly fail to be influenced by the realism of Masaryk; and as a teacher of economics, he also had some sympathy with the Social Democrats. All this increased his scepticism about the future of Austria-Hungary, so much so that, as soon as the war broke out, he decided that the time had come to put paid to it and he sought out Masaryk with this in mind. Austria-Hungary had identified itself with Pangermanism; both must be defeated. In the end, the West must win; and the Czechs and Slovaks must triumph with them. He was very quickly at the heart of the Mafia, coming abroad only when it seemed that there was no further possibility of doing anything at home. Once abroad, he became the lynch-pin of the movement, Masaryk himself maintaining later that without him there would have been no independent Czechoslovakia.

The Mafia kept its end up at home as best it could under the careful leadership of the Realist Přemysl Šámal, but from the middle of 1915 the main Czech and Slovak effort was centred abroad. In May Denis had started *La Nation Tchèque* in Paris as a means of publicising the Czechoslovak case to the French public. Later Beneš took it over. Masaryk used the occasion of the quincentenary of the martyrdom of Jan Hus on 6 July 1915 to make a speech in Geneva advocating the destruction of Austria-Hungary and the establishment of an independent Czechoslovakia. In August, Sychrava began to publish, first in Annemasse and then in Paris, *Československá samostatnost* (*Czechoslovak Independence*), a newspaper designed to unite all the Czechoslovaks abroad. In September, a Czechoslovak Foreign Committee was established in Paris, with Masaryk as chairman and Beneš as secretary, and two months later it declared war on Austria-Hungary. The following February, Masaryk was received by Aristide Briand, the French premier, at which point it was judged the moment had arrived to go further and officially establish abroad a Czechoslovak National Council.

This was an important development. There were National Councils already in the Czech Lands and in Slovakia, although they were effectively defunct by 1916. Now the political exiles were not only assuming the title of a National Council, but doing so as a Czechoslovak body. They had taken their time, not least out of respect for the position of the politicians at home. By 1916, however, they had to recognise that most of the Czech and Slovak leaders at home were either in prison, or disinclined to believe in victory for the Allies, or virtually without influence, and that many of the rank-and-file Young Czechs, Agrarians, and Social Democrats had come to the conclusion that Austria-Hungary would survive the war and that ultimately the most they could hope for was autonomy for the nationalities. Masaryk and his colleagues had to take full responsibility for the struggle to destroy Austria-Hungary and create Czechoslovakia. Short of resigning their task, they had no alternative. Yet it was also an act of great courage. A diminutive group of politicians and assorted helpers, lacking serious support at home, took on the job of dismantling Austria-Hungary at the very moment in 1916 when it seemed as if the Allied powers were losing. Further, if they were short of prominent figures on the Czech side, they were practically without them on the Slovak side. No important Slovak politician had come to the West. This as much as anything convinced Masaryk of the need to champion the Slovak cause alongside the Czech. In the circumstances of 1916, with Russia on the defensive, all the spirit had gone out of the Slovak national movement. It was up to those Czechs who were in the West to stake out a future for the Slovaks. However, there was one important Slovak on the National Council, the legendary Milan Štefánik, a young astronomer in his mid-thirties, who had studied in Prague between 1897 and 1904 and, at the instigation of Šrobár, had come in contact with Masaryk. He had then emigrated to France, travelling to most parts of the world on behalf of the French ministry of marine. He had become a French citizen and a Knight of the Legion of Honour. After the outbreak of war he joined the French air force and fought in battles over the western front and over Serbia in 1915. In the same year, he tried to get in touch with Masaryk and at last, in December, met Beneš. He was soon firmly a part of the movement. He had many influential friends in French government circles; he had a glamorous appeal for his fellow countrymen; and he sincerely believed in the Czechoslovak idea. Masaryk and Beneš were determined to fight for a Czechoslovak state anyway; but the arrival of Štefánik gave them a Slovak partner of genuine stature and enabled them to act for the Slovaks as well as the Czechs despite the absence of support from many of the older-established politicians.

The arrival of Beneš and the addition of Štefánik were fillips to Masaryk's cause. There were others. From the spring of 1915 onwards, Czech and Slovak soldiers on the eastern front, and later in Italy, began to desert in increasing numbers. At a time of mounting Allied losses in the field they represented a growing asset to the *émigrés*. They added an element of power to Czechoslovak political arguments. From about the autumn of 1915 the very existence of idle manpower was of positive assistance to Czechoslovak propagandists. Propaganda itself, or rather the ideals behind it, also acquired a sudden value. Once the Allies had failed to achieve the military victory they confidently expected, they turned to the business of defining their war aims as a means of maintaining domestic morale and acquiring additional allies. It was a short step from championing the restoration of Belgian independence to looking with favour on the national aspirations of the suppressed peoples of central and eastern Europe. In October 1915, Masaryk was able to transfer his own activities to London, leaving Beneš to continue the good work in Paris, and to give the lecture inaugurating the School of Slavonic Studies on the bold subject of 'The Problem of Small Nations in the European Crisis' with no less a political person than Lord Robert Cecil, the under secretary of state for foreign affairs, taking the chair. Although it was a further twelve months before he could persuade his friends to begin publishing *The New Europe*, dedicated to national self-determination, he nevertheless found the tide running increasingly in his favour during 1916.

Against this background, and given the changing character of the war in 1915-16, Masaryk also found the Czech and Slovak immigrants in the United States a developing asset. The Czechs had been quicker than the Slovaks to band themselves together and begin campaigning for an independent national state. In 1915 the Czech National Association redoubled its efforts to arouse the enthusiasm of all the Czech communities, to strengthen its contacts with the exiled leaders in Europe and raise funds for them, and to persuade the American public of the justice of their cause. They also tried to find common ground with their Slovak brethren, but this was none too easy. It was not just that the Slovaks were slower to seize the opportunity the war presented. Like their relatives and friends at home, the Slovaks in America were in two minds about the future; they all agreed that Slovakia should become autonomous, but only a small group was convinced from the start that it should end up within some kind of Czechoslovak state. In April 1915, however, the Slovak League entered into negotiations with the Czech National Association for a common front, and in October the two organisations reached an agreement to work for an independent Czechoslovakia with a federal constitution. They even set up a common Executive Committee of Czechs and Slovaks in America. Yet the American picture was still not one of complete unity. Apart from disputes arising from local circumstances, there were others that stemmed from visits by pro-Tsarist Czechs and Slovaks from Russia. Nonetheless, more and more funds found their way to Masaryk to help him both with his diplomacy and with his propaganda. The signatures of American Czechoslovaks were appended to the first declaration of the

Czechoslovak Foreign Committee in November 1915, and representatives were sent to its successor, the Czechoslovak National Council, in 1916. The support for Masaryk in 1916 was ill-assorted but widespread.

Support was also to be found among the Czechs and Slovaks in Russia. Yet they provided a clear example of the difficulties he had to overcome if he were to be successful. There were about 100,000 settled or working in Russia at the outbreak of the war. Almost a thousand at once found their way into a Czechoslovak unit of the Russian army and earned themselves an enviable reputation for courage and skill during the winter of 1914-15. In the course of 1915 they and the emerging leaders of the Czech and Slovak communities tried to enlarge the force but, by the end of the year, they had not even doubled it. In spite of Russian losses and the easy availability of the increasing numbers of Czech and Slovak deserters, the Tsarist government was unwilling to authorise an enlarged Czechoslovak force, not least because of the political implications of such an act for the future of the multinational Russian state. When the Russian army mounted a fresh offensive in 1916, the Czechoslovak soldiers again fought with bravery and enhanced their reputation, but they achieved no more than a temporary change in the Tsar's attitude. Masaryk enlisted the energetic assistance of the French government, but was no more successful. It was one thing to have the support of his co-nationals, another to make an impact on the Tsarist government. Of course, not all the Czechs and Slovaks in Russia backed him. They had come from widely scattered areas at home, at different times, to settle in even more widely scattered areas in Russia. Their politicians were divided, some of them as late as 1916 still canvassing the idea of autonomy for their homelands within the Russian empire. The Tsar and his aides were adept at using such differences of opinion to delay their decisions. Communicating with the Czechs and Slovaks in Russia was also a problem. In the summer of 1916 Josef Dürich went to Russia to improve communications and to start direct negotiations with the Tsarist government. Someone had to go, and Dürich seemed a good choice. Formerly an Old Czech and latterly an Agrarian deputy, he had been sent to the West in 1915 with the agreement of both Kramář and Švehla, and in February 1916 he had been appointed as one of the two vice-presidents of the National Council. Unfortunately, he shared Kramář's Neoslav opinions and he immediately aligned himself with the conservatives in Russia, eventually establishing, with Tsarist support, a separate national council with himself as its leader. This not only stymied the expansion of the Czechoslovak military force in Russia; it spread confusion among Czechs and Slovaks everywhere else, including the United States; and it reduced Masaryk's standing in Paris and London.

Nevertheless, the potential for improvement in Czechoslovak fortunes remained unaffected, and Masaryk and his small group of devoted followers were not the people to dissipate it. On the contrary, Štefánik, the other vice-president of the National Council, went off in hot pursuit of Dürich and managed to secure the loyalty of most of the colony to the leadership in the West. From late 1916 onwards, Masaryk's struggle to create an independent Czechoslovakia out of the ruins of Austria-Hungary gained both in direction and in momentum. It was not an easy operation and it suffered reverses, but it gradually won successes and with a resurgence of the national movement at home it triumphed in the end.

The first success came at the turn of the year. In December 1916 the Central Powers proposed peace negotiations, and President Wilson, to whom the offer was addressed, requested both sides to declare their war aims. From the Czechoslovak point of view this was opportune if the Allied Powers could be persuaded to give genuine support to their case; otherwise it was dangerous. Through meetings at the Quai d'Orsay and articles in the French press, Beneš worked hard to win French and so British backing. Allied opinion was already tilting in favour of national self-determination as a war aim, but it was by no means certain that the Czechoslovaks would come within the definition. Beneš, however, was persistence itself. When the Allies gave Wilson their answer in January 1917, it included the Czechoslovaks as one of the peoples to be liberated from foreign rule. The form of words used showed that Allied statesmen were not clear who the Czechoslovaks were; and the peace negotiations flopped. Nevertheless, where the Czechoslovaks might have lost their case altogether, they had succeeded in asserting themselves as recognised suppliants. To the Allied statesmen the occasion might be unimportant; but for the Czechoslovaks it represented a major breakthrough.

Masaryk in Russia and America, and Recognition of Czechoslovakia

Another breakthrough followed shortly afterwards. The collapse of Tsarism in March 1917 and the emergence of the Provisional Government, dedicated to refashioning the state and winning the war, transformed the position of the Czechoslovaks in Russia. In April the Czechoslovak Rifle Regiment was authorised to recruit prisoners-of-war and transform itself into the Czechoslovak Army Corps. At the same time, all Czechs and Slovaks in Russia were allowed to acknowledge Masaryk and his Council as their legitimate government—a considerable step forward. The entry of the United States into the war, also in April 1917, seemed equally to promise well. However, Wilson did not immediately declare war on Austria-Hungary, and various difficulties arose in Russia. The high command was less enthusiastic about a Czechoslovak Army Corps than the government and put obstacles in the way of its recruiting. The unit that went into action on the eastern front in July 1917 still numbered only 7,000 men. Nevertheless, its minor triumph at Zborow altered the situation once more. So did Masaryk's presence in Russia during the summer and autumn. By the time the Bolshevik Revolution disabled Russia the Corps numbered almost 30,000 men. In the days of big armies, this might seem nothing. In a period of big losses, it meant more. When the soldiers were highly motivated and very successful in battle, 30,000 was a sizeable force, the factor that elevated Czechoslovakia from a possible war aim to an international reality.

It was his awareness of this that took Masaryk to Russia in the first place. He did not go to break down the high command's conservatism or raise the Czechoslovaks' morale. He knew that there was nothing immediate he could do about America and that, in any case, the Czechoslovaks there would continue to send money. He knew that Beneš was more than able to continue diplomatic negotiations in Paris, London, and Rome. But Russia had just gone through a change of government. Its support was still essential to the winning of the war, and anything he could do to retain it would be to his people's advantage. Russia was also in the midst of what might well be a real revolution, so its impact on the peace settlement would be all the greater. The Czechoslovak case could not be left to go a-begging; and the new Russia was more likely to be sympathetic to it than the old. But there was much more to Masaryk's mission. The French government's interest in the raising of a Czechoslovak force in Russia had first been aroused in 1916, not so much for the use that could be made of it on the eastern front but for its possible transfer to the troop-hungry western front. The Provisional Government had balked at this; but when Masaryk sailed for Russia in May 1917, he went with the blessing of the British government for the idea as well as of the French. This was immensely important. Russia must be kept in the war; and its favour must be sought for the peace. In all the uncertainty of mid-1917, however, the effective centre of the war still seemed to lie in the West. The place in which to defeat Germany and Austria-Hungary was in France and Italy, not in the Ukraine. The West also seemed the better place to influence the peace settlement. In the course of 1917 the process of defining war aims seemed to run against Czechoslovak interests. The freeing of Czechoslovakia from foreign rule disappeared from the statements of Western ministers; the best that emerged anywhere in the middle of the year was the hope put by A. J. Balfour, the British foreign secretary, that the Austro-Hungarian nationalities would be 'allowed to develop on their own lines'. To convince the French and British of the desirability of granting independence to the Czechoslovaks, a military presence was essential. Masaryk went to Russia, above all to secure the transfer of the Czechoslovak Army Corps to the western front. As he boosted its numbers, and as in the autumn he persuaded the Russians to transfer a token force, he could reflect that he had made another advance on the road to Czechoslovak independence.

Retrospectively, Masaryk's activities in Russia, and subsequently in America, took on the appearance of a well-prepared and well-executed plan. Because of their glamour, they also overshadowed others' achievements. Certainly his purpose and pressure were consistent from the start; and equally, his role as leader cannot be disputed. At the same time, however, there was much improvisation; and the whole effort was really that of a team. Masaryk arrived in Russia in May; he did not intend to remain for long, but he did not leave until the following April. Such was the dislocation caused by the unexpected. During all that time he was in touch with his colleagues, but it was Beneš who maintained the steady diplomatic pressure in the West and Štefánik who began to drum up support in the United States.

The delay in Masaryk's departure from Russia was the result of the Bolshevik Revolution. Even before the revolt broke out there had been rumblings in the Czechoslovak Army Corps. For a month or more there had been little fighting with the Germans and no obvious sign of transport to the West. In the disintegrating political situation, Czechoslovak soldiers were sometimes tempted to take sides. With the Revolution, morale sank lower and impartiality weakened. Masaryk found himself in difficulty. He managed to restore the spirit of his troops and impose neutrality upon them; he got the token force away through Archangel and began to make preparations for the others to go through Siberia. Yet with the Russian army collapsing and the German poised to make a great advance, there was a case for keeping the Corps on the eastern front. Masaryk had discussions to this end with Polish and Ukrainian representatives. He also found himself under French and British pressure to put the Corps at the disposal of a ring of small dissident states from the Baltic down to the Caucasus to contain the Germans and prevent them moving as reinforcements to the West.

In December, however, the picture changed once again. The bolsheviks began peace negotiations with Germany and Austria-Hungary. The Rumanians followed suit; and a month later the Ukrainians also sued for peace. Britain was reluctant to admit that things had changed and was only with difficulty persuaded to evacuate another minor force through Murmansk. But Masaryk was convinced that the Corps could now serve no purpose in Russia and devoted all his energy to the preparations for its exodus across Siberia. In the meantime, Beneš and his colleagues had been hard at work in Paris, trying to persuade the French government to authorise the establishment of a Czechoslovak army on French soil, under the general control of the French high command, but otherwise autonomous, and including the Corps from Russia. Because of the critical situation on the western front the French government eventually agreed. A presidential decree of 16 December 1917, amplified by a general instruction of 7 February 1918, gave the Czechoslovaks what they wanted. It only remained for Masaryk to reach agreement with the bolsheviks on the eastward movement of the Corps. The way was cleared by the Treaty of Brest-Litovsk on 3 March, which finally took Russia out of the war, and on 26 March the Soviet government gave the Corps permission to proceed to Vladivostok. The Czechoslovak volunteers in Russia could then sail to France to join their compatriots in the struggle to liberate Czechoslovakia. And Masaryk could proceed to America.

In fact, the Czechoslovak Army Corps never got to France; it was still spread out across Siberia when the war ended. It is doubtful whether the outcome would have been different if Masaryk had stayed in Russia. As it was, he had to move on. He wanted to prepare the way for the Corps. He also had specific tasks before him in the United States. Others had gone there ahead of him. Vojta Beneš, Edvard's elder brother, had been sent there by the Prague Mafia as early as 1915 and had since worked assiduously for the national cause by raising money, giving lectures, and generally acting as the liaison between the American Czechoslovaks and the National Council. In the summer and autumn of 1917 Štefánik had visited the United States, principally to recruit volunteers for Czechoslovak units in France. Since the American army was itself recruiting among Czechoslovaks, whom it rightly regarded as Americans, he had found his task complicated; but he had succeeded in getting permission to recruit those it did not want and had collected two or three thousand men. The immigrants themselves had become more enthusiastic and united with America's entry into the war and had done much to educate public opinion about their cause. But in the spring of 1918 there was still much for Masaryk to do. Štefánik, for example, had got on well with ex-President Theodore Roosevelt, but not with Woodrow Wilson. The main task confronting Masaryk was to educate America to the need to establish a Czechoslovak state at the impending peace conference. The war had still to be won. Brest-Litovsk might delay an Allied victory, but American entry would clearly make it inevitable. The peace conference might, so Masaryk thought, be as much as a year away, but the Czechoslovaks would have to be ready to substantiate their claims. The best way to do that would be to have the support of America in advance. Early in 1918 that looked far from certain.

The United States had not made its declaration of war on Austria-Hungary until early December 1917. Even after that, hostilities were somewhat formal. Its real enemy was Germany, which had torpedoed many of its ships and interfered in its domestic affairs. Officially, Austria-Hungary was cast in the role of Germany's unwilling partner, a power to be detached. Throughout the later part of 1917, Wilson had Colonel House, his confidential adviser, and a team of specialists investigate the proper terms for a peace settlement. When Wilson then brought out his Fourteen Points on 8 January 1918, he did not contemplate the destruction of Austria-Hungary: its peoples were simply to be accorded what he termed 'the freest opportunity of autonomous development'. This fell far short of what Masaryk wanted, but Wilson was very anxious for the moment not to cause more disruption to the *status quo* in Europe than would result from the revolution in Russia and the defeat of Germany. When none of the Allies dissented from Wilson's moderate view, it was clear that Masaryk faced a gargantuan task.

He was not without friends and helpers in the United States. His wife and all but one of his children stayed in the Czech Lands throughout the war; and it was the intervention of American friends that secured his daughter Alice's release from prison in June 1916. When he arrived in Chicago on 5 May 1918, he was welcomed by 100,000 Czechs and Slovaks in what was the largest Czech city outside Prague. When he reached Washington four days later, he was received by an old acquaintance, Charles R. Crane, industrialist and patron of Slavonic studies. Crane and another good friend and sympathiser, Professor Herbert Adolphus Miller, rapidly introduced him to a variety of influential officials and members of Congress. On 19 June House introduced him to Wilson himself. And all the time, the scenes at Chicago were repeated, if on a slightly smaller scale, at other cities and towns. All this support was vital. It was only through influential intermediaries that Masaryk's arguments could come to the notice of the White House, the State Department, and experts preparing papers for the peace conference. It was because of the backing of American Czechs and Slovaks that his representations were given a fair hearing. The 1912 election had taught Wilson that he could not neglect the American Poles. Now that America was at war with Germany and Austria-Hungary, he was wide open to pressure from other east European immigrant groups. Masaryk used his advantages well.

America's entry into the war gave an enormous boost to the Czechoslovak organisations. It was respectable to be anti-German; it was patriotic to raise funds for the war and make plans for the peace. Catholic and socialist groups that had held aloof from the movement for a united, independent Czechoslovakia at once began to lend support to it. The beginning of 1918 saw a crescendo. From 9 to 12 February the Czech National Association and the Slovak League held a conference that was attended by representatives of virtually all the Czechoslovak groups throughout the country; and on 10 March they set up a sixteen-member American section of the Czechoslovak National Council to act both as their own executive and as agency for the main body in Paris. It was this group that, before Masaryk arrived, submitted a preparatory memorandum to the State Department and that, on his arrival, deputed its chief officer, Karel Pergler, to act as his secretary. For his part, Masaryk was keen to spur on the enthusiasm that he found in the United States and to make the organisation more effective. Hence his whirlwind tour of centres of Czech and Slovak settlement. Hence his visit to Pittsburgh, where on 30 May he appended his signature to the famous Pittsburgh Agreement, looking forward to a unified Czechoslovak state in which the Slovaks would have considerable autonomy. By the beginning of June he was the undisputed leader of a single-minded movement that could not be left unheeded. It was for this reason as much as any that he was received by Woodrow Wilson on 19 June. However, to see the President was one thing; to win him for the Czechoslovak cause was another.

At their first meeting, the subject of independence for the Czechs and Slovaks does not appear to have arisen. Masaryk's primary aim at this stage was, if possible, to get American help in shipping his troops from Russia to France. This was essential to his whole policy; it was also a useful opening gambit. The Czechoslovak Legion, as the troops were now called, had suddenly become news. On 14 May some of them had become involved in a brush with Red Army recruits at Chelyabinsk in Siberia; this led to a direct confrontation with the local soviet and then, in rapid escalation, with the

Bolshevik government. Immediately, the Legionaries reached the international headlines. Immediately, too, the Czechoslovaks in America won recognition as their compatriots. It was clearly to Masaryk's advantage to discuss the Legion with Wilson. It was also inevitable that he should; Wilson was intensely concerned at what was taking place in Russia for its effect both on the course of the war and on its outcome. Indeed, most of the conversation seems to have been taken up with Russia. The Soviet Union, which already existed, was important; Czechoslovakia, which was simply an idea, was not. Masaryk achieved nothing, not even a promise of possible American transport. In fact, he suffered a reverse. Wilson and a number of his advisers, like some Allied politicians and soldiers, appeared to be developing such an interest in getting Russia back into the war that it began to look as if the Legion might get stuck there.

Masaryk was not disheartened; the philosopher had great patience. Ultimately, his efforts were rewarded. Yet the breakthrough was as much the result of changes in Europe. The incentives for dismantling Austria-Hungary—or desisting from shoring it up—were not always as clear to Allied statesmen as to the nationalist politicians thrown up by the subject peoples. Memories of Balkan rivalries and ethnic wars were too fresh. That was why Masaryk, for example, was so keen to establish the unity of the Czechs and Slovaks in Paris and Pittsburgh. But the real question went wider. There were disagreements between the Czechoslovaks and the Poles and between the Yugoslav leaders and the neighbouring Italian minority. The destruction of Austria-Hungary seemed more likely to balkanise the area than to stabilise it. Fortunately from the nationalities' point of view there were men like the French deputy Henri Franklin-Bouillon or the Italian premier, Vittorio Orlando, as well as Wickham Steed and Seton-Watson, who were aware of the dangers of quarrels and managed to dampen them down. Three Czechoslovaks also played an important role, Beneš, Štefánik, and Sychrava. It was as a result of all their efforts that a Congress of Oppressed Peoples was held in Rome from 8 to 11 April 1918. This produced a series of resolutions in favour of the total independence of the peoples of Austria-Hungary. What gave importance to the resolutions was the unity they represented. Even in the middle of the German spring offensive, the Allies might have disregarded them if they had emanated from a single national group; but they could not when they stood in the name of the representatives abroad of virtually two-thirds of the population of Austria-Hungary. In the Czechoslovak case the Congress of Rome was followed on 21 April by a pact authorising the establishment of a volunteer corps on Italian soil as part of the army being assembled in France. More significant than the military achievement was the diplomatic fact that it resulted, not from a unilateral decree (as was the case with the creation of the Czechoslovak army in France), but from an international treaty negotiated between the Italian government and the Czechoslovak National Council and signed for the two sides by Orlando and Štefánik. In May, Beneš was cordially received by Georges Clemenceau, the French premier, by Balfour and Cecil, and again by Clemenceau, and given to understand that both the French and the British governments fully sympathised with the views expressed at the Congress of Rome. On 29 May, before Masaryk visited Wilson, the United States also declared its sympathy; it could not fall too far behind the Allies. In fact, it went a step ahead by declaring its sympathy in public. The others followed suit on 3 June and even started out on the road to acknowledging a separate state. On 29 June, the French government officially recognised the Czechoslovak National Council as 'the supreme organ governing all the interests of the nation and the first basis for the future Czechoslovak government'. Beneš and his colleagues in Europe had been able to make more progress there than Masaryk in America and were therefore able to help him.

It was, however, after Masaryk's first visit to Wilson that the United States made its next significant move. On 28 June the State Department amplified its previous statement concerning the Rome resolutions, declaring its conviction that all the Slavs ought to be free of Austro-Hungarian rule. This was a notable advance in Wilson's position; and it followed not only Masaryk's visit, but a letter from him to the State Department. Yet what Masaryk requested on his visit was transport for his troops, which he did not get; and what he asked for in his letter was official recognition, which also he did not get. It again took events in Europe to force the pace of American recognition. The latest American statement was hardly a day old when partial French recognition was given. Beneš had not necessarily been more assiduous, but he had certainly been more successful. He went on to win a further triumph. Through negotiations in London with Balfour and Cecil, he secured a declaration on 9 August that Britain would regard the Czechoslovaks as an Allied nation and recognise the National Council in the same way as France. This was not only a tribute to his skill. It was a sign of growing political confidence in Britain as the military situation improved. It also reflected the reputation the Czechoslovak army was beginning to build for itself on the western front and in Italy. Above all, perhaps, it was an indication of the usefulness of the Legion in Russia. Among the British public, as among the American, it was acquiring a legendary fame. However, British, like American, statesmen were less concerned with its glamour than with its power in the middle of the Russian vacuum; and the National Council that controlled it would clearly be a valuable ally. At any rate, Beneš's success and the factors producing it had their influence upon Washington. Ultimately, so too had Masaryk. With the British declaration to cite, and with the Czechoslovak Legion to point to, he was able to persuade the State Department to go one better than Britain and, on 2 September, to recognise the Czechoslovak National Council as a '*de facto* belligerent government'. This was what he and his team had been working for all along. Similar recognition soon came from China and Japan. Improved recognition came from France and Italy—and *de jure* recognition from Russia. What did it matter that Masaryk had still not found transport for the Legion? The Legion, like the rest of the new army, had been intended to win recognition; it had won it.

The Czechoslovaks at Home and Independence

The part played by the soldiers should not be underestimated. Some of them were volunteers from Russia or America or elsewhere abroad. However, the majority were civilian conscripts who had voted with their feet to leave Austria-Hungary and fight against it. In a way, they represented public opinion in the Czech Lands and in Slovakia. The Allies were aware of this. As the war went on, they were also conscious of the increasing restiveness of those remaining behind. This was an important factor in their conversion to the idea of an independent Czechoslovak state.

The middle of the war was a dark period in the political life of the Czech Lands and Slovakia. The most active leaders of the Czech and Slovak peoples had either gone abroad, or been imprisoned, or been otherwise put out of harm's way. In 1916, old-style politics were almost impossible. In practice, the only expressions of opinion allowed were declarations of loyalty to the Habsburg throne. Some of these embarrassed Masaryk and the movement abroad, since they were genuine expressions of the timidity of the politicians remaining at home and of their need to reach an accommodation with an Empire that in their opinion would survive the war. But things changed in 1917. For one thing, the privations of war became much more widespread, and shortages of food in particular much more prevalent. Inevitably, disaffection intensified. The news from abroad also made an increasingly powerful impression: the progress of the National Council, the democratic notions of the Allies, the February Revolution in Russia, the military involvement of America, all these finally had repercussions on popular opinion. The national movement, temporarily cowed, found its courage and its spokesmen. At first, incidents were scattered and unorganised. A demonstration of 8,000 confectionary workers in Prostějov at the end of April led to the deaths of twenty-three of them. In the middle of May, Jaroslav Kvapil, the drama director at the National Theatre who was also a leading figure in the Mafia, and more than 200 other writers and artists issued a manifesto condemning collaboration with the Austrian regime. There was a strike of 3,000 Prague metalworkers at the beginning of June, calling for reform. And so it went on into the autumn and winter until, in the wake of the Bolshevik Revolution, demonstrators began demanding immediate negotiations for peace. However, alongside these spontaneous manifestations, there was an increasing number of organised actions. Learning that the Austrian diet was to be reconvened, Beneš got a message through to the remaining Czech deputies who used its opening on 30 May to demand what looked like autonomy, but amounted to independence and unity with their Slovak brethren. Through the Mafia, Beneš continued to advise them, and on 6 January 1918, two days before the Fourteen Points, they joined their colleagues from the local diets in demanding independence for the Czech Lands and Slovakia and a seat for the new state at the peace conference.

From that point on the two streams of development moved, both separately and together, in the same direction. On 22 January 1918 the Social Democrats, who had now replaced Šmeral with the tough Vlastimil Tusar, and the National Socialists called massive strikes throughout the Czech Lands; in Prague alone 60,000 men and women came out in favour of 'peace, freedom, and bread'. From 8 to 11 April the resolutions of the Rome Congress were directed as much at the oppressed nationalities as at Allied governments. On 13 April a great assembly of politicians and writers came together in Prague to take a national oath, prepared by the socialist František Soukup, and recited by the novelist Alois Jirásek. On 16 May the occasion of the fiftieth anniversary of the National Theatre was used for an impressive demonstration in favour of national self-determination. In May and June several regiments mutinied, and there were bitter strikes in Plzeň and elsewhere. Eventually, on 13 July, the two streams of the movement coalesced when a Czechoslovak National Committee was formed in Prague to work with the National Council abroad for a united independent state. The movement at home had come alive. The thirty-eight seats on the Committee were divided up in proportion to the strength of the political parties at the 1911 election, thus emphasising continuity. Kramář, released from prison the previous year to attend the reconvened diet, was made chairman, Švehla and Klofáč vice-chairmen, and Soukup secretary, thus spanning the spectrum from right to left. And the whole group began operating like a shadow government in close contact, through the Mafia, with the leadership abroad.

The Slovak movement also came to life. The early part of the war had seen it less active than the Czech, and its weakening spirit had been temporarily destroyed by the retreat of the Russians and repression by the Magyars. Some of its leaders had gone to Russia. In June 1915, Pavlů, a convinced supporter of the Czechoslovak idea, had begun to publish *Čechoslovák* (*The Czechoslovak*) in Petrograd, and it had compensated for the lack of discussion at home. However, the real centre for debate on the future of Slovakia had been the United States. Up to a point this had also been true for the Czechs; but for them there had been less at issue. They had had to weigh autonomy against independence; but the Slovaks had had to decide whether to go it alone or to co-operate with the Czechs and fight for a unified state. This was why as late as 1918 agreements like that concluded at Pittsburgh were considered so important. Despite the unfavourable conditions produced by unrelieved repression, 1917 saw the debate inaugurated in Slovakia itself. The two Russian revolutions undoubtedly had greater impact on Slovakia than on the Czech Lands; geographical proximity and similarity of social conditions were enough to ensure that. There were strikes and mutinies; and soldiers deserted to the mountains. There was never a successful Mafia in Slovakia; but the Czech Mafia brought news about developments in Paris, London, and Washington. In circumstances where the situation in Russia was confused, if not menacing, Czech progress in the West was inevitably attractive, particularly to those who were already favourably inclined to a Czechoslovak solution, mainly Hodža, Šrobár, and Lehocký. Even Hlinka and Juriga mustered pro-Czech sympathies. But it was into the spring of 1918 before there were open political manifestations of the revived national sentiment. At Liptovský Sv. Mikuláš, on 1 May, Šrobár persuaded the Slovak Social Democratic Party to adopt self-determination for all the peoples of Austria-Hungary as its official policy and, in particular, to demand self-determination for the Slovak branch of the Czechoslovak nation. A similar pro-independence, pro-Czechoslovak unity line was adopted on 24 May when the Slovak National Party, which included everyone except the Socialists, met secretly at Turčianský Sv. Martin. Magyar control of Slovakia was still too rigorous for the politicians to be able to publicise their aims. Nonetheless, hostility to the regime became more intense and obvious during the summer, particularly through strikes, until preparations were made in secret in September for a Slovak National Committee along the lines of the Czech one, to head the local resistance and to co-operate with the leadership abroad.

By the autumn of 1918 the outlook for the Czechoslovak nation was totally different from what it had been at the beginning of the war or even just a few months previously. The Allies were about to triumph. Austria-Hungary was about to disintegrate. The Czechoslovak National Council was in an almost invincible position. It was internationally recognised; was highly skilled politically; and had an army of its own; and the fact that part of the army was bogged down in Russia was, in the particular circumstances of the time, an added strength. It had influential support in all the Allied capitals. It had a powerful and well-organised pressure-group in the United States; and from the same source it received generous financial backing. Last, but most important, it had widespread popular and political support at home. The time had come to take the last few steps. On 14 October Beneš told all the Allied governments that the National Council had constituted itself a Provisional Government. On 15 October France gave it recognition, and the other powers quickly followed. Diplomatic relations were established and representatives appointed. But Beneš had another reason for increasing the pace. On 4 October the Central Powers sued for peace on the basis of the Fourteen Points. It was essential for the Czechoslovaks to take some dramatic and decisive action to underline the fact that much had happened since Wilson stated his Fourteen Points, and to show that bogus autonomy was not enough and that only independence would suffice. It was the same need that pressed Masaryk into action. He had not rested content with Wilson's earlier recognition of his Council as a *de facto* belligerent government. Throughout September and early October he had worked hard to produce practical co-operation with other immigrant organisations and central European politicians in the United States. He had also prepared a declaration of independence. The peace overture from the Central Powers, and Beneš's reaction to it, inevitably made him realise the importance of ensuring that Wilson's reply did not accept something less than Czechoslovak independence. He sent an advance copy of his declaration to Wilson on 16 October, and the final copy on 18 October—just as Wilson was completing his reply. In fact, Wilson said that it was no longer up to him; the Czechoslovaks, whom he had recognised, must decide their own future. In the event, that was all that was needed. The Czechoslovak Provisional Government in Paris issued its declaration of independence on the same day that Wilson's terms were sent to Vienna. On 27 October Vienna conceded defeat; and on 28 October representatives of the Czechoslovak Provisional Government and of the Czechoslovak National Committee from Prague met in Geneva to declare that Czechoslovakia was no longer part of Austria-Hungary, but an independent state. On the same day a similar proclamation was issued in Prague; and two days later, the National Committee in Turčianský Sv. Martin declared that Slovakia was part of the independent, united state. In the end, everything went with a rush, even with a bit of confusion. But enough happened for 28 October to become the national day of the Czechoslovak people.

BOOK TWO

CHAPTER 8

Establishing Czechoslovakia

Introduction

IN CZECHOSLOVAK TERMS, 1918 was a revolution. Before the war the Czechs and Slovaks were kindred peoples in separate sectors of a German and Magyar-ruled state. At the end they came together in an independent state. Their history was no longer that of separate, if related, national movements, but of a nation striving to express its identity and to maintain its independence. They were, of course, the same peoples, and they inherited problems and opportunities alike. But the framework within which they dealt with the one and made use of the other was quite different. They were a nation and they were independent; the history of Czechoslovakia as such had begun.

The world into which the new state was born was also radically different. The principle of national self-determination had triumphed. Its application barely extended beyond Europe and the Americas, and even there it was only imperfectly applied. Many of its ostensible champions paid mere lip-service to it. On the other hand, it was enshrined in the peace settlement and in the concept of a league of nations. It was legitimate for Czechoslovakia to be a nation and to fight to remain one.

Initially that was none too difficult since the distribution of power in the world had also changed drastically. Almost unbelievably, Austria-Hungary had collapsed, and despite fears and alarms the Habsburgs were never to return. The United States had thrown its power into the settlement of Europe's affairs and, if it was shortly to withdraw, it was to leave Germany, would-be successor to Austria-Hungary in central Europe, apparently soundly defeated. Tsarist Russia, an uncertain ally to its fellow Slavs and long-standing opponent of nationalism, had also collapsed. If the Soviet Union was something of an unknown quantity, it appeared to support self-determination, and it was in any case likely to be burdened with problems of its own for some time to come. Britain had committed itself to European and international stability as never before. If there were doubts about its sincerity, there were none about the commitment of France to the new order in Europe. National self-determination had broken one French enemy, Austria-Hungary, and could contain another, Germany. It was a situation in which Czechoslovakia could entrench its independence.

To maintain it in the longer run was to prove much more difficult. The world remained dedicated to national self-determination, and Austria-Hungary found it impossible to recover. But the United States went off to be self-determined in its own peculiar isolationist way. Germany used the principle to assist its recovery as a power and to undermine Czechoslovakia's existence. Britain and ultimately France grasped it as a shield for their unwillingness to fulfil their obligations towards Czechoslovakia. Russia employed it as an aid to defensive westwards expansion, against the interests of small nations. In 1938-39 Czechoslovakia lost its independence in a world that seemed to have reverted to the imperialism of pre-1914, or worse. The Second World War, however, accelerated the growth of nation-states. The principle of self-determination spread rapidly to Asia and Africa. When Czechoslovakia joined the League of Nations, it was one of forty-two members. When it joined the United Nations, it was one of fifty-one members. Yet the problem of maintaining even fairly basic independence was greater than ever before. The super-powers had arrived, complete with alliances and economic agreements and areas of influence. In 1948 Czechoslovakia slipped almost inevitably into the Russian sphere and virtually lost its independence. Came 1968 and there were a hundred and twenty-six members of the United Nations; but Czechoslovakia could not determine its domestic policy, let alone slide out of the Russian zone of Europe. Yet neither could it be destroyed. Its independence might be limited, like that of so many other small nations; but in 1968 the world was still a world of states, not of old-fashioned empires or modern federations.

As far as the Czechoslovaks were concerned, the international scene after 1918 was not all change. In particular, Czechoslovakia had not lost its strategic importance. The Czech Lands were still the fortress heart of Europe. They were valued highly by the French as a bastion in Germany's rear and as a staging-post to Russia. They were then envied by Hitler for the reverse reason, as well as for their usefulness in any invasion of Poland or the Balkans. Later, both Stalin and Truman were aware of their crucial importance in the Cold War struggle over Germany. If Czechoslovakia's military importance then declined in the nuclear age, its ideological importance continued to grow. Even more in 1968 than in 1948, it was obvious that, whatever way Czechoslovakia

2 The Frontiers of Czechoslovakia before the Rise of Hitler

went, the rest of eastern Europe might follow. The Czechoslovaks had won their independence in 1918, but they could not escape their geographical heritage, no matter how hard they tried.

The history of the Czechs and Slovaks after 1918 is thus the history of the independent state of Czechoslovakia and of its struggle to survive in a world that blessed it in principle but was less kind to it in practice. There was another struggle, however, the struggle to become a nation in the full sense of the word. The two were not separate or disconnected. Hitler used the Sudeten German minority, just as Stalin used the Czechoslovak Communist Party, to cripple Czechoslovak independence. But the battle for nationhood existed in its own right. It was both ethnic and social.

The vagaries of history and the decisions of the peace conference gave Czechoslovakia an ethnically mixed population. In 1921 the Czechs and Slovaks comprised only 65.5 percent of it; Germans made up 23.5 percent, Hungarians 5.5 percent, Ruthenians 3.5 percent, Poles and some others the rest. Ethnically speaking, Czechoslovakia was a small reverse image of the Habsburg Empire. The painstaking attempt to find a *modus vivendi* with the Germans failed in 1938 and they were expelled in 1945. In the same year, the Ruthenians, and the area they lived in, were simply transferred to the Soviet Union. From then on, the Czechs and Slovaks numbered about 95 percent of the population and could claim to be the nation. Yet, from the outset the Czechs and Slovaks were not one nation; they were but kindred peoples thrown together by long suffering and common triumph. Tension was often high before 1945, and the fusion thereafter was somewhat artificial. The federal solution of 1968 recognised that the state would not fall apart, but the nation had some way to go before it was forged completely.

In the half-century between independence and 1968 a vast amount of energy was expended in trying to solve the ethnic problem. The framework was new, the problem old. This was also true of the struggle to unite the nation socially. Population growth continued, though there were two breaks, the one associated with the political disruption of 1918 and the other (and greater) with the national redistribution of 1945. This helped to maintain the pressure for economic development, particularly industrial. But 1918 added its own pressures. A new economy had to be created out of fragments surviving from Austria-Hungary, and it had to be productive enough to support independence. 1918 also increased the pressure to rise in the social scale; independence would have achieved little if it had not made openings for those below. All this, as well as the influence of socialist ideas rising within Czechoslovakia and gathering strength abroad, moved the new state towards reducing the differences between rich and poor, towards creating a single nation. The expulsion of the Sudetens in 1945 accelerated the process by enabling the Czechoslovaks to turn their attention from the national struggle to the social one. It only required the intervention of the Soviet Union to enforce social levelling after 1948, and to arouse the anger of a nation united against it in 1968, for the entire process to be as complete as perhaps it can be.

The Frontier

Czechoslovakia came into existence as a legal entity on 28 October 1918, but territorially it was still undefined. The Western governments had recognised the Czechoslovak people's right to independence; their advisers had prepared memoranda on possible frontiers for the new state and had sifted memoranda from Czechoslovak spokesmen. But military exigencies, as well as political differences, had prevented the governments from reaching any kind of agreed position on what was by common consent a most difficult problem. In the circumstances it was easier to leave a settlement to the peace conference. The armistice with Austria-Hungary was based on the principle of national self-determination, but it made no attempt to map out what this would mean in practice.

For their part, the Czechoslovak leaders had definite ideas, and they had tried to get them across to the Western powers from the first moment when Masaryk made contact with Seton-Watson in Holland in October 1914. Before he was arrested, Kramář had been advocating a much more ambitious scheme than Masaryk's, one that would have extended the frontier well into Germany by reverting to the position in the fourteenth century. However, it was the moderate view that prevailed. The area sought embraced the historic provinces of Bohemia, Moravia, and Silesia (apart from the sector with a Polish minority), and the Slovak-speaking part of northern Hungary. From an ethnic viewpoint this was not a national frontier. It pulled Germans, Magyars, and Poles into the new state along with Czechs and Slovaks. The fact was that an ethnic frontier was simply impossible. Centuries of population movement, and in particular of German migration, had produced too many mixed areas for any line, let alone a just one, to be drawn between Czechs and Germans or Slovaks and Magyars. This was another reason for Western indecision. But from 1914 onwards the Czechoslovak argument was never based on ethnic considerations alone.

Until 1914 there had been two strands in Czechoslovak thinking. State rights, the restoration of autonomy to the historic provinces of Bohemia, Moravia, and Silesia, had originally been the political platform of the German aristocracy, but it had been taken over first by the Old Czechs and then by the Young. The newer parties, including Masaryk's, had inclined rather to autonomy for national groups, a scheme that would have left part of the historic provinces under German autonomous government. It was this ethnic line of thinking that had supported autonomy for the Slovaks in close linkage with the Czechs. The two strands had never been wholly distinct, but the outbreak of war in 1914 brought them inextricably together. It was now a question of independence, not autonomy. The Czechoslovaks must be in a position to protect their new status. They must have strategically defensible frontiers; they must have an economically viable territory. In the west in particular, the new state must occupy the position formerly held by the independent kingdom.

Behind this reasoning there was a degree of emotionalism. The one-time flourishing kingdom had been suborned by German immigration and destroyed by Habsburg aggression. The clock should now be turned back, and a Czechoslovak state, albeit with a series of minorities, should be allowed to spread to the limit of the old frontier. There was even an element of revenge. The Germans had lorded it over the Czechs for three hundred years (the Magyars over the Slovaks for even longer); the boot should now be put on the other foot. Some of the statistics produced were downright inaccurate: the number of Germans in the new state was underestimated by almost a million. There was also a certain amount of double-think. The German minority was to be included with the new state for historical reasons; but in the face of similar arguments, Hungary was to lose its Slovak territory. Yet the same picture had its other side. The Czechoslovak argument was national, strategic, and economic, rather than crudely historical. The Germans' statistics were at least equally faulty; they overestimated their strength in the new Czechoslovak state by more than a million. There was also a touch of genuine idealism in the Czechoslovak approach. The Germans of the historic provinces represented the outdated bureaucratic ineptitude of the Habsburgs and, more recently, the aggressive Pangermanism of imperial Germany. In contrast, the Czechoslovak national movement drew its inspiration from the democratic Western tradition and would therefore, or so it was argued, create a new kind of multinational community in the new state. There was even talk of adopting the Swiss model for its constitution, though this was more well-intentioned than realistic. Through every Czechoslovak argument, however, ran the need to create something viable. Austria-Hungary had been a failure; Germany could still be a menace; Czechoslovakia must be able to survive.

It worried the Czechoslovak leaders that no specific frontiers were mentioned in the Austro-Hungarian armistice. Their government had been recognised. The terms of recognition gave them a right to make representations to the peace conference then being organised in Paris. They were able to argue their point as well as any group, and they had several concessions they were perfectly willing to make. But recognition had come practically at the eleventh hour. Differences between the Western governments could rebound against them. Even recognition, let alone sympathy for their cause, could disappear as rapidly as it had come. Just after the end of the war the public mood in the West was as favourable to the Czechoslovak cause as the official attitude, but anything might happen in the longish spell before the conference was due to meet. The Austro-Germans and the Magyars were quick to argue their own case for national self-determination. The military situation in central Europe, which could determine the political, was very fluid. It was quite conceivable that the Austro-Germans and the Magyars, who were angry at their unexpected defeat, could turn it to their advantage. Nor could the Czechoslovaks expect help from the Soviet government, which did not wish to participate in the peace conference. It had also become embroiled with the Czechoslovak Legion still in Russia and was, if anything, hostile. Partly for that reason, too, there was no immediate prospect of getting the Legion transported to central Europe. In four years of war, the Czechoslovaks had advanced a long way; but they could certainly not afford to rest on their oars with the cessation of hostilities.

To begin with, the Czechoslovaks were united in their approach to the frontier question. Masaryk was the first President of the new state. Different shades of opinion were united under him, with Kramář as prime minister and Beneš as foreign minister. They acted together firmly. Masaryk was the symbol of good sense abroad and unity at home; Kramář kept passions cool; Beneš negotiated the actual settlement. The immediate problem was the lack of a military presence. The Western powers could not agree whether to send troops. The Austro-Germans and Magyars made hostile noises and appeared ready to fight. There was a real danger that Czechoslovak authority might be confined to a limited area of the Czech Lands. Most of the seasoned Czechoslovak troops were in Italy or France, or stretched across Siberia. But fresh troops were raised at home, and approval was obtained for assigning them officially to the French command so that they could operate as an Allied force in entering areas claimed by the Germans and Magyars. In the face of Austro-German protests and Anglo-American scruples it did not prove too easy to enter the German parts of the Czech Lands. Of tremendous assistance was the French desire for a powerful buffer-state; but ultimately of equal assistance was the Anglo-American fear of decomposition in the old Austria-Hungary if bolshevism were allowed to spread in the chaos of the post-war period and the hardship of a long cold winter. By the end of December 1918 Czechoslovak troops had occupied the Czech Lands in their entirety, on condition that this did not prejudice the final settlement. If anything, the occupation of Slovakia proved more difficult. In the moment of defeat, Hungary separated itself from Austria and established a moderate government in the hope of preserving the Hungarian kingdom from national self-determination. Czechoslovak soldiers trying to advance into Slovakia were repulsed; and some confusion in the armistice terms seemed likely to keep them out for good. It was again French self-interest that opened the way to eventual occupation. Indeed, it was almost solely a French success. Hodža, sent to Budapest on behalf of the government, was completely outmanoeuvred. The British government appears to have held aloof and the American to have played ostrich. The French government—not without Czechoslovak prompting, of course—

acted unilaterally, and at the same time as sanctioning occupation of the whole of the Czech Lands, announced that Hungary had withdrawn from Slovakia—which, at French military dictation, it did. By the end of the year Czechoslovak troops were in possession. By dint of some negotiation and a series of *faits accomplis,* the Czechoslovaks made a reality of their territorial claims before the peace conference met.

In retrospect, the story is not altogether a pleasant one. But it was a hard world and had been so for a long time. If the Czechoslovaks had not moved, or the French had not moved for them, then the Czechoslovak state might have amounted to no more than a truncated part of the Czech Lands, probably without Slovakia. A major battle for the nation would have been lost, and the next one would really have been over before it had begun; the mini-Czech state would have been weak and defenceless, a very easy prey for its stronger neighbours. Nothing was taken that had not previously been asked for, and adjustments could still be made. The Czechoslovaks had had too long a history of policies stymied and concessions withdrawn to be willing to leave so much to the peace settlement. Possession was two-thirds of ownership; for once in their history they could argue their case from a position of real strength.

The peace conference met for the first time on 18 January 1919. Beneš and Kramář appeared before the Council of Ten, as the inner group were styled, on 5 February. The so-called Commission on Czechoslovak Affairs sat from 28 February to 12 March, on which date it presented its almost unanimous findings on the Czechoslovak frontier. There were still several stages for the appropriate treaties to go, but by and large the geographical shape of the new Czechoslovak state was settled. It was not nearly such plain sailing as the quick timetable might suggest. Kramář, who as prime minister was senior to Beneš and responsible for drawing up the papers, stretched the Czechoslovak claims beyond the frontiers of occupation. Success had gone to his head, as it had with others of his less elevated countrymen. The Commission would simply not accept his extravagant claims, and it took all Beneš's moderating approach to undo the damage. That in itself raised problems, since Beneš's willingness to make minor concessions opened the way to unreasonable demands. The American delegates raised more difficulties than anyone else. They were committed to self-determination but, like their master, Wilson, they were not very sure what it really meant. They also believed in viability, and ultimately came to much the same conclusions as everyone else. They did utter warnings about future problems, but in the end they reserved their position on only one point, insisting that Cheb ought to go to Germany. Strangely enough, this was also Beneš's view, but it was the French who carried the others with them. Indeed the whole operation was more of a French success than of a Czechoslovak. The French were now thoroughly convinced of the need to buttress Czechoslovakia as a major ally in central Europe. They very quickly obtained support for Czechoslovak possession of the historic provinces as a whole, and although there was some tough arguing, most of it was concerned with points of detail—or with Slovakia. It was rather ironic that Slovakia, not possessing a historic frontier, raised more heat than the Czech Lands. Yet it was natural enough, since its frontier called essentially for an ethnic decision. This gave the Americans in particular an opportunity to discuss matters of principle that were barely susceptible of settlement. Perhaps surprisingly, it was in this area that the British delegates did most to promote a sense of reality by insisting on the Czechoslovak need for internal rail communications. In general it was the French who pushed, supported by the British, while Kramář and the Americans just about cancelled one another out; and behind them all was Beneš, young in years but old in experience, gently negotiating towards acceptance of the already existing occupation situation.

There were still some obstacles to be overcome. When the Commission's report was presented to the three great political figures of the conference, it looked for a time as if Clemenceau would not get the French government's way; Wilson and Lloyd George began arguing in favour of an ethnic frontier. But whereas Wilson was rather confused and Lloyd George could not formulate a clear alternative to the Commission's plan, Clemenceau was clear-cut and single-minded in pursuit of viability. Face to face with reality, the ethnicists could not win. There were in any case other pressing problems to worry the Big Three. The Franco-German frontier still had to be agreed; and it was a big issue. There was a whole series of east European frontiers to be agreed. The civil war in Russia was at its height. To cap everything a bolshevik revolution in Hungary in March 1919 appeared to challenge the right of the powers at Paris to settle anything. There was much to be said for moving quickly on lesser issues. On 4 April, House (who was standing in for Wilson), Lloyd George, and Clemenceau agreed to accept, not the adjusted historic frontier between Germany and the Czech Lands but the existing 1914 frontier. This abandoned the Commission's refinements but gave Czechoslovakia its essential requirements. Thereafter there could be little argument. The threat of a bolshevik rising in Austria propelled the conference to a speedy agreement on the Austro-Czech frontier. On 12 May the three leading statesmen accepted the Commission's proposal, the one-time historic frontier with some adjustments in favour of Czechoslovakia. The Czech frontiers with Germany and Austria were eventually enshrined in the appropriate treaties—Versailles on 28 June and St-Germain on 10 September.

The Slovak frontier with Hungary took rather longer to embody in a treaty. Trianon was signed only on 4 June 1920. The bolshevik revolution in Hungary in March 1919 certainly moved the peace conference to act on one half of Czechoslovakia's frontiers, but it delayed and divided the conference on the other. A military clash between the Czechoslovaks and the Hungarians made the situation worse. The Czechoslovaks were forced to fall back and were rescued only by a strong line from the conference. The Big Three in fact accepted the Commission's proposed frontier on every point but one as early as 12 June. But the Czechoslovaks' prestige had fallen considerably. The collapse of bolshevism in Hungary in August did little to help. The new government appeared to be intent on a Habsburg restoration; and the gradual disintegration of the peace conference, which had been somewhat disorganised from the start, provided opportunities for Hungarian efforts to have the frontier revised. The Czechoslovak possession of the disputed territory, plus the blessing given by the Big Three, held the line. But before Trianon was finally agreed, the Slovak frontier had already become a question of post-war foreign policy rather than of peace-making.

This was probably to be expected. There was naturally no love lost between the Magyars and the Czechoslovaks. The delay in peacemaking gave the Magyars their opportunity not only to argue the terms but also to play one power off against the other in a typical post-treaty way. There was no love lost between the Germans and the Czechoslovaks either, but the peacemaking process was so quick in their case that there was little opportunity to make foreign politics, though some were tried. What was less expected was a long international struggle to settle the Czecho-slovak-Polish frontier. Before the war, the Poles had been as much an oppressed people as the Czechoslovaks, and the war was their opportunity too. Indeed, during the war there was a remarkable degree of co-operation between the leaders of the two peoples. It was Masaryk's hope that independence would lead to increasing co-operation and that Poland and Czechoslovakia, together with Yugoslavia and Rumania, would ensure peace in eastern Europe. He even contemplated a Polish-Czechoslovak federation. But a dispute immediately arose concerning Těšín. This duchy formed the eastern part of Czech Silesia; its population was mixed Czech, German, and Polish, with the Poles undoubtedly in the majority. A historical argument would have assigned it to Czechoslovakia; conversely, an ethnic case would have given most of it to Poland. However, the situation was complicated by the fact that Těšín was rich in coal, was a centre of heavy industry, and carried the main railway connecting the Czech Lands with Slovakia. This made it valuable to both states, but fractionally more vital for Czechoslovakia. Before the peace conference met, Beneš had secured general Western diplomatic support for a compromise plan assigning most of it to Czechoslovakia, but allocating a small sector in the east to Poland. Unfortunately from Czechoslovakia's point of view, Polish troops quickly took over some two-thirds of it and neither Czechoslovakia nor the Western powers could do anything about it. Since Těšín also had an important role in supplying coal to the whole of central Europe, there was some sympathy for the Czechoslovak case. But this was quickly dissipated when Kramář's government took unilateral action by invading Těšín in January 1919. Sympathy swung behind Poland, and even Beneš was unable to assuage the wrath of France, Britain, and more particularly the United States. In February the Czechoslovaks had no option but to agree to the sending of a control commission to Těšín to hold the ring to the greater advantage of Poland. This time the Czechoslovaks had not managed a *fait accompli;* they had sharpened the hostility of the Poles, and lost credibility with the peace conference. Since the control commission did nothing constructive, and since the peace conference gradually fell apart, the Czechoslovaks were saddled with one more foreign policy issue, whereas it ought to have been disposed of in the peacemaking. It was an issue that even got entangled with Hungarian politicking. In the end, on 28 July 1920, the conference of ambassadors, all that remained of the peace conference, made a decision to divide Těšín, giving the coalfields and the railway-line to Czechoslovakia, but leaving the city itself to Poland. In the midst of its war with Russia, Poland could scarcely reject the imposed settlement. Czechoslovakia had gained almost all it wanted, but there lay ahead as much hostility from the Poles to the north as from the Magyars to the south.

Ruthenia

There was one other area the peace conference dealt with, what came to be known as Sub-Carpathian Ruthenia. Geographically, it could reasonably be described as an extension of Slovakia, since it was separated by high mountains from Rumania and Poland and bore the same physical relationship to Hungary as did Slovakia.

Ethnically, it was distinct. It did contain some thousands of Slovaks; but it had as many Rumanians, rather more Germans, and many more Magyars. More than 60 percent of its population, however, was of Ruthenian stock, and thus much more akin to the Ukrainians than to the Czechs or Slovaks. More remote than Slovakia, it was also more backward. More backward, it was less able to resist the pressure of late nineteenth-century magyarisation. National feelings existed in 1914, but of a national movement there was virtually nothing. Abroad, however, the situation was rather different. In particular, there was a large settlement of Ruthenians in the United States. More than 50,000 had emigrated there in the last decade before the war—and the population at home was hardly more than 500,000 at the outbreak of war. Similar factors influenced them as influenced other immigrants in the United States to campaign on behalf of their countrymen at home. A particular factor was the distinctiveness conferred by their membership of the Uniate (or Greek Catholic) Church. This prevented them from being absorbed in the Russian or even the Ukrainian community, just as language kept them apart from other kindred Slav groups. Once the war and especially American involvement in it gave them the opportunity, their minds turned to thoughts of independence. In ethnic and religious terms this was probably the only thing that made sense. In terms of viability, however, independence made no sense at all. Autonomy was the next alternative, and in the chaos that spread over eastern Europe with the outbreak of the Russian Revolution and the approaching disintegration of Austria-Hungary, calls for autonomy became quite common even in Ruthenia itself. There were neighbouring peoples who cast envious eyes upon Ruthenia and sought after its hand in autonomous marriage. The independent Ukraine that emerged after the Bolshevik Revolution had its expectations. So had post-armistice Hungary and post-independence Poland. Rumania had its share of Uniates and grew in ambition as it drove back the Hungarian bolsheviks. Yet in the end Ruthenia went to Czechoslovakia.

Geographical links and ethnic confusion had caused Slovaks to look eastwards even before the war. Ruthenia, like Slovakia and the Czech Lands, had enjoyed a place in Kramář's scheme of a vast Russian domain in eastern Europe. In the first half of the war, however, Masaryk had not thought of including Ruthenia in his new state. However, in Russia during the Revolution his attitude began to change. In a fluctuating situation, Ukrainian nationalists seemed willing to accept the inclusion of Ruthenia in Czechoslovakia. In the United States Masaryk found himself further involved in the future of the area. He was approached—not against his will—by a number of Ruthenian spokesmen, in particular by Dr Gregorij Žatkovič, lawyer son of the first editor of the newspaper of the 80,000-strong Greek Catholic Union. At that point, in the late spring of 1918, Žatkovič saw three possibilities: for preference, the Ruthenians could be independent on their own; failing that, they could unite in independence with kindred peoples in Galicia and Bukovina; or as a last resort, they could perhaps seek autonomy within another state. Masaryk was now alive to the importance of Ruthenia to Czechoslovakia, not in ethnic but in strategic terms; if nothing else, it was a bridge to Russia. He could also point quite properly to the difficulties such a tiny state would face on its own and to the advantages of co-operation in eastern Europe. In July, Žatkovič formed a National Council of American Ruthenians in Homestead, Pennsylvania, and reiterated the three possibilities. On 21 October 1918 he put his position to Wilson, who told him quite plainly that the first two alternatives were impracticable and unacceptable and that he should negotiate the third with Masaryk. Clearly Ruthenia was too small to survive independently, and there were other claimants to both Galicia and Bukovina. Autonomy across the mountains seemed rather illogical; that left autonomy within Hungary, which was part of an enemy state and likely to be dismembered, and within Czechoslovakia, which was emerging as a favoured newcomer. The choice was now clear. On 26 October, Masaryk and Žatkovič concluded an agreement in Philadelphia that bound them to work for the inclusion of Ruthenia in Czechoslovakia on the basis of guaranteed national autonomy for the Ruthenians.

This was almost but not quite the end of the story. Two-thirds of the Uniate churches canvassed voted in favour of the Philadelphia agreement. But at home in Ruthenia the situation was less clear. In the three months following the armistice, three local councils appeared, one supporting autonomy within Hungary, another within the Ukraine, and a third within Czechoslovakia. Naturally enough, each enjoyed a degree of external support, and all three together seemed to cloud the position. From the viewpoint of the Commission on Czechoslovak Affairs, however, the position was not cloudy. Even the American representatives were convinced. Beneš's arguments were readily accepted. Ruthenia could not be left to the oppression it had endured from the Magyars; it could not be allowed to become a springboard for bolshevik aggression; its accession to Czechoslovakia would not only benefit that country's stability, it would contribute to general peace in eastern Europe by providing a corridor from Czechoslovakia to Rumania. The Commission's report on 12 March 1919, therefore, recommended the inclusion of autonomous Ruthenia in Czechoslovakia. Although there were still bickerings to come, linked closely with arguments about the Hungarian frontier, the essential decision had been made. The bolshevik revolution in Hungary in March, the likely fate of the Ukraine with the outbreak of the Polish-Russian war in April and the entry of Czechoslovak soldiers into Ruthenia also in April, all combined to unite the three councils into one, meeting at Užhorod on 8 May 1919 in the presence of Žatkovič and approving the link with Czechoslovakia.

The inclusion of Ruthenia in Czechoslovakia was almost an afterthought. An ethnic case had never been put forward, and was never made. The Ruthenians were not supposed to be integrated, and they never were. After twenty years they passed out of Czechoslovak history, to spend a brief spell in Hungary before being incorporated in the Soviet Union in 1945. In the circumstances it was really rather odd that they became attached to Czechoslovakia. From the Czechoslovak point of view the explanation was partly altruistic, partly strategic. If the Ruthenians had no alternative, they could join the Czechoslovak experiment. More to the point, in the political vacuum left by the First World War Ruthenia had a strategic value that grew with time. It provided a link with Rumania, an early ally. It kept Hungary and Poland apart as relations with both of them deteriorated. In face of the danger from a recrudescent Germany, it held out the promise of a link through Rumania with Russia. However, in 1945 the Ruthenians could pass out of Czechoslovak history. They could link themselves with kinsmen across the mountains. The whole strategic situation had changed. The Soviet Union had filled the political vacuum, and Czechoslovakia had no need (or no opportunity) to secure Ruthenia for its strategic value. Nevertheless, in the eyes of the Czechoslovaks, both before and after 1918, what was important territorially was not Ruthenia, but the Czech Lands and Slovakia. These they got—and kept.

If Ruthenia came to them easily, it was partly because the Western powers were concerned to see them, rather than the Russians, hold a crucial wedge of territory. Much of the peace settlement had an anti-Soviet flavour, and this applied to the Ruthenian aspect of the Czechoslovak settlement. Strategic considerations, one part of the viability argument, played a considerable role in determining the whole frontier, especially in the minds of the French. Equally important, however, were what might be called the promises of good behaviour. These did not have to be extracted from the Czechoslovaks. Not every Czech and

Slovak was high-minded; some were to stoop very low. But Masaryk, Beneš, and their more important colleagues were determined from before the creation of the state to be fair to its minority population. The peacemaking powers, however, could not overcome their doubts about some aspects of the settlement, without a guarantee of fair treatment for minorities. This became all the more necessary in face of complaints from the dispossessed. The Germans, for example, made a whole series of protests. Immediately after the armistice, they set up autonomous governments in various parts of the Czech Lands, hoping to be united with Austria or Germany or even in time both. By the end of the year their territory was occupied by Czechoslovak soldiers, and naturally they objected. Subsequently prevented from voting in the Austrian elections, they arranged protest meetings for 4 March 1919, only to fall foul of the Czechoslovak police and lose over fifty killed. This time their protests were echoed by the Austrian government. Germany was more cautious, but unofficial protests came from individuals and organisations in Bavaria and Prussian Silesia. In the case of the Magyars, the complaints were louder and longer. The bolshevik regime was itself a form of protest, and later governments kept the stream of objections going hopefully until well into 1920. The powers in Paris needed something, even if only to quieten their own consciences. On 20 May 1919 Beneš submitted a memorandum about the nationalities in Czechoslovakia. It promised that Czechoslovakia would become a 'sort of Switzerland', though taking account of its 'special conditions'; that it would provide universal suffrage under proportional representation; that it would make public offices open to all and make the official language in any area that of the majority, though reserving 'a certain special position for the Czechoslovak language and element'. This was a genuine intention, which also satisfied the Western powers. In addition, the Czechoslovaks signed the standard minorities treaty that all the newly independent nations agreed to, enshrining minority rights. For its part, Ruthenia was guaranteed its autonomy and self-government, in so far as 'compatible with the unity of the Czechoslovak state', and its own special diet. Czechoslovakia had won its frontiers; and it had promised not only to observe the right of its minorities but to make of itself something of a state of nationalities, at least so long as this did not endanger its Czechoslovakness.

Czech-Slovak Relations

The shape of the new Czechoslovakia was not ideal. Neither were the circumstances of its birth. A century of racial strife did not make for tolerance or magnanimity, nor four years of bitter carnage for dispassionate peacemaking. The collapse of several empires and the triumph of umpteen nationalisms raised more problems in 1918 than had been known since 1815. Most of the peacemakers also had domestic problems to cope with. It was remarkable that so much justice and commonsense went to the making of the new state.

Czechoslovak statesmen had their own domestic problems. The most urgent was the working relationship between the two peoples. Wartime declarations had generally implied that the state would be unitary and centralised. The Pittsburgh Agreement had envisaged a kind of federation in which Slovakia would have its own administration, diet, and law courts. It represented the political wishes of the Czech and Slovak immigrants in the United States and was signed by Masaryk. But it recognised that it was for the Czechs and Slovaks at home after the war to make their own decision. In fact, there gradually emerged a Slovak autonomist group under the leadership of Hlinka. He accepted the Turčianský Sv. Martin declaration but re-established his Slovak People's Party. He was not anti-Czech, simply pro-Slovak. He was not separatist, but autonomist. Several factors, however, combined to vitiate a federal settlement and to push politicians like Hlinka into near opposition.

Initially there was some confusion. While discussions were still proceeding in Prague, a provisional Slovak government was established at Turčianský Sv. Martin on 4 November. Its president was Šrobár, for over twenty years champion of Czechoslovak unity, and it included three other leading figures with similar views, Ivan Dérer, Anton Štefánek, and Pavel Blaho. It did not have a fully liberated territory over which to exercise authority and had to look to Prague for military assistance. So ten days later, in face of continuing Magyar intransigence, it was dissolved, and its functions were assumed by the provisional Czechoslovak government established in Prague, of which Šrobár was made a member. In difficult circumstances this raised no particular objection. Šrobár was given both power and responsibility as minister for the administration of Slovakia. Then with the enforced retreat of the Magyar forces, he established headquarters in Bratislava. This had its unfortunate side, however. None of his colleagues was assigned a place in the central government, with the exception of Milan Štefánik, who was unfortunately absent in Russia with the Czechoslovak Legion. Hlinka had not won a place even in the short-lived Slovak government, and for this and other reasons felt somewhat slighted. Nevertheless, the ministry in Bratislava set about the task of constructing the necessary administrative apparatus in Slovakia. It appointed Slovaks to head what were in fact mini-departments of state and to be *Župani* or administrators in the counties. All the men appointed had been prominent in the national movement, though the converse was not true—notably in the case of Hlinka. However, one way or another it looked as if something near autonomy would emerge.

External factors intervened. A Magyar-inspired railway strike was broken by getting Czech railwaymen to keep the service running, but the presence of Czech workers in what, it was felt, ought really to be Slovak jobs evoked considerable Slovak resentment. The constant Magyar threat undermined Czech tolerance of Slovak demands. Accidents intervened. The death of Štefánik in May 1919 as he was returning to Bratislava by plane was an irretrievable loss in terms of leadership. History intervened. The obvious political and cultural superiority of the Czechs at this stage encouraged many of them, often with the best possible motives, to go into Slovakia as teachers, lawyers, and officials, to the frequent annoyance of unqualified but aspiring Slovaks. It also encouraged Czech politicians to assert excessive claims to the leadership of the whole Czechoslovak state. The National Assembly that was established in November 1918 had 256 deputies, but only forty of them were Slovaks; the addition of a further fourteen Slovaks in March 1919 did little to right the balance. Personalities also intervened. Though there were faults on both sides, the growing coolness between Šrobár and Hlinka did nothing to help Czech-Slovak relations. Indeed it tended to magnify other differences. In particular, it pushed Hlinka towards extremes both of attitude and of action. He moved from an autonomous to a separatist point of view. He also joined forces with a politically dissident priest, František Jehlička, who in 1906 had been elected as a Slovak deputy to the Hungarian diet but had abandoned his seat for the bribe of a professorship in Budapest and was now a pro-Magyar separatist. In the late summer of 1919, in company with Jehlička, he went to Paris to plead for a plebiscite in Slovakia to lead to its separation from Czechoslovakia. *En route* he stopped in Warsaw and received advice from Polish leaders. In fact, he soon found himself acting as the agent, witting or unwitting, of a Hungarian-Polish conspiracy to break Czechoslovakia or at least to whittle away its eastern frontier. Fortunately he drew back in time to avoid the fate of Jehlička (who spent the rest of his life abroad), but not before he had damaged the cause of Slovak autonomy within Czechoslovakia beyond immediate repair.

The settlement as it emerged was not autonomy, and was not satisfactory. In February 1920 the Constituent Assembly enacted a law abolishing the historic Czech Lands and the 'Land' of Slovakia and, instead, dividing the whole of Czechoslovakia into a series of twenty-one *Župy* or districts. The six new *Župy* in Slovakia replaced the previous seventeen and in practice as well as in theory gave the Slovaks a kind of identity. But since the *Župy* system was not in the end put into practice in the Czech Lands, many Slovaks saw it as a cheap political stratagem. Each *Župa* had an elected assembly, but much power lay with nominated officials. This, too, was seen as an anti-autonomy device. The separate ministry for Slovakia was retained in Bratislava, but its various sub-sections became more and more subordinate to their head offices in Prague. Given the historical disadvantages of Slovakia, there was much to commend the paternalistic attitude Prague adopted. On the other hand, it clearly represented a centralist triumph and, however much it satisfied the temporary need for government, it was not a contribution to the welding of the nation. In the elections of 1920 Hlinka's party secured almost one-fifth of the recorded votes.

One of the features of life after 1918 that most irked the Slovaks was the presence of large numbers of Czechs in prestigious positions. It was disappointing to have disposed of the Magyars to find sympathetic but nonetheless somewhat alien Czechs in their place. But decades of magyarisation had deprived most Slovaks of the kind of education that would have fitted them for high positions. Perhaps a thousand were ready to go into government service or to take up jobs in university, schools, or law offices. Nor should Slovak discontent be overemphasised. For the mass of the people life in Czechoslovakia was an infinite improvement on life in Hungary. At a different level, the majority of Slovak politicians were not only willing to work with the Czechs, they were really anxious to do so; and the united Czechoslovak Social Democratic Party won twice as many Slovak votes in 1920 as Hlinka's party. There was a genuine desire to establish a Czechoslovak nation. Moreover, many Slovak difficulties were not peculiarly Slovak; they were really nationwide. Framing a constitution—and a host of other things, such as building an economy—had to be looked at in the broad to benefit everyone. Using up-to-date parlance, Slovakia might be a vastly underdeveloped region; but Czechoslovakia itself was a developing country that still had a long road ahead of it.

The Constitution

Giving political form to the relationship between the Czechs and the Slovaks was important, but it was still peripheral to settling the constitution of the new Czechoslovak state. In this, there were several determinants. In the first place, there could be no question of a monarchy. The Czech Lands might have lost their independence and their king together almost three centuries before, but all their experience of the Habsburgs since had inclined them to distrust monarchical institutions. There was no surviving claimant to the throne, and the possibility of a Russian substitute had gone for good with the Revolution. Anyway, the German monarchy had collapsed as well as the Austrian and the Russian; and the British was inimitable. A crown might have been the prize of every self-respecting new nation-state before 1914, but the First World War changed all that. Thereafter, the one possibility was a republic. The fact that two of the three major victors, France and the United States, were republics, made the possibility a certainty.

The second inescapable determinant was that the new state had to be democratic, however defined. The three major victors were, in their various ways, democratic. In its own view, so was the new Soviet regime. The war aims and the peace terms of the Western powers were shot through with democratic slogans, as was the propaganda of the Russian government and of the Comintern. If a defeated Germany had to be democratic, greater still was the obligation on a triumphant Czechoslovakia. In any case, the whole pressure of the national movement had long been toward some kind of representative government; there could be no turning back now.

The third determinant—the outlook of Masaryk and Beneš—was no less powerful. By 1918 they were the unquestioned leaders of the national movement. There were other major figures and very many minor ones; but Masaryk and Beneš dominated the movement. On certain points, their views might differ. In age, they were more than a generation apart; Masaryk's foreign experience was more American, Beneš's more French. But their differences were of emphasis, not on fundamentals. They were both republicans and democrats. They were also both realists. They might look to Western models, but they saw deficiencies in both the United States and France. They saw, too, that the American constitution was peculiarly American, and that the French was not only European in concept but, in alliance terms, physically nearer. They also knew how long it had taken to make the American constitution manageable and how often the French had been under threat. Finally, they were deeply conscious of the politics, the personalities, and the weaknesses of their own national movement. To declare a republic was easy. To shape a democracy was a more delicate task, one in which they had to draw on both the experience of other countries and the realities of their own. In so doing, they were helped by their combined wealth of knowledge and wisdom, but they were also children of their time. They were constitution-making in the given atmosphere of a Western victory and a Bolshevik menace. They could not escape the present or foresee the future.

The final factor was the political situation at home. This had the effect of making the new state unitary, but it had other results as well. The Czech political parties had emerged in the context of the Austrian system which in the end had yielded to adult male suffrage. The new system would have to advance on that, give women the vote, and, more important, acknowledge the parliamentary supremacy the Habsburgs had fought against to the last. There were other specific Habsburg abuses to be got rid of, affecting the liberties of politicians and individuals. The new system was also one to be determined by the politicians of the day. The National Committee formed in July 1918 comprised thirty-eight members, selected in such a way as to represent the balance of the parties in the elections of 1911. The National Assembly established in November 1918 comprised 256 deputies, not elected on a fresh ballot but chosen on the same principle. The men who fashioned the Czechoslovak constitution were the men who had officered the national movement for a decade or more, not unknowns thrown up by the uncertain fortunes of a post-war election.

One of the first acts of the National Assembly was to name Masaryk provisional President of the new state. When the proper constitution came into operation in 1920, he was elected first President. He was twice re-elected, in 1927 and 1934. This was both inevitable and significant. The President was elected, not by popular vote, but by the legislature. He was responsible to the legislature in the way that no Habsburg monarch had been and he had a more intimate relationship with it than an American President. At the same time, like a French President, he was elected for seven years, which added to his power. Unlike a French President, he could be re-elected for a second term, which added still more to his power. An exception was made in the case of Masaryk to allow him to serve for more than two terms, and even though he retired after only a year of his third, he brought so much prestige to the office and then held it for so long that he gave it an authority beyond the merely constitutional. When Beneš became President in 1935, he too was an inevitable choice. He probably had less popularity than Masaryk, and times had certainly changed; so he was able to exercise less authority. Nonetheless, even in his time the presidency carried more weight in the government of the country than had ever been intended.

On the whole, this was beneficial to Czechoslovakia. The President was the subject of parliamentary choice and control; he had few real powers of his own; but he had reserves and could exercise genuine leadership. It was certainly beneficial with statesmen of the calibre of Masaryk and Beneš. There were, however, at least two disadvantages. The President was often expected by his own people to be capable of the frankly impossible; and he was frequently seen abroad as almost a dictator who could carry through unpalatable policies with little regard for parliamentary opinion. For their part, neither Masaryk nor Beneš overestimated their presidential authority; and certainly the other politicians did nothing to amplify or exaggerate it. The first provisional prime minister in November 1918 was Kramář, and his appointment was also full of significance. Next to Masaryk's, his had been the most important name before the war, and at the end it was still the best known on the home front. The prime minister of the new state was not to be a nonentity, either then or later. Kramář resigned within eight months, his conservative views no longer in favour with the majority of his colleagues. His successors, however, particularly men of the calibre of Švehla, Jan Malypetr, and Hodža, were not cyphers to be pushed aside. The new Czechoslovakia was a parliamentary democracy; the prime minister and the cabinet were responsible to the legislature; and the legislature was unlikely to let them lose their authority to the President.

The National Assembly that hammered out the constitution was unicameral. However, the legislature that it established was bicameral. A single body to express the will of the nation at the moment of its birth was one thing; but government over a longer period, it was felt, would necessitate checks and balances. This was the commonplace view even in societies as different as the United States and the Soviet Union. Since Czechoslovakia opted against federalisation, it could not really follow the American and Russian examples and have a state- or people-based second chamber. There was no Czechoslovak aristocracy and nothing but distaste for the hereditary principle as practised by the Habsburgs. Instead, the Czechoslovaks decided to adopt the French model of a second chamber based on age. The minimum voting age for the chamber of deputies was twenty-one, for the senate twenty-six. The minimum standing age for the chamber was thirty, for the senate forty-five. The senate was also smaller, half the size of the chamber, with 150 members to the lower house's 300. In theory, the senate also ran for eight years to the lower house's six, although in practice they were dissolved together. Otherwise, the two were similar. The whole system had a certain logic to commend it. Primacy lay with the chamber of deputies; the senate did no more than exercise a delaying power, and it therefore acted as a steadying influence. In financial matters, complete primacy lay with the lower house. Disputes between the two were uncommon, so uncommon as to raise the question whether the second house was really necessary. The fact was that, in terms of the distribution of seats among the parties, the senate was largely a mirror of the chamber of deputies. Indeed, since many of the deputies tended to be middle-aged, even the difference of years became something of a constitutional myth. By being a trifle cumbrous, the system may have thrown extra power in the direction of the presidency. On the other hand, even if the check seldom had to be used, it was always there. The constitution provided a series of safeguards for individual parliamentarians' rights, but the existence of the senate was a protection for the whole system. It guaranteed that the legislature would not lose its position by abusing it.

Age restrictions were almost bound, indeed were intended, to make the entire legislature somewhat conservative, at least in the sense of conserving the revolution. This did not make it unrepresentative of popular views. In fact, in adopting proportional representation, the Czechoslovaks produced a legislature that was ultra-representative. They ignored the majority principle of their Western mentors, and they reverted instead to the teaching of one of the original Young Czechs, Karel Sladkovský. The proportional system they introduced was mathematically exact and, in election after election, secured a remarkably accurate reproduction of all shades of Czechoslovak political opinion, including minority divisions. It was designed to do just this, not only to make government responsive to all of the people in the best democratic tradition, but to forge co-operation among divergent interests, both social and ethnic. In a limited way it succeeded. It had beneficial side-effects too. Deputies and senators were freed from local constituency pressures, at least in the early years. On the other hand, the system had one very unfortunate result. It encouraged a multiplicity of new parties and even the splitting of old ones. In the first general election of 1920 no less than twenty-three parties competed and seventeen actually secured seats. This would not have mattered greatly had one party managed to win a majority or even a sizeable block. As it was, the Czechoslovak Social Democratic Party came first with no more than seventy-four seats in the chamber of deputies, approximately one-quarter of the total. And in no other election in the inter-war period was this number ever reached, let alone surpassed. Inevitably, resort was had to coalitions that were not only inimical to the spirit of proportional representation but tended to be cumbrous and stifling. They produced slow progress, and sometimes none, and in a sense they defeated the purpose of the legislature which was not only to represent but to govern. Further, coalitions tended to remove decision-making from the legislature to the people organising them, sometimes the party managers and sometimes the cabinet itself. It was the deals not the debates that counted. Finally, the cumbrousness of coalitions frequently forced the President to take initiatives that were not strictly his to take, and that were not made easier by the state of affairs which forced him into action. Yet, returning the initiative to the President made the constitution work.

Proportional representation had an important bearing on the Slovak question. It protected Slovak separatism and enabled Hlinka's People's Party to get a fair return from the votes cast for it, so that it increased its number of deputies in the chamber each election. The position of the Catholic Church in the new state was also of some importance to the Slovaks but was not immediately settled. Of greater concern was the system of local government. The establishment of *Župy* in 1920 appeared to undermine the unity of Slovakia and further to reduce its chance of autonomy. In fact, the division of Czechoslovakia into what amounted to French-type prefectures was not specifically aimed at Slovakia. It was a product of Czech tidiness and of admiration for something else French. It was directed against all local loyalties, in particular the centrifugal provincialism that was associated with the former diets. Partly because of provincial loyalties the system never worked in the Czech Lands, and in 1927 it was completely altered throughout Czechoslovakia. Provinces were allowed to reappear, and each of them—Bohemia, Moravia-Silesia, and Slovakia—was permitted its own provincial governor, administration, and diet. In this way Slovakia recovered a degree of unity, but not very much autonomy, no more in fact than the Czech Lands. Czechoslovakia remained centralised. The provincial governors and administrations were appointed by the central government, as were one-third of the members of the provincial diets. The same central restrictions were imposed at the level of district government. At the grassroots level of communal administration there was much more genuine self-government, and seven larger cities or towns had a special charter status. Essentially, however, the local government system everywhere in Czechoslovakia was intended to promote the authority of the central government and reduce the influence of former loyalties. It was not an attack on the Slovaks as such, any more than on the Czechs. It was meant to consolidate the concept of Czechoslovakness.

The Minorities

Proportional representation was equally important for Czechoslovakia's minorities. It was never suggested that the Germans, Poles, and Magyars would be turned into Czechoslovaks in the ethnic sense. Czechoslovakia was envisaged as a state made up of Czechoslovaks and minorities. But it was expected that the minorities would become full citizens of the Czechoslovak state, and it was solemnly agreed that they should have certain guaranteed rights. These were set out in the special Minorities Treaty that amplified Beneš's promises to the peace conference on 20 May 1919; and the constitution-makers proceeded to make sure that they were given effect. Universal suffrage and proportional representation were solemnly promised; so they were duly given. Six German parties entered the 1920 election and between them won 72 seats in the chamber; three Magyar parties won 10 seats. Separate schools were promised; so provision was made in the Schools Law for separate elementary schools wherever minorities could produce an attendance of forty. It was promised that, in practice, German would be the second language of the country. Under the Language Law, a minority language was accepted as the official language in areas where two-thirds of the people spoke it. Where one-fifth of the people spoke it, it could be used both for public instruction and for official communication.

There were other aspects of the minorities legislation. Forced denationalisation, for example, was prohibited. But quite apart from whether all the laws and all the articles of the constitution would be observed, there were blemishes: Beneš made it clear in Paris that the Czech and Slovak languages would enjoy a special position. In the event, this went beyond their use on banknotes and in the army. They were made a basic requirement for all public appointments, which tended to operate against the minorities. Beneš also promised that Czechoslovakia would become a 'sort of Switzerland', which clearly it did not. Indeed, it could be argued that the centralist view taken of government had little to do with the Slovaks and everything to do with the problem of minorities. If the *Župy* system was abandoned, it was partly to prevent some of them becoming Swiss-type minority-dominated cantons. If provinces were resurrected, it was to submerge the minority groups among the Czechoslovaks. If the reins were kept on the provincial and district administrations, the purpose was also to check possible minority aspirations. On the other hand, the minorities were allowed a remarkably free hand at commune level (though every commune had to have an official Czech or Slovak name). When Beneš made his promise, he added a rider to the effect that the 'special conditions' of Czechoslovakia would have to be considered. In short, his promise was qualified. It was, in any case, unrealisable. Conditions for cantons on the Swiss model simply did not exist in Czechoslovakia; and, for the record, Beneš never mentioned cantons.

Consistent with the integrity of the Czechoslovak state, the constitution-makers went a long way to protect minorities. It might even be said that they went almost too far, for it was the platform provided by proportional representation that ultimately enabled the Sudeten Germans to destroy the state. However, the limiting factor in the post-war period was the questionable loyalty of the minorities, particularly the Germans. Nothing they did, however comprehensible, was in any way calculated to make the Czechoslovaks think that they would respect the integrity of the state. It was perfectly understandable that the majority of the Germans should not wish to find themselves in Czechoslovakia. Some of them had behaved very well in the days of the Habsburg Empire, but it cannot have been easy for most of them to contemplate at best sharing the new state with people whom they had been used to treating as inferiors. Since there was no definable ethnic frontier, some Germans had to remain in the new state. Since the ethnic shading began far across the only viable frontier, more Germans than should ideally have been the case had to face a future in Czechoslovakia. The peace conference could accept this and agree to some limit on self-determination as a means of promoting international stability. But it was natural that the Germans to be stranded in Czechoslovakia should see things rather differently and demand self-determination for themselves. Their leaders refused to take part in the work of the National Assembly and proceeded generally to stir up trouble. One consequence was the demonstration and deaths of 4 March 1919. This did nothing to endear the Germans to their fate. But by the same token, the policy of abstention and disaffection that produced such a tragic result did nothing to enamour the Czechoslovaks of the Germans. The Germans still refused to take part in the work of the Assembly, leaving it to continue on its own with the crucial job of constitution-making. When the constitutional framework finally emerged in 1920, it certainly had its shortcomings as far as the Germans were concerned. Yet however much sympathy might legitimately be extended to them, both because of the decision to assign them to Czechoslovakia and because of the conditions they met there, the fact remains that they did nothing to try and improve their lot, either by calming Czechoslovak fears or by helping in the actual business of determining the constitution. In the circumstances, it was remarkable that they did not fare worse. The Czechoslovaks might really have paid them back for centuries of misrule, or for the war, or for their subsequent posturings. As time went on, the Czechoslovaks were much criticised for the arrangements they had made for them. Yet, quite apart from what the Germans had done before the war or might themselves have done if they had won, few of Czechoslovakia's critics conducted themselves after 1918 with as much tolerance and fairness as Czechoslovakia.

Politics and Economics in the New State

The declaration of independence on 28 October 1918 and the accession of Slovakia to the republic two days later were followed by widespread scenes of Czechoslovak rejoicing. The return of Masaryk to his homeland in December 1918 was the occasion for even wilder scenes of enthusiasm. But to negotiate the treaty of Trianon took until June 1920. The constitution was approved a little earlier, in February 1920, and the first general election took place in between in April. The intervening twelve to eighteen months were not easy for the Czechoslovak people. Peacemaking proved complicated, and at one stage it involved a renewal of the war through fighting in Slovakia. Constitution-making was hardly easier and produced a state of civil tension between the Czechs and the Germans. The conditions of life showed no improvement; food, clothing, and housing were all short. The country also went through its first major independent political crisis and embarked on a tentative programme of social and economic reform.

The two were connected. Before the war the Czech Lands in particular had had as wide a range of parties as almost any other modern country. The differences between them were primarily social or occupational. But the circumstances of alien rule had driven them together to form a single national movement with a common social aspiration, to get rid of the Germans and to be their own masters. Victory on the national front in 1918 undermined their old unity. National revolution was supposed to lead to social revolution, but the nature and extent of the latter were in question. Political differences reappeared. Democratic propaganda and communist revolution raised the hopes of some parties and the fears of others. A National Assembly representing the old political parties was bound to hear acrimonious debates when non-national social and economic issues were being discussed. A National Assembly charged to produce social and economic reform as well as a new political structure was bound to engender crises.

About some reforms there was no serious dispute. It is to the credit of the Habsburgs that they had introduced a rudimentary scheme of social insurance. The new Czechoslovak government had a foundation upon which to build, and social welfare in one form or another had come to be accepted as a part of normal government activity in every civilised country. Before 1918 was out, the National Assembly had passed laws setting up a scheme of unemployment assistance and regulating working conditions. The 8-hour day and the 48-hour week became standard for all employees in business, industry, and agriculture. The employment of children under fourteen was prohibited, and restrictions were placed on the types of work open to adolescents and women. However, on the question of land reform there was deep disagreement. The issue was basically social, not economic. In 1918 as few as 150 families with estates of more than 5,000 hectares apiece held more than a tenth of the total arable and forest land in Czechoslovakia. At the other end of the scale almost a half of the peasants in the Czech Lands held as little as half a hectare, and in Slovakia two-thirds of the peasants were totally without land. There was no dispute about the urgent need for land reform. Since most of the large landowning families were of alien nationality, there was little disagreement about dispossessing them. The argument started below the 1,000-hectare mark. The State Rights Democrats, or as they were now styled, the National Democrats, of whom Kramář had become leader, represented the oldest, most conservative and monied strain in Czechoslovak party politics. In the National Assembly they were still one of three bigger parties. As far as they were concerned, expropriation should cease below 1,000 hectares. At the opposite extreme were the Social Democrats, the second of the bigger parties, who wanted confiscation without compensation of all lands above 50 hectares. Somewhere between the two positions were the Czechoslovak and Slovak People's parties. Their Christian Socialist outlook and widespread artisan backing made them more egalitarian than the National Democrats, but less doctrinaire than the Social Democrats. The Slovak People's Party was also very anxious to protect church lands. The third of the bigger parties was the Agrarian, guided by Švehla who was now the influential minister of the interior. His concern and that of his party had for years been to represent the interests of the peasantry in general, which meant in practice to foster the growth of a well-to-do independent peasant proprietor community. For this reason they were nearer to the Social Democrats' position. They wanted to maximise the amount of land available for distribution, but not to minimise the size of farm to which some of their supporters might some day aspire. Thus the balance of forces in the National Assembly and the provisional government in the debates of early 1919 was towards a much lower figure than 1,000 hectares, and as positions hardened, Kramář's popularity and that of his party both declined.

However, there remained serious differences between the Agrarians and the Social Democrats over the distribution of the land to be expropriated. Naturally enough, the Agrarians wanted to parcel it out among their supporters, particularly those most able to make use of it—the better-off peasantry. Naturally also, the Social Democrats wished to use the expropriated lands to form co-operative farms for the poorer peasants. It was an acute ideological conflict. Both parties also reacted to the international situation and its possible local repercussions. In the first quarter of 1919 the peace talks in Paris had only begun. The Czechoslovak Legion was still intermittently engaged in the Russian civil war. Béla Kun seized power in Hungary and began directing communist propaganda against the Czechoslovaks. There was no saying how Czechoslovakia might fare in the peace negotiations, or whether it might be engulfed in a vast international ideological war. Neither the Agrarians nor the Social Democrats shared the anti-bolshevik views of Kramář and his colleagues; but neither welcomed the prospect of communism spreading to Czechoslovakia. Both responded differently, however. The Agrarians thought to delay land reform, and Švehla's mind turned to possible means of introducing restrictive legislation. The Social Democrats took exactly the opposite attitude. There was a full-scale government crisis. Czechoslovak political unity seemed about to break at its first social test.

It was Masaryk's intervention that settled the crisis and preserved the state. The two parties could not agree, and neither had the upper hand. Masaryk had no alternative but to arbitrate and his prestige and skill were such that he could hardly fail. It was a tough baptism for the Czechoslovak people. It was also a strange foretaste of the pattern of parliamentary-presidential politics to come. The whole episode was in fact important in a number of ways. There was the settlement itself. The basic Land Reform Law was passed immediately, on 16 April 1919; this represented a Social Democratic victory. The top limit of holdings was fixed at 150 hectares of arable, or 250 mixed; this was nearer the Agrarian position, but was not quite a defeat for the Social Democrats. The land actually expropriated was to go to peasant farmers and landless peasants, to Legionaries and war-wounded, and to associations and institutions of various kinds. This was essentially the Agrarian solution, yet with just a touch of concession to the Social Democrats. Compensation was to be paid to the dispossessed, and here the Social Democrats definitely lost. This particular law, of course, was only the first of a series. As such, it was a reasonable compromise that, at least in theory, prepared the way for far-reaching reform. Even if it did not go far enough, it nevertheless initiated a social revolution.

However, there was more to the episode. It really marked the end of Kramář and almost the end of his party. His attitude to the Soviet Union and to land reform were already making him unpopular. Strikes and demonstrations in May against high prices and shortages did not improve his image. The establishment in June of a Slovak Soviet Republic in eastern Slovakia, supported by Béla Kun, added to his difficulties. Finally, in the middle of the month, the first local elections in the Czech Lands placed the Social Democrats at the top of the poll with 30 percent of the votes, the Agrarians second with 20 percent, and the National Democrats as low as fifth with a mere 8 percent. The signs were clear for Kramář to resign, which he did early in July. At the general election in 1920 his party gained only 19 seats, and in subsequent elections down to 1935 it fared worse. The new Czechoslovakia still had an indigenous right wing, but its power was broken.

The new prime minister was the Social Democrat Tusar. At thirty-nine, he was twenty years younger than Kramář, as well as more in tune with the popular mood. He had wide practical experience as a trade union official, as a journalist, as a deputy in the Austrian diet, and finally as first Czechoslovak ambassador in Vienna. By temperament, too, as well as by experience, he was more of a negotiator than a revolutionary. He was therefore well suited to healing the wounds left by the battles of the previous few months. He was equally well suited to the task of working with the Agrarians. For this was another consequence of the land-reform crisis. If one of the three largest parties had registered its disagreement and gone into decline, the remaining two had come to terms and created the prototype for the kind of 'red-green' coalition that was several times tried in the inter-war period. Neither the 'red' nor the 'green' was to be true to its colour. The Social Democrats were to lose their left wing in 1921 when it broke to form the Communist Party. As a result of land reform, the Agrarians were to retain the support of the peasantry at large, but at the same time to become more and more the party of the well-off farmers. But the original 'red-green' coalition did represent a Czechoslovak mood. Neither party in 1919 was strong enough to assume command or to oust the other. The same was true in the general election of 1920 when the Social Democrats won 74 chamber seats, the Agrarians forty. Leaving other parties aside, the fact was that among the Czechs and Slovaks as a whole there was too even a balance between town and country, workers and peasants, for any one party to emerge with a commanding majority, too wide a divergence of economic interest for any one party to represent everyone, and too close an identity of social interest for the two major parties not to co-operate. In its first major political crisis Czechoslovakia achieved much and learned more; in particular, it learned the art of political compromise.

If the new state was to survive, let alone progress, it required far more than political reconstruction. In the immediate post-war situation there was a daunting series of economic problems to solve. More fundamentally, there was a new economy to shape. The first set of problems really stemmed from the war. Industry had been redirected to military production, agriculture had been deprived of much of its labour to fight (or to desert) at the front. The Allied blockade had further reduced the availability of machinery and consumer goods. Industry and agriculture were both working below pre-war standards by 1918, and recovery was difficult. It was hazardous enough in the established countries of western Europe. Czechoslovakia was a new entity in the troubled area of central Europe. It had to find its own currency and to fight off inflation, to cope with shortages, and to deal with unemployment, while all the time struggling to settle its frontiers, hold back its enemies, calm its minorities, and draw up its constitution. Gallant efforts were made, for example by Rašín, the first finance minister, but during 1919 industrial output continued to fall and food prices to rise. Currency measures helped and the situation began to improve in 1920. But the real problem was the long-term one.

In one sense the new state had a tremendous industrial advantage. It emerged in 1918 with about 21 percent of Austria-Hungary's territory, about 25 percent of its population, and about 70 percent of its industry. Some of the individual percentages were remarkably high: porcelain, 100 percent; glass, 92; sugar, 91; foodstuffs, 87; woollens, 80; chemicals, anthracite, and cotton, 75 percent each. Some of the others were very close runners: paper, 65; lignite, 63; iron, 60; brewing, 57. This made Czechoslovakia certainly the best-endowed economically of the emerging central European states. But it also had its problems. Its industry had been built up to serve a large protected Austro-Hungarian market. In a toughly competitive and often autarkic world it now had to find export markets. In some cases it also had to find new sources of raw materials to replace those now situated in foreign countries. Its balance of industries was also wrong; two serious lacks, for example, were electrical goods and light engineering.

A further problem was that most of its industry was located in the west. If 39 percent of the population of the Czech Lands worked in industry, the figure for Slovakia was only 17 percent. Since Czechoslovakia as a whole already had more industry than it knew how to handle, there was little incentive to develop more in Slovakia. Indeed, the pressure was really the other way round. Slovak industry was much less competitive and its labour force much less highly skilled; the rational thing was to run it down. Nor was it even a case of an industrial western half and an agricultural eastern half being complementary. Agriculture in the Czech Lands was well developed from before independence, particularly in those sectors supplying industry. If after independence the balance of trade in agricultural products was only a little adverse, credit was due not to Slovak output, but to Czech. In the development of individual areas of its farming, Slovakia was anything from thirty to eighty years behind the Czech Lands. Man for man, its output was only a third of that in the Czech Lands. If Czechoslovakia had to face a hard economic road internationally after 1918, it faced a harder domestic one. Communications were no help. Most Czech roads and railways ran south to Vienna, most Slovak south to Budapest. East-west links were very poor, and the internal provision of roads and railways in Slovakia abysmal. Czechoslovakia was born with an unbalanced and disjointed economy.

There were sundry other problems. Of certain industries in the Czech Lands a biggish proportion was owned and worked by Germans. Thus of 1,793 textile factories of various kinds that fell within Czechoslovakia, as many as 1,231 were in German hands, and of twenty-one glass factories, no less than sixteen were German. In principle there was nothing wrong with this; but in practice, textiles and glass suffered more from the loss of the Austro-Hungarian market and the onset of fierce international competition in 1918 than any other industries, which meant, regrettably, that the Germans suffered unduly. Other problems still lay in the future: it was 1921 and 1924 before fresh United States immigration laws effectively cut migration from Czechoslovakia and particularly from Slovakia and removed a traditional economic safety-valve. One of the biggest difficulties facing the new state immediately, however, was how to secure domestic control of Czechoslovak industry as a whole. By the time

Czechoslovakia achieved its independence, perhaps a third of the capital in its industry was its own. Much of the rest was Austrian and Hungarian. Money apart, the actual running of most Czech and Slovak factories was done from head offices in Vienna and Budapest. This was a state of affairs fraught with danger. In the unhappy conditions of post-war Austria and Hungary even the most longstanding industrial and commercial enterprises might crash. If they survived, they could proceed to run Czechoslovak industry in the interest of Austria and Hungary. There was a whole Czechoslovak economy to create; but it could only be done if Czechoslovakia controlled its own industry either through the government direct or through private enterprise.

In economic terms, independence was not the end but the beginning. There was much to do to recover from the war, much more to overcome the long-term problem. The politics of 1918-20, and the nature of the society they reflected, determined that the solution would not be sought through socialism (though in 1920 a beginning was made to the nationalisation of the more important railway companies). Equally, however, they determined that the government would assume a leading role. In the formative period, Tusar's government showed this by passing a Domestication Law in December 1919 which instructed all companies operating exclusively in Czechoslovakia to move their offices and officials there and all foreign companies having factories in Czechoslovakia to run them separately there as independent companies. By arrangement, Czechoslovak banks were on hand to bring about capital transfers. It was the start of the process that gave private enterprise, under government guidance, a major say in shaping the Czechoslovak economy. It was also in a way the start of the process that was to unite the different sections of the Czechoslovak economy and enable the whole to face up to the changed nature of the post-war world. Czechoslovakia had its problems; it also had its opportunity.

CHAPTER 9

Czechoslovakia in the 1920s

International Security

By the middle of 1920 Czechoslovakia had secured its frontier and settled its constitution. It had begun to shape its social and economic destiny. Industrial production was at last rising, unemployment falling, and shortages diminishing. Bitter political disputes and severe economic crises lay not far ahead, but in the meantime there was a sense of achievement and optimism. Life was more than getting back to normal; it was finding new and better norms. Music and the arts had revived. New opportunities in education had been created with the establishment of universities in Brno and Bratislava and the founding of technical high schools in Prague and Brno alongside the earlier German ones. The war was over at last; there was no more fighting in Slovakia, and the Legionaries were returning from Russia. The League of Nations had met for the first time and the peace might be lasting.

One of the rights the constitution left to the President was that of nominating and dismissing the prime minister and other members of the cabinet. This was the legal position; in fact, real power lay with the ruling coalition. However, in one respect the President was able to assert his prerogative. Both Masaryk and Beneš were successful in securing the appointment of non-political foreign ministers of their own choosing. Masaryk's choice, inevitably, was Beneš himself. By the middle of 1920, with the war and the peace behind him, Beneš really personified the nation's foreign policy. Like the rest of his countrymen he had a sense of achievement, and possibly more than most of them he was optimistic. On the other hand, he was a realist who knew that optimism could survive only if the conditions that had nurtured it could be maintained or improved upon. This was the task he set himself as soon as the last of the treaties was signed.

Czechoslovakia had been created out of the ruins of the Habsburg Empire. If it was to survive for long, no one must be allowed to bring the Empire to life again. This was the primary tenet of Beneš's policy. It had both a negative and a positive side.

Specifically, on the negative side, the reappearance of the Habsburgs themselves had to be prevented. Here the danger lay not with Austria, which had represented the more reasonable half of the Empire and which seemed to be escaping more rapidly from its past, but with Hungary whose position was exactly the opposite. After the overthrow of Béla Kun, Hungary in fact declared itself still a monarchy, and two serious attempts were made, in March and October 1921, to restore Charles of Habsburg to the throne. Sympathy for a restoration was to be found even in France, but opposition was much more widespread; it was too early yet to upset the peace settlement. Beneš was able to find enough international support to force Charles to withdraw, though Hungary still went by the style of a monarchy. However, the positive side of Beneš's policy was more important and far-reaching. This was to promote co-operation among the so-called successor states. The policy included Austria which, once the initial shock of defeat and dismemberment was over, was glad, for economic reasons, to improve relations. At the end of December 1921 an agreement was reached between the two countries. Austria accepted the new frontiers, the two promised to put any dispute that might arise to international arbitration, and Czechoslovakia gave Austria financial help. But the rock on which this co-operative policy was based was the Little Entente. The concept of an alliance between the Czechoslovaks, the Yugoslavs, and the Rumanians was not new. It followed from the friendship that developed between them as subjects, or in part subjects, of the same oppressive Empire; it followed from the intellectual leadership Masaryk gave before the war to small but influential numbers of South Slav and Rumanian students; it followed from wartime discussions and a somewhat similar view about peace. The alliance was also a natural one, for all three had a vested interest in preventing a Habsburg restoration. Its completion was nonetheless an achievement, most of the credit for which should go to Beneš. Czechoslovakia signed its treaties with Yugoslavia and Rumania in August 1920 and April 1921, and the other two signed theirs in June 1921. Local defence of the *status quo* was thus assured, and was strengthened when Czechoslovakia and Austria came to terms. However, the Little Entente and the agreement that followed it had a wider purpose. They were meant to lay the foundation for co-operation in central Europe, both political and economic, that would provide not only a substitute for the vanished Empire, but an improvement on it.

Beneš also managed to extend this combination of security and co-operation to Poland, at least for a while. Masaryk's original hope that Czechoslovak-Polish relations would flourish at the end of the war had been shattered by the Těšín dispute. Even after the Western powers had imposed a settlement in July 1920, relations between the two states remained distinctly cool. They differed fundamentally over Russia, and Poland at first saw fit to support Hungarian efforts to bring back the Habsburgs. But Czechoslovak support for Poland in the Silesian dispute in 1921 contributed materially to an improvement in relations. At the end of that year the two governments signed an agreement giving up claims to each other's territory, thus preparing the way, it was hoped, for positive co-operation. But Beneš's interest in Poland was not simply connected with the future of the Little Entente. It was linked with his legitimate fears about the future of Germany. If a Habsburg restoration was unthinkable, so equally was German revisionism. One of the main criticisms of the Habsburgs had been that they became linked with Pangermanism. Even with the Habsburgs gone, Pangermanism could still present a serious threat to Czechoslovakia, and it was therefore necessary to prepare defences. Beneš saw Poland as one of them. In looking to Austria he saw that it too had an importance in terms of Germany. The peace settlement's veto on an Austrian *Anschluss* with Germany would have to be supported. One way of helping to ensure this would be to come to terms with Austria, as Beneš did, in the hope of taking its mind off an *Anschluss*. The containment of Germany was the second tenet of Beneš's policy.

This was clearly something that Czechoslovakia could not achieve alone. It had played its part in bringing down the Austrian and German empires. But the burden of the battle had fallen on the Western powers, and upon them would obviously fall the burden of containing Germany. In this context, the withdrawal of the United States from anything but a minor role in Europe was a matter of real regret. Beneš could not exploit the relationship that Masaryk had established in the last year of the war. In Britain, Beneš had useful contacts, and Czechoslovakia could rely on a wide measure of understanding and sympathy. Once the peace was settled, however, Britain resumed its offshore island attitude and intervened in the affairs of Europe only where its vital interests seemed likely to be affected. Unfortunately, from the Czechoslovak point of view, this meant that Britain was not automatically committed to containing Germany to the extent that France was. There was the League of Nations, of which Italy was a member as well as Britain and France, and which was dedicated to everything that Czechoslovakia stood for, from self-determination itself to the peaceful settlement of international disputes. Beneš was an ardent Leaguer. He was anxious to uphold its authority and improve its procedures, both as a matter of principle and in the interest of Czechoslovakia. From the very beginning he worked assiduously towards this end. He served spells both as Chairman of the League Council and as President of the Assembly. Indeed, he was more than once in trouble at home for spending too much time on League business abroad. But he was also a thorough realist. The League might be one means to peace and security for Czechoslovakia. But at the end of the day, the support of the Western powers would be crucial; and in the circumstances of the time, that essentially meant France.

In general, it was reasonable for Beneš to depend on France. France had been Czechoslovakia's staunchest and most helpful advocate both during the war and at the peace conference. Its determination to contain Germany amounted almost to an obsession. If there was a danger in the dependence, it lay partly in this obsession, which was an embarrassment, and partly in the French difficulty of choosing at times between conflicting east European interests. Fundamentally, however, the link with France was sound and, anyway, it was inescapable. Yet it was not thoughtlessly or hurriedly forged. At the Genoa conference in the spring of 1922, Beneš attempted, with the backing of the Little Entente, to negotiate a common Franco-British approach to Germany, and when his attempt foundered in face of growing animosity between the two powers, he did not adopt the French line. In the Ruhr crisis in 1923 Beneš once again did not follow the French lead but took a sensible neutral stance. The dangerous situation in Germany, following the French occupation of the Ruhr, and the blandishments of France in its isolation did encourage Beneš to change his attitude slightly. In January 1924 Czechoslovakia signed its first-ever treaty with France. The two countries concluded a mutual guarantee, and in particular they promised joint action to prevent a Habsburg or a Hohenzollern restoration and endorsed the veto on an Austrian *Anschluss* with Germany. At the same time, however, Beneš made it abundantly clear that Czechoslovakia would not support aggression; the treaty was to be entirely defensive, whatever the French might perhaps hope for. The year 1924 forced another slight change of policy. It was the beginning of the period in which Stresemann guided German foreign policy on a course of fulfilment coupled with revision, of acceptance of part of Versailles coupled with negotiation for the removal of the rest. The danger that Czechoslovakia might suddenly find itself in an area of revision caused Beneš to seek some more general support than that of France. He was very active in the negotiations that led to the Geneva Protocol, presented to the League in October 1924, which underwrote the peace settlement, in particular by making arbitration compulsory for all future international disputes. Unfortunately, because of the fall of the Labour government in Britain, the Protocol was never ratified; the Conservatives opposed the extension of Britain's role in the preservation of European peace and were in any case becoming increasingly disenchanted with Versailles. In this atmosphere, Stresemann's proposal in 1925 for a mutual guarantee of Germany's frontier in the west represented a most serious threat to Czechoslovakia in that it put in doubt Germany's eastern frontier. With some support from the Little Entente, with none from Austria, but much from Poland, Beneš tried first to head off what in October became the Locarno Treaty and then to lessen its damaging effect on Czechoslovakia. In its own interest France secured a promise of German entry into the League as a guarantee of good behaviour, and this was of advantage to the Czechoslovaks as well. However, in company with the Poles, with whom they had now signed a broad agreement, the Czechoslovaks won two important concessions of their own. They got an arbitration treaty with Germany, under which frontier disputes were to be settled by compulsory arbitration, and they negotiated a full-scale treaty of alliance with France. The die was cast. As from 1925 Czechoslovakia was firmly dependent upon France.

Under the terms of the treaty the two countries promised to lend each other immediate aid and assistance in the event of German aggression. From the Czechoslovak point of view this was basically satisfactory. It did not conflict with other Czechoslovak reciprocal commitments, either to the Little Entente or to the League; it reinforced and complemented them. It was a specific and firm guarantee from the most involved Western power against the major potential danger. Considered alongside the Franco-Polish alliance, it represented security. It became the lynch-pin in Beneš's policy for safeguarding Czechoslovakia, and in October 1925 it looked as if it would be sufficient. The tragedy was that it was necessary. Locarno was a step forward in Germany's acclimatisation to Versailles; but it was undoubtedly a step away from its acceptance of its frontier in the east, including that with Czechoslovakia. It was a piece of eastwards revisionism that the British government seemed practically to encourage. That Beneš was obliged to seek a French alliance as a means of security was evidence of real insecurity. To win it was a triumph; to have to do so was a sign of how frail Czechoslovakia's position still was. However, no one could then doubt the genuine value and trustworthiness of a French alliance. In the mid-twenties, Czechoslovakia could feel that it was coping successfully with a fluid situation.

Beneš also worked hard in this period to normalise Czechoslovakia's relations with Russia. In theory, this ought to have been easy. Two Slav peoples with a record of friendship and both shaking off the shackles of the past ought to have been able to come together in sympathy and co-operation. During the war, and even as late as Brest-Litovsk, their relations had been reasonably good. The accidental involvement of the Czechoslovak Legion in the Russian civil war, however, made friendly relations impossible. From the middle of 1918 until early in 1920 the Legion was strung out along the Trans-Siberian railway, in effect operating a private state within the Soviet Union. Some of its units did get involved on the side of the Whites, but for the most part it simply fended off the Red Army and waited for its transport. The delay was not really its fault. Without ships it could not go eastwards. The new Czechoslovak state had none; and nobody else would provide any. To have gone westwards would have been to get further involved. Admittedly, Beneš was not above employing the presence of the Legion in Siberia as a bargaining point during the peace conference. Admittedly, Kramář was anxious to see it fully committed to intervention on the side of the Whites and had powerful support for this, particularly among the French. Partly for this reason, however, Kramář had to resign in the middle of 1919. For his part, Beneš was determined to get the Legion home and resisted all the pressure exerted on him to involve it in the Polish-Russian war which started up in April of that year. In January 1920 the Legion surrendered Admiral Kolchak, the most successful White leader, and the following month began to sail home in Japanese ships. Until then all thought of normal relations with the Soviet Union was out of the question.

Even after that it was scarcely easy. The affair was one that took time to forget as the two governments contemplated normalisation. Ideological differences as well as civil war memories made it difficult for East and West to come to terms anywhere, and this was as true in the Czechoslovak case as in any other. Yet, once Britain broke the ice by concluding a trade agreement with Russia in March 1921, the way was open for others to follow. Even when Russia caused consternation by coming to separate terms with Germany at Rapallo in April 1922, the way was not barred. Indeed, from the Czechoslovak point of view it became all the more important to reach an accommodation. France might still be hostile to Russia, but Czechoslovakia was not a French satellite. Britain might be upset at the Russian action, but it was much more realistic in trying to appreciate the Russian point of view. Czechoslovakia could afford to offend French susceptibilities; it could also profit from following a British lead, particularly one that corresponded with its own inclination. More important, however, was the need not to let Germany use the Soviet Union as a tool to break the peace settlement and destroy Czechoslovakia. Accordingly, in June 1922, Czechoslovakia concluded an interim agreement, recognising the Soviet Union *de facto* and laying the foundation for the development of economic, cultural, and political relations. It was both halfway house towards the relationship Beneš wanted and a safeguard against Germany.

Beneš was quite clear that Czechoslovakia needed a wide range of guarantees for its continuing independence. By 1925 he was just as clear that the main one had to be France. From this point of view any agreement with the Soviet Union took second place. It was a matter of power, not a question of ideology. But Beneš still worked hard to get beyond the interim agreement. In 1924 both Britain and France granted the Soviet Union *de jure* recognition. Beneš tried to follow suit. Yet even after the conclusion of Locarno he failed. Given the danger which that treaty presented to the Soviet Union as well as to Czechoslovakia, he might have been expected to succeed. Failure did not lie on the Soviet side. The fact of the matter was that Beneš could not carry his own government with him. Czechoslovak foreign policy was getting to the stage where domestic politics had more and more impact on the shape it took. If the national question affected relations with Germany, the social question affected relations with Russia. In this as in so much else to do with Czechoslovak foreign policy the pattern set by 1925 was to persist down to 1938. Czechoslovakia was to approach Munich, its faith residing in France and its people divided over an incomplete agreement with the Soviet Union.

Czechoslovakia lived dangerously. Born of war and still young, it could expect little else. Nevertheless, in the period 1920-25 Beneš did everything possible to cocoon it so that it could build in peace on the domestic foundations laid in the years 1918-20. Indeed, until the Wall Street crash changed the entire international situation, Czechoslovakia enjoyed a remarkable term of peace in which to get on with its nation-building.

Economic Development and Social Improvement

By European standards, Czech and Slovak casualties in the First World War were not high. The number of people inhabiting the area of Czechoslovakia decreased a little both during and just after the war; it was 1924 before the 1914 figure was reached again. But the decline was due initially to a wartime drop in the rate of marriages and births, and subsequently to migration abroad from the

German' areas. Between 1920 and 1930 the population of Czechoslovakia grew by a million, from thirteen to fourteen. This absolute increase, however, concealed a slowing-up in the natural increase. In fact, the birth-rate was declining, even in Slovakia, and the rise in numbers resulted from other factors, including the return of some Germans and the disappearance of outlets for emigration. Czechoslovakia was undergoing the standard experience of an advanced west European country. This was true in other respects as well. The towns continued to prove attractive. In the decade 1920-30, in round numbers, Prague grew from 675,000 to 850,000, and Bratislava from 110,000 to 155,000. These increases of approximately 25 and 40 percent were high. They represented the standard west European rush to the bigger cities. But the rise in the percentage of the population as a whole in towns of more than 2,000 inhabitants was considerably lower, some 2.1 in the west and 2.2 in the east. The movement from the countryside was tailing off.

The growth in population was reasonable. Yet the slow-down in its rate was healthy: Czechoslovakia stood in need of capital more than of manpower. The continued drift to the towns was essential. But its slow-down also had a healthy aspect: as a result of land reform, agriculture was becoming more attractive. In fact, land reform proceeded in uncertain stages, and the acreage involved was not very spectacular. In the western half of the country less than a tenth of the arable land changed hands, and in the eastern half not quite a quarter. But by 1930 all the big landholdings had disappeared. Small holdings of up to 2 hectares had decreased in number by about 12 percent over ten years till they comprised 43 instead of 49 percent of the total. All other sizes of holdings up to the permitted maximum of 150-250 hectares had increased in number. There were, for example, about 37,000, or 17 percent more holdings of from 5 to 10 hectares in 1930 than there had been in 1921. All told, holdings of between 2 and 20 hectares comprised almost 53 percent of the total as against the previous 47 percent. It would be fair to say that by 1930 Czechoslovak landholdings were rather fewer in number, but slightly larger in size. This meant that there was not enough land for everyone who wanted to get it; about 30 percent of those claiming under the land reform acts had to be turned away empty-handed. But those who were lucky had a better deal and felt less inclined to migrate to the towns.

Some did very well indeed. The 4 percent of the total number of farms that owned more than 20 hectares could afford to hire labour and, in some instances, management. Farms of from 5 to 20 hectares could generally support an entire family and were undoubtedly the backbone of agriculture in the new state. Farms—if they could be called that—below 5 hectares were increasingly inadequate, and income had to be supplemented in some other way, by running a shop, working at a craft, or acting as hired labour. The real pinch was below the 2 hectare mark. At that level, matters were often made worse by the scattered nature of the holdings. Under the land reform acts consolidation was voluntary, and particularly in Slovakia most of the smallholdings remained scattered throughout the inter-war period. This was uneconomic and hurt the peasantry, but it was popular. The poorer peasants were simply opposed to any rationalisation that appeared to threaten their private property.

In the 1920s, no one did really badly. One of the things that helped was the co-operative movement. This was an indigenous Czech growth from the 1890s that now took root in Slovakia as well and was very active in providing loans for machinery, in bulk-purchasing fertilisers, in opening up new insurance schemes, and in making a beginning on grading and marketing. The secret lay in self-help for limited purposes not affecting ownership. Altogether, the number of co-operatives of various kinds grew by half in the period 1920-30. However, the usefulness of the co-operatives decreased as the size of the holdings diminished. The really poor peasants could profit little from them. Agriculture prospered nonetheless. There had been a big drop in output during the war because of a lack of labour and a shortsighted government policy. In four years the production of potatoes had gone down by a half, of grain by three-fifths, of beet by two-thirds, and of hops by as much as six-sevenths. In general, agricultural productivity had dropped to less than half its pre-war level. There was therefore a lot of leeway to be made up. For the first few years high prices provided the required incentive, as well as lining the pockets of the larger farmers and at least patching those of the smaller. A large-scale educational programme organised by the ministry of agriculture extended the tradition of sound Czech husbandry, in particular to Slovakia. Neither measure was sufficient, however, in face of the international economic situation. With recovery, the value of the Czechoslovak crown increased, and Czechoslovak farm products therefore became more expensive for foreign countries. Austria and Hungary were now numbered among the foreign buyers and Czechoslovak agriculture had to export or fall back again. As the war gradually receded, world food prices declined and a number of Czechoslovakia's neighbours resorted to dumping. Czechoslovakia was not self-sufficient in food; so the farmers' market was threatened at home as well as abroad. The challenge on both fronts was met partly by an improvement in productivity. In the period 1926-30 productivity rose to a level some 28 percent higher than in the pre-war period 1909-14. This was a considerable achievement and augured well for the future, not least since it included an 18 percent improvement in Slovakia. It also meant that even the small farmers could live above the margin, though, as always, the poorer peasants did rather less well, especially in Slovakia. The other measure used to meet the foreign challenge was not such a happy omen. In 1926 the first tariffs were imposed on imported foodstuffs, particularly cereals. For the next two years prices and products on the market both increased; farmers and agriculture both prospered. But counter-tariffs and falling prices lay a brief distance ahead.

At the end of the 1920s the balance-sheet in the countryside was pretty sound. With land reform, life was satisfying; with good prices, it was rewarding. Inevitably there were blemishes. Proportionally more land changed hands in Slovakia as a result of land reform than in the west. For the same reasons as in the west there was something of a rise in agricultural productivity. Unfortunately, it was less of a rise. Anything that was good in the Czech Lands was not quite so good in Slovakia; anything that was bad in the Czech Lands was much worse in Slovakia. The fact was that, whatever the overall statistics, and whatever the particular position in the west, there was still too high a proportion of the Slovak people living in the countryside. The actual figure was 74 percent, which compared poorly with 52 percent in the Czech Lands. True, many of those who remained on the land were happy to do so, much better-off than they could have imagined. Others simply had no alternative—no Budapest, no United States, and no Slovak boom-towns. Some went west, but there was a limit to the number of Czech boom-towns. There was even a reverse trend. Czech peasants migrated from Orava, ceded to Poland, to take up farming on formerly Magyar land in southern Slovakia. Inevitably also, some of the most fertile expropriated land in the south went to Magyar peasants. The laws of inheritance combined with the lack of alternative outlets to subdivide many of the tiniest holdings into even tinier ones, whose miserable owners were in effect landless peasants who lived at subsistence level off seasonal earnings. To be fair, there were also hard times in the west of the country. There were Czech peasants who envied the lands that were given to Germans, and who were even more annoyed at some of the huge forests left with their aristocratic owners contrary to the land reform laws. But Germans deserved lands, and some forests were better left with those who could continue to cultivate them. If Czech wheat, beet, and hops did well, so did Slovak maize, vines, and tobacco. Since Czech farmers exported more of their agricultural products, they suffered more from swings in prices. And there were certain improvements in the quality of countryside life that applied everywhere. Electricity and piped water were slower to spread in Slovakia than in the Czech Lands. But the 48-hour working week, averaged out over the year, applied to both areas, as did the new health, disability, and old-age insurance. Finally, one of the happiest features of the post-reform Czech Lands applied almost as much to Slovakia: the comparative absence of social division. There were better-off and worse-off, but there was no unbridgeable gulf between them. There were no excessively rich and no impossibly poor as in so many other parts of eastern Europe, or as in Czechoslovakia itself before independence. Instead, there was a social cohesion that made the country think as one, particularly in relation to the towns. This was one of the great achievements of the new Czechoslovak state.

Czechoslovak agriculture as a whole made an important contribution to exports, almost 20 percent of which in the mid-1920s comprised food and drink. Since it could not supply all the needs of the country, it also left a gap for imports, more than 20 percent of which comprised food and drink. For its own consumption it required fertilisers from abroad, but its companion, forestry, made at least a compensating contribution to exports through timber, wood-pulp, and paper. But the backbone of the Czechoslovak export trade was industry. In the mid-twenties, 60 percent of it was in manufactured goods. In fact, the disparity was increasing all the time; by 1929 food and drink accounted for 11 percent of exports compared with 71 percent for manufactured goods. Land reform was something new; agricultural wellbeing was important; but industrial prosperity was crucial.

Between 1920 and 1921 industrial production increased. So also did exports. This was the predictable result of growing stability at home and lagging recovery abroad. But there was a sharp reversal between 1921 and 1922 and a clinging depression in 1923. Over the two-year period output was down by about 25 percent and exports by more. This was partly the result of a deflation, designed to raise the value of the crown, which seriously reduced the level of demand both abroad and at home. It was also the outcome of the gradual satiation of the European market. The effects were widespread but were particularly serious in some of the basic industries such as iron and steel, glass and textiles. A number of quick-growing post-war enterprises simply disappeared. But the crisis also had its beneficial consequences. For one thing, it put paid to the policy of deflation which had made sense in the first year or two after the war but had been carried too far. In 1925 the crown was finally stabilised at its late-1922 level. This revived the home market and made export prices more attractive to foreign buyers. The crisis also awoke both industry and government to the rigorous demands of post-war competition. Czechoslovakia had become a manufacturing island; it no longer had a hinterland market to cushion it from competition. Industry realised the need for more mechanisation, particularly in coal-mining and engineering. It began to turn to oil and, above all, to electricity as sources of energy. It resorted to new materials such as synthetic dyes and artificial silk. It also started the serious process of rationalisation and consolidation. Throughout the 1920s small enterprises, comprising up to five employees, continued to dominate such sectors of light industry as foodstuffs and clothing. But in heavy industry, concentration increased. By the late twenties, metallurgical factories, employing over 2,500 workers each, accounted for 20 percent of heavy industry's work-force and 55 percent of its consumption of energy. Half a dozen companies almost dominated heavy industry, among them the Prague Iron Company and the Škoda works at Plzeň. Marketing organisations got under way, and much more research was directed towards consumer needs and the possibility of establishing new industries. Five banks, in addition to the vast Živnostenská, played a leading role in encouraging and financing all these changes, and from 1926 onwards government taxation policy greatly facilitated industrial investment. Apart from a slight setback in 1926, production increased steadily between 1924 and 1929, until in the latter year it stood at over 40 percent above the pre-war level. It was a healthy record.

So was the record of exports, which rose in much the same way. In this field, however, the Czechoslovaks had much less control. They profited from the shut-down of the Ruhr, but suffered from the inflation of the mark. In the later 1920s they were helped by the loan-based prosperity of their east European neighbours, but they began feeling the pinch of German competition and British retaliation. In 1929 their exports fell slightly, though they still maintained a trade surplus. In general they were anxious to avoid foreign debt and, since independence, they had kept loans to a minimum. Subsequently this was to have some advantages, but they could have accelerated their modernisation with rather more help from abroad. As it was, Škoda linked itself with the French Schneider-Creusot company; British capital supported Czechoslovak banking; and the first Czechoslovak state loan in 1922 was issued both in London and in New York. The total service on foreign debts amounted to no more than 5 percent of the annual value of exports, which was considerably less than in the case of any other east European country. The Czechoslovak economy was geared to maintaining independence.

A severe test lay ahead with the onset of the world slump. But in the twenties, difficulties had already emerged. Slovakia presented a peculiar problem. By and large, the trade cycle affected it in the same way as the Czech Lands; but since the industrial base was smaller, the depression was more obvious and the subsequent boom less significant. The depression of 1923 eliminated at least two of the dominant pre-war factories, the ironworks at Krompachy and the sheet-metal works at Zvolen. The boom of 1924-29 produced an electrical machine and cable industry and not very much else. Nevertheless, there were encouraging signs. There was a sizeable increase in Danube traffic. A river fleet was built up, based in Bratislava, and the volume of goods handled there and in Komárno grew tenfold in the period 1921-30. In the mid-twenties, rationalisation and consolidation spread eastwards. Competitiveness was increased in the working of minerals and in the provisions industry. But what was more obvious to Slovaks was the disappearance of over 200 factories that had previously employed a quarter of the work-force, and the gradual movement of industry westwards. Two important railway links were constructed between the Czech Lands and Slovakia, the Horní Lideč-Púchov and the Veselí-Nové Mesto lines; and although less than a hundred miles of new track were laid in the Czech Lands, other tough new lines were constructed in the centre and east of Slovakia. But the west-east links appeared too late to make the Krompachy and Zvolen works competitive; freight costs via Bohumín or on private lines were something the Czech metal industry did not have to meet before sending its products abroad. And the new internal Slovak lines were partly strategic, and still just a drop in the bucket. In defence of the Czechs it must be pointed out that rationalisation and consolidation affected them similarly; that competition was bound to eliminate first the most out-of-date and the least economical, which meant mainly Slovak plants; and that the capital available for investment, in railway-building for instance, was rather limited and had to be spread over many projects. It could be argued that an attempt should have been made to put additional effort into Slovakia as the most deserving area. However, it made more economic sense in the first years of independence to build on existing strength and so to maximise the benefit for everyone. Yet it was unfortunate that this obviously coincided with Czech self-interest. Whatever the rights and wrongs of the situation, the proportion of the Slovak population working in industry of all sorts in 1930 was 18 percent, whereas the Czech proportion was 40 percent. Oddly enough, the increase over the decade in each case was only one percent.

To distinguish between the Czech and Slovak experiences with industry during the 1920s is somewhat artificial. Conditions within the Czech Lands were not uniformly better than within Slovakia, and vice versa. Differences were in fact exaggerated by separatist politicians. The same was true of the German experience of life within Czechoslovakia. One example was land reform. Most of the expropriated estates belonged to Austro-German aristocrats. Compensation was calculated at a diminishing rate on pre-war values expressed in new Czechoslovak crowns. There is no doubt that the deprived landowners suffered both by expropriation and by compensation. 1918, after all, was a social revolution, and the same thing would have happened to the landowners even if they had all been Czechs, as some of the lesser ones who suffered were. But the expropriated greatly overstated their case, submitting a memorandum to the League of Nations in September 1922. In the event, the whole land reform was not carried through: ownership of many of their breweries, for instance, was never transferred. Nevertheless, the complaints continued and spread downwards to their former employees and to German peasants in general. The entire land reform, it was claimed, was anti-German. In a sense this was true. That was why it went further than elsewhere in eastern Europe. On the other hand, if there was to be reform, it was bound to hit the German landowners; and on balance it treated the remaining Germans in the same way as the Czechs. There were certainly land office staff who misapplied the reforms to the disadvantage of German claimants; but actually, since they were political appointees, they sometimes did the same to fellow Czechs. Corruption apart, there was inevitably a lot of anti-German feeling; yet there were many Czechs who left the land office aggrieved, and there was at least one German group, the foresters, who suddenly found themselves really free men at last. Some German complaints about land reform were genuine, others were invented. Probably they were all to be expected. There was a long tradition of struggling over land; recently it had been much intensified. In a society only partly industrialised, land was a fundamental issue.

German industry in the 1920s was a similar issue. In one sense, it was indistinguishable from either Czech or Slovak. They were all part of the one internationally exposed economy, and they all went through the same booms and slumps. However, German industry was different in that a large part of it was particularly linked with foreign markets. This accentuated both the booms and the slumps, but it was the slumps that were remembered. In the immediate post-war period, lignite, textiles, porcelain, and glass from the German areas sold better than most goods from elsewhere in Czechoslovakia. On the other hand, during the 1923 depression they fared worse, and business losses and unemployment were proportionately higher. This was not the consequence of discrimination. But the Germans, and particularly the businessmen, thought otherwise. In the first place, it was discrimination that they were in Czechoslovakia at all. In this they had an arguable point, though at that stage they would have been no more protected or prosperous in Austria or Germany. In the second place, they blamed Rašín for all their problems. Certainly as minister of finance until his assassination in January 1923, he was the main architect of the deflation policy that was partly responsible for the depression. Certainly as one who had been imprisoned by the Austrians in 1893 and sentenced to death by them in 1916, he never claimed to be pro-German. Yet his deflation policy had certain advantages, and it affected everyone, Czechs and Slovaks included. Rašín was also responsible for a capital levy, which affected mainly rich Germans, and for the partial repudiation of war-loans, which affected many more. Yet in both cases Czechs too were involved. The capital levy was part of the social revolution and, since there were more rich Germans, they were bound to be harder hit. The partial repudiation of war-loan had its economic aspect, but was rather more an anti-German measure, regrettable no doubt, though understandable in the mood of victory. Yet the Czechoslovak government inherited 42 percent of the Austrian state debt (and 16 percent of the Hungarian) and had to pay the Allies a liberation debt, but still did not repudiate the war-loan in its entirety. In any case, by the mid and later 1920s, Rašín was dead and exports were fast picking up. German industry participated fully in the boom—and a very successful tourist industry also sprang up. Ironically, the main difficulties that were encountered in this period were the result of the Germans' own folly. They largely refused to become involved with Czech banks and made serious losses in the Weimar Republic. The German areas were an economic problem, but it was not the result of Czech discrimination and it was not made more soluble by the behaviour of the Germans themselves.

All Czechoslovakia's problems were capable of solution, given time. The general rate of economic growth was possibly too weak. If the movement to the towns was slowing down, it was not just the attractiveness of agriculture; but rather the insufficiency of industry. At the same time, the national economy was able to provide for a basic labour force that increased from 5 to 6½ million and to reduce the secondary labour force from 1½ million to a million, a considerable triumph. There were also pleasing signs of diversification in the occupations of the population. There might be only a one percent increase in the proportion employed in industry throughout the country in the decade 1921-30. But in the west the proportion employed in transport and allied occupations went up from over 5 to over 7 percent, and in the east from almost 4 to almost 6 percent. The corresponding figures for banking, insurance, and trade were from almost 6 to almost 8 percent, and from almost 4 to almost 5 percent. In the east there was also an interesting one percent increase in the public services and a corresponding decrease in personal services. In addition, there were definite signs of a reduction in the social differentiation of the population in the cities and towns as well as in the country. Communist statistics note the growth of the working class in the Czech Lands as from more than 54 to more than 60 percent of the total, with a minimal growth in the capitalist class from under 5 to under 6 percent. For Slovakia the statistics read from almost 43 to almost 48 percent, and from 4 percent to a mere fraction above it. Czechoslovak society was modernising at a reasonable pace.

No modern society has been without unemployment, and Czechoslovakia in the 1920s was no exception. At the peak of the depression in January 1923 the unemployment figure stood at 400,000; but the annual return was 200,000 and continued to drop (with the slight exception of 1926) down to 1928-29 when it hovered around the 40,000 mark. By contemporary standards this was rather impressive. So was the index of real wages, which fell a little in the mid-twenties and then proceeded to climb back. The out-of-work were not forgotten. The 1918 scheme of unemployment assistance was augmented in 1925 when the trade unions were brought in to help administer and provide extra funds. The system of employment agencies was improved. Finance was made available to help builders hire the unemployed. This was done through the ministry of social welfare, which also provided funds for road-making and other forms of relief work. The general level of social concern was high. By 1929 all the regular labour force was covered by various forms of insurance, dealing with sickness, injury, disability, and old age. Behind this lay a complex of modern hospitals, sanatoria, and rest homes. There were flaws, some bureaucratic, most financial. Levels of payment were not really high enough. Czechoslovakia lacked the money, but its performance was at least the equal of any in Europe.

Political Stabilisation

The economic and social development of Czechoslovakia in the 1920s was determined by a wide variety of factors—the legacy of the past, the hopes raised by independence, the pressure of circumstances, domestic and foreign. The evolution of the political parties was also crucial for this as for every aspect of the nation's policy. In the early days, for instance, there was unanimity on the overriding need for a crash housing programme, but as time went on, there was division on the priorities to be accorded to industry and to agriculture. However, despite stresses and strains, the political system survived. One reason was that the new state emerged from the years 1918-20 less socially disparate than Austria-Hungary and more socially cohesive than its immediate neighbours. The high degree of political awareness helped, although the Slovaks were less experienced. A further factor was the high literacy rate: in the 1921 census only 3 percent of Czechs proved illiterate and only 14 percent of Slovaks; by 1930 the figures had fallen to one and 6. The age structure of the population provided both balance and enthusiasm; two-thirds were between fifteen and sixty, one-third between twenty and forty. There was also the widespread and deep sense of achievement in winning independence as well as the chastening awareness of the continuing threat to it. And finally, there was the leadership of a small group of men, of whom Masaryk had most prestige and was the most important. Yet the political fabric had to withstand some early shocks.

The first major political crisis had come and gone in 1919 over land reform. Another arose almost immediately with a challenge from the left. The socialist movement throughout Europe was in turmoil. The success of the Bolshevik Revolution in 1917 and the founding of the Communist International in 1919 had split it ideologically and by 1920 it was falling apart. The struggle was reflected within a number of local movements. Most Czechoslovak Social Democrats were sympathetic to the Russians, and much of what the Communists were now doing seemed to be in the interest of the Russian people. On the other hand, much of what Lenin preached was alien to the Marxist tradition in which they had been reared and unsuited to an advanced society like their own. Their reformist attitude was adequately represented by their leader, Tusar. However, a few of those who had been in Russia as prisoners or Legionaries came back converted to communism. As early as May 1918, Alois Muna, a Social Democrat, founded a Czechoslovak Communist Party in Moscow. Returning home in November 1918, more than a year ahead of most of his fellows, he tried to swing the Social Democratic Party to the left. He was unsuccessful; but because of the base he established in Kladno, long a radical industrial area, he could not be expelled from the party. The left-wing case was also taken up by Šmeral, who had been ousted in the later part of the war and was now glad to find a respectable anti-nationalist cause, and by others who were later to earn fame, such as the Kladno stonemason Antonín Zápotocký. Throughout 1919 they refrained from challenging the right-wing leadership, sensing the majority mood and anxious not to create a mere splinter group. But the following year was different.

A left-wing programme appeared in January 1920. Unity was preserved for the elections in April in which the Czechoslovak and German Social Democrats between them accounted for not far short of 40 percent of the votes. But victory increased left-wing restiveness. It was worth challenging the leadership; and with Tusar premier of a coalition government there was a necessary challenge to make. Šmeral, however, was anxious to avoid dividing the party. He preferred to continue working for a majority grip on it. He was willing to accept the Comintern's demand that all national sections should oppose reformism. He was an internationalist, but not a bolshevik; he believed in proletarian unity, but also in parliamentary democracy; he was still in the longstanding Czechoslovak tradition. Despite a trip to Moscow and talks with Lenin, he did not change his view. Zápotocký and others felt differently. Ideologically they supported the Comintern; they also felt that the moment was ripe when the Red Army had just fought its way to the gates of Warsaw. Lenin and the Comintern also thought their opportunity had come; and when the Red Army was beaten back into the Ukraine in late August, they pressed all the harder for an immediate takeover of the Social Democratic Party in a strategically placed Czechoslovakia. This was the challenge from the left.

Tusar and his colleagues sensed it coming. Like Šmeral, they were reformist parliamentarians, but in contrast to him they were strongly nationalist and anti-Comintern. They were not anti-Soviet—simply opposed to bolshevism in Czechoslovakia for the advantage of Russia. As 1920 slipped by, and particularly as the Social Democratic Party congress approached in September, they saw support for the left growing, and they also saw that it was not Šmeral who would make use of it, but Zápotocký and the Comintern. They resolved to meet the challenge. Realising that the majority of the delegates to the congress were Comintern supporters, they postponed it; with a majority on the executive they could legally do so. They agreed to make loyalty to the Comintern incompatible with membership of the party; as the executive, they had the right to interpret the rules. In other words, they delayed the congress to purge the party. It was an extreme action to take. They might have been wiser to campaign at grass roots, or wiser still to have taken up the challenge a long time before. But Tusar had been preoccupied as premier and was no more anxious than Šmeral to split the party. When the challenge came, however, he was in no doubt about what it meant. In Russia the bolsheviks had destroyed the mensheviks and established a dictatorship, ostensibly in the interest of the proletariat, manifestly to the advantage of none but a few. Tusar and his colleagues had no wish to meet the fate of the mensheviks themselves, or to see Czechoslovakia suffer from a narrowly sectional dictatorship. It was too happy and democratic a country for that. So they took the risk of dividing the Socialists.

The left wing went ahead with their congress and elected their own executive, so that there were now in effect two parties. Tusar felt constrained to resign as premier in mid-September. He could not possibly continue to run a coalition government when his own minority party was divided and one section was dedicated to the overthrow of the parliamentary system. He also had to be free to fight the party battle. The left wing organised an action committee of workers in Prague to seize the party headquarters in *Lidový dům* (The People's House) and to turn the party newspaper, *Právo lidu* (The People's Right), into their own organ, *Rudé právo* (Red Right). They retained the party name since under Šmeral's guidance they were still anxious to take over the entire legacy of Social Democracy. They rejected collaboration with the bourgeoisie in a parliamentary government, but they deferred a decision on joining the Comintern. It was a clever, sustained challenge to the old leadership and to the Czechoslovak state.

Tusar and his colleagues retaliated in November by summoning a party conference of their own and by resorting to legal action to recover the party's property. It was an interesting confrontation: force on the left, law on the right; Šmeral, the attorney, on the left, Tusar, the trade unionist, on the right. The courts decided in favour of the official leadership, which immediately sought police help to recover its property. On 10 December the left wing called a general strike and produced a whole series of demands, including one for the government's resignation. In Kladno, Zápotocký established a Central Revolutionary Committee and, with Šmeral swept aside, the scene was set for an attempt at a bolshevik-style *coup d'état*. There were ugly scenes in a number of industrial centres throughout the country, and several people were killed. But within five days the strike had collapsed. It never became truly widespread even in the towns, and it left the countryside virtually unaffected. It acquired a measure of rank-and-file Social Democratic support; but the left found nothing like the backing for violent action that they had had for sentimental propaganda. From other parties they encountered straightforward hostility. Outside they heard only the sympathetic cries of the Comintern. They vastly overreached themselves. And Czechoslovakia's political structure, momentarily threatened, emerged much stronger than before.

It was a little while before the left officially constituted themselves a separate Communist Party. Zápotocký and Muna were among those imprisoned; and Šmeral was still unwilling to make the final break. He was under pressure from left-wing Slovaks and Germans who rapidly established their own parties and was severely criticised by Moscow. In May 1921 he finally agreed to the establishment of a Communist Party, but only on the basis of mass membership (he claimed 300,000 supporters), a reformist approach, and a federal structure. In fact, it took five months of bitter criticism from the Comintern, of intense pressure from Hungarian and German Communists, and of skilful talking from Lenin before the deed was done. In October, the Czechoslovak Communist Party was established in Prague and admitted to the Comintern on essentially bolshevik principles. It was revolutionary, not reformist; it was unitary, not federalist; Czechs, Slovaks, Germans, Magyars, and Poles were all to be members of a single party and world movement whose aim was the overthrow of the bourgeoisie. There was to be no particularly Czechoslovak road to the proletarian paradise. All that Šmeral could salvage was his mass membership and his personal preference for tolerance.

Strangely enough, these two idiosyncracies were to make the Czechoslovak Communist Party significantly different from most and to perpetuate its moderate popularity for some years to come. It won 41 seats in the 1925 election and managed to hold on to thirty in 1929. But international socialism was irrevocably split, and the Soviet Union was preoccupied with its own economic transformation. Conditions had not been ripe for revolution in 1920, and by and large life improved as the twenties wore on. There was no likelihood of a Communist *coup*. The position of socialism in general was much weaker after 1920. Tusar abandoned politics and became Czechoslovak minister in Berlin, where he died in 1924. In the inter-war period no Social Democrat was ever again prime minister. Rudolf Bechyně was an influential member of the *Pětka*, the five leaders of the coalition parties active behind-the-scenes in smoothing the working of government from 1920 down to 1926; a minister of education from 1922 to 1924; and from 1925 to 1926 both minister of railways and deputy prime minister. But the party could not regain its strength. From 74 seats in 1920 it dropped to twenty-nine in 1925; and in 1929 its recovery was by a mere 10 seats. It could therefore not exert the influence it had in the formative years 1919-20, and in the period 1926-29 it had no place in government at all. There was no retreat from the path of social betterment; but there was no great advance. The socialisation of industry on which the party had set its sights could not be achieved. The state extended its ownership to such public services as telephones, railways, and even the airline, and encouraged municipal enterprises; but it stopped short at that. Perhaps it was for the best; socialisation was untried, and not at all to the majority's taste. But it is a haunting thought what might have happened if external pressures had not forced the Social Democratic split.

When Tusar resigned in 1920, Masaryk exercised his prerogative by appointing a cabinet of bureaucrats, with a senior official, Jan Černý, as prime minister. This was designed to hold the ring while Tusar settled his party problems. It was an effective stratagem, even if one disliked by the left-wing Social Democrats whose revolution was thwarted by Černý's firm action. When the crisis was past and the disposition of the parties was clear, a new government was formed on a proper coalition basis. The Social Democrats could not lead it but were reasonably represented in it. But for Masaryk's stratagem, they might have been totally excluded from a coalition formed in their time of disarray. However, the predominant influence in government now moved steadily to the Agrarians.

After the Social Democratic débâcle they were in fact the best-placed party. In 1920 they won 40 seats, which made them the second largest; in 1925 they raised their number to forty-six, which made them the largest, and they retained their place in 1929. In a sense they represented the other half of the community, the farmers; and although they suffered from splits between Czech and Slovak members and between rich and poor, they drew great strength from their widespread rural support. They also had able leaders and a strong financial base in the Živnostenská Bank. They did not immediately take over from Černý; but from October 1922 to September 1938 every prime minister, with one brief exception, was an Agrarian. They were in an enormously influential position. On the other hand, they were neither able nor did they try to have things all their own way. Their parliamentary numbers were too small to form a government themselves, and their leader in the 1920s was essentially a man of moderation.

In the period 1922-25 Švehla presided over a government that included Social Democrats and that, with the aid of the *Pětka*, guided the country away from the depression of 1923 and negotiated the comprehensive social insurance law of 1924. But before the election of 1925 he broke with the Socialists on tariffs. Imposed on agricultural imports, these were meant to benefit the farming interest. The Agrarian argument was quite plausibly that it would not help industry to destroy farming, and that the two interests had much in common. Cheap sugar from Cuba and Java, for example, hurt beet-processers as much as beet-growers. But the Socialist concern was almost entirely with cheap food and industrial competitiveness. So Švehla found his courage and stood by Agrarian policy. The election was a little indecisive. The Socialists lost seats, the Agrarians gained. It was not at once obvious whom Švehla could pull into a coalition. Černý was again put in charge of a caretaker government while Švehla went abroad for a short rest and Hodža organised a fresh party alignment. The government which emerged was divisive in the sense that it left out the Social Democrats and ended the 'red-green' (or really the 'green-red') coalition. It was an Agrarian dominated government. On the other hand, it promoted the growing prosperity of the period 1926-29 which benefited everyone. And it was cohesive in that it aligned other groups with the existence and policies of the Czechoslovak state.

For one thing it settled the troubled religious issue. Before 1918 the Catholic hierarchy had too often been associated with Habsburg policy and Austro-German and Magyar nationals. Despite personnel changes in 1918 some anti-establishment feeling was inevitable even among the many devout Catholics. For historical reasons there was a strongly independent streak in Czech Catholicism in particular, and some Catholics established an independent Czechoslovak Church. It was therefore not easy for the Catholic Church and the Vatican to accept the new order. The Protestant Churches were well represented among both Czech and Slovak leaders. The influence of Marxism and atheism was considerable. And immediately after the war there were iconoclastic outbursts which were unnecessarily offensive to quite moderate Catholics. So it was sometimes rather hard for rank-and-file Catholics, too, to accept the new order. Matters came to a head in July 1925 when the papal nuncio left Prague in a huff and the Czechoslovak government broke off diplomatic relations with the Vatican—an altogether unhappy situation. Šrámek, leader of the Czechoslovak Populists who represented the Catholic interest, was a member of Švehla's 1922-25 government, but was unable to achieve any amelioration. In 1925, however, things did change dramatically. The election raised the number of Czechoslovak Populists in the chamber from 21 to 31 and made them the second biggest party in Švehla's 1926-29 government. With the Social Democrats out of the way it was possible for Švehla to negotiate a settlement with the Catholic Church. A law of June 1926 authorised the payment of state salaries to the clergy (a privilege later extended in a modified form to the Protestant Churches); and a *modus vivendi* worked out with the Vatican in January 1928 recognised both the special position of the Catholic Church in Czechoslovakia and the limitations upon outside interference.

Švehla also managed to bring Hlinka's Slovak Populist Party into his government and to achieve a marked improvement in Czech-Slovak relations. Between 1920 and 1925 the Slovak case was argued within the government by Slovak members of nationwide parties, such as Dérer of the Social Democrats. Hlinka remained out on a limb and even quarrelled with Šrámek. In January 1922 he introduced his first bill proposing Slovak autonomy; yet two months later he appointed to the editorship of *Slovak* a certain Béla Tuka, a forty-two-year-old ex-professor born in Slovakia but of Magyar parentage and outlook, who lost him friends even among his own party faithful. However, in the 1925 election the Slovak like the Czechoslovak Populists scored a success and increased their membership of the chamber to twenty-three to become, though with just a third of the votes, the largest Slovak group. Obviously the other parties had not achieved enough for Slovakia. But the religious question had an additional importance since the Slovak bishops were still regarded by the Vatican as being subject to the archbishop of Esztergom in Hungary. For whatever reason they triumphed, the Slovak Populists could not be ignored. They could also be at least partly appeased by the settlement of the religious question; the *modus vivendi* freed the Slovak bishops from Hungarian authority. But Švehla's main achievement was to abolish the *Župy*, to make Slovakia one of the four provinces, and at that small price to get two of Hlinka's lieutenants, one of them Father Jozef Tiso, to take up government office.

Švehla's final and perhaps most important cohesive achievement was to smooth the entry of the first Germans to the Czechoslovak government. Adjusting to the existence of Czechoslovakia had been difficult for both sides, but clearly more so for the Germans. From early on there were some prepared to try, notably the German Social Democrats. However, it was the progressive normalisation of Austria's and Germany's relations with their former enemies that gradually tilted the balance, along with the steady improvement in life within Czechoslovakia. The election that took place in the year of Locarno and of the German-Czechoslovak Arbitration Treaty gave two of the German parties most interested in activism, as it was called, substantial gains in their representation. The Agrarians won 24 as against 13 seats, and the Christian Socialist Party thirteen as against nine; and between them they held just over half the total of German seats. From the Czechoslovak point of view there were obvious party advantages to be gained from the admission of 'Agrarians' and 'Populists' to the government. But the prospects both for internal harmony and for standing in the world were the real attractions. To pass an improved language law of advantage to the Germans was not to grant a concession but to prepare a better future for all the citizens of Czechoslovakia.

There were blemishes and worrying signs in these years. In helping to construct the new coalition, Hodža showed considerable talent. But he also revealed an excessive personal ambition that apparently involved him in negotiations with the German minister in Prague and that caused him to scheme to have Švehla oust Masaryk as President in order to have himself succeed Švehla as premier. Halfway through the term of the new government, Tuka initiated a campaign to take Slovakia out of the republic; in so doing, he enlisted Hungarian and other foreign help; and he swept the faithful Hlinka with him. Nevertheless, Švehla's achievement was considerable in strengthening Czechoslovakia's political stability and unity. The future was full of promise. Unfortunately, tragedy lay ahead in crises for which Czechoslovakia was not responsible.

CHAPTER 10

From the Wall Street Crash to Munich and Prague

The Internal Repercussions of the Crash

PARLIAMENTARY ELECTIONS WERE HELD in Czechoslovakia on Sunday, 27 October 1929. They produced a slight swing from centre-right to centre-left and changed the nature of the government back to 'green-red'. They therefore left the political situation only marginally different. But they occurred in the middle of the Wall Street Crash which began on the Thursday and reached a new low on the Tuesday. So the economic situation the new government had to face was different to the point of being almost catastrophic. The international repercussions of the Crash were even more disturbing and ultimately proved destructive of Czechoslovak independence. 1929 was an unhappy turning-point.

In part, the crisis in Czechoslovak agriculture predated 1929. World prices for farm products had been falling for some time and had taken a serious dip over the winter of 1928-29. But the Wall Street Crash pushed them down very much faster. Between 1928 and 1934 the prices received by Czechoslovak farmers fell all told by over 40 percent. The volume of produce going on to the market actually increased, but the total return to the farmers decreased year by year. Consequently, personal consumption dropped by about a third; indebtedness almost doubled. Bankruptcies, public auctions, and mortgages became increasingly common. The smallholders, who formed the majority of the farmers, were particularly hard-hit.

Industry was in a more prosperous state than agriculture in 1929; so it was less quickly affected by the spreading depression. But eventually it suffered more than the industry of any other country. Industrial production in western Europe as a whole declined by somewhat less than 30 percent in the years down to 1932. In Czechoslovakia the decline continued into 1933 and went beyond the 40 percent mark. Indeed, in some sectors it was nearer 60 percent. Prices, however, did not fall as far as in agriculture, going down by less than 30 percent. Despite this, suffering was widespread in the period 1929-34. Income from capital went down by a third. Wages fell by almost a fifth. At the peak of the crisis in 1933 unemployment topped the million mark, so that a quarter of the families in the country had no breadwinners. Many other workers were on part-time. Thousands of small businesses went into liquidation. Many officials, clerks, and teachers were pensioned off or paid off.

Falling prices for their products reduced the farmers' demands on industry. Falling incomes reduced the urban dwellers' demands on agriculture. The link between the two depressions was often more direct: hop-growers and brewers suffered together. It was difficult to foresee an end to the downward spiral. Imports decreased, from almost 20,000 million crowns in 1929 to just over 6,000 million in 1933. This might not have been so bad if exports had not decreased as well, from between 20,000 and 21,000 million crowns in 1929 to under 6,000 million in 1933. Czechoslovakia's economy was dependent on foreign trade, and its prosperity was contingent upon a favourable balance. In fact, a favourable balance of 500 million crowns in 1929 was converted into an adverse one of 200 million in 1933.

Nothing Czechoslovakia might have done before or immediately after 1929 could have saved it from the effects of the Crash. No industrialised or trading country escaped; and Czechoslovakia was both. The collapse of the *Kreditanstalt* in Vienna in May 1931 deepened the crisis by destroying the last vestiges of European financial confidence. There was nothing Czechoslovakia could do to prevent Britain from devaluing sterling in September 1931 or introducing imperial preference in 1932. But it had to suffer the consequences; in 1932 Czechoslovak exports to Britain declined by 70 percent. The economic autarky that swept central Europe and further cut Czechoslovakia's exports was something quite outside its control. Perhaps Czechoslovakia was too quick, in 1930, in raising its own tariffs on agricultural imports and too late, in 1934, in devaluing its currency. But by and large Czechoslovakia was simply acting as blindly and ineffectively as every other country.

Nevertheless, a combination of government policies and private initiatives gradually produced economic recovery. It was inevitable that a government led by Agrarians should think first of the agricultural interest. One Agrarian prime minister succeeded another after 1929; František Udržal to 1932, Jan Malypetr to 1935, and Hodža to the eve of Munich in 1938. The raising of tariffs in 1930 led naturally to the grain monopoly instituted in 1934. The government raised the price of imported grain; it then bought up the entire domestic surplus at a guaranteed price. Initially the scheme went astray, for it encouraged farmers to overproduce; but a poor harvest in 1936 and stricter controls thereafter made it work reasonably satisfactorily. The import bill was reduced from almost 2,000 million crowns in 1928 to less than 200 million in 1936, and much of the grain surplus was sold abroad. In 1934 home prices began rising, and this, coupled with the guaranteed sale, gave grain-producers their first taste of returning prosperity; so much so, in fact, that other, mostly smaller, farmers started campaigning for a monopoly in cattle and poultry. By 1938 this was on the way, and the agricultural interest could claim to be doing fairly well.

Successive governments also encouraged the diversification of crops. International competition prevented hops and beet from regaining their pre-1929 ascendancy, so some emphasis was shifted to fodder-producing and food-processing crops. The output of mangels was almost doubled in the last five years before Munich, and the output of coleseed for cattlefeed and margarine was increased a dozen times over. From a self-sufficiency point of view, Czechoslovakia remained dangerously dependent on the import of fertilisers, but in terms of its agricultural output it was within about 10 percent of being self-supporting. What the government could not do on its own, it did in collaboration with the co-operative movement. The number of co-operatives of different kinds grew by a fifth during the 1930s, their capital increased, and the links between their central organisations and the Agrarian Party gradually tightened. In 1938 many of the problems of 1918 remained to be solved. The large farmers fared better than the small, the Czech better than the Slovak. The pauperisation of the small peasants in Slovakia was a matter of particular criticism. Crop yields exceeded those in France but lagged behind those in Germany. Czechoslovak agriculture, however, was both relatively prosperous and progressing satisfactorily, and it had substantially recovered from the effects of the Crash.

Agricultural autarky made industrial recovery difficult. It became harder to sell manufactured goods to countries that had traditionally sent Czechoslovakia their own farming products. Sales to the Danubian countries were particularly sluggish. For political as well as economic reasons the government was anxious to reinvigorate trade with the other two powers of the Little Entente, but despite goodwill purchases of Yugoslav wheat and the fortuitous need to buy Rumanian oil, Czechoslovak exports to Yugoslavia and Rumania in 1938 were only two-fifths in money terms of what they had been before the depression. Not all the responsibility lay on one side; Yugoslavia, Rumania, and many other countries also practised an exchange control designed to protect and restore their economies in the wake of the depression. For this among other reasons Czechoslovakia's trade with Germany made no better a recovery and its industry could export no more than two-fifths in money terms of what it had formerly managed. On the other hand, immense and largely successful efforts were made to increase Czechoslovakia's industrial exports to non-exchange control areas, particularly to Britain and the United States. The government twice devalued the currency, in 1934 and 1936, to make manufactures more competitive, and private industrial concerns sent out enthusiastic selling-teams. By 1938 exports to these areas were back to over four-fifths in money terms of their pre-1929 level.

This was a considerable achievement, particularly in absolute terms. By the time of Munich, Czechoslovakia was exporting a greater volume of manufactures to the non-exchange control areas than before the Wall Street Crash. The whole industrial recovery was remarkable. Taking 1929 as the base year, the index of industrial production fell from 100 to as low as 60 in 1933, but by the end of 1937 it was up again to 96. Both these achievements owed much to the diversification of industry. Despite the steady introduction of new enterprises over the years the Czechoslovak economy was still dominated before the depression by a small group of basic industries of the old type. It was the need to escape the disastrous consequences of this over-concentration, to create new jobs and find new markets, that drove the government to encourage and business to capitalise a sizeable expansion in the electrical equipment and precision instrument industries and a mushroom growth both in the production of motor-cars and in the output of rubber and leather goods. Škoda, Praga, and Tatra cars were to be found all over Europe in the late 1930s and as far away as Canada and India. The Bat'a shoe combine, which had surrounded itself with a major town at Zlín in Moravia and a minor one at Poprad in Slovakia, exported factories and shops as well as footwear. The share of the non-European world in Czechoslovak trade almost doubled from about 15 percent in 1929 to not far short of 30 percent in 1937. Before it was broken at Munich, Czechoslovakia had begun a promising new stage in its industrial revolution.

The revolution was not to get very far, but it made its mark on Czechoslovakia's economic recovery. By the end of 1937 the country had a favourable overall balance of trade of 1,000 million crowns, which was an improvement on the 500 million of 1929 even allowing for the 30 percent devaluation of the currency. However, in money terms, the total turnover in foreign trade was only about 23,000 million crowns as against somewhat over 40,000 million in 1929. Czechoslovakia had a better balance, but on a smaller turnover. The accounts looked healthy, but the economy still had its ailments. The recovery in industrial production lagged several points behind the average for most other advanced countries. National income was rising steadily, but was barely three-quarters of what it had been immediately before the Crash. The population had grown more than half a million since 1929 and opportunities for emigration had disappeared; cost-awareness and new machinery had reduced the proportion of labour going into many products. It had therefore proved difficult to reduce, let alone eliminate, unemployment, and in 1937 there were at least 400,000 unemployed, including professional people and skilled workers. The real value of wages had begun to rise again, but they were not yet back at their pre-devaluation, never mind their pre-depression, level. The number of cartels and syndicates had increased since an act of 1933 recognised their right to regulate production, marketing, and prices. By the year of Munich, however, many of them were said to operate more in favour of their shareholders than in the interest of expanding the economy. It was also ominous that some of the recovery in industrial production and in exports was the consequence of rearmament; four times as many arms were exported in 1937 as in 1929. Yet even this boost was not enough to stave off a recession over the winter of 1937-38.

Perhaps the most unfortunate aspect of the depression and its aftermath was that industry in the predominantly German regions was especially hard-hit and particularly slow to recover. It was frequently alleged that this was entirely the consequence of deliberately discriminative Czechoslovak policies. In fact, the decline in textile and glass exports began before 1929, largely because of Japanese competition. The collapse of scores of German enterprises after 1929 was the inevitable result of their preferred dependence on capital from Weimar Germany. Some of the workers who lost their jobs, particularly away from the frontier areas, were not Germans, but Czechs. The continuing shortfall in textile and glass exports in the late 1930s almost exactly mirrored the situation in other industrialised countries, including Britain, France, and the United States. The Czechoslovak government made particular efforts to increase its trade with Germany, and although it had immense difficulty in securing a limited agreement in 1934, it ensured that at least a half of the Czechoslovak exports in the deal came from the German regions. Some industries in these regions also suffered less and recovered more quickly; this was true of chemicals, for example. The important tourist industry picked up a little in the mid-thirties—more than its Slovak opposite number. But its failure to return to a pre-1929 level was purely and simply the result of German foreign exchange controls which the Czechoslovaks several times tried but failed to soften. It was nonetheless unfortunately true that, throughout the 1930s, the proportion of the population unemployed rose along with the proportion that was German.

The International Repercussions of the Crash and Internal Politics

Not everything of importance that happened internationally after the Wall Street Crash happened because of it, but the international balance certainly became progressively worse from the Czechoslovak point of view. The United States itself lost most of the little interest it had retained in the outside world and, with the inauguration of Franklin D. Roosevelt as President at the beginning of 1933, it embarked on the double task of rebuilding its own prosperity and keeping out of other countries' troubles. Japan, buffeted first by the United States' loss of business confidence and then by its rising tariffs, could not restrain its own soldiers from sweeping it into Manchuria in 1931 and out of the League of Nations in 1933. Britain entered the crisis in 1929 with a Labour government dedicated to the principles of collective security, but in 1931 it acquired a so-called National government that by 1933 was deeply committed to financial retrenchment at home and the economic appeasement of Japan abroad. France, less immediately affected by the Crash than free-trading, world-funding Britain, still proclaimed its faith in collective security in 1933 and promised to stick by its European agreements. But the Soviet Union, isolated from the rest of the world as much economically as politically, never ceased to proclaim the depression other countries suffered from as proof of their social bankruptcy and of its own ideological supremacy. And Germany, tied to Wall Street by the loans required to pay the Anglo-French reparations bill, disintegrated economically in 1929 and struggled through the three years of political convulsion that on 30 January 1933 made Adolf Hitler the chancellor of a Nazi state dedicated to refashioning and excelling the power and glory of former German empires.

Even if there had been none of these changes in the outside world, the period of depression would still have left its mark on Czechoslovak politics. The early years saw strikes, marches, demonstrations, shootings. There was less violence with the recovery of the later 1930s, but prosperity had still not returned to its pre-1929 level. In the elections of 1935 the Communist Party was able fractionally to increase its percentage of the votes cast, the Social Democratic Party lost only slightly; together they represented almost a quarter of all the voters in a multi-party society. The left had no shortage of targets to attack. The Bat'a shoe combine, for example, was responsible for a third of Czechoslovakia's output of footwear in 1929 but for as much as nine-tenths by 1937. In the same period it increased its share in the export of footwear from a half to nine-tenths. It was Bat'a that made Czechoslovakia the world's largest exporter of leather footwear and the third largest of rubber. The Bat'a concern also built up its own sources of energy, chemicals, machine-tools, and even of food; it turned to allied trades, like the manufacture of tyres; and by the end of 1937 it employed half as many workers in its factories abroad as in those at home. It was not the only near-monopoly in Czechoslovakia; there were dominant syndicates in coal and steel. But in contrast to them, it was not several but a single concern, with most of its vast capital in the hands of one family, and with aggressively expansionist tendencies at home and abroad. Whatever its contribution to Czechoslovakia's recovery from the depression, therefore, the Bat'a shoe combine could not but appear to the left as an archetypal capitalist, imperialist monopoly. The rationalisation of its labour force on mass-production lines and its combination of concern for the physical wellbeing of its workers and antipathy to their organisation in trade unions completed its condemnation in the eyes of the left. But there were other easy targets. The seven largest banks, including the Živnostenská with its close Agrarian links, between them held about 90 percent of the domestically owned investment in Czechoslovak industry and agriculture. Czechoslovakia exported capital, but at less than a third of the rate at which it imported it. Perhaps as much as 20 percent of the capital in Czechoslovakia was foreign-owned; in the Škoda works alone more than 50 percent belonged to the French Schneider-Creusot company. The left could easily lambast the small class of domestic and foreign capitalists who seemed to control the Czechoslovak economy and the destiny of its working class.

Yet the left was not united. It had split in 1920 and its division became irreparable in and after 1929. Following the election of that year the Social Democrats joined the government coalition and stayed with its various versions through the years of depression and recovery down to the very eve of Munich. In theory they remained devoted to the overthrow of capitalism and the promotion of the proletarian revolution, but in practice they tempered the policies of the Agrarian-led governments in the interest of industrial rehabilitation and the relief of the distressed. That there was so much government-ordered or inspired action to reactivate the economy and to ameliorate unemployment was partly to their credit. In a time of near national disaster their humanitarian and practical traditions overcame their ideology. With the Communists it was quite different. The 1920s for them had been a period of ideological indecision and of bickering with the Comintern. In 1929, however, even before the elections and the Wall Street Crash, everything changed with the appointment of a new secretary-general. Klement Gottwald was one of the young generation of Communists. He was thirty-three to Zápotocký's forty-five. A carpenter by training and a Socialist by background, he did not really emerge until after the war, first as a shop steward and then as a journalist. He was an enthusiastic advocate of the split from the Social Democratic Party, and born near Brno, he was very active in the early twenties among the Slovak Communists and in the important industrial centre of Moravská Ostrava, thus acquiring a breadth of national and social experience that was to stand him in good ideological stead. By 1925 he was a member of the central committee of the Communist Party of Czechoslovakia and in 1928, critical of the national divisions within the party and of its residual Social Democratic reformist ideas, he found himself much favoured in Moscow and elected there to the executive committee of the Comintern. Finally, in February 1929, supported by the Comintern through a fierce internal struggle, Gottwald became secretary-general and began a tough but successful campaign to bolshevise the Czechoslovak party on the Russian model. Elected to the chamber of deputies later that year, he made it clear to his non-communist colleagues that 'we go to Moscow to learn from the Russian bolsheviks how to wring your necks', and he proceeded to create the kind of organisation that he believed would eventually do it. One or two old-stagers, like Zápotocký, remained with the leadership. Even Šmeral was recalled from semi-disgrace in Outer Mongolia to give a few years' respectability as an elder statesman. But some of the founder members, including Muna, either withdrew or were expelled, and the new men at the top were mostly left-wing youngsters in the Gottwald mould, Rudolf Slánský, Jan Šverma, and the German Bruno Köhler. Membership of the party, which had stood at 150,000, was cut by more than half as some left and others were weeded out. Gottwald's aim was a revolutionary corps, not a supporters' club. The traditional local branches were replaced by factory cells, and Gottwald handed them a policy of exploiting the economic crisis to overthrow the bourgeois coalition government, then immediately to nationalise industry, ultimately to collectivise agriculture, and generally to promote the wellbeing of all the nationalities within Czechoslovakia, if necessary up to the point of the dissolution of the state. It was a policy that attacked the Social Democrats as much as their middle-class urban and rural partners in office and questioned the whole basis of Czechoslovakia as a national state. It was also a policy that led inevitably to the nomination of Gottwald in May 1934 as the sole challenger to Masaryk in the presidential election.

The slogan Gottwald campaigned under was 'Not Masaryk—but Lenin'. This was a political leader, manoeuvred into position from outside, advocating a foreign ideology. In the election held in the assembly he was hopelessly defeated, winning little more than the votes of his fellow Communists. On account of a pamphlet published with his slogan as its title he was later charged with treason; but in August 1934 he evaded arrest and escaped to the Soviet Union. For all that, the Communist Party in its Gottwald period still represented an internal political reaction to the Crash and its economic consequences in Czechoslovakia. Gottwald's accession to power predated the Crash, but his bolshevisation of the party was concurrent with the depression. And in the parliamentary election of May 1935, even with Gottwald still a fugitive abroad, the party slightly increased its share of the vote. There was enough truth in its economic, social, and national strictures and sufficient attraction in its proffered policies for it to appeal quite genuinely to one in ten of the voters, Czechoslovak and German. The attitudes and position of big business were grist to its mill. The converse was also true. After the Crash, and irrespective of its international political repercussions, there was at least the beginning of a polarisation in Czechoslovakia's domestic politics.

There was a detectable movement to the right among some members of the Agrarian Party. Juraj Slávik, minister of the interior in the government Udržal formed in 1929, found himself taking up an increasingly hard-line position against Communist agitators and demonstrators. He was left out of the government Malypetr formed in 1932. In 1934 Kramář's party, the National Democrats, withdrew from Malypetr's government and established a so-called National Union along with a quasi-fascist party, the National League, that had won three seats in the 1929 election. Kramář acted as its president, and František Hodáč, a former secretary of the Industrialists' Association, as its tactician and financial backer. In the 1935 election the National Democrats raised their number of seats from fifteen to seventeen though the National League lost all its three existing seats. However, another quasi-fascist party, the National Front, won 6 seats. Between them, these extreme right-wing groups took almost 8 percent of the votes cast, not far short of the Communist proportion. Another increasingly right-wing party that did better in 1935 than in 1929 was

Hlinka's Slovak Populist Party. Its membership of Švehla's government and Tuka's eventual conviction on a charge of treason probably accounted for its loss of 4 seats in 1929. But it immediately began to recoup its popularity by ascribing Slovak suffering during the depression to godless, Marxist-inspired, self-centred Czech policies; and despite the flirtations of two of its rising leaders, Fedor Ďurčanský and Karol Sidor, with Hungarian and Polish politicians, it won back 3 of the 4 seats in 1935 and totted up about 7 percent of the votes. The right, variously defined, was a more powerful factor in Czechoslovak politics by 1935 than it had been in 1929.

However, the right was not a cohesive force and was not particularly fascist. When in November 1935 Masaryk announced his intention of resigning as President and recommended Beneš as his successor, there was a half-hearted right-wing attempt to defy his wishes. A number of Agrarians put forward a certain professor Bohumil Němec as an alternative candidate, but even Hlinka's party voted for Beneš in the December election and Němec received less support than Gottwald had the previous year. Agrarian extremists were anti-communist, not fascist; Hlinka's party was anti-Czech. Even the National League and the National Front were not fascist. In so far as they were anything, they were anti-German. The leading figure in the League, Jiří Stříbrný, was a former National Socialist cabinet minister, dismissed for misconduct; the leading figure in the Front, Rudolf Gajda, was a former general, cashiered for indiscipline and disloyalty. Neither could give convincing corporate flavour to their alleged political ideologies.

Equally, whatever the strength of extreme left and extreme right in Czechoslovak politics, either absolutely in 1935 or in comparison with 1929, polarisation was on the wane. Many politicians who were regarded as reactionary voted for Beneš; so strangely enough did the Communists. There were all sorts of explanations: on the one hand, the absence of unbridgeable social gaps between different Czechoslovaks; on the other, the basic cohesion of those in the centre, the Agrarians, the National Socialists, and the Social Democrats. But an ever more important reason for the retreat from polarisation was the rise of a German threat within Czechoslovakia linked with the threat from Hitler outside.

Even if there had been no Hitler, the tide of anti-Czechoslovak feeling in the German districts would have run high after 1929. Activism had been a triumph for the commonsense of the 1920s, but the two German parties that entered the government in 1926 accounted for only just over half of all the German deputies. When the Social Democrats took the place of the Christian Socialists in 1929, much the same was true. With a rate of unemployment higher in what was more and more coming to be known as the Sudetenland than elsewhere in the country, activism became much less popular even with the rank-and-file of the parties professing it. Outside, it became almost the equivalent of treason. Violent German national feelings at the end of the war had been somewhat assuaged by the growth of prosperity within Czechoslovakia in the post-war decade. They were bound to revive with the onset of the depression. In any case, the Sudetenland had considerable claims to be regarded as a birthplace of Nazism. It was among the Germans of the pre-war Czech Lands that there had appeared the first All-Austrian German Workers' Party, opposed to Czech political and social advancement in Austria-Hungary and infused with a mixture of Pangerman and socialist ideas. In the Imperial elections of 1911 three of its candidates had been elected in Bohemia and Silesia. Before the end of the war it changed its name, and it was under the new title, German National Socialist Workers' Party, that its Czechoslovak section emerged in November 1918 as one of the more vociferous opponents of the inclusion of the German districts in the Czechoslovak state. In the parliamentary elections of 1920 it won 5 out of about 70 German seats, in 1925 seven, and in 1929 eight; not a large party, but growing; the number voting for it in 1929 was about 200,000. It was also becoming more extremist in its views, campaigning for a Pangerman state to include the Sudetenland and taking on an anti-semitic attitude that had been largely absent before. It was also gathering the support of other organisations such as the closely-knit Comrades' Union and similar student groups and the Gymnastic Union, an old-established physical culture and ethnic propaganda society which leaders of the Comrades' Union, like Konrad Henlein and Ernst Kundt, gradually penetrated. Indirectly, the National Socialist Workers' Party was also assisted by the fortunes and attitudes of two other German groups. The German National Party, possibly the most vociferous opponent of the Czechoslovak idea in 1918, lost steadily during elections—from 12 seats in 1920 to ten in 1925 to seven in 1929. As it lost, its views, too, became more extreme and contributed to the general hardening of the Sudeten attitude. So did the views of the Christian Socialist Party which became increasingly hostile to what it saw as the leftwards, secularising swing of the Czechoslovak government. Raising the number of its mandates from thirteen in 1925 to fourteen in 1929, it gave up its brief flirtation with activism and swelled the chorus of nationalist protest beginning to gather around the National Socialist Workers' Party. All that was needed was the depression.

Escalating unemployment immediately gave the National Socialists credibility and widened their support. Bankrupt businessmen and ruined shopkeepers were just as ready fodder for their propaganda. People's Sportsclubs and the National Socialist Students' League paraded in para-military uniform and pulled in the tough and the young. And of course support came from the Nazis in Germany. The connection predated 1929. Sudeten National Socialists attended the German Nazi Party rallies. They were not subservient; they were faring too well for that. After 1929, however, the Nazi star was in the ascendant in Germany and the Sudeten National Socialists found themselves being drawn into a major Nazi plot. In 1930 Joseph Goebbels and Baldur von Schirach, among others, addressed political rallies in Prague. In 1931 preparations went ahead for the seizure of power in Germany and the Sudetenland, and in Austria as well. An indigenous movement acquired substantial outside backing and put the Czechoslovak government in a position where it had to take positive action.

It was not too hard for the government to decide what to do. The Sudeten National Socialists were still a minority party in parliamentary terms and were bitterly opposed by the two activist parties, particularly the German Social Democrats. The Nazis were not yet in power in Germany. In domestic and international terms the two anti-democratic and anti-Czechoslovak groups were opposed to everything the government stood for and everything that enabled it to stand. In the course of 1931 it banned the wearing of para-military uniforms and the visits of supporting speakers from Germany. In the spring of 1932 it disbanded the People's Sportsclubs and the National Socialist Students' League, and in the autumn it secured their leaders' conviction on charges of conspiracy against the republic. Even after Hitler's coming to power it pursued its campaign against local Nazism, and in October 1933, after further trials, the National Socialist Workers' Party anticipated its own disbandment (and that of the German National Party) by dissolving itself one day ahead of the official decree.

This disposed neither of Sudeten economic grievances nor of National Socialist ideas. The Czechoslovak government continued to wrestle with the problems of the depression, but unemployment, now at its height throughout the country, was still at its most devastating in the German regions. National Socialist aspirations simply found a new instrument. Hot on the heels of the disbandment, Konrad Henlein established a new organisation, the Sudeten German Home Front, which was not directed from Germany, nor ostensibly National Socialist. Henlein appealed for Sudeten German unity within the

1 Prague before the First World War: Václav Square in 1890

2 Bratislava just before the First World War — the edge of the Jewish quarter beneath the castle in the Old Town

3 Masaryk (*third from left*) with the Czechoslovak Army Corps in Russia in 1917

4 Štefánik (*centre*) with American Czech and Slovak helpers in Washington in 1917

5 Czechoslovak Legionaries in Russia in 1918

6 Beneš returns to Prague in 1919 after successfully pleading the Czechoslovak case at the Peace Conference

7 Before the First World War: a demonstration in Prague against rising prices

8 After the First World War: harvesting in one of the more prosperous and developed regions of Slovakia near the Danube

9 Before the First World War: a strike in northern Moravia against evictions from factory houses

10 After the First World War: Masaryk homes for children and the aged on the outskirts of Prague

11 Before Munich: a demonstration in Prague 'For the unity of the nation, the safety of the republic, democracy, and peace'

12 After Munich: Henlein thanked by Hitler in Berlin for his crucial role in the destruction of Czechoslovakia

13 The Czech Protectorate: Heydrich takes charge of the historic crown jewels from Hácha

14 The Slovak Republic: Tiso, accompanied by Ribbentrop, returns through Salzburg from a briefing session with Hitler, followed by Tuka, his newly imposed foreign minister

15 Jan Masaryk (*wearin* *glasses*) with Ivan Maisk (*on his right*) in Londo in 1941

16 Beneš with Roosevelt Washington in 1943

17 Citizens of Prague build barricades in May 1945 during their rising against the Nazis

18 Beneš and his wife appraise the new order of things in August 1945 — Husák addressing a crowd in Banská Bystrica

19 Clementis (*right*) and Kopecký (*second from left*) discuss import questions with film workers in 1946

20 Novotný (*left*) joins in the applause for Gottwald (*second from right*) after the communist assumption of power in 1948

21 Mission completed: people's militia units played a vital role in the Communists' rise to power in 1948

22 Slánský with Svoboda and Gottwald (*left to right*) some time before his arrest

23 The mid-1950s: the massive statue of Stalin that kept watch on the citizens of Prague

24 The mid-1950s: bystanders in Prague appraise a product of the capitalist West

25 Novotný's presidency: traditional transport still in use in eastern Moravia

26 Novotný's presidency: industrial development in Slovakia, the ironworks at Podbrezová

27 Husák, Svoboda, Dubček, and Kriegel (*left to right*) lead the

28 Smrkovský (*centre*) visits a Czech steelworks in 1968

29 Soviet liberator in May 1945

30 Soviet invader in August 1968

31 Smrkovský (*left*), Dubček (*second from left*), and Černík (*fourth from right*) nearing the end of their service on the Communist Party Central Committee in September 1969

32 Svoboda, Brezhnev, Kosygin, Husák, and Strougal (*left to right*) at Prague airport in January 1972

democratic framework of the Czechoslovak state. On the other hand, he kept secretly in touch with Berlin and simply dissimulated in public to avoid prosecution for treason. He was also sensible enough to realise that he could exploit the electoral system to the Home Front's advantage. Throughout 1934 he scrupulously avoided a confrontation with the Czechoslovak government while building himself up as the natural champion of the aggrieved Sudetens. In time for the 1935 elections he secured a subsidy from Berlin, but he was careful to use all the public paraphernalia of Nazi electioneering in a somewhat muted fashion and even changed his organisation's name to the Sudeten German Party to make it more acceptable as a participant in a democratic exercise. His tactics were entirely successful. He was not himself a candidate, but preferred to stand aside and maintain a certain mystique. His party emerged with two-thirds of the German votes and 44 out of the 46 German seats. The activist Social Democrats and Agrarians tumbled from 37 to 16 seats; and only one other German party survived, the Christian Socialist, which found itself with six deputies in place of fourteen. In fact, the Sudeten German Party emerged as second by only one seat to the Czechoslovak Agrarians.

In May 1935, therefore, Czechoslovakia awoke to an essentially new situation. Hitler was more than two years in power. Yet the Sudeten National Socialists had been disposed of, and their place had appeared to be taken by a rather more subdued group, opposed to the Czechoslovak government but still loyal to the state and just one among several Sudeten bodies. The right wing of the Czechoslovak Agrarian Party had seen fit to talk with the Home Front in 1933 and again in 1934 with an eye eventually to forming a coalition of the right irrespective of nationality. As recently as April 1935, Masaryk had overruled a cabinet majority (that included Beneš) favouring the dissolution of the Home Front, and had allowed it to participate in the elections as the Sudeten German Party in the hope that, however well or badly it did, it would settle down and play the part of a normal parliamentary group. The extent of Henlein's political connection with Berlin, and the fact of his financial relationship, were both unknown in Prague. However, the shock and size of his electoral victory in May 1935 were sufficient to alert the Czechoslovak parties and public to the new danger suddenly facing them of a sizeable Sudeten minority overwhelmingly backing what now seemed to be a likely domestic ally of Hitler. It was little wonder that there was a retreat from polarisation among the Czechoslovak parties and that in the December presidential elections the majority decided on Beneš as Masaryk's successor. For some time there had been a growing awareness of a common external threat in Hitler; Henlein added the necessary internal coagulant.

Munich

The period 1929-35 was inevitably one of preoccupation with internal affairs. Recovery from the slump and maintenance of political stability were overriding issues. However, the emergence of the Sudeten German Party switched public preoccupation to foreign policy, and the election of Beneš to the presidency put at the head of the state a man whose personal and official concern for the previous twenty years had been predominantly with Czechoslovakia's standing in international affairs. For the next three years the main problem facing the Czechoslovaks was their own survival as an independent national state.

Before Hitler came to power in Germany there had been alarms and excursions. The German attempt at a customs union with Austria in 1931 was one. If it had not been blocked by Franco-British intervention, it would have left Czechoslovakia in a position of virtual Pangerman encirclement. But the real danger came with Hitler. He had prepared no detailed plan for the conquest of Europe; he had not thought much about Britain or even the Soviet Union. However, his hostility to the Versailles settlement and his immediate Slav neighbours was not in doubt; and his Nazi ideology added thrust to the revisionist expansionism that had begun to colour the policy even of his Weimar predecessors. In January 1933 there was no certainty that Hitler would remain in power; there was always the possibility that he might become more temperate. Yet the balance of probabilities made it sensible for Czechoslovakia at least to take precautions.

The risk of a Habsburg restoration had largely disappeared; or rather, it was now subsumed in the threat from Germany. If Hitler could absorb Austria, he could control Hungary. The independence of the former subjects of the Habsburg Empire would be in jeopardy. It was natural for Czechoslovakia to turn to its partners in the Little Entente, and just as natural for them to turn to Czechoslovakia. Indeed, they had the additional reason that for some years Mussolini had been stepping up his meddling in the Balkans. In January 1933 Beneš made proposals for strengthening the organisation of the Little Entente and for extending its activities. In March a Permanent Council was established to coordinate the foreign policies of the three powers, and in January 1934 an economic pact was agreed to pave the way for cooperation, even integration, among them. There was an urgency in Beneš's policy that derived from Hitler's mounting threat. By a combination of blatant terror, political adroitness, and economic improvement, Hitler strengthened his hold over the German state and people during 1933 and 1934. He also took the first steps designed to upset Versailles and create his own new order in central Europe. In October 1933 he took Germany out of the Disarmament Conference and the League of Nations and embarked on rearmament in earnest. In January 1934 he detached Poland from the encircling ring France had built around Germany in 1925 by concluding with it a non-aggression treaty; and a month later he arranged a commercial treaty with Hungary that tied it effectively to the German economy. In July he failed in an attempt to seize Austria by promoting a Nazi *coup*, but one failure in a row of successes did little to add to the security of Czechoslovakia. In face of the autarky practised by his Little Entente partners as well as by his own country, Beneš found it hard to promote co-operation, and Czechoslovakia's position looked increasingly hazardous.

There was a passing comfort to be drawn from the attitude of Italy. Memories of wartime assistance lingered in Czechoslovak minds, and they had not been completely soured by the aggressiveness of Mussolini's foreign policy in the 1920s. In May 1934 Mussolini concluded the so-called Rome Protocols with Austria and Hungary as a demonstration against Germany, and in July he sent some troops to the Brenner as a warning to Hitler not to intervene militarily in Austria after his unsuccessful conspiracy. Italian interest in central Europe could act as a counterpoise to German. On the other hand, Mussolini could be as dangerous as Hitler in the long run. In the spring of 1933 he tried to father a four-power pact, the effect of which would have been to secure Franco-British support for the revision of Versailles, to the advantage of Germany in Poland and of Italy in Austria, and for the exclusion of Russia from Europe. It took a major effort on the part of Beneš and his Little Entente colleagues to persuade the two Western powers to let the pact die. Throughout 1934 Mussolini continued to promote his designs in the Balkans, and in October Italian-trained Yugoslav terrorists assassinated both the French foreign minister, Louis Barthou, and King Alexander of Yugoslavia, just arrived in Marseilles on a visit of friendship to France. Czechoslovakia could expect little support from Italy in the long run.

To some extent, the Balkan Entente that was established in February 1934 on the pattern of the Little Entente was a check on Germany and a barrier against Italy. It included Greece and Turkey in addition to Yugoslavia and Rumania. But it became ever more clear to Beneš during 1934 that the security of Czechoslovakia must depend increasingly on the French alliance, coupled if possible with an alliance with the Soviet Union. France was just emerging from a period of civil turmoil, but it was still the one great power opposed heart and soul to the recrudescence of the old Germany. The international position of the Soviet Union was rapidly changing. Internally it was in the midst of its bitter industrialisation and collectivisation programme that endeared it no more to outside powers than had its original Bolshevik Revolution. But although it had looked with favour on the Nazis in their rise to power, it was much disturbed by the actions of Hitler in power and afraid of his likely intentions against itself. All Hitler's actions, not least his Polish treaty, seemed calculated to increase Soviet disquiet; and Germany and Russia, brought together in friendship by their common post-war misfortunes, began rapidly drifting apart. By the same token, France and the Soviet Union began drifting together. What emerged in the spring and summer of 1934 was a complicated French proposal for a kind of eastern Locarno. But Britain showed even less enthusiasm for this than for a similar French proposal in 1925; Germany turned it down abruptly, and Poland followed suit. Beneš supported the idea ardently. Politically he was no champion of the Soviet Union. At heart a Social Democrat, he disliked bolshevism. On the other hand, he could appreciate what the bolsheviks had done for Russia and what Stalin was doing; in any case, it was their business, not his. Nor was his support for the French plan based solely on the need to restrain Hitler. He was a passionate believer in the general atmosphere of security international agreements could bring and in the possibility of educating malcontents to acceptable norms of international behaviour. In June 1934 he finally persuaded his cabinet colleagues in a time of growing awareness of Czechoslovakia's difficulties to grant *de jure* recognition to the Soviet Union. And when the eastern Locarno suggestion foundered in September, he supported the admission of Russia to the League of Nations and went on to advocate the conclusion of individual alliances to deal with the German menace. What eventually tilted the balance, however, was not action by Beneš. In March 1935 Hitler announced that a German air force was already in existence and, a little later in the same month, he went the whole hog by announcing the reintroduction of conscription to build up an army of half a million men. On 2 May France and the Soviet Union signed a treaty of alliance promising each other aid in case of unprovoked aggression. A fortnight later, Beneš achieved his aim by negotiating a linking treaty with the Soviet Union for Czechoslovakia.

The treaty with Russia was signed on 16 May. Three days later the parliamentary elections gave Henlein his majority among the Sudeten Germans. One event may perhaps have helped produce the other. Certainly, after Henlein's victory the Soviet pact was all the more necessary. A revitalised, revisionist, rearming Germany now had a powerful ally within Czechoslovakia. Czechoslovakia needed external support. Nevertheless, its position was still far from secure. In the first place, the implementation of the Soviet pact was dependent on the prior implementation of the French one. If Czechoslovakia were attacked, France would have to come to its assistance before Russia would. This condition was inserted partly at Russia's request. Ideologically and from experience the Soviet Union had no particular reason to trust France, and it did not wish to be left alone defending Czechoslovakia against a German onslaught. But the condition was equally important for Czechoslovakia. Even Beneš had no wish to have his country's fate settled in isolation with Russia. He was prepared to look for assistance where it could be found; he was anxious to forge links between East and West; but in the last resort he was a Westerner. Even if Beneš had wanted to waive the condition, the political situation in Czechoslovakia would not have allowed him to. In May 1935 there were right-wing Agrarians prepared to talk coalition politics with Henlein, while Gottwald, the Communist Party secretary, was absent in Moscow as a political refugee. By the time Beneš became President in December, Hitler's antics had sufficed to bring the political extremes closer together; but even then there would have been little support for the idea of possibly going it alone with communist Russia.

The second weakness in the Czechoslovak position, and really the major one, was the uncertainty beginning to surround the attitude of France, despite its alliance with the Soviet Union. In the course of 1935 it became increasingly likely that Italy would try to score a cheap triumph by invading Abyssinia. When the attack came in October, it was Beneš who presided over the plenary session of the League that decided to apply sanctions to Italy. The moment was one to be savoured. The League had come alive in defence of a small power; France and Britain had proved willing to oppose fascism and resist aggression. But France showed itself a reluctant supporter of sanctions and, more than any other state, was responsible for sabotaging them. By December, when Pierre Laval, the French foreign minister, tried to organise a Franco-British deal with Italy, sanctions were dead. And Czechoslovakia was discomfited. The French position was understandable, no doubt. The alliance with Russia had served to widen the rift between left and right in internal politics. Militarily, the French government felt unable to cope effectively with two opponents and was convinced that the more dangerous one now was Germany. It had more than once been given reason to believe that Italy could become a counterweight to Germany, and it saw no cause to jeopardise the possibility at this stage. But whatever the explanation, the conclusion was the same. Things might be different in the Czechoslovak case where an alliance against Germany was involved; but France was clearly an unreliable power in times of international danger. By May 1936 there was an overrun Abyssinia to prove it.

Another factor influencing France was the line taken by Britain, and this was a further Czechoslovak weakness. Britain genuinely favoured sanctions against Italy. The conquest of Abyssinia might threaten its own imperial position. On the other hand, it was not anxious to go to the point of war. War might be unpopular and would be expensive. To fight Mussolini might perhaps be to lose an influence on Hitler. And the Conservative government was already committed to a policy of weaning Hitler away from aggression by diplomatic manoeuvre and physical concession. To use Mussolini might be one such manoeuvre. An Anglo-German naval treaty, drawn up in June 1935, was already one such concession. Against this background, France wished to prevent Britain getting embroiled in a distracting imperial adventure; hence its sabotage of sanctions. It also wanted to involve Britain more in dealing with Hitler; hence its welcome for Britain's loss of interest in Abyssinia. All this, too, was perfectly understandable. But it had serious consequences for France and, more particularly, for Czechoslovakia. Britain did show more concern for the problems of Europe; but it lent its weight not to resisting Hitler but to appeasing him and, where necessary therefore, to adjusting French policies. The new situation was evident as early as March 1936 when Hitler made a sizeable breach in Versailles and violated the treaty of Locarno, which his predecessors had signed of their own free will, by remilitarising the Rhineland. It was a direct challenge to the French security system pivoted on an unfortified German frontier. The French government was technically not free to act alone; Versailles and Locarno were British commitments as well. It lacked the courage or foresight to take a strong line, and it let the British view prevail. Hitler was not forced to withdraw. And from that moment on French policy was decided more in London than in Paris.

From the Czechoslovak point of view this was most unfortunate. In terms first of its independence and then of its security, France had usually led and Britain sometimes followed. For Britain to take the lead spelled danger. It had always resisted an eastern Locarno and was specifically opposed to a Russian alliance. Its commercial and strategic interests lay elsewhere than in eastern Europe. In so far as its press and public opinion were aware of individual countries in central Europe, there was more sympathy for dispossessed Magyars and more liaison with Polish aristocrats than there was identification with middle-class Czechoslovaks. On the other hand, Britain still had a reputation for international fair play; and even if it was tolerant towards Germany and ill-disposed towards alliances, it had entered the fray in 1914 with a rather similar record. Whatever might be thought of some of his actions, its foreign secretary, Anthony Eden, was apparently a firm League supporter and he had both visited Prague officially and shown understanding for the Czechoslovak point of view. Nothing was without hope.

The final weakness in the Czechoslovak position was the deteriorating situation in eastern Europe. Beneš wanted the Franco-Soviet-Czechoslovak alliance system to be the nucleus for a whole series of pacts. Despite his efforts he could hope for little from Poland, which imagined itself a great power able to handle Germany on its own and which disliked only one state more than Czechoslovakia—and that was the Soviet Union. He did have high hopes of Yugoslavia and Rumania, while Hodža, prime minister since December 1935, campaigned for a Danubian economic federation to include both Austria and Hungary. In May 1936 Beneš was able to chalk up one success: the Little Entente powers declared their solidarity with the forces of law and against those of anarchy. He went on to negotiate with Nicolae Titulescu, the Rumanian foreign minister, a draft treaty arrangement to enable Soviet troops to cross Rumanian territory on their way to give France and Czechoslovakia assistance in a possible war with Germany. Unfortunately, right-wing anti-Russian forces in Rumania secured Titulescu's dismissal in August. This was the signal for Milan Stojadinović, the Yugoslav prime minister, to retreat to safer ground, internally and internationally; in September he began to negotiate a secret agreement with Hitler. The Little Entente appeared to have gone into reverse. Hodža's plan hardly got into gear. There were no negotiations with Hungary. Early in 1936 there were conversations with Schuschnigg, the Austrian chancellor, but they had made little progress when Mussolini intervened in March to renew and extend the Rome Protocols to bind Hungary and Austria much more closely to Italy. The July Agreement between Germany and Austria, which recognised the Protocols but bound Austria to co-operation with Germany as well, followed in November by the announcement by Mussolini and Hitler of the Rome-Berlin Axis, seemed to leave Czechoslovakia not merely alone in eastern Europe, but surrounded.

1935-36 was a period of profit and loss for Czechoslovakia. Internationally it got off to a good start with the conclusion of the Franco-Soviet-Czechoslovak treaty system. But setback followed setback down to the Rome-Berlin Axis. Internally there were fluctuations. Henlein's success was a blow. But Beneš's virtually unanimous election to the presidency was a victory. The economy was recovering and there was a remarkable degree of social cohesion. It was possible in the spring of 1936 to pass a series of laws to establish a restricted frontier area in the Sudetenland, to place controls on unreliable individuals, and to apply the death penalty for espionage. Yet strains reappeared among the Czechoslovaks themselves. Gottwald returned from Moscow under an amnesty; while backing the defence of Czechoslovakia, he swung the Communists away from co-operation with the government on most political matters. Rudolf Beran, who became president of the Agrarian Party in 1935, grew fearful of the Soviet connection and of German hostility, and began to put more feelers towards Berlin and towards Henlein as 1936 wore on. Against this background Henlein played a very skilful game. He emphasised the Sudetens' national identity and cultural aims, but almost imperceptibly introduced Nazi political paraphernalia. He came to secret understandings with various propaganda agencies in Germany itself so that he could both strengthen his position in the Sudetenland and follow the parent party line. In August 1936 he went to Berlin and was received by Hitler and other German leaders. In a deteriorating international and internal situation he made it difficult for the Czechoslovak government to do anything but negotiate concessions with him. Just to make sure, he repeated in July 1936 a trip he had first made to London in December 1935 to win sympathy for his moderation. Prague might resist the hostile bluster of Berlin, but it could not ignore the friendly advice of London.

As President, Beneš could not continue to be foreign minister. He was succeeded in due course by Kamil Krofta, an established historian who had entered the foreign service just after the war and had become deputy foreign minister in 1927. Krofta was a quiet but skilled negotiator of independent mind. But he was steeped in the Beneš tradition of foreign policy; and hitherto the junior partner, he could not suddenly emerge as the senior. He also had no separate party political standing, which as far as Beneš was concerned was partly the reason for his choice. In any case, the international situation had become so grave that, even if Beneš had wanted to reduce his own initiative and responsibility in foreign policy-making, he would not have been able to do so. Moreover, now that Masaryk had retired, Beneš was the leading survivor from the war-time revolution that was being directly challenged. He could not evade his duty. Lastly, in an age of total war and total diplomacy, foreign policy-making, especially in a state like Czechoslovakia, was as much a question of defence capabilities and of party relationships. The foreign minister had a role; but the President was the only person with the ultimate constitutional and individual authority to do the job.

One thing he could and did do was urgently to review the country's defences. He accelerated work on a Maginot-type series of fortifications along the Czechoslovak frontier with Germany. He supervised the re-equipment of the army with the latest weaponry produced in the Škoda armaments works. He set up a supreme defence council to plan for the war that might come, to build up the air force, to mechanise the army and reorganise its units, to expand the officer corps, and to exercise the reserves. By 1938 the Czechoslovak forces were at least as efficient and well-equipped, man for man, as the German. At the heart of Beneš's policy was not only his determination to play a full part in the alliance, but above all to be ready, if it proved necessary, to fight alone.

The next thing he had to do was to deal with pressure from Germany and Britain. The winter of 1936-37 was an ideal moment for Hitler to apply pressure; it had been his best year yet, and better things might lie ahead. He sent two emissaries to Prague to negotiate the isolation or, preferably, the neutralisation of Czechoslovakia and to secure for himself the right to intervene on behalf of the Sudetens. It was a slightly different version of his successful Polish policy. Beneš was only too well aware of the danger of getting caught helpless in Hitler's web. He indicated his interest in continuing the negotiations, but only on the basis of refurbishing the 1925 treaty of arbitration; he was also prepared to discuss internal questions, but not to negotiate about them with anyone outside. And there, in January 1937, the matter rested. By that time, British pressure was taking over. Eden was careful to avoid responsibility for advising Beneš to negotiate a settlement with Henlein and therefore with Hitler. However, after Henlein's mission to London, Eden twice got the message to Beneš in the summer and autumn of 1936 that negotiations made obvious sense. And the message still stood at the beginning of 1937. It was one thing for Beneš to avoid a trap. But to stand up and say no to talks was virtually impossible. Beneš's reputation rested on his willingness to negotiate; and so, it seemed to him, did British interest and therefore French and Soviet help.

Beneš was in any case aware of the need for changes in the conditions under which the Sudeten Germans lived. They were better treated, he rightly maintained, than any other minority in eastern Europe. But they had genuine economic grievances; and reforms were required in administrative practices, in the distribution of official posts and contracts, and even in the direction of autonomy. If concessions were called for anyway, all the more need to make them soon as evidence to outside powers that Czechoslovakia meant to put wrongs to right. There was also a strong case for trying to undermine the position of the Sudeten German Party by removing the grievances that had partly accounted for its electoral triumph. The same reforms, too, could apply to other groups, including the Slovaks, who might welcome decentralisation as much as the Sudeten Germans. For all these reasons, Beneš authorised Hodža to enter into negotiations, early in 1937, with the German Agrarians, Christian Socialists, and Social Democrats. By late February, agreement had been reached on a series of important points, from proportional participation in government services to the placing of public contracts with Germans in German districts. The activists were satisfied. So were some foreign powers. But Henlein was angered.

His ultimate aim was the destruction of Czechoslovakia and the incorporation of at least the Sudetenland in Germany. He was not yet clear when this might be possible, but he saw his own function as preparing the ground locally for eventual outside intervention. In the spring of 1937 it was too early for Hitler to act, but in the meantime Henlein could not allow a genuine settlement of Sudeten grievances. He had to excite his countrymen to clamour for more and to make the Czechoslovak government look unreasonable and unbending. So while Berlin poured abuse on Prague, he introduced a series of draft laws in the National Assembly aimed at establishing totally separate corporations for all the Czechoslovak nationalities. He outbid the activists and outplayed the government. Beneš could not agree to a settlement that would dissolve the state, but he could not so easily persuade foreign governments that this would be the inevitable outcome of Henlein's proposals or that, if it were, it would be such a bad thing. Henlein understood this and therefore adopted the tactic of raising his bid, when necessary, to outshine the activists and wrong-foot the government at the same time. Throughout 1937 he kept up the pressure of propaganda and of incidents; and in October he went off to London again to win sympathy for the Sudeten cause and to malign Beneš.

Beneš's reply was essentially to press on doggedly for a fair settlement. Opportunism and duplicity were neither in his nature nor within his purview. He now found it difficult to work with the activists as Henlein sabotaged their mutually agreed points and pushed even moderates towards extremism. In September 1937 he therefore authorised Hodža to start discussions with Henlein. This was an important departure. The object was still the same, a fair settlement. But the discussions themselves were extra-constitutional in the sense that the National Assembly was the proper arena for considering and deciding on political reforms. Beneš was taking a risk in granting a special position to Henlein. He was practically acknowledging him as the leader of a state within the state, a risk all the greater because of Henlein's obvious link with the Reich. He was also taking a risk with many of his own colleagues. Hodža, as an Agrarian, might be willing to talk; but others in the centre and on the left regarded Henlein as a virtual traitor. On the other hand, Beneš was being a realist. Henlein had power in the Sudetenland and backing in Germany; he could hardly be wished away. He was the man with whom a fair settlement had to be made—or with whom in the end a rupture had to come. He was also the man whom the British thought to be reasonable—or who had to be shown to them to be unreasonable.

The British factor in Beneš's policy suddenly became much more important in May 1937, the month in which Neville Chamberlain became prime minister and began imposing his will on British foreign policy, particularly towards Hitler. Appeasement was unwillingness to face another and unnecessary war. It was regret at the causes and the outcome of the previous one. It was concern for social progress in Britain and elsewhere in Europe, a wish for retrenchment, a fear of revolution. It was reasonably well-intentioned and horribly ill-informed. In practical terms it meant avoiding the anti-German diplomacy of pre-1914 and reversing the anti-German decisions of post-1914. Amends should be made to Germany, and France should be restrained. Russia should be fended off from Europe, and Italy admitted to a new four-power condominium that would keep European peace, hegemony, and prosperity for generations. The nation-states of Versailles, upstarts and interlopers, should be coaxed into the German sphere of influence, and all would be well. It was not a purpose Chamberlain could achieve overnight. It was not one that required the immediate removal of Eden. British pressure for change in central Europe could build up slowly in the summer and autumn, and Eden could assent to it as a continuation of his own policy, if in stronger measure. But it was something Beneš could not ignore.

It was not pressure, as he saw it, that he had to give into. He had to go along with it to the extent that it was aimed ostensibly at the same kind of fair settlement he himself wanted. He had to accede to it because of Britain's importance and, so he thought, its passing indifference to its vital interest in central Europe. What would restrict his freedom of action would also temper Henlein's demands. If, as a result, Henlein came to terms, then little would have been lost. If, however, Henlein proved unreasonable, Beneš would gain British support, for Chamberlain would realise the importance of Czechoslovakia as a barrier against German expansion to the Mediterranean and the Middle East, traditional areas of British imperial concern. There were attendant risks, as Jan Masaryk, the ex-President's son and minister in London, was careful to point out. But once France had all but subordinated its policy to British inclinations, Beneš had precious little alternative. In the last resort, he and his countrymen could go it alone; but it would be foolish to do so before the last resort, since it might never come. Beneš, no more than Masaryk who knew them better, could believe in 1937 that the British would push the Czechoslovaks into hopeless surrender in 1938. It was realistic in several ways to start talks with Henlein in September 1937.

The talks, as Henlein intended, produced no result other than a reiteration of opposing points of view. He was still preparing the ground for intervention. Following his visit to London in October, he worked the Sudeten public into a frenzy over alleged police brutality and eventually, in late November, went off to present his record to Hitler. Perhaps the time was ripe for action. Hitler, in fact, was not quite ready. 1937 had been a year of economic consolidation and military preparation, but his operational plans were still defensive. On the other hand, he soon would be ready. Earlier in the month he had indicated to an intimate group of ministers and generals that he might go on to the offensive and take Austria and Czechoslovakia in 1938 if the circumstances were favourable. About the same time as he saw Henlein, he also conversed with Lord Halifax who had come to Germany on a private visit as Chamberlain's unofficial emissary. His conversation led him to conclude that Britain and France would not intervene if he moved carefully against Austria and Czechoslovakia. It was still too soon to encourage Henlein in his provocative actions. There was some highly placed internal opposition to be got rid of; British overtures had to be further encouraged. Early in February he deposed the dissidents; and in early March, after the resignation of Eden, the British came up with an official overture. Hitler could therefore move quickly; and it was Austria, somewhat fortuitously, that provided him with his first opportunity. On 11 March he moved his troops into Austria and found himself positioned to deal with a now part-encircled Czechoslovakia. Henlein could be given the go ahead.

Beneš was almost as surprised as everyone else by the *Anschluss*. Hitler had moved quickly. Mussolini had uttered not a syllable of protest. Britain and France had stood idly by. Part of the Czechoslovak frontier, still imperfectly fortified, was suddenly exposed. But apart from expediting the work of reinforcing the frontier, Beneš persisted in his previous policy. There was little else he could do and no realistic alternative. In any case, he had become more deeply involved with British pressure. Halifax's visit to Hitler had produced joint Anglo-French advice to go further and faster in coming to terms with Henlein's demands, and the preparation of new proposals was under way when Hitler struck at Austria. Chamberlain would do nothing more than warn Hitler that a new policy thrust might have far-reaching consequences. He refused outright to give a guarantee to Czechoslovakia. Succeeding French governments spoke more reassuringly, but nonetheless joined the British government in urging concessions. Eden's resignation was a serious loss, but even Masaryk could offer no better advice to Beneš than going along with the British government while trying to influence the British public. The Social Democrats apart, the German activist parties went over to Henlein. Gottwald uttered warnings and called for closer relations with the Soviet Union. Beneš did try to persuade the French high command to start tripartite talks with the Russians and discreetly undertook bilateral negotiations. Yet no one could suggest an alternative course but to continue talks, or an alternative German body to talk with than the Sudeten German Party. Either there would be a settlement—less fair now to the Czechoslovak position—or Henlein would be unmasked and the British would stand against him.

Possibly Beneš's greatest disadvantage was that he had to act in public while Henlein could act partly in secret. There was no proof at the time that when Henlein went off to see Hitler at the end of March he was appointed Hitler's deputy and told always to demand more than the Czechoslovak government could yield; or that he was recommended to return to London to maintain the sympathy felt there for his cause. Still less was there any public knowledge of Hitler's military preparations for a lightning attack on Czechoslovakia. What was known was Henlein's speech at Karlsbad on 24 April. In this he put forward eight demands that skilfully combined the reasonable (for example, equal rights with the Czechoslovaks)—to impress Chamberlain—and the unattainable (for example, freedom to practise Nazism)—to embarrass Beneš. What was less widely known were the honeyed words of the German diplomatic corps; but they were still taken reassuringly in the quarters where it mattered. And what was known only in privileged circles in London on 14 May was Henlein's performance as the honest man in search of a fairminded, independent solution. Against this false background it was hard for Beneš to win credit for his openly gradualist policy. His proposal at the end of March to consolidate all legislation on minorities was treated with scorn; and as a result of an Anglo-French ministerial conference at the end of April, he was urged early in May to take Karlsbad seriously and negotiate towards a state of nationalities as an alternative to the unitary state. There was a temporary improvement at the end of May. During the third weekend of that month Hitler chanced a sudden move against Czechoslovakia, and Chamberlain reacted to the point of threatening him with war in case of aggression. But the crisis was barely passed when the British government began to regret its over-impulsive action. Hitler secretly chose 1 October as the latest possible date for his invasion of Czechoslovakia, and Henlein strengthened and intensified his private contacts with Berlin and London. But to Chamberlain the situation still seemed one in which Hitler and Henlein were acting with restraint and in which the pressure must be put on Beneš. Alternatively, the situation was more dangerous since Czechoslovakia had recalled some reserves during the crisis and must therefore be badgered into a settlement in case it should behave foolishly again. No one could prove that Hitler had moved his army to the Czechoslovak frontier; but the Czechoslovak government had organised its mobilisation openly.

However, it was not simply a matter of secrecy versus publicity. Beneš and Hodža continued to discuss a possible compromise with Henlein and his colleagues. They suspected the Sudetens and were anxious to expose their duplicity. But although Chamberlain possibly suspected Hitler, he was not anxious to expose him. He wanted a peace settlement, not a showdown. What concerned him, therefore, was not that Beneš had now moved from the concept of a minorities statute to that of a nationalities statute, but whether whatever plan came from Beneš would have settlement value. Thus a long retreat lay ahead of Beneš. Whenever Henlein demanded more, Chamberlain pressed for more; and there was no certainty of an end short of the destruction of Czechoslovakia. Just after the May crisis the British government applied a new round of pressure on Beneš. The Czechoslovak government made further concessions and then, in face of Henlein's ambivalence, made ready to publish its plan. Now desperately afraid of a showdown, Chamberlain more or less forced Beneš to invite Lord Runciman to Czechoslovakia as investigator and mediator. A Liberal peer with governmental and commercial experience, Runciman was more naturally inclined towards the Sudeten Germans, especially their well-to-do, hunting-and-shooting aristocracy; he had also had his advice from Chamberlain. So despite moments of sympathy for the Czechoslovaks, he too applied pressure to push Beneš, early in September, to the stage where he conceded the Karlsbad demands in all but name. Even this 'Fourth Plan' was not enough. Privately admitting that his original requirements had been met, Henlein broke off the negotiations on a pretext and fled to Germany. He had played out his role, forcing Beneš back, pulling Britain on. The invasion date was approaching fast. It was now up to Hitler to take the leading part. On 12 September, at the Nuremberg Party Rally, it was Hitler, not Henlein, who spilled out abuse against Czechoslovakia and foreshadowed a military confrontation. Beneš was worried, but he could feel pleased that he had at last exposed Henlein as nothing other than Hitler's agent. Chamberlain was also worried, but distinctly not pleased. So he simply took the matter out of Henlein's hands and out of Beneš's by flying to Berchtesgaden on 15 September to discuss peace with Hitler. Since Hitler had now taken on the bidding, his demand was for more than Karlsbad, for more than Beneš could yield. He demanded the cession of the Sudetenland to Germany. But since Chamberlain had not changed and was still desperate for a settlement without open violence, he soon had the combined weight of the British and French governments behind an ultimatum to Beneš in the early hours of 21 September to accept cession or be left to face Hitler alone.

Beneš had moved cautiously and painstakingly from one concession to another in the fervent hope that he would be able to manoeuvre Henlein and Chamberlain into accepting a reasonable compromise that would give the Sudetens satisfaction but maintain an integral Czechoslovakia. But the destruction of Czechoslovakia now stared him in the face. This had always been a possibility, and he had always said that he would resist it. In a few hours in the middle of the night he had to decide whether to resist, whether to say no to the Anglo-French plan of destruction. There were many factors to influence his decision. He had recently been clarifying the position of the Soviet Union. There was no doubt that throughout the spring and summer it had been helpful in its public pronouncements and its private actions and that it would honourably fulfil its treaty obligations. Beneš did not really want it to do more; he was a man of the West and, if necessary, exclusively so. There were also genuine doubts about Soviet capabilities after the purges and given the difficulties of transport through Poland or Rumania, Poland was likely to refuse. The Little Entente was teetering on the edge of collapse, with Rumania just clinging to the possibility of allowing the Red Army to use its single-line track to go to the assistance of Czechoslovakia. But intervention by Russia and co-operation from Rumania hung on the certainty of assistance from France. Beneš had gone to great lengths to ensure this. He had kept in touch with a wide spectrum of French politicians, but had done nothing to ruffle the susceptibilities of the two right-of-centre leaders, Edouard Daladier and Georges Bonnet, who had become prime minister and foreign minister in April. He had accepted their advice to negotiate with Henlein; he had fallen in with their wish to pay heed to Britain and not to press military negotiations with the Soviet Union. In the uncharted sea of appeasement the one light he had thought he could rely on was the French treaty. Yet he had at least suspected that France's willingness to honour its obligation would depend on the attitude of Britain. He had not simply gone along with British wishes. He had argued the Czechoslovak case at length, not least with Runciman, and over and over again he had tried to relate Germany's threat to Britain's interests. Masaryk had been assiduous in trying to muster support in London; and champions from the First World War, like Seton-Watson, had done their best to help. Nevertheless, on the morning of 21 September, he knew he had failed. It was no longer simply pressure; it was no longer just on behalf of Henlein; it was quite crudely an ultimatum on behalf of Hitler—and delivered as toughly by France as by Britain. He had been defeated not by his enemies but by his friends.

But Beneš never lost a battle, because he never really gave up. In any case, he was not fighting for himself, but for his people. Out of the ultimatum he secured the promise of a guarantee for the remainder of the Czechoslovak state. With a firm treaty broken, perhaps the promise of a guarantee was of slight value. On the other hand, Britain would be a guarantor as well as France, and for a state whose shape they would have determined. In addition, as Beneš saw it, the Anglo-French plan was really an incident in a longer struggle. If Hitler wanted to destroy Czechoslovakia in a war, he would not be stopped by any Anglo-French plan. He would reject it and, sooner or later, would be exposed for the deceitful aggressor he was. Britain and France would have to stand and fight and so support the integrity and independence of Czechoslovakia. In the meantime, Beneš could continue to make propaganda in London and Paris. Unfortunately, Beneš overestimated Hitler and underestimated Chamberlain. At his Godesberg meeting with Chamberlain on 23 September, Hitler did ask for more: the cession was to be quick, brutal, and entirely to his advantage. He still wanted his war. Yet at Munich on 29 September he retreated a little: the cession could be more orderly. He also did without his war. Chamberlain persisted so much in thrusting on him the essentials of what he wanted that he finally realised he could have a bloodless victory. Without the loss of a soldier and with an immense accretion of personal prestige, he could have a broken Czechoslovakia covered by a totally useless guarantee; he could also have an ostracised Russia and a humbled France, a fawning Italy and a grateful Britain.

Beneš was not invited to the conference; and his representative was kept outside, to be informed subsequently of the Munich decision. This time it was a four-power ultimatum. If Czechoslovakia rejected it, Hitler would be free to attack while the other governments simply looked on. Chamberlain cleared his conscience with the hope that it would not be necessary to bomb civilians. The onus was therefore on the Czechoslovak government to accept the terms and paralyse their country, or reject them and risk its destruction in a German war. Or rather, the onus was on Beneš. He took advice; he talked with his ministers and he listened to his generals. He had been doing that for the past six months. But he did not consult the National Assembly. It was not only that there was too little time. Whatever the constitution might say, the character of Czechoslovakia in 1938 was such that, in its moment of crisis, it was for Beneš to decide. At least since the *Anschluss* he had been doing just that, and there was no escaping his obligation now.

Czechoslovakia was militarily strong. The mobilisation that preceded Munich put a million well-trained men in the field. Their equipment was at least as up-to-date as that of the German army, and indeed, once captured, it made the German army strong enough to conquer the greater part of Europe in 1939-40. The frontier fortifications were not complete, but later immensely impressed the Germans. In any case, the plan was to abandon Bohemia, if need be, and to retreat to Moravia and eventually to Slovakia. The Second World War was to prove what even a small army could do from the mountains. Army morale was high; ever since the *Anschluss*, individual army officers and groups of senior staff had made intermittent appeals for the government to take a strong line, and on the morrow of Munich the general staff specfically pleaded with Beneš to go to war. But Beneš's reply was straightforward and unequivocal. The army was right to state its views and to reflect those of the people at large; but as President he had to consider all aspects of the crisis, and despite Czechoslovak readiness to fight, the international balance was clearly still such as to force him to accept the Munich agreement. The German army was poised to attack; the German people had been promised a victory over Czechoslovakia. The British and French governments had washed their hands of Czechoslovakia; the two peoples would not easily understand it if the Czechoslovak government turned down the chance for their country to live in peace and justice. Italy could make no difference at all to the situation. Poland and Hungary were moving in to claim their minority areas inside Czechoslovakia. The United States was trapped in its neutrality laws and too far away to be of any help; with the best intentions in the world President Roosevelt had made his contribution to Czechoslovakia's plight by encouraging peace talks. There remained Russia. Despite French failure to honour their treaty, there was just a chance that the Soviet Union might assist Czechoslovakia on its own. Soviet aircraft might be able to ferry troops and supplies to Slovakia. But Beneš smelled danger. The Western powers would say that Hitler had been right all along, that Czechoslovakia was an outpost of communism and should be offered no mercy. In fact, they would not only still their consciences over Czechoslovakia; they might even lend Germany active assistance against Russia. Beneš had no more wish to endanger Russia than to destroy Czechoslovakia.

He was also particularly anxious to avoid the fate of Spain, a civil war with disastrous outside intervention, or the other way round, outside intervention leading to civil war. In a sense, war against Germany with Anglo-French support would still have produced a civil war. Henlein had used Reich German money, Nazi terror tactics, and all the techniques of the twentieth-century political agitator to whip up enthusiasm for his policies. At the local elections in May and June he had won more than 90 percent of the Sudeten German votes. However, even if he had used more conventional methods, he would still have had widespread popular support. Sudeten grievances, Hitler's success, Czechoslovak provocations, all would have combined to ensure that. War with Germany in September 1938 would have meant war with the majority of the Sudetens, though there were signs of division in their ranks in the middle of the month. More seriously, it might have meant a Czech-Slovak split. Hlinka's Slovak Populist Party had voted for Beneš as President in December 1935, and under the growing internal and external German threat had remained a basically loyal supporter ever since. But the opportunity presented by the government's discomfiture in the past six months had not been entirely permitted to pass. Soon after the *Anschluss* some of its leaders associated themselves with Henlein's autonomy demand. A tougher line on autonomy won the party two-fifths of the local votes cast in May and June. A delegation of American Slovaks brought the original of the Pittsburgh Agreement to Bratislava (and received encouragement from the Polish government on the way); and at a vast open-air meeting on 4 June Hlinka demanded that Slovakia be given its autonomy. Beneš and Hodža (himself a Slovak) made it clear that any concessions to the Sudeten Germans would involve a change in status for the Slovaks as well. But Hlinka died in August and was succeeded in the leadership of the party by the rather more extreme Tiso (though there were others more extreme than him). Contacts were strengthened with Henlein. The Populists were not in open rebellion in the days of Munich, though perhaps on the brink of a serious conspiracy. In the face of the Nazi threat the mass of the Slovak people were ready to fight for their country, and all the more so as the Hungarian government began making revisionist pronouncements. But Beneš could not be wholly sure how far Czech-Slovak relations would stand the stress of war.

One thing he certainly suspected was that a war fought with Russia alone would strain Czech-Slovak relations too much. At its Bratislava rally in June the Populist Party had made a ceremonial burning of the text of the Czechoslovak-Soviet Treaty. The devout Catholicism of the Slovak peasantry, quite apart from the right-wing approach of most Slovak parties, might provoke a reaction against a government prepared to co-operate with communists. This indeed was a fear he had about the whole of Czechoslovak society. He had lost Western help; if he now went to war with Soviet help, there might be a right-wing reaction and a Communist rising. The arrival of the Red Army could well be the signal for a civil war. It is impossible now (as it was for Beneš then) to say how far the Agrarians, for example, would have gone. It is also impossible to say how much Beneš knew then of their double-dealing over the past few months. It was not so much that Hodža had almost lost his head during the May crisis. Since then he had several times invited the French and British governments to apply pressure to Beneš and other colleagues as the only means of breaking their resistance to concessions and avoiding war. The last time was when he invited the ultimatum that was delivered on 21 September. Other Agrarian leaders, like the party chairman, Beran, and the head of the Živnostenská Bank, Jaroslav Preiss, had been in surreptitious contact both with the Runciman mission and with the German embassy in Prague in an effort to find some kind of settlement short of a Nazi attack that Hitler would have to accept. Their stamp was on the cession compromise that was eventually agreed. All these Agrarians knew that their actions were close to treasonable. Their motives were many. They had their persons and property to protect. In the belief that they could get better terms, they went willingly along the path that Beneš was forced to traverse reluctantly. But they had always been anti-communist and anti-Soviet, and they were anxious to avoid at any cost a situation in which Czechoslovakia could be taken over by the

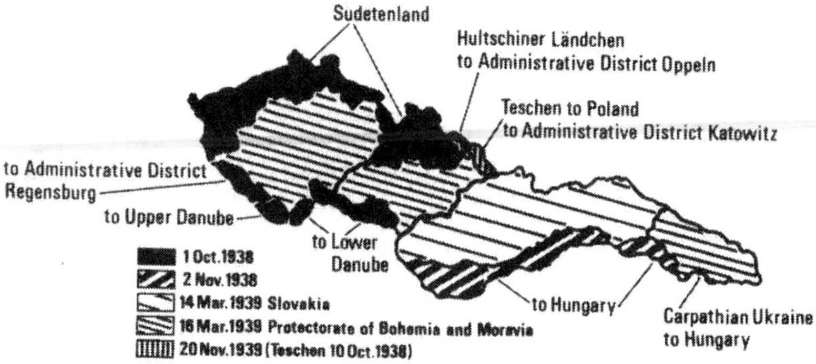

3 The Results of Munich 1938-39

Communists with Soviet help. Beneš may not have known the details of the Agrarians' activities, but he was aware of their political attitudes and had reason to fear a civil war. On its side, the Communist Party had recently assumed the mantle of patriotism. Many rank-and-file members were indeed patriots to the core, but Gottwald had spent most of his near decade of leadership maligning Czechoslovak society. Even when he began to address rallies on the need to resist Nazism, he still prophesied revolution at the side of the Soviet Union. In May and again in September he acted as intermediary to reassure Beneš of Stalin's loyalty. If the Red Army were to come to Czechoslovakia, it would be hard for the Communist Party not to assert its special position. Beneš could imagine nothing more disastrous than a German-Russian war fought over Czechoslovakia and producing civil strife between Agrarians and Communists of the kind that had mutilated Spain.

Considerably more than half the Czechoslovak people did not

back Henlein, or Hlinka, or Hodža, or Gottwald. Rich industrialists like Bat'a were as anxious to fight Germany as the thousands of ordinary citizens who paraded demonstratively in the streets at the time of the Anglo-French ultimatum or the Munich diktat. As Beneš knew, the Czechoslovak army would give an excellent account of itself. Resistance, at least in the early days, would be infectious. Perhaps most of the people would rally. But Czechoslovakia on its own would be defeated. With Russia on its side it would still be defeated, or it would end up a Communist state. Beneš did not want his people to die, still less to die in vain. He did not want the survivors to be either Nazi or Communist. Despite all Britain and France had done, he still wanted his country to be of the West. The only course, as he saw it, was to accept Munich under duress and so to save his people to fight another day. He was quite convinced, and told his generals so, that it was only a question of time before the West would have to turn and fight. At that point, Czechoslovakia would be on the victorious side, and the right one. It was hard to explain to his people. It would have been impossible to decide in the assembly. Beneš knew it was the proper course and took the onus upon himself. It was the logical outcome of his entire policy.

Prague

The Munich period is full of nagging questions. Many of them concern the other powers. In the case of Czechoslovakia the most important is what would have happened if it had been decided to say no to Munich. It was touch and go. Just after the Anglo-French ultimatum of 21 September Hodža resigned in favour of a government mainly of officials, presided over by general Jan Syrový, one of the legendary heroes of the Czechoslovak Legion. This was inevitably less preoccupied with the niceties of politics than Hodža's government had been and was highly patriotic. It might have tipped the balance in favour of war. On the other hand, officials were employed to execute, not make decisions. Immediately after acceptance of the Munich terms there was talk among some of the younger politicians and army commanders of overthrowing the Syrový government and declaring war. But the talk lasted a day or two and then faded. Mobilised soldiers and demonstrating civilians thought of war. But there were neither generals nor political leaders to be found to overthrow Beneš's decision. In the end, virtually everyone realised that, right or wrong, it was the only decision possible. Czechoslovakia had been betrayed and was deserted. It could fight gloriously, even lengthily, and then die. Alternatively, it could live to fight another day.

Beneš thought that that other day would come in May or June 1939 when he expected Hitler to attack Poland. He hoped the rump Czechoslovak state would still be intact, no more mutilated than it had been by Munich. That was indeed part of the reasoning behind his whole policy. He himself was prepared to go abroad, as Hitler soon demanded. It represented a weakening of Czechoslovakia. On the other hand, he would leave behind him a competent government that could keep in touch with him pending the outbreak of war. Nor was a fighting exile something new to him. He had it in his blood from the First World War. For the moment, certainly he would not engage in acts of public hostility towards Germany. He would quietly prepare for the Second World War and his struggle to restore his shorn country to its previous state.

However, although Beneš's reasoning was sound enough in the context of whether to submit or to resist, his acceptance of Munich inevitably changed many things. The Czechoslovak people as a whole was stunned; betrayal and impotence were terrible things to bear. The five-power international commission established in Berlin to stake out the frontier line between Germany and the Czech Lands settled everything in Germany's favour by an automatic four-to-one vote; the Czechoslovak representative was a helpless embarrassment. Poland snatched Těšín. Within a month, Hungary was able to carve off a large southern slice of Slovakia and Ruthenia by exploiting the rivalry between Germany and Italy. The surviving Czechoslovak state was down to 70 percent of its former area and 67 percent of its former population. It had lost over a million Czechs and Slovaks to Germany, Poland, and Hungary; yet it still contained almost half a million Germans, Poles, and Hungarians within its attenuated frontiers. Its territorial loss was not compensated for by any corresponding gain in ethnic homogeneity. It also had to provide for half a million refugees. Its only defensible frontier around the Czech Lands, as well as its defence works, were now in German hands. Its 'waist', between the Czech Lands and Slovakia, had been slimmed to under 40 miles, and two of its main west-east railway-lines had been completely severed. Slovakia apart, the country was wide open to any invader. Economically, the situation was worse still. Over 40 percent of Czechoslovakia's industry had been concentrated in the lost territories. The country was now without 67 percent of its metal-working plant and 50 percent of its coal, to give two vital examples. In agriculture the loss of arable land was 33 percent, of forest 26 percent. The biggest single blow was the loss of 60 percent of the hop-fields. The most serious consequences of industrial and agricultural losses were felt in trade, investment, and employment. Much of what had hitherto been internal trade became import-export business, subject to tariffs, and many of Czechoslovakia's best export lines passed to the account of Germany. Germany's share of Czechoslovakia's trade increased; Jewish and Western money fled abroad, German poured in. Unemployment grew, and authorisation had to be given for 40,000 workers to take up labouring jobs in Germany. But the economic losses also compounded defence problems. One way and another, the rump state was no more ethnically pure; but it was militarily much less defensible. Little wonder its people was numb.

There were additional humiliations; the loss of historic sites like Chod in Bohemia and Devín in Slovakia and the expulsion of Beneš were just two instances. The burden of defeat was all the worse because there had really been no battle. In the Czech Lands there was a noticeable drawing together. The number of parties was reduced to three: the National Unity Party, which was under Agrarian leadership and attracted the majority of politicians; the National Labour Party, which embraced Social Democrats and some National Socialists; and the Communist Party, which was finally outlawed in December 1938. The same phenomenon was exhibited in other fields, among the trade unions for example. It represented determination, bewilderment, and fear. It also represented a certain disillusionment with the politics of the first republic that had brought only self-destruction upon Czechoslovakia. The same attitude was reflected in the enabling law the Assembly passed in December that gave the President and his cabinet full legislative powers for a two-year period. Imitation of Western democracy had palpably been as damaging for Czechoslovakia as reliance on the Western democracies. In any case, politics was becoming too tricky for all but the most ambitious politicians. It was best to leave it to two parties, or to the leaders of one. The Czechs had lived in their independent democracy for a mere twenty years. For three hundred years before that they had lived through various forms of autocracy. They had not forgotten how to lie low. German pressure also worked in the same direction, towards authoritarianism, the expulsion or imprisonment of troublemakers, and censorship. Finally, there were Czechs to be found, willing, even anxious, to take the lead in the new situation. They were men like the ageing Emil Hácha, renowned lawyer and judge, ready to make the best of what might be a less bad job than it appeared. He succeeded Beneš in the presidency in October. Or they were men like Beran who had long felt, in opposition to Beneš, that Czechoslovakia should follow a course of near friendship with Germany to avoid the Scylla and Charybdis of East and

West. He succeeded Syrový in the premiership in December. By the end of the year, Czechoslovakia was not only smaller and more exposed as a result of the capitulation at Munich; the politics of the Czech Lands had swung much more to the right than Beneš expected.

The extent of the swing in Slovakia had been even more unexpected. After Munich the majority of the Slovak people were still faithful to the republic; they had no wish to live under the hegemony, still less the rule, of Germans, Poles, or Hungarians. On the other hand, for twenty years they had accepted Czech leadership and authority, and in the end it had brought them defeat without a fight. Their desire for autonomy within the republic had been much weaker than often claimed; but once the republic had effectively failed them, it became much stronger. In any case, the Czechs who now governed in the name of the second republic were obviously not to be compared with those of the Masaryk and Beneš generations. After Munich, therefore, there was at least a sentiment in favour of autonomy. In fact, all the negotiations with Henlein had encouraged the idea that the Slovaks could expect the same degree of decentralisation as the Sudetens; and there were many quite reasonable critics, Czechs among them, who had long held that some measure of Slovak autonomy would strengthen the state. The initiative after Munich, however, lay not with the men of reason, Czech or Slovak, but with the Slovak Populist Party. Although they had not gone to the point of treason, a number of Populists had been in touch with Germans, Poles, and Hungarians as well as with the Sudeten politicians, and the whole party had been pushing for the kind of autonomy claimed at Bratislava in June. They were therefore poised for action. They considered a number of possibilities: a union with Poland or Hungary, or both; a union with Bohemia and Poland, or Bohemia and Hungary; independence under a German protectorate or an international guarantee. In the end, they chose autonomy within the second republic. The international situation seemed to allow nothing else; the internal situation seemed to suggest that the Czechs were now too weak to hold the upper hand in a federal Czechoslovak state and the Slovak Populists not yet sufficiently strong in Slovakia itself to push for absolute separation. Everything was arranged at a meeting in Žilina on 5 October. The Communists were not interested. The Social Democrats attended and tried both to restrict the authority to be devolved on Bratislava and to secure the participation of all parties in Slovakia in the autonomous government. The Populists might realise their limitations, but they would not deal with a Marxist party. They chose the alternative, which was to come to terms with the Agrarians. A new government and assembly were established, autonomous in everything except defence, foreign policy, and national financing. Tiso became the minister for Slovakia and, as well as two Populists, agreed to bring two Agrarians into his government. Prague agreed at once, glad that the Slovaks did not want to press further. And so, within a matter of days, Slovakia had won a remarkable degree of local independence and set up a government with no greater limitation on the evolution of its views than that provided by Beran's Agrarians.

The swing to the right was then very rapid. In a matter of days Communists and Socialists were both outlawed. On 8 November all the other political groups were forced into the Slovak National Unity Party with the Populists dominating it. On 15 December it won 97.5 percent of the votes in the election to the new Slovak diet. Slovakia had become a one-party state of the right. The Czech Lands were on the same road. And the new Czech-Slovak federation was already very different from the rump Czechoslovak state Beneš had fervently hoped would persist. In fact, it had already taken irreversible steps towards its own destruction.

Hitler had both lost and won at Munich. He had not actually destroyed Czechoslovakia, but he had put himself in a position to do so whenever he was ready. However, he was not immediately sure when he could act. His directive to his forces on 21 October bade them prepare for the defence of Germany, the liquidation of Czechoslovakia, and the occupation of Memel. On 24 November he added the occupation of Danzig. He had not yet made Czechoslovakia top priority, or fixed a date. Action around Poland might take precedence. Beneš was not being ingenuous in expecting Hitler to give Poland priority over Czechoslovakia. However, during December, Hitler's sights began to concentrate on Czechoslovakia. There were many reasons. Most important was continuing appeasement by Britain and France; next in line, the traditional resilience of Poland. But the altered situation inside Czechoslovakia also played its part. František Chvalkovský, the new Czechoslovak foreign minister, had visited Hitler in October and shown no real resistance to being subservient to him. Of more consequence, Ďurčanský, the Populist minister of the interior in Slovakia, had been to see Göring twice and Ribbentrop once to make it clear that Slovakia wanted to go beyond autonomy within Czechoslovakia to independence in association with Germany. For the moment, Hitler had advised the Slovaks against change, but he had begun to cultivate Ďurčanský and others like him. He knew he had willing servants when the time came. The Slovak elections of

15 December appeared to bring the time a little nearer; Ďurčanský's party was almost completely triumphant. And on the same day, the Enabling Act was promulgated in the Czech Lands. Two days later, Hitler ordered his army to prepare for the occupation of the rump Czechoslovak state on the assumption that it would meet little resistance. And in the new year he began his campaign in earnest. He stirred up the Germans remaining inside Czechoslovakia to make old-style Sudeten demands. As January rolled on, he bludgeoned Chvalkovský who came to Berlin to try and remove Sudeten and Reich German grievances. And early in February he started prompting the Populists to prepare for a declaration of independence. Within a month, he was presented with the opportunity he wanted. Bratislava had been full of conspiracy and Prague full of suspicion. On the night of 9-10 March, Hácha dismissed Tiso. Perhaps losing his nerve, or finding his conscience, Tiso at first declined to establish an independent state. But he and Ďurčanský were almost forcibly taken to Germany and harangued by Hitler on the evening of 13 March; back in Bratislava next morning, they lost no time in declaring Slovakia independent. In the Czech Lands the Germans manufactured the usual incidents and appealed to Hitler for help. Against the background of Slovak rebellion and Sudeten complaint it seemed essential to Hácha and Chvalkovský to go direct to Hitler to save what they could. But on the night of 14-15 March they were ruthlessly bullied into telephoning their colleagues not to resist the entry of German troops into the Czech Lands. By the evening of 15 March Hitler was in Prague, and all that remained was for him to declare the Czech Lands the Protectorate of Bohemia and Moravia. Post-Munich Czechoslovakia had ceased to exist.

Only Hitler was happy with the outcome. He had won a victory of great historical, economic, and strategic significance. The British government was initially relieved to have got rid of an embarrassing commitment to participate in an international guarantee, but it was soon forced by public and political opinion to reverse its hapless policy of appeasement and to take at least an apparent stand against Germany. Inside Czechoslovakia, the Sudeten Germans were happy—they were now the top dogs—but no other group was totally satisfied. The Ruthenians had been the least integrated and the least well catered-for of all Czechoslovakia's nationalities. Like the Slovaks, they had taken the chance of autonomy in October 1938. But in March 1939 what they got instead of the independence they wanted was occupation by the Magyars and absorption within Hungary. The Slovak Populists were a little happier. They were free of Prague; they had avoided rule from Budapest; they had a tangible form of independence. Yet even for them, matters did not work out right in March. They were under German protection; they had to garrison German forces. At best, as they saw it, their fate was the least of a number of evils. For its part, the central government in Prague had been hopelessly outplayed. It had taken on the Slovak challenge and given Hitler his much-wanted chance; it had sent its troops into Slovakia and left the Czech Lands largely defenceless. Hácha and Chvalkovský themselves had walked naively into a trap. The truth was that they, like Beran and the others, had really hoped for some reward from their policy of co-operation with Hitler, whereas they had simply facilitated his seizure of their country. They might defend their record, but they could hardly be pleased with it.

Beneš was certainly unhappy. He was perhaps a little too hard on those he had left behind him after Munich. They had contributed to the dissolution and subjugation of the Czechoslovak state. However, in all the circumstances, there was perhaps little else they could do. German aggression and British appeasement would probably have done the job anyway. What saddened Beneš was that he would now have to start his struggle without a country and that, until it was victorious, the Czechoslovaks would have to suffer a very great deal. The Czechoslovak people were unhappiest of all. Self-determination had brought them independence just two decades before. The same principle had now been misapplied by the Germans and the British to terminate their independence. All their efforts had been for nothing; and they were the ones who were left to face up to Hitler and the Nazis. In December 1938, even before the total extent of the tragedy was apparent, Karel Čapek, deservedly the internationally best-known of Czechoslovakia's writers, died in Prague in his forty-ninth year; they said it was of pneumonia, but everyone knew it was of a broken heart.

CHAPTER 11

The Resurrection of Czechoslovakia

The Struggle for Recognition

THE EVENTS OF MARCH 1939 ended the Munich fiction. As far as Hitler was concerned, he had now liquidated Czechoslovakia, and he could proceed to deal with Poland. As far as Beneš was concerned, his policy of concessions had failed. He had not saved even part of his country for the war against Hitler. At the same time he need no longer pander to the Anglo-French view of Germany. He could repudiate all that had happened and begin the new struggle for independence. At the end of the inevitable world war, Czechoslovakia would be resurrected in its former shape and would resume its historical development where it had left off.

In a sense, it was a familiar situation. Beneš was in the United States when Hitler marched into Prague. It was from Chicago, the heart of Czechoslovak America, that he disowned Munich and attacked Hitler. Before the war broke out, he was in London to begin organising political action abroad; and hardly had the war started, when he went over to Paris to expedite military action. But the situation was not the same as it had been in 1914; and the outcome was also to be different from that of 1918.

In one way, the situation was easier. Czechoslovakia had been independent for twenty years; it did not have to prove to the United States or Britain or France its right to exist. On the other hand, the United States was neutral. Even when Britain and France went to war in September 1939, they were half-hearted in their efforts and somewhat disinclined to repudiate Munich. The situation with respect to Russia was even worse. As a result of the Nazi-Soviet Pact of August, it was actually at peace on the side of Germany. And Nazi Germany looked a much tougher enemy than had the Central Powers in the First World War.

The lesson of 1914 was that the support of outside powers was essential to final success and that their support would only be won if the Czechoslovaks were well organised and could offer a contribution to the defeat of Germany. The fact that an old campaigner like Beneš was abroad helped immensely. There were faces missing. Lev Sychrava, for example, the great propagandist of

1914-18, was in a concentration camp. So were some post-war figures, like Krofta or Petr Zenkl, National Socialist mayor of Prague. But Beneš was able to assemble quite a battery of personalities in the West, men such as Šrámek or Hubert Ripka, an outstanding National Socialist journalist. He also had the talent and charm of Jan Masaryk, well known on both sides of the Atlantic. He had the services of most of the legation staffs in Washington, London, and Paris (although the Paris minister caused him some difficulties) and the use of their offices. This was an improvement on the beginning of the First World War. Some of his top civil servants also escaped to the West to participate in the struggle, though others were less fortunate; from the former presidential chancellery Jaromír Smutný got away, but his superior, Emil Sobota, was imprisoned and eventually tragically murdered.

Beneš therefore had a political organisation from the start of the war. Yet as in the First World War, it suffered somewhat from internal tensions. Hodža came to London; but the suspicions concerning his pre-Munich activities were now so widespread that he could not really take an active part in the new movement and went off, on his own preference, to the United States. Initially, the Communists were an even greater problem. Gottwald himself and several other key figures escaped to the Soviet Union and fell in with Soviet neutrality. One or two others, like Zápotocký, were captured while attempting to escape. Another group went briefly to Paris before joining the leaders in Moscow. Finally, a small group including the Slovak Vladimír Clementis ended up in London. Beneš had discussions with both the Paris and the London groups with a view to winning their co-operation. However, the Paris group in particular were prepared to co-operate only if Beneš transferred his exile headquarters to Moscow to await the great communist revolution that would come in the wake of European exhaustion in war. Beneš could not be party to a one-sided view of the future and in any case he expected that the Soviet Union would be drawn into the war, willy-nilly. The talks failed. The London Communists remained sullenly aside; and all those gathered in Moscow took to attacking Beneš and his colleagues as tools of Western capitalism. As Anglo-French fortunes worsened disastrously in 1940, Beneš found himself unable to accept the backing of exiles on the right and attacked by those on the left.

Nevertheless, Beneš was well supported abroad. Most of the Czechoslovak army intelligence group stole over to London. Several generals, including Sergej Ingr and Rudolf Viest, and many officers and soldiers escaped to France where they had old-established contacts with their French opposite numbers. It was much easier to find the nucleus of an army abroad now than it had been a couple of decades before. But Beneš was very much aware of the need for support at home since, in the end, that had been crucial in the First World War. Here the situation was most difficult. Munich had virtually destroyed public confidence in Britain and France and had seriously undermined Beneš's personal position. The events of March 1939 and Beneš's speedy reaction to them did do something to restore his prestige, but little to renew the credibility of Britain and France. The guarantee given to Poland contrasted with the betrayal of Czechoslovakia, and its irrelevance to the defence of that country in September 1939 was treated with cynicism and even with glee. Their confrontation with Germany went some way to revive respect for the two Western powers. But rising confidence on one score was seriously offset by disillusionment on another. Czechoslovak Communists might be able to follow and approve the motives of the Russian government in signing the Nazi-Soviet Pact, but the great majority of the people were puzzled and afraid of the consequences. The partitioning of Poland by Germany and Russia, the wasted months of the 'phoney war' when Britain and France seemed to be more anxious to get back to peace than to enter the fray, and Hitler's subsequent triumphs were factors accelerating the decline of domestic morale. Those who felt confident enough, or who had sufficient courage, went abroad, if they were not first arrested and put in prison or shot. March 1939 also had the effect of dividing public opinion. Physical separation and differing internal political conditions made Beneš's liaison task with the Protectorate and with Slovakia at least twice as hard.

Resistance within the Protectorate began the moment German troops entered the country. But it was very limited and mainly preparatory. Hitler and Henlein had poured out enough threats for the Czechs to be afraid of what was likely to happen. The leaders of the Sudeten German Party had in fact been preparing basic long-term plans for the expansion of German settlement in the Protectorate and for the absorption or expulsion of the Czechs. Yet the occupation was so sudden and so non-political that the Czechs were taken off-guard by its speed and surprised at its mildness. There were arrests and deportations, but mainly of Czech Communists and German refugees from Nazism. The Gestapo were kept discreetly in the background, and Czechs were employed to make the arrests. In fact the Protectorate retained its own President, prime minister, and government throughout the war. The first Protector was Konstantin von Neurath, Reich foreign minister until February 1938 and a diplomat of the old school. Karl Hermann Frank, perhaps the evil genius behind Henlein, became his deputy, but otherwise the Sudetens were kept out of positions of influence. Gajda, the nearest Czech approximation to a fascist, was given no special support. To some extent, Hitler was improvising and experimenting, but he was above all anxious to exploit Czech resources. The Hermann Göring works, for example, was assisted into the position of controlling most of the Czech armament and steel industries. The entire Czech stock of weapons was seized, but otherwise the economy was run in such a way as to increase industrial output and foreign currency earnings. This meant postponing the customs union originally proposed and offering Czech industrialists a variety of incentives to co-operate. Trade with the West fell off even before the outbreak of war, but there was an increase in trade with the Soviet Union. The result was something of an industrial boom in the period 1939-40 and its continuation, at least in heavy industry, for another winter. Even when the customs union was finally enforced in the autumn of 1940, it gave Czech industry, and therefore industrialists, a special place at the heart of the Nazi new order in Europe. Prices rose faster than wages, which hurt the interest of workers in particular. On the other hand, there were more jobs available, including for their wives; and the Germans did force several wage rises for the lower-paid. In terms of rationing, the Czechs fared little worse than citizens of the Reich. There was no doubt about who was running the show, but Hitler so organised the first two years of the Protectorate that he did not provoke the Czechs into violent or widespread resistance.

All this made it difficult for Beneš to elicit strong support from his countrymen at home. It was not that they had either come to like the Germans or to take real pleasure in the advantages of the Protectorate. It was simply that they were politically dispirited and not yet driven to the point of material desperation. They might make all sorts of symbolic demonstrations of their Czechoslovak patriotism. They certainly hoped and believed that the Protectorate would be destroyed some day and Czechoslovakia be resurrected. But they had no heart for open rebellion and little for secret resistance. By and large they supported the policy of Beran's successor as prime minister, general Alois Eliáš, who anticipated German needs and for some time therefore managed to stave off more extreme demands from Hitler himself and from his Sudeten and right-wing Czech supporters. On the other hand, the activities of the Gestapo and the army and the steady infiltration of the German bureaucracy gradually encroached on what little autonomy remained and stimulated opposition. The struggle for power between Neurath and Frank, and between German and

Sudeten moderates and extremists generally, turned modest Czech displays of opposition into bitter incidents. A peaceful demonstration in Prague on 28 October 1939, Czechoslovak National Day, was met with police violence. The funeral of one of those killed, Jan Opletal, was attended by 3,000 of his fellow students who went on to sing patriotic songs. On 17 November nine officials of the National Student Union, most of whom, ironically, supported co-operation with the German authorities, were shot without trial, and the universities and other places of Czech higher education were shut down. The Czechs were still too cautious to do anything rash. Indeed, the lesson of October-November 1939 was to avoid public demonstrations. But popular bitterness went deep and provoked the disenchantment that was to be the backbone of resistance. It was not long after this that three distinct groups in the underground came together to form a kind of co-ordinating unit, the Central Leadership of Home Resistance, one of whose main functions was to strengthen the link with Beneš. Eliáš, who appears to have kept in touch with Beneš, now began to doubt how long he could play his role of staving off pressure, and, in agreement with Beneš, took more and more steps in favour of resistance.

Even so, Beneš was without some of the support at home that he would dearly have liked. The Nazi-Soviet Pact turned a nascent Communist resistance movement into a dispirited minority attempting to excuse non-resistance with Marxist sophistry. In Slovakia the position of the Communists was different but no happier. They could initially attack the Tiso government and not fear a direct German response, but they were completely hamstrung when the Soviet Union gave it *de jure* recognition. At first there was generally less resistance in Slovakia than in the Protectorate. There was more positive internal support for the new Slovak political dispensation than for the Czech, and German interference was less immediately obvious. Slovakia became essentially the Czech path to the West, particularly through Hungary and Yugoslavia. Many Slovaks, who did not feel like fleeing themselves, used their normal contacts with local officials and with foreign diplomats to help Czech politicians and officers on their way. From the start, however, there were some resistance groups that were either pro-Czech or anti-Tiso. One such group that was both was centred around Ján Lichner, an Agrarian deputy who had for several months been a minister in the autonomous government that followed Munich. He regretted complete separation from the Czech Lands and the ousting of his party from all power, and through a wide network of friends in high places at home and abroad (of a kind just not available to his counterparts in the

Protectorate) he negotiated about Slovakia's future with Beneš in London, Hodža in Paris, and others elsewhere. As a result of betrayal and pressure from Germany, he had to escape abroad in May 1940; but he had provided a useful link and he left others behind to form the nuclei for resistance in due course. As in the Czech Lands, too, the atmosphere was beginning to change. A series of economic agreements, forced on Slovakia in December 1939 and January 1940, put its industry virtually in German hands. And in July Hitler himself compelled Tiso to remove the comparatively moderate Ďurčanský and to promote the now pro-Nazi Tuka. The openly alien tendencies of the reconstructed Slovak government at last gave genuine body to the resistance movement.

For all that, Beneš did not find it easy to claim to represent the whole Czechoslovak people. Quite apart from the different attitudes of Czechs and Slovaks, all that had happened and was happening made much more difficult the whole question of the Czech-Slovak relationship. Hodža and others talked of a Czech-Slovak-Polish federation at the end of the war. Lichner favoured Czech and Slovak equality within Czechoslovakia, but vehemently opposed the old centralist system. The Slovak Communists discussed an independent socialist Slovakia alongside Soviet Russia. But Beneš's talent combined with the fortunes of war to make him at least appear to the outside world to be leader of his people. Hodža went off on his own to America. The Communists sulked on the side with Stalin. In July 1940 Lichner joined Beneš in London. One way and another a united front was maintained abroad, linked with growing support at home. In the meantime, Beneš forged ahead with the task of winning Franco-British recognition. As early as October 1939 he secured the permission of the French government to establish a Czechoslovak army on French soil, and it soon built up to a single division and a sizeable air force unit. In November and December he won Franco-British recognition for a Czechoslovak National Committee. This fell short of his hopes; but whereas the French government was willing to sanction the raising of troops, it was less willing than the British to take any action that might admit to its having been wrong at Munich. So Beneš had to await the fall of France before he could secure the recognition of his committee as the Czechoslovak Provisional Government. The British government made its formal announcement in July 1940 as the Czechoslovak forces from France began regrouping on British soil. There was still some way to go. Britain would not commit itself to the future frontiers of Czechoslovakia and, although noting that the new government was representative, it would not admit legal continuity with the government before Munich. But the search for outside recognition had been more quickly successful than in the First World War.

To that extent, things had been easier. But in the middle of 1940 and over the winter of 1940-41 the situation as a whole was not particularly hopeful. Britain was undefeated but alone. The Provisional Government was recognised, the resistance movement was gathering strength; but abroad or at home, the Czechoslovaks could do little themselves. In the previous war, first the Russians, then the Americans, had lent their support. Now neither was involved. From philosophical conviction, from a specific conversation with President Roosevelt in May 1939, and from the evidence of American action as the war continued, Beneš was confident that the United States would ultimately be involved. There was certainly no doubt about American public or official sympathy for the Czechoslovak case. Shortly after Munich, Czech and Slovak groups in various parts of the United States had begun to arrange sympathy meetings. After the events of March 1939 the former Czechoslovak National Council was resurrected to bring the groups together and to support the Czechoslovak Struggle Abroad, a political and financial organisation which co-operated with Beneš in his activities in Europe. The two organisations had their difficulties; they suffered in particular from differences of view both between Czech and Slovak groups and among the Slovaks themselves on the question of independent Slovakia. The Slovak League, faithful to its view of the Pittsburgh Agreement, stood aloof. Nevertheless, the American Czechoslovaks were successful in building up a favourable climate of opinion that expressed itself in material as well as emotional terms. At the time of Munich, Roosevelt had acted contrary to Czechoslovakia's best interest, and many of his envoys in Europe had been hostile. But Czechoslovakia's eventual plight in face of aggression gradually changed the official American mood. Protected by its neutrality laws and not directly responsible for the Czechoslovak tragedy, it was no doubt easy for the United States government to refuse to recognise the establishment of the Protectorate and the separation of Slovakia. But the friendly mood took a concrete form in the continued recognition of the Czechoslovak legation and consulates in America and the tolerance eventually extended to the American activities of the Czechoslovak Provisional Government. By the spring of 1941 Beneš felt the moment had come to start negotiations for full recognition of his government.

The negotiations came to fruition in July. The United States did not commit itself to any particular frontiers, but although neutral, it did recognise a warring government abroad, and recognised it as definitive, not as provisional. This was a considerable step, at least commensurate with its neutral help to Britain. In fact, United States recognition followed definitive British recognition, also accorded in July 1941. And both followed recognition by the Soviet Union. Beneš had always been convinced that it, too, would become involved in the war. At Munich he had done what he could to keep it out of the wrong war, one in which it would have to face German and even Western might on its own. He regretted but understood the Nazi-Soviet Pact. He regretted Soviet participation in the carve-up of Poland, but saw the advantage of having Russia closer to Czechoslovakia. He regretted the inaction and hostility of the Czechoslovak Communists at home and abroad, but did everything possible to keep open the door for eventual co-operation. In the dark days of 1939 and 1940 it was clearly difficult to bear Communist attacks as well as Soviet neutrality. On the surface, the expulsion of the Czechoslovak minister in Moscow and the dispatch of a Soviet mission to Bratislava were cruel blows. Yet Beneš managed to keep in secret contact with the Soviet government, to assure himself about the safety of those Czechoslovak troops who had fled to Russia through Poland, and even to secure the transfer of some of them to the West. More convinced than the Czechoslovak Communists or the Soviet government that Russia would soon be dragged into the war, he also did what he could, particularly through Robert Bruce Lockhart who was accredited to him, to accustom the British government to the idea of a Soviet alliance. So when Hitler struck eastwards in June 1941 and Churchill offered Stalin all possible support, Beneš was quick to negotiate definitive recognition for his government, a new Czechoslovak-Soviet alliance, and permission to raise an army on the Russian front. Within a matter of weeks the situation had been transformed. The Czechoslovak government in exile was completely accepted by three great powers, of whom two were now locked in combat with Germany and the third was virtually so. By the end of 1941 the United States was also at war, and Beneš seemed, if anything, to have led the Czechoslovak government into a better negotiating position than its predecessor had enjoyed at any time during the First World War.

There was still a long way to go, but Russo-American involvement was to lead inescapably to the defeat of Germany. It was also to have a more immediate harvest. Beneš was able to exploit British concern for an alliance with the Soviet Union, and its conclusion, to get British agreement in August 1942 to the virtual annulment of Munich. Partly for the same reason, he managed to persuade Charles de Gaulle, on behalf of the National Committee of Fighting France, to go further a month later and declare Munich null and void from the moment it had been signed under duress. This was important for the independence of Czechoslovakia and for its frontiers. It was even more important for Beneš, both personally and as a statesman, since it shifted the burden of Munich from his conscience and from his reputation. But Russo-American entry into the war had far more fundamental and far-reaching consequences for Czechoslovakia. In contrast with the previous war, Russia as well as America was still to be in it at the end and was to be at least as important as America in shaping the peace. Both were to remain in Europe and in international affairs generally after the war. The Anglo-French renunciation of Munich, therefore, was the end of a chapter for Britain and France as well as for Czechoslovakia. They were never to be as influential again, certainly in the fortunes of Czechoslovakia. And Czechoslovakia was to face the task of regaining and retaining its independence in the context less of Anglo-French-German relations than of Russo-American rivalry. Internally, too, the situation was to be different. The old left was to emerge greatly strengthened; the old right was to disappear, leaving the centre to meet the new situation alone. In the aftermath of Germany's assault on Russia and Japan's attack on America, Beneš obliterated Munich. But he was also called upon to lead Czechoslovakia into the age of the super-powers and the Cold War.

The Shift to the East

Much that happened in the middle years of the war was of crucial importance for the later history of Czechoslovakia. The German invasion of Russia transformed the attitude of the Communists to resistance in the Protectorate and raised the morale of most Czechs at home and abroad. The hopes and desires of the government in London and the leadership in Prague came together in a growing number of acts of sabotage and subversion in the summer and autumn of 1941. This obviously annoyed Hitler, already worked up by the success of his attack in the east. Something had to be done to teach the Czechs a lesson. The time had also come to advance his racial policy in a showpiece region. One way to do this was to appoint a new Protector, since Neurath was no racialist and was in any case increasingly at loggerheads with Frank. Accordingly, at the end of September, Hitler announced the appointment of Reinhard Heydrich, the Gestapo leader who had been entrusted, among other tasks, with the final solution of the Jewish question. Heydrich immediately arrested Eliáš and had him condemned to death for treason. He began the systematic removal of Jews to death camps and rounded up several hundred of the more important participants in the resistance, including most of the leading figures. He browbeat Hácha; he persecuted the intellectuals; but he wooed collaborative workers and farmers as those most suitable to be assimilated into the Reich. In January 1942 he carefully packed Hácha's government with reliable turncoats, of whom there were sadly enough. He then proceeded to circumvent it by running the country through the body of Czech bureaucrats who took their instructions from a handful of top German civil servants. Finally, he started the process of scrutinising the Czech population as a whole for suitability for assimilation. In sum, he induced bitterness but enforced submission.

This was an unhappy development from many points of view, not least from that of Beneš's government. There was a sense of impotence in face of the suffering of Czechs at home, and a sense of disappointment at the disappearance of the last remaining vestiges of Protectorate autonomy and of bitterness at the collaboration of the few. There was genuine understanding of the traditional attitude of the mass of the Czech people, which was neither to collaborate nor to resist, but basically to live intelligently to fight another day. At the same time, it seemed essential to demonstrate the hostility of the Czechs at home to the regime imposed upon them in order to maintain the negotiating power of the government abroad. Czech agents trained in Britain had been parachuted into the Protectorate before Heydrich's appointment as acting Protector. More followed, and despite some misgivings among resistance workers in Prague a plan for his assassination was allowed to develop. On 27 May 1942 he was injured in a bomb attack, and a week later he died. Retribution was swift and vicious. On Hitler's direct orders, the Gestapo, the police, and the army were all employed in searching out the perpetrators. Thousands were arrested and hundreds shot, frequently whole families. On the flimsiest of evidence the village of Lidice was selected for special treatment. On 10 June its 173 male inhabitants were cold-bloodedly shot in a farmyard; its 198 females were sent off to Ravensbruck concentration camp; of its 98 children, 81 were later killed as racially unsuitable and the remaining 17 placed with German families. Its buildings were burned and flattened; and 26 inhabitants absent at the time were caught and executed later. The agents responsible for the assassination were finally betrayed and died fighting in the Orthodox church of St Cyril and St Methodius in Prague on 18 June. The following day Eliáš was executed, and several days later the 24 adults of the hamlet of Ležaky were also murdered. Before the war was over, the Nazis committed worse outrages elsewhere. But such coolly calculated revenge was almost unique.

In a tragic fashion, scarcely anticipated, the assassination of Heydrich made Czechoslovakia's mark on the international diplomacy of the war. The resistance movement in the Protectorate was penetrated and virtually destroyed for some time to come. Even the Communist network was penetrated. But the name of Lidice in particular caught the sympathy and attention of the still free world and made sure that Czechoslovakia's case for independence would not be forgotten. It certainly aided the negotiations for the annulment of the Munich agreement in the summer of 1942. It also decided the fate of the Sudeten Germans. Czech animosity towards the Sudeten Germans was high enough after Munich and it rose higher still after Prague. But after Lidice it was simply irreversible. The terror was instigated and prosecuted by Germans from the Reich, but many Sudeten Germans openly urged them on. In any case, by that stage it was emotionally difficult to distinguish one German from another. Among the exiles, Beneš had always been an ardent exponent of a reasonable settlement of the Sudeten problem within Czechoslovakia. Munich undermined his faith but did not completely destroy it. He felt that the German minority would have to be reduced in size but not necessarily removed from Czechoslovakia altogether. In any case, in the early years of the war, he had to negotiate with the British who, at every stage, showed a strong interest in safeguarding the position of the Sudetens; that, after all, had been their moral pretext for forcing Munich on him. Unlike the resistance leaders in Prague, therefore, he was neither anxious nor able to advocate expulsion. His moderate policy ran into opposing hostilities. He hoped to include Sudetens in his government abroad, but he found Wenzel Jaksch, president of the Sudeten German Social Democratic Party, unwilling to abandon the idea of a separate Sudeten unit within liberated Czechoslovakia. He tried to persuade his cabinet to accept at least a distinct Sudeten area after the war, but found very little support. As early as May 1941 Ripka spoke out publicly in favour of expelling the Germans. Things changed with Russia's entry into the war. Beneš had less need to look over his shoulder at Britain; and in August 1941 he adhered to the principles of the Atlantic Charter, only provided that they did not establish a German right to self-determination. But things really began to alter as reports came in of the Heydrich regime. Even Jaksch had a change of heart and offered to co-operate without conditions. Yet Beneš had to decline. It was too late for co-operation, too late in fact for his own idealism. The last straw was the butchery that followed the assassination of Heydrich. Beneš himself could no longer stick to his notion of a mixed state; the Germans would have to be expelled. In the summer of 1942 he secured the agreement of Britain to the principle of transfer. The tragedy of Lidice made Czechoslovakia a homogeneous state.

The problem of how to fill the vacated Sudeten areas was in due course to be taxing. In the meantime, there was still the problem of persuading the Soviet Union and the United States. Soviet agreement was obtained at diplomatic level in London in June 1943. The Russians already had an eye on population transfer as a useful instrument for their own east European policy. Anyway, they did not like to be outdone by the British, and still less by the Americans. American agreement, at least to a radical solution, came during Beneš's visit to the United States in May and June 1943. In their emotional way, the Americans were almost more anti-German and pro-Czechoslovak than Beneš. Indeed, everywhere he went, he was royally received. He had several long conversations with Roosevelt and, as an old European hand, was listened to with attention; his views on Russia were especially sought. At the end of it all, Beneš was satisfied, not only that he had won approval for the expulsion of the Sudetens, but that he had raised the standing and enhanced the future of his country. In short, he had achieved the purposes for which he travelled to America. However, he also confirmed the impression with which he set out for the United States, that Czechoslovakia's future was more dependent on the Soviet Union.

Before going to visit Roosevelt, he sought answers to a number of questions about Soviet policy in Europe and elsewhere. He liked to keep himself informed, and it specifically helped his negotiating position in the United States. But he was also well aware of the new balance of power in the world and of the need not merely to win support from both Russia and America but also to know the latest state of play between them, at worst to avoid mistakes, at best to help play along. Czechoslovakia would not profit from the disagreements of its friends. He received helpful replies through the accredited Soviet envoy in London, Alexander Bogomolov. He also enquired whether the Soviet Union would be prepared to conclude a long-term alliance with Czechoslovakia, incorporating a guarantee that neither would interfere in the other's internal affairs. This was the question that was bound to be uppermost in his mind. It was part of his national heritage and personal experience to be aware of the importance of Russia to his country, in particular *vis-à-vis* Germany. Its support would be as necessary after the war as during it. But he was enough of a student of history and politics to be every bit as aware of the Russian tradition of expansion and the communist theory of revolution. Any alliance, therefore, had to have a built-in guarantee against interference. He received an encouraging reply through Bogomolov, to prepare a draft treaty. Accordingly he could talk realistically as well as helpfully in Washington.

Short-term aims apart, everything Beneš told Roosevelt was calculated to contribute to Russo-American understanding. The future of Poland was only one point of dispute. Beneš gave the best possible interpretation of Russian intentions and offered the proposed Czechoslovak-Soviet alliance as a model of how Russia's neighbours, including Poland, could come to terms with it and at the same time preserve their independence and their friendship with America. Roosevelt and his advisers agreed readily, in fact so readily that Beneš concluded that they would not give continuing support to what was then an unreasonably extreme Polish position. This augured well for Russo-American relations, but not for Poland. Despite apparent American support, and despite the powerful Polish-American lobby, the Polish government abroad would eventually have to reach an accommodation with legitimate Soviet ambitions. The message for Czechoslovakia was crystal clear. The United States had helped to give birth to Czechoslovakia both during and after the First World War. It would help to resurrect it during the Second, and subsequently, in balance with the Soviet Union, to maintain it in reasonable independence. However, despite the influence of the Czechoslovak-Americans, who were less numerous than the Polish-Americans, the United States would certainly not back Czechoslovakia against the Soviet Union. Beneš told Roosevelt that he hoped to make a treaty with Russia and that this would involve a certain influence on the internal affairs of his country. Roosevelt approved.

Roosevelt may have been naive in the expectations he had of the Russians. He may have underestimated his own country's quest for empire or his countrymen's sense of ideological mission. However, from Czechoslovakia's point of view, America was very distant compared with Russia. American interest was heart-warming, but Russian proximity stark reality. Roosevelt or no Roosevelt, Beneš had no option but to seek an accommodating alliance with the Soviet Union. There was a further factor. During the First World War Masaryk had been able to capitalise on the great Czech and Slovak trans-Atlantic migration. But the flow had stopped, and the original immigrants and their children were increasingly American. In the Second World War, at least after 1941, the equivalent influence was that of the Czechoslovak Communists in

Moscow. Indeed, their impact was greater. They were not migrants, but politicians temporarily in exile. They had enjoyed considerable popular support, they had continuing links with the resistance, and they had a tremendous sense of mission backed by the revolutionary fervour and growing military success of the Soviet Union. From the very first, Beneš had wanted to include the Communists in his government. In defeat and exile a united front made obvious sense. Czechoslovakia had existed on coalitions,and the situation was unlikely to change immediately. It was Beneš's duty as President to promote coalitions. His personal experience and political views made it easier for him to co-operate with the left than with the right. In any case, Munich and after had discredited the right in Czechoslovakia; and the future seemed to many in Europe to lie rather with the left. Before 1941 Beneš had tried to work with the Communists; after 1941 he still wanted to, and in any case he had no possible alternative.

Some would argue that Beneš was also naive in the trust he put in Russian goodwill. He was always an optimist; and the middle of the war was high-tide for optimism. On his return from America, the British argued against his going to Russia and concluding an alliance. Out of respect for Churchill and Eden he delayed his visit for six months until after the Moscow conference of foreign ministers and the Teheran meeting of Churchill, Roosevelt, and Stalin. But he could not delay for ever for Britain's sake. It was not easy to forget the past. Some of the ministers who had supported Munich were still in the British government and were as unfriendly to Czechoslovakia and as suspicious of the Soviet Union now as they had been then. In military terms Czechoslovakia remained a far-away country, and in relative terms Britain was likely to become a second-class power. In any case, Britain had already concluded its own alliance with the Soviet Union, and Beneš was entitled to think that he was following a pattern of West-East friendship. Finally, even the British government was convinced that his plan was worthwhile when the two conferences made it optimistic too. When he eventually reached Moscow in December 1943, Beneš was received as royally as in the United States. He had a number of meetings with Stalin, all relaxed and friendly. He was in his own way an important visitor, an intimate of Roosevelt, a friendly east European. Even Stalin had his passing moments of humanity and idealism, and after the battle of Stalingrad and the conference at Teheran he could afford to be jocular and generous. Beneš came away with his treaty, much assured; some have insisted, much deluded. There is no doubt that Stalin made a profit. By accepting an alliance, he reassured the Americans and to some extent the British. He obtained a lever for pressure on Poland, and a supporter in applying it. He signed a treaty that could be used against its co-signatory; and if he promised not to interfere in Czechoslovakia's internal affairs, he did not say that he would not work to the same end through the Czechoslovak Communist Party. Yet Beneš made a profit too. He got a written assurance of Soviet non-interference—something in writing he needed. Without it, Czechoslovakia might not have retained its independence down to 1948. He got it within the framework of West-East talks. To him this condition was fundamental. If the talks had led to more lasting co-operation, then his country would have remained independent much beyond 1948. He also secured agreement on several other matters of some importance, although only verbally. For example, Stalin promised that Czechoslovak units would cross their own frontier along with the Red Army, and that the latter would transfer liberated territories to the new local civilian administrations as soon as they could be brought into being. Beneš knew he would have to accept a Soviet alliance; he went to Moscow to get the all-important details settled, if possible in writing. He was a man of diplomatic agreements, not a deluded idealist.

One of the many uncertainties in 1943 was the relationship between the Soviet government and the Czechoslovak Communists then living in Moscow. The Soviet government had amply demonstrated its controlling power in 1939 at the time of the Nazi-Soviet Pact. But in May 1943 it had disbanded the Comintern, for over twenty years its chosen agent for directing foreign communist parties. So in December, Beneš could not be entirely certain who spoke for whom. In negotiating with the Soviet government, he had also to take account of its possible influence on his own Communists. If he could restrain the one, he might curb the other. However, the uncertainty made it all the more necessary for him to talk to the Communists. In contrast with the period 1939-41, they were now in a very buoyant mood. They could run with, instead of against, national feelings at home. They could boast the support of the first country to halt Germany on the continent. They could champion national as well as social revolution; and with Soviet military support, they looked like being successful champions. Late in 1941 they had agreed to some of the London Communists joining what was called the State Council, an advisory body of a fairly representative kind that played the role that would have been played at home by the National Assembly. However, late in 1943, they rejected Beneš's invitation actually to join his government, but at the same time insisted that, before returning home, it would have to be reshaped. Gottwald, of course, was a purist. He it was who had brought the Czechoslovak Communist Party into line with the prevailing Stalinist principles before the war and who had kept it there since. His membership and later his secretaryship of the executive committee of the Comintern had further strengthened his orthodoxy, as had two sojourns in Moscow. He was therefore not the man to temporise with non-communists, and he saw no reason to do so. He knew Beneš to be an experienced politician with an unrivalled reputation at home and abroad. He could not therefore ignore him, and temporarily at least he had to co-operate with him. But he could still attack him, privately and publicly, for his policy of submission at Munich and for his long co-operation with the Eliáš government in the Protectorate; these were easy targets for someone without the responsibility of deciding what to do at the time. And Gottwald could still make demands; after all, it was Beneš who had had to seek him out in Moscow, not vice versa.

However, Beneš went to see Gottwald, not in a spirit of humility or defeatism, but of confidence and realism. Yet, whatever he expected, he clearly found Gottwald and his colleagues in rather a tough mood. This war was different from the previous one and would have to be followed by a revolution, which would entail a great swing to the left and the end of the parties of the right. A network of national committees should prepare the revolution and provide the basis of administration. A national front government should formulate and execute a united post-war policy. It was strong meat. And it brought home to Beneš the real danger of a serious split between the two groups of exiles and, what was worse, of a civil war at home after the war. He himself did not find it impossible to agree in principle. He was disappointed that Gottwald would not consider the merging of the various socialist parties, which would have softened Communist rigidity. But he was prepared to agree that the first prime minister of the national front government should be a Communist, since Gottwald accepted the need for elections within six months of victory to determine who would be the next one. And he saw the other proposals as according fairly well with Czechoslovak traditions in the new historical circumstances. At the same time, he was clearly concerned about how the scheme would work out in practice and about how it would be received by his colleagues back in London. He had come to Moscow determined to bring the Communists into the fold, wanting to work with them, knowing he had to, and anxious to do so on generally acceptable terms. Once there, he was left in no doubt as to their strength and resolution, the difficulty of securing their co-operation, and the danger his failure would involve. If he could not negotiate a common policy between the non-communists in London and the Communists in Moscow, then the

Communists would go it alone with the assistance, clandestine or open, of the Soviet government and the Red Army. The only result of that would be a Communist victory, which he did not want, or a bloody civil war, which he had done so much at Munich to avoid.

In talking with the Communists, Beneš was not living in some idealistic dream-world. In the spirit of 1943 he certainly entertained hopes of them, as of Stalin. But essentially he had to work as much with the reality of Communist prospects, as with that of Soviet preponderance in eastern Europe. He tried to tie them down to an acceptable common policy. Home from Moscow, they might mellow. His efforts had some success; in particular, the agreement on elections was a guarantee that democracy would prevail. Yet even Beneš was not entirely reassured, however much he might preserve his optimism in public. When he left Moscow, he felt that he could really still not rule out the possibility of a civil war.

By the end of 1943 the whole Czechoslovak situation had changed. There was little doubt that Germany would be defeated or that Czechoslovakia would be resurrected. Only the details of the expulsion of the Sudetens still had to be settled. But the future now depended much less on Britain and France than on America and Russia, and much more on the latter than on the former. The balance of Beneš's effort was moving from negotiating for national independence to directing a social revolution. Beneš remained the acknowledged leader of the Czechoslovak people, but as he had previously been undermined from the right, he was now being challenged from the left. Whatever he did had to be accepted as much by Gottwald in Moscow as by Šrámek in London. The aim and pattern of the Second World War struggle was now quite different from the First.

By the end of 1943 the centre of gravity of Beneš's activity had shifted eastwards. So had the centre of resistance inside Czechoslovakia. Within the Protectorate, hatred for Germany was much fiercer after 1942 than before, but it tended to be mainly passive. Lidice reinforced the Czech tradition of living to fight another day, and calculated bouts of Nazi terror acted as reminders. Hitler remained conscious of the urgent necessity of Czech industrial output and so made sure that he never actually pushed the Czech people to the point of open defiance. Despite police harassment, the resistance movement regrouped, but non-communist or Communist, its activities were limited, at least until early in 1945. Indeed, the two main factions took up rather much of their time in rival manoeuvres for post-war position.

In Slovakia, the tide of resistance rose as the war progressed. The faint glitter associated with autonomy faded in 1941 when it involved active participation in fighting against Russia. Troops dispatched to the eastern front began deserting with the first Red Army successes. Within Slovakia, disaffection slowly spread through most political and social groups until it even touched the fringe of the puppet government itself. The Communists, freed from the embarrassment of the Nazi-Soviet Pact, also participated in the growing resistance movement. Fugitives from a dozen occupied countries joined the small partisan groups in an area only loosely under German control. Agents were parachuted in from Britain and Russia. There was no consolidated organisation, and initially there was wide variation in aim, apart from the defeat of Germany and the overthrow of Tiso. At one extreme, Šrobár, old hand from the first republic, favoured the reincorporation of Slovakia in Czechoslovakia on pre-war centralist terms. At the other, local Communists talked loosely about a Slovak Soviet Republic. Up to 1943 Beneš's main concern was to guarantee the resurrection and maintain the integrity of Czechoslovakia. This meant that he constantly re-emphasised Czechoslovak nationality and put to one side any detailed discussion of future Czech-Slovak relations. However, while he was securing general agreement to the unity of the Czechoslovak state, he found he also had to give some consideration to Slovakia's specific position. So too had Gottwald while awaiting Beneš's arrival in Moscow. Developments in Slovakia forced the pace. In February 1943 a group of Social Democrats, led by Juraj Kapinaj, worked up a memorandum for Beneš that basically declared their loyalty to him and to the idea of a return to the first republic. In August, Šrobár called a meeting of senior Agrarians, army officers, and even the chairman of the Slovak diet, and sent Beneš a message in effect promising the overthrow of the Slovak government, the establishment of a national committee in the fashion of the First World War, and the establishment of Czechoslovak unity on 1918 lines. However, several younger Agrarians, notably Jozef Lettrich, took a different view. They saw that the experience of the previous five years had given the Slovaks a taste for, at the minimum, equality with the Czechs, and a strong feeling for social change to bring Slovakia out of its backwardness. They were therefore prepared to negotiate with the Communists. In July 1943 Gottwald sent Karol Šmidke and Karol Bacílek as special advisers to the Slovak party. Bacílek was arrested, but Šmidke worked with two local men, Gustáv Husák and Ladislav Novomeský, to set about building a new central committee and a new party policy. Away from Moscow, they were subject to the same pressures as Lettrich. If the Communists were to make a major impact, they would have to abandon all thought of a Soviet Republic. On the other hand, there was a middle course that would bring them wide support. In September they entered into an agreement with Lettrich and his colleagues; three from each group formed a Slovak National Council charged with the task of preparing a common programme for liberation. By December, when Beneš and Gottwald came together, the new Council had its plan ready. It would do everything it could to free Slovakia; it would seize power and hold on to it until new representatives could be elected; it would work along with the Czechoslovak government in London and with the whole movement abroad. Its aim was a Czech-Slovak society in a state of Czechs and Slovaks joined together on a basis of equality. In its foreign policy it would be friendly with all Slav states, above all the Soviet Union. It would build a democratic society with social and economic justice for all. It would maintain religious toleration but prevent ecclesiastical interference in the government and policies of the state.

The Slovak National Council agreement was quite a remarkable document. Tiso's government was clearly disintegrating; it was unpopular and kept in power only by the military force of the nearby German army. It had failed essentially because it was an extremist answer to the Slovak problem. Other somewhat extremist answers were on offer, a return to pre-war conditions or a Soviet Republic. What emerged through Lettrich and Šmidke, through the unlikely combination of an Agrarian and a Communist, was a compromise tailor-made for genuine Slovak needs. It was bound to win widespread support in Slovakia and to make an impression on the exiles. In the Moscow talks, Beneš was reluctant to abandon his formal position of trying to restore the pre-war relationship, since, in agreement with his Slovak ministers in London, he had given his backing to Šrobár's plans. But under pressure from Šmidke, Gottwald went a long way to meet the Slovak National Council's views. However, after conferring with his ministers and weighing the advantages of the Slovak National Council agreement, Beneš finally gave it his blessing in March 1944. The Lettrich-Šmidke axis had succeeded, at least in principle, in securing a change of position for their fellow countrymen in the post-war republic.

They had also succeeded in putting additional fire into the resistance movement in Slovakia. They won further recruits themselves and aroused other groups to greater action. Slovakia had finally found its soul. In that sense, the war was the making of the Slovaks, but Slovakia also became a centre of exile and foreign controversy. Beneš was the acknowledged leader of the Czechoslovak struggle. He was determined to remain leader, and determined to lead, all the more so after his meetings with Stalin and Gottwald. He therefore did everything possible to assert his position in Slovakia and to encourage the resistance to effective action. Early in 1944 the Šrobár group selected lieutenant-colonel Ján Golian, regional chief-of-staff at the army headquarters in Banská Bystrica, to be its military commander and to prepare a revolt. In March, Beneš reminded it of his presidential standing by approving Golian's appointment and his preparations for an uprising. The Slovak National Council was also looking for army support and alighted on Golian. It came to terms with him in April, but was dismayed to find that he still took orders from London. The Council was willing to co-operate with Beneš, but not necessarily to be subject to him in the field. Beneš continued to send Golian instructions. So, in June, the Council established a military council made up of two politicians and two officers, one of them Golian. This did not deter Beneš; he appointed Golian military commander of all Slovak resistance forces and gave further encouragement to the proposed insurrection.

If there was to be a rising, the moment was obviously approaching. In its westward drive, the Red Army was getting nearer the Slovak frontier. Towards the end of June it began a vast new offensive aimed at clearing Russia and entering Poland, and its southernmost wing passed through Lvov before July was out. In August the Warsaw rising began. Red Army officers were already operating with some partisan units, and their function was clearly to facilitate and prepare for the arrival of their comrades. Golian was also anxious to assist the Red Army; but he was more anxious still that it should assist him. He had fellow officers ready to take over command of the two Slovak divisions in eastern Slovakia and of other military and para-military groups. On behalf of Beneš and the National Council he reached working agreements with some partisans to accept his leadership. He also tried to win the support of the Red Army and in the end managed to make his plans known through the Czechoslovak government and its military mission in the Soviet Union. Militarily, the Russians were anxious to stir up whatever trouble they could behind the German lines. But they seem to have been concerned about the actual preparedness of the Slovak army and about the strategic difficulty of helping it. At least they promised to send arms. Politically, it is impossible to say exactly what the Russians thought. What Golian was preparing on behalf of the Czechoslovak government and the Slovak National Council was a military *coup d'état,* not a communist-style revolution. Golian's allies included right-wing politicians and many of his supporters were from the middle class. On the other hand, Stalin and Gottwald had come to terms with Beneš, and Šmidke with Lettrich and Golian. The war saw the Russians with many strange bedfellows. Certainly they must have had their reservations. Some experienced Ukrainian partisans were parachuted into Slovakia and produced several incidents ahead of plan. Šmidke, flown to Moscow on 4 August as one of two emissaries from the Slovak National Council, did not win agreement to the idea of a rising until 23 August when Gottwald approved it. Stalin was perhaps as determined to be cautious as Beneš to be inflammatory. The Slovak revolt was already a part of politics.

Suspicions were understandable. They were made more understandable by another ploy that emerged in the summer. General Ferdinand Čatloš, Tiso's defence minister, indicated his willingness to bring Slovakia over to the Soviet Union's side, and Šmidke communicated his proposal to Moscow. Stalin was apparently interested; one instrument might be as good as another. Beneš was annoyed at what was a challenge to the standing of the Czechoslovak government. The incident had the makings of a serious rift, but was soon swept aside by events. Golian had prepared two plans. The first assumed that the Slovaks would have the initiative when the Red Army drove for the frontier; there would be a general rising and the two Slovak divisions in the east would open the Dukla pass. The other assumed a premature German occupation, in which case the main aim would be to hold the area around Banská Bystrica. The Germans might have intervened anyway; but the sudden rush of partisan attacks on important communications and the partisan murder of the German military and diplomatic mission on its way back from Rumania forced their hand. On 29 August, with the inevitable agreement of Tiso, the German army moved in in force. Golian proclaimed the Slovak uprising.

It was one of the finest and yet saddest episodes in the modern history of the Slovaks. The National Council ruled from Banská Bystrica for two months. At one time Golian commanded 50-60,000 insurgent soldiers and was assisted by 15-20,000 partisans. The civilian population of central Slovakia participated widely. The British and Americans sent small missions from Italy and such supplies as they could ferry in. The Russians flew in the second Czechoslovak parachute brigade and still more supplies, and in the second week of September the Red Army took the offensive in the Carpathians. Gottwald dispatched Šverma and Slánský, two of his most trusted colleagues, to lend support. The Czechoslovak government sent in general Viest, its deputy defence minister, to take over direct command. Unexampled deeds of heroism were done, and a legend built for decades to come. Yet the uprising was plagued with difficulties from the start. It was the second or defensive plan that the Slovaks had to implement. They had no chance to seize Slovakia and control it; they had no advantage of surprise. They had to defend restricted areas, and it was the Germans who caught them not fully prepared. In particular, the two Slovak divisions in eastern Slovakia were virtually cut off from the rest of Golian's forces at the very beginning of the German attack, and only about a third of their number ever reached him. The Slovaks were also outgunned and out-tanked from the start and eventually outnumbered. They often had the advantage of the terrain, but in sharp contrast to the Germans, they suffered from divided leadership. Šrobár manoeuvred for power within the National Council, of which he became joint chairman with Šmidke. The Council rejected František Němec, the civilian minister whom the Czechoslovak government sent out to represent their interests in Slovakia; Šmidke and Husák found it difficult to co-operate with Šverma and Slánský, their Moscow comrades. In short, the men on the spot did not easily accept the exile theorists. Worst of all, the insurgent troops and the partisans did not see eye to eye, militarily or politically, and fought increasingly on different lines. Mounting hardship brought out the greatest extremes of heroism in face of the enemy, but also encouraged mutual suspicion. Divided counsels invited defeat. Unfortunately, there was no greater co-operation outside Slovakia. It took the Soviet government more than a week to react to the fact of the Slovak uprising, and it did so only at the urgent prompting of Gottwald. Even when the Red Army began its drive for the Dukla pass, it made rather slow progress. It did not reach the top until early in October, and by the time Banská Bystrica fell it was not very far through. Russian pressure was crucial to Slovak success, and there were those who said at the time that it was not mounted soon enough or maintained hard enough. Russian supplies were also strangely slow to arrive, unlike fresh partisan commanders and Communist advisers. The British and Americans complained about difficulties the Russians put in their way when they offered to fly in supplies. Certainly, the uprising was sprung prematurely. The Soviet government had not been convinced anyway; and the Red Army was given a tough task and met determined resistance. Anglo-American efforts were mainly directed elsewhere. Whatever the reasons, Russian support was insufficient to save the Slovak rising. The Warsaw rising collapsed at the beginning of October in circumstances of similar helplessness, suspicion, and controversy, and this did nothing to raise the flagging hopes of the Slovaks.

They knew the odds against them and began to fear that they, too, would be left to face them almost alone, as in the end, they were.

Banská Bystrica fell on 27 October 1944. The Germans proceeded to take their inane reprisals: in five sizeable towns there were mass killings; more than sixty villages were burned down, and several thousand people were transported to concentration camps. A number of leaders, including Viest and Golian, were captured, sent to Berlin, and then shot. The uniformed members of the American military mission were also executed. The Slovak uprising was crushed, but not so the Slovak resistance, for before his capture, Viest had ordered as many soldiers as possible to take to the mountains, and they found the partisans already there. Over the winter, they suffered much. Among the more prominent casualties was Šverma. But they greatly harassed the German army and, with the Slovak uprising itself, contributed to the Red Army's victorious advance in the spring of 1945. Moreover, the whole episode left an indelible mark on subsequent Slovak and Czechoslovak history. Whether intentionally or not, the Soviet Union had allowed the Slovak revolt to collapse. When the Red Army invaded Slovakia, it met mainly Communist partisans. This had immediate political consequences and also intensified the suspicions aroused in the autumn of 1944. Bad memories as well as good were to prove important in the political infighting of the coming years; but the basic demands of the Slovak rebels for national, social, and economic justice could never be ignored again for any length of time by politicians of any nationality or party. The Slovaks had lost a battle, but they had found out why they were fighting.

One side-effect of events in Slovakia was the enlivening of the resistance movement in the Protectorate. A more direct consequence was a serious challenge to Beneš's position. His type of Slovak revolt had failed; he had been unable to establish a monopoly of power in a vital part of his own country. Others were contemplating a revolution and hoping to seize power for themselves. The initial challenge came from the Soviet Union on the question of Ruthenia. Its attachment to Czechoslovakia in the first place had been accidental, and its subsequent relationship had been uneasy. Beneš was committed as a matter of politics to the restoration of Czechoslovakia with its pre-Munich frontiers. His fear was that to yield in one area would be to create a precedent for pressure in another; but in principle he had no objection to a different future for Ruthenia, if the Ruthenians wanted it and it was not disadvantageous to Czechoslovakia (as attachment to Hungary in 1939 was). He hinted at changes in Moscow in 1943. He understood the

Russian, or rather the Ukrainian, interest in the area, and after the experience of Munich he rather favoured a common frontier with the Soviet Union. But in 1944 there had been no specific negotiations. He therefore sent Němec on from Slovakia to Ruthenia at the end of October as representative of the Czechoslovak government's authority, and was dismayed when in November Němec ran into difficulties with the Red Army. The Moscow understanding about transferring power from the liberating soldiers to the new civil authorities had been given written form in May; but the reports reaching Beneš showed that the Red Army was in fact helping to set up alternative pro-communist authorities to demand incorporation in the Soviet Union. His protests in Moscow were met with a cynical misapplication of the recently concluded alliance: the Soviet Union could not interfere in what was clearly Czechoslovakia's internal affair. In January 1945 Stalin so far relented as to assure Beneš that, since the Ruthenian people had raised the question, it would have to be dealt with, but that, since he also did not wish to damage the interests of Czechoslovakia, it would have to be settled between the Czechoslovak and Soviet governments. Beneš accepted this procedure, conscious of the fact that he had already lost Ruthenia and that the important issue now was to safeguard Slovakia. What concerned him about the earlier Ruthenian procedure was not so much that it would lose him the territory as that it would act as a precedent. At least there could not now be an immediate transfer of Slovakia to Russia by popular demand. At worst, there would have to be government negotiations. To give up Ruthenia might also placate the Russians and make them less liable to cast their eye on Slovakia. The Czechoslovak government in London saved something of its political position. But the challenge had been quite serious and might come again.

Beneš flew to Moscow in March 1945. Despite pressure from the Soviet foreign minister, V. M. Molotov, he firmly refused to complete the negotiations about Ruthenia before his return to Prague. It was one way of protecting Slovakia. Another was to make it clear that, when he did negotiate, he would not accept any change in the dividing-line between the two areas. His visit to Moscow was partly occasioned by the need to head off another challenge to the position of his government. The attitude of the Moscow Communists to the Ruthenian affair had been ambiguous. There was the chance that, in the wake of the Slovak collapse and the Red Army advance, they would abandon co-operation with the non-communist majority and establish a government of their own. Alternatively there was the possibility that the Soviet government would instruct the Moscow or other communists to put themselves in office. It was not simply a question of power in Slovakia; the stake was more and more obviously the whole of Czechoslovakia. In January Russian troops liberated Košice, in March Banská Bystrica. There was no time to be lost. The Slovak National Council was reactivated in Košice in February and took on itself the running of the freed territory, including the setting-up of national committees. Šrobár and Novomeský shared power; so there was no certainty that the Beneš line would prevail. Nor indeed was there a guarantee that the Communists would not take over. Beneš had to go to Moscow to come to terms with Stalin. As they had agreed, he also had to arrange with Gottwald the composition of a new government. He then had to go on to Košice to establish it on Czechoslovak soil. The only sensible way to meet possible challenges was to go home with a united government. Two members of his London government appear to have counselled him otherwise; but the rest submitted their resignations in readiness for an inescapable trip. In common with Beneš, they recognised that Czechoslovakia would be freed from the east by the Russians, not from the west by the Americans, and that their quickest and only way home was therefore through Moscow. Equally they recognised that they must conclude the best bargain they could with the Russians and the Communists. At one extreme, it might be beneficial; at the other, there was no alternative. Everything had shifted eastwards for Czechoslovakia.

Beneš achieved most of what he wanted to in Moscow; he was received with less deference and saw more of Molotov than of Stalin; but he won important promises. The Soviet Union would supply arms to expand the Czechoslovak army and would not seize Czechoslovak property. There was still considerable cordiality and many reassurances of Soviet non-interference. There were also frequent references to continuing East-West friendship which, to Beneš, was still crucial to the survival of Czechoslovakia, whatever its relationship with the Soviet Union. For their part, the talks with Gottwald produced a united government and a common programme. Both were subsequently much criticised and still provide a subject for historical controversy. But at that stage in the military balance, the most likely alternative would have been a Communist government and a Communist programme.

Inevitably the first decision was to reduce the number of parties. It was not simply that there had been a surfeit before the war. Since Czechoslovakia was to be a homogeneous state, so far as possible, there could be no German, Magyar, or Polish parties. Since the Agrarians had played a treacherous role in 1938-39, and since the Slovak Populist Party was guilty of outright treason, neither of them could be allowed to practise. Only six parties were to be allowed to exist, not an unreasonable number. The decision, however, left some elements of the population not directly represented and also two parties in peculiar opposite positions. There was a Slovak Communist Party as well as a Czechoslovak one. But the Slovak Social Democratic Party, that had merged with the Slovak Communist Party at the height of the Slovak revolt, was not permitted to reappear. In addition, it was decided to include all six parties in the National Front government. It had been the practice of the first republic to govern by coalition; it was the spirit of victory to assume that there could be no parties in opposition. The distribution of offices could not be based on any objective measure and was obviously the outcome of some very tough horse-trading. The new prime minister was Zdeněk Fierlinger, a career diplomat and Social Democrat of twenty years standing. Since 1937 he had been minister in Moscow and, despite the interregnum of 1939-41, he had gradually swung closer to the Soviet and Communist points of view. He was officially on the Socialist left wing and therefore a suitable compromise candidate, as being poised between the two major groups, non-communist and Communist. On the whole, the Social Democrats did badly. Before the war they had been second only to the Agrarians; in the National Front government they won a mere three out of twenty-five offices. Three went to the National Socialists (including Ripka), and three to the Czechoslovak Populists (including Šrámek). Four went to the group christening itself the Slovak Democrats, including Lichner from the London government and Šrobár, now sharing power in Košice. The Communists secured the biggest individual share, a total of eight, four of which went to the Czechoslovak party (including Gottwald) and four to the Slovak (including Clementis). There were also four non-party members of the government, brought in somewhat in the pre-war way as experts. The two most important were Jan Masaryk, who was appointed foreign minister, and general Ludvík Svoboda, who had commanded the Czechoslovak army units in Russia and who was now appointed defence minister. These were balancing appointments; if anything, Masaryk was a westerner, Svoboda an easterner. However hard the bargaining, the final spread of offices showed a rough justice; the Communists had eight, but they were in a minority, which remained true even with the addition of sympathisers like Fierlinger. It was, however, a sizeable minority, and the Communists won the crucial ministry of the interior. On the other hand, six of the twelve members of the London government became ministers in the new one, and the foreign ministry was very important.

Naturally enough, too, nine of the twenty-five appointees were Slovaks. By and large, the government that emerged from the discussions in Moscow was representative of the Czechoslovak struggle abroad and of such minimal direct contact as it had with the people at home. In any case, elections lay ahead.

The programme that emerged was similarly representative. The discussions centred on a memorandum prepared by the Moscow Communists; but the ministers from London and the representatives from the Slovak National Council came well prepared to put their respective views. The most serious arguments concerned the future position of Slovakia and the character of local government, but there were no insurmountable differences. Essentially, both the London and the Moscow groups were responsive to the international situation and to domestic circumstances and moderated what might otherwise have been irreconcilable views. The non-communists agreed to government control of key industries, including power, and of finance, including insurance. The Communists agreed to peasant ownership as the basis of land reform. Certainly, there was much that was easy to agree on: the prosecution of traitors and war criminals, the expulsion of minorities (except in the case of individuals with anti-fascist records), and the confiscation of their property; reconstruction, the expansion of the social services, and an extension of education. There was also the ultimate sanction of elections: an elaborate scheme was devised of first a Provisional, then a Constituent, Assembly. Decisions now could eventually be changed. However, for whatever reason, compromise prevailed. With minor amendments, the proposals for local government were accepted. The Slovak National Council originally wanted a declaration of the equality of the Slovak and Czech nations within the framework of an indivisible state, and recognition of itself as representative of the will of the Slovak people and as both government and parliament for Slovakia. On Gottwald's prompting, it eventually accepted a declaration of the principle of the equality of the Czechs and Slovaks in their mutual relations and of the standing of the Council as national representative of the Slovaks and bearer of the supreme state power in Slovakia. Though something of a retreat and deliberately vague, leaving room for further negotiation, it enabled agreement to be reached on a common policy.

Beneš and his colleagues returned to their country on 3 April 1945. They set foot first in Košice; and significantly, it was there that they announced their new government and its programme. The Košice programme, as it was subsequently called, was essentially middle-of-the-road socialism. Everything would now depend on how it was interpreted and implemented. That in turn would depend on the balance of forces inside and outside the country. As a compromise, it contained the seeds of its own success or destruction. Although a domestic affair, it nevertheless hung on harmonious international relations. The Košice programme stated explicitly that Czechoslovak foreign policy would be based first of all on the Czechoslovak-Soviet alliance and then on a concomitant friendship with all Slav and democratic nations. But it made equally clear that this new orientation would have to be based on friendly relations with Britain, America, and France. In April 1945 that still seemed possible.

The Prospect in 1945

Beneš returned to Prague on 16 May 1945. Czechoslovakia was liberated. He was in fact preceded by his government which reached the city on 10 May. He had led the struggle abroad for the whole of the war, and he was now prepared to assume a presidental role and allow his cabinet more freedom of action. However, they were all preceded by the Red Army, which entered Prague on 9 May. Three weeks before that the American army liberated Plzeň and almost went on to free Prague. But on orders from above, it stopped reluctantly in its tracks. There was therefore no question of who had freed Czechoslovakia and its capital. So neither President nor government enjoyed a really free hand.

In that context, what happened in Prague before the arrival of Soviet tanks was glorious, but unavailing and rather sad. In contrast with Slovakia and the Slovaks, the Czech countryside and people were not formed for large-scale partisan warfare, though there were small groups engaged on scattered raids in the spring of 1945. However, at about the beginning of the year a number of resistance workers came together in Prague to form a Czech National Council, repeating that of the First World War and imitating the one recently formed in Slovakia. At the end of April it organised itself more formally and began to make preparations for a revolt. Its president was Dr Albert Pražák, a professor in the Masaryk tradition; the member who subsequently achieved most political fame was the Communist Josef Smrkovský. Its keynote was courage with caution. There must be a rising in Prague to assist the advance of the Red Army, to drive out the Germans, to round up their collaborators, and generally to help the old city raise its head again; but it must not be summoned too soon. The citizens were almost unarmed; the German army was dangerous with its back to the wall. In time, the right moment began to look like 7 May. But in the event, shortly after midday on 5 May, the radio station started broadcasting appeals for help, and within a few hours there was fighting in the streets. The populace was impatient; some of the militia and police were unwilling to await the orders of a Council that had not yet acquired great prestige. Yet the Council took command, and by the time the Red Army reached the city four days later, the Germans had begun to withdraw. In these four days there were innumerable instances of individual heroism and an exhilarating spirit of defiance on the barricades. But the Germans would have left in any case; and before they did, they had the chance to kill perhaps 5,000 Czechs. They might possibly have wreaked worse havoc if they had been unopposed; but the SS certainly used the opportunity presented by civilian resistance to do some particularly brutal and cold-blooded murder. There were completely innocent children and long-imprisoned political figures who might have survived the last few days of the war but for the revolt. Clearly, pent-up hatred could not be suppressed for ever; and Prague wrote its name in the resistance roll of honour. However, the real tragedy was that, unlike the Slovak National Council, the Czech Council was given no special place in the new political firmament. In contrast with 1918, history had been fashioned from the East.

At the same time, the weakness of the Czech National Council represented more than the firmness of the military and political forces arriving from Košice. Six years of German dictatorship had deprived the Czech Lands of a whole layer of political leaders, some killed, others imprisoned, and yet more discouraged before they ever became involved. Several did emerge from concentration camps to catch up on the experiences and mood of their countrymen. But time was required to train a new layer, and mentors were in short supply. This applied to all social groups. But the middle-class intelligentsia had suffered particularly, so that the new state lacked precisely those who might have done most to implement middle-of-the-road socialism. On the other hand, the events of 1939-45 had made an inroad on the business class. With every year of the war, Germany had increased its economic drain on the Protectorate. As one means of achieving this, it had intensified the concentration of Czech industry that had begun before the war. In the metallurgical industry, for example, 900 firms fell to about 600. Altogether, about 17,000 smaller businessmen lost their independent enterprises. German interests took over many large undertakings either by insinuating members on to their boards or by direct confiscation. This second method was the one employed against the Jews who were said to have owned about a third of the country's assets before the war. At the end of the war, the business class was almost as much German as Czech. Once its German members were swept out by defeat, it was therefore too small a class to offer serious opposition to middle-of-the-road socialism. The expulsion of the Sudeten Germans also contributed to the removal of a property-owning group, as did the veto placed on the Agrarian Party. All this was grist to the mill of the National Front government. Yet an emaciated right threatened to produce an overweening left that might in the long run jeopardise moderation.

In Slovakia the war ultimately produced more political leaders than persecution and retribution eliminated. In addition, German economic policy increased considerably the number of small businessmen since it created a high demand for industrial products and permitted some enterprising Slovaks to acquire confiscated Jewish undertakings. But the number had been so small before the war that this merely helped to correct the previous social imbalance. The end of the war also eliminated the big property-owners who had mostly been German or Magyar. The social spread in 1945, therefore, was reasonably likely to support socialism of the Košice variety. The left also came stronger out of the war, but right and left were united in looking forward to an improved status for Slovakia. It was not precluded, however, that failure to achieve this might result in a division between them on other Košice points.

There were further results of the war that made the Košice programme apt and yet, at the same time, implied possible threats to it. In whatever way the majority of Czechs managed to survive the occupation, or Slovaks the invasion, the war left a fierce hatred of all things German. The new government's promise to expel the Sudeten Germans struck a responsive domestic chord. A state with no more than a tiny handful of loyal Germans also promised to be one that could solve its other problems. It could concentrate on questions of Czech-Slovak relations; it could utilise confiscated property to gain control of its industry, or confiscated land to satisfy the yearnings of its peasantry. But before the government could extend its writ to the whole of the liberated territory, the local population took the law into its own hands in several places and either drove the Germans out and looted their property or subjected them to brutal treatment—behaviour that challenged the whole spirit of Košice. In the economic sphere, Czechoslovakia was left impoverished and dislocated by the war. It did not suffer as much, say, as Poland. But damage to factories from bombing, and to buildings in Slovakia and Silesia from fighting, was serious enough; rail and road transport was reduced to half of its former effectiveness. The economy of the Protectorate, and indirectly that of Slovakia, had been harnessed to Germany's war effort. This increased the output of heavy industry in the Protectorate, but rather retarded that of light industry and building. It also developed mining and the production of chemicals in Slovakia to meet a mainly military demand. So Czechoslovakia was left with an industry, the parts of which were less well-matched than before the war, and the whole of which was unsuited to post-war requirements in foreign trade. The extensive use of labour, the non-replacement of old machines, and sheer worker resistance reduced productivity. In agriculture both productivity and output declined, though this was due more to peasant non-co-operation than to lack of German interest. Finally, all the uncertainties and upsets of liberation brought the economy to the verge of collapse. One way and another, the Košice promise of economic reconstruction was universally welcome. At the same time, it was clearly one that would be hard to fulfil, and just as clearly one whose non-fulfilment might jeopardise the whole balance of post-war forces. The war-time concentration of Czech and Slovak industry and the germanisation or magyarisation of its ownership greatly facilitated its nationalisation under the Košice programme. In the same way, vacant possession made land reform easier than it might have been. Yet both circumstances obviated the need for the returning politicians and the Czech and Slovak public to think seriously what their new socialism was or where it might lead. The gradual appreciation of the unresolved conflict that Košice obscured might impose a greater strain on the National Front government than it could bear, whatever the intentions of the various groups comprising it.

For the majority of Czechoslovaks at home the war was a long and humiliating emotional experience, all the more so coming on top of Munich. Liberation in 1945 was a sudden emotional release. Everything was wonderful. Beneš had wiped clean the stain of Munich. Germany was defeated. West and East were allied in victory, and both gave their support to Czechoslovakia. America had abandoned isolationism; Russian communism was mellowing. There would never be another Munich; and there was nothing else to fear. Gottwald had returned with the same programme as Beneš. Czechoslovakia could pick the best of West and East, of liberalism and communism. It could construct a new future free of the international dangers and internal wrangles of the past. Much has since been written of the blindness that Beneš is supposed to have shown, or the evil that Gottwald is supposed to have concealed, or vice versa. Neither was either blinkered or wicked. Both had their illusions and their aspirations. But both felt that liberation was a great opportunity, and that the Košice programme would be widely beneficial. So, with similar illusions and aspirations, did the majority of their countrymen. The fine-sounding phrases of the Košice programme suited the public mood. Those who had collaborated one way or another were now less happy; Hácha died in prison before he could be tried. There were also some who felt that the war had made Beneš go too far, or that Gottwald had not used the war to go far enough. All these people might threaten the middle way of Košice, if the euphoria of 1945 were to pass. The whole public might threaten it, if they were to feel themselves deceived. The war had taught them the art of undercover politics and justifiable sabotage. In fact, something of the public euphoria began to pass quite early. The American army had failed to rescue Prague; Russian soldiers had raped and stolen. Everything would depend on whether the Košice spirit could be put into practice.

CHAPTER 12

From Liberation to Communism

The Implementation of Košice

THE GOVERNMENTS OVER WHICH BENEŠ PRESIDED were, at least up to 1947, remarkably balanced in attempting to implement the Košice programme in both home and foreign affairs. This was the consequence partly of the personalities involved and partly of the suitability of the programme for Czechoslovakia's particular historical situation. The direction of pre-war development and the circumstances of post-war reconstruction both called for a guided democracy, a controlled economy, and a foreign policy based on East-West co-operation. Perhaps 1946 was the high-point. When the breach finally came in February 1948, it was provoked from inside, and impetus was provided by personal disputes and unresolved issues. But the pressure came from outside and began to build up as early as 1947. If compromise was difficult in the world at large, it was out of the question in Czechoslovakia.

For the first few months the provisional Czechoslovak government ruled without any public control over its policy and actions, a normal situation in a liberated country. The situation was remedied in October 1945 with the setting-up of a provisional National Assembly of 300 members. This exercised only nominal control, however, in the double sense that the government employed its considerable prestige to do what it wanted and that the Assembly itself reflected the prevailing balance of power rather than public opinion. Theoretically, the 300 were elected by the three provincial national committees for Bohemia, Moravia-Silesia, and Slovakia. In practice, each of the six political parties chose 40, and the remaining 60 were selected by organisations such as the trade unions or appointed for their individual abilities. At this stage, too, the provincial national committees were not elected, but were selected by district national committees set up in the wake of the invading Russian army and representing either local pressure-groups or the same balance of political forces as the government. The entire system was rather bogus. On the other hand, the National Front government was popular; an assembly

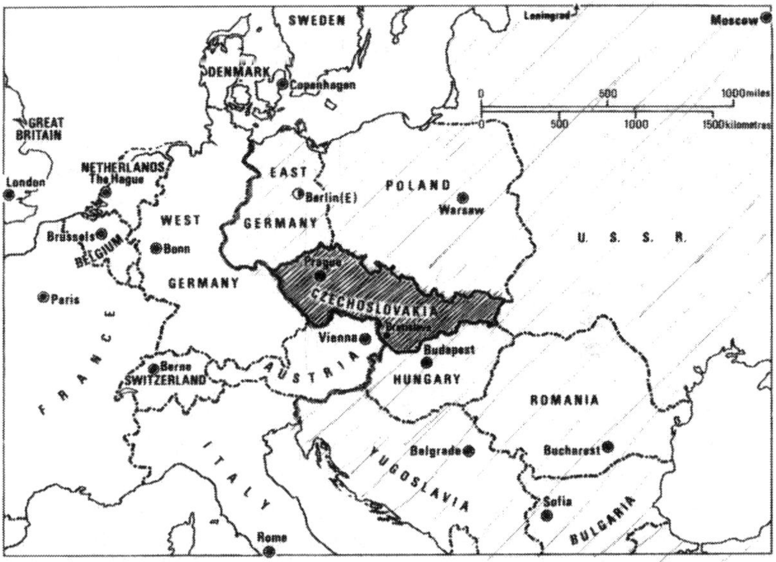

4 The Frontiers of present-day Czechoslovakia

that reflected it, therefore, had some claim to represent the popular will. In any case, it was a major task of the provisional government and the provisional assembly to organise proper elections.

These were held in May 1946. For the most part they followed the customary Western democratic practice. As before the war, voting was by genuine secret ballot; it was direct and based on a system of proportional representation. There were some less happy features. Unsubstantiated charges of wartime collaboration could be used to remove voters from the lists. It was open to voters to opt for the so-called empty ticket if they did not like any of the parties that were standing; but the only parties allowed to stand were those that acceded to the National Front. However, under this procedure, two new Slovak political groups were permitted to put up candidates for election; these were the Freedom Party and the Labour Party, the first winning three seats and the second two. Moreover, the National Front restriction was in conformity with Košice and apparently no particular heartbreak to the majority of the Czechoslovak public. There was a feeling that Czechoslovakia had suffered too much from the pre-war multiplicity of political parties and that the lack of an opposition as such was compensated for by the diversity within unity of a National Front government. It could be influenced to the right or to the left, but it could not be overthrown. In the event, less than one percent of the electorate registered disapproval by voting for the empty ticket. And the actual distribution of seats showed that the system was responsive to changes in the public mood. The Communists emerged with 114 as against the 98 members they claimed in the previous Assembly. This represented an overall rise, but their fortunes varied as between the Czech Lands and Slovakia. The position was distorted by the assignment of more seats in the new Assembly to the Czech Lands than to Slovakia. But the Czech Communist Party now had 93 seats as against 51, the Slovak 21 as against 45. In fact, the Slovak political scene was dominated by the Democratic Party which won 43 of the 69 Slovak mandates.

The new Assembly was innovative in several ways. Its voting age had been reduced to eighteen. It differed from its pre-war counterpart by being unicameral. Yet it remained a constituent assembly whose function was as much to embellish the constitution as to influence the government. It was given two years in which to fulfil its task of construction, but in fact the job was incomplete when the government split in February 1948. The task was a difficult one since the existing constitution was no more than an amalgamation of pre-war laws, exile edicts, and post-war acts. However, both before and after the elections of 1946 new constitutional features assumed importance. The old centralised system of local government had been eliminated by Košice. The new scheme of national committees meant a complete reversal, with much more local initiative. The provincial, district, and local committees took to themselves frequently quite extensive powers and, up to 1946, sometimes acted above the law. There was an improvement, however, in the middle of 1946. Separate elections were still not held, but at all levels the committees were reorganised in accordance with the results of the Assembly elections. This made them somewhat more representative and rather more responsible and opened up the possibility of a real improvement on pre-war days.

One thing the new constitution-makers did not have to deal with was the minorities question. The great powers finally approved the orderly transfer of the Sudeten Germans at Potsdam in July 1945. Within fifteen months the complicated process was virtually complete and only about 200,000 Germans in special categories still remained. The number now is not very much more than half that. There was therefore no special need for the protection and representation of the most troublesome minority. On the other hand, the question of Czech-Slovak relations had become more pressing. The Košice programme deliberately left much that was vague. But the Slovak National Council immediately began to act as the supreme legislative authority, except in all-state matters where it accepted the authority of Beneš to legislate in agreement with itself. It also appointed a board of commissioners to act in effect as a Slovak government. There were obviously several ways in which the equality of the two peoples could be given effect. But this particular outcome seemed to challenge the Košice balance. In negotiations between the Czechoslovak government and the National Council in June 1945 a list was drawn up of twenty major all-state matters in which the Council was allowed no say, and the position of the board of commissioners was reduced to that of an executive. Nevertheless, the Council enjoyed greater power in Slovakia than any comparable body in the Czech Lands. It acted as the provincial national committee, and it performed a much more active function than either of its provincial counterparts in Bohemia and Moravia-Silesia. However, a year later there was another change. The reorganisation of National Council membership after the elections to the Assembly converted a slight Communist majority to a sizeable Democratic one and added Communist distrust to old-established Czech susceptibilities. A new agreement of June 1946 gave the government in Prague the almost unrestrained right to decide which matters lay within the competence of the National Council, to approve the appointment and actions of the commissioners, and to make all senior administrative and legal appointments. On the other hand, the Slovaks were left with the guarantee that there could be no constitutional change affecting Slovakia without the agreement of a majority of their sixty-nine representatives. It was not a permanent answer, nor a particularly happy one. But the problem of Czech-Slovak relations was an old one not capable of lightning solution; the Košice formula was deliberately evasive; and the settlement of June 1946 at least prevented an open breach between Czechs and Slovaks or within the government. Progress was still possible.

There were allegations both then and later that politics in the post-war years had little to do with constitutional forms and practices. This was true in the fundamental sense that Košice had laid down guidelines from which there could be little deviation. Up to a point it was true in other senses as well. The first Czechoslovak republic had inherited a bureaucratic tradition from the Habsburg Empire. Civil servants were powerful and patronage was fairly widespread. Since few Communists had been patronised, it was inevitable after 1945 that the Communist Party should seek to make good its deficiency in influence. The result was not only a swollen civil service, but one that was highly politicised, leaving ministers and deputies with sometimes less, sometimes more, power than was properly their due. The new army, organised around the Czechoslovak forces that had fought on the Russian front, was also more political than its predecessor. Its two top men, general Svoboda who was defence minister and general Bohumil Boček who was army chief-of-staff, were both easterners though not Communists. General Heliodor Píka, who was deputy chief-of-staff, was a westerner, formerly head of Beneš's military mission to Moscow. The air force was mainly western-trained and commanded by westerners. Yet though politics were played by the armed services, one influence tended to offset another; and the President exercised a controlling involvement in senior appointments. After the experience of wartime, the police were in need of some weeding-out. The man responsible, as minister of the interior, was Václav Nosek, one of the diminutive body of London Communists, who established the new National Security Corps and overstaffed it with political sympathisers. He instituted various small and rather more clearly political forces, but withdrew most of them under non-communist pressure. Nosek did not really go as far as his detractors alleged or as his political masters may have wished. But he certainly gave the police something of an extra-legal role in Czechoslovak politics. His activities were curbed, however, by the vigilance of the ministry of justice, presided over by the National Socialist Prokop Drtina. Indeed, unconstitutional political interventions appeared by and large to cancel each other out. As much as anything, they were growing-pains.

There was one particularly new political force in post-war Czechoslovakia whose activities had constitutional standing. Trade unions and strikes were nothing new. But the trade union movement as a whole in the inter-war period was incredibly fractionalised. The nearest it came to cohesion was the linking of about 500 of its 700 unions in some nineteen districts. The trouble was that the craft principle still operated and that in addition each political party and nationality felt it had to have its own union in every craft; but the experience of the Protectorate changed things. The Nazis reduced the number of unions to two, one for private, the other for public, employees. This showed the drastic steps that could be taken, but also illustrated the continuing danger of division where even two unions could be played off against each other. The strengthening left-wing atmosphere among resistance workers at home and the leftwards swing of the struggle abroad gave the final push. The Košice programme made provision for a united trade union movement and promised it official standing as guardian of the interests of the working class. In April 1946 the separate Czech and Slovak movements were brought together to form the United Revolutionary Trade Union Movement with its own central council and with the right to participate actively in executive and legislative discussions on labour matters and to be represented on all public bodies that were not elected. Factory branches were also given virtual control of factory councils, a new feature in the running of Czechoslovak industry, and in that way acquired access to factory militia, groups of armed workers first deployed against the beaten Germans and never stood down. The trade union movement, therefore, exercised a considerable and constitutionally quite proper influence on the development of industry and on working conditions. Occasionally it had its disagreements with officialdom, as with employers; but by and large it reflected the composition and attitudes of the government. Its president was Zápotocký, the veteran Communist; its general secretary was Evžen Erban, a Social Democrat; its policy was Košice. However, particularly with its access to force, it had the makings of a threat to the middle way.

Mass organisations were something of a feature of the new Czechoslovakia. The Union of Freedom Fighters and the Union of Czechoslovak Youth were only two examples. All of them played a role in influencing public opinion and, through the political figures associated with them, in shaping government policy, at least within Košice principles. Pressure-groups on this scale are common in most modern societies, and just as extra-constitutional. Indeed, the *Sokoly* and the Legionaries had established the tradition in Czechoslovakia long before 1945. What had kept the pre-war pressure-groups under control and what did the same for those emerging in 1945 was the free expression of individual and collective views. All the post-war political parties had their own newspapers; there was no censorship of the press. Many organisations had their political journals; there was no censorship of books. To that extent there was freedom of the written word; there were many battles between, say, *Rudé právo* and the National Socialist *Svobodné slovo* (*Free Word*). Yet only National Front parties and approved organisations were allowed to publish, and no individual or group of individuals could set up business on their own. Criticisms were also expected to be within the Košice framework, though that usually left ample room for manoeuvre. Censorship by restricting the supply of newsprint was possible and was occasionally said to have been exercised by Václav Kopecký, the Communist minister of information. As before the war, broadcasting was in the hands of the government, and here again there were frequent allegations concerning Kopecký's bias. However, the fact that the allegations could be made was witness to overall freedom of expression, and so long as it could be sustained there was no great danger from the pressure-groups. But obviously the situation was delicate.

For two years this hybrid Czechoslovak semi-constitution worked. It survived the elections of 1946 despite the allegations of Communist intimidation and bribery in the Czech Lands and of Catholic subversion in Slovakia. It produced a new government after the 1946 elections. Gottwald replaced Fierlinger and the Communists acquired nine as against their previous eight portfolios. Yet though both membership and leadership were more obviously on the left, policy did not immediately change. The years 1945-47 saw the steady implementation of the Košice programme. 1945 was a period of recovery made possible with much internal effort and the generous assistance of UNRRA and the next two years witnessed considerable industrial progress. Taking 1937 as the base year with an index of 100, industrial production stood at 50 in 1945, 69 in 1946, and 88 in 1947. The rate of progress varied, being greater in the Czech Lands than in Slovakia and more marked, for example, in chemicals than in textiles. The advance in agriculture was perhaps more noteworthy. In 1946 output was between 80 and 90 percent of the pre-war level and, but for a disastrous drought, the percentage might have reached the 100 mark in 1947. In foreign trade, comparisons with pre-war are impossible to obtain, but its value doubled between 1946 and 1947, although a reasonable surplus was converted into a slight deficit. One way and another, the whole economic performance was quite impressive. In appraising it, the drop in population must be taken into account. The pre-war population of about 14½ million in the Czech Lands and Slovakia had been reduced by almost 2½ million by 1947. Industry had to operate with a much smaller labour force and, apart from several thousand key workers who were allowed to remain, had to run the former Sudeten factories without Sudeten employees. Sudeten industry, too, had been particularly high on the list of exporters. On the other hand, there were fewer mouths to feed and a smaller agricultural output went further. In sum, industrial growth was all the more remarkable and agricultural growth, at least to the end of 1946, quite sufficient.

Some of this success was the result of old-fashioned measures like the currency reform of November-December 1945. Some of it was attributable to nationalisation. Decrees issued in October 1945 nationalised all banking, finance, and insurance, and altogether some 60 percent of manufacturing. Heavy industry was almost wholly nationalised, food-processing only partly so; in-between it depended on the size of the plant or on the number of employees, the limit being in the region of 400. Through the ministries of finance and industry the government exercised a supervisory function; but the new national enterprises were run by regional and managing boards appointed by the government in consultation with unions and other interested parties, and they were mostly expected to operate on a competitive basis. At the worker level, factory councils ensured at least some participation by unions in management. Government interest remained powerful, however; without it, rationalisation might not have been as extensive as it was—in the chemical industry, for instance, some 80 independent companies with about 100 separate factories were reduced to ten national enterprises. And the government took a fairly firm hand in guiding the whole economy. At the same time as reorganising industry, it set up an economic council comprising the appropriate specialist ministers, the governor of the national bank, the president of the trade union movement, and two or three similar functionaries. The council itself established a secretariat, the central planning commission, which acquired a state planning office to assist it. In fact, there was quite a battery of politicians and bureaucrats to lay down detailed guidelines in the public sector and, with the same purpose, to allocate scarce resources to the private. Under this kind of organisation economic growth edged forward through 1946 to fulfil one of the Košice promises, progress through a middle-of-the-road socialism.

But the better life was not as quick in coming as the people had expected and the government had hoped. There was therefore pressure to speed things up. Košice had said nothing about a planned economy. But planning had supposedly accelerated the economic development of Russia, and it was even being discussed in the West. An elaborate apparatus was already in existence, and in the course of 1946 it produced a report whose information and conclusions could easily be adapted to construct Czechoslovakia's first economic blueprint. In October 1946 a law was enacted that set in motion a two-year plan designed to raise industrial and agricultural production to respectively 110 and 100 percent of their prewar levels by the end of 1948 and to correct the imbalance between different sectors of the economy and different areas of the country. It was an ambitious exercise, exceeding but not contravening Košice, and it added a further stimulus to expansion. It undoubtedly contributed to the continuing industrial growth of 1947.

Nationalisation had a social as well as an economic end. The reallocation of property was intended to destroy the business class (although its Czechoslovak members were given compensation). Another such action was the programme of land reform. The first stage was begun immediately after liberation: the transfer of land confiscated from the Sudetens, the Magyars, and such Czechs and Slovaks as were proved or deemed to have been traitors. The area confiscated amounted roughly to 25 percent of all agricultural and forest land. Most of the agricultural land went to individuals in lots of from 8 to 13 hectares, and the greater part of the forest to the state forest administration. The lucky individuals had to pay the state an amount varying from the equivalent of one to the equivalent of two harvests within 15 years. The second stage came in an act of July 1947, revising the land reform of the first republic. Among other things, this made it possible to confiscate land in excess of 50 hectares, and it has been estimated that a further 4 percent of all available land was transferred in this way in lots of from one to 2 hectares. Acts were also passed to reduce rents, to prevent excessive subdivision of farms, to transfer uncultivated properties, and to help small farmers with machinery. On balance, the whole programme was a sensible if short-term and, to some, unhappy solution to the problem of inequality in the countryside. Unfortunately, much remained to be done. And this was true in other areas of social improvement. There was talk of bettering pre-war social insurance, but it was 1947 before a joint commission of the United Revolutionary Trade Union Movement and the National Front sat down together to hammer out proposals. However, the promise of a comprehensive social policy, made at Košice, was clearly on its way to being honoured.

From the very beginning Czechoslovakia adhered to the foreign policy set out in the Košice programme. Genuinely friendly ties were developed with the Soviet Union and, internationally, nothing was done with which it could possibly quarrel. It was not difficult to support the Soviet line. Over Germany, for example, Czechoslovakia was bound to take as tough a stand. If anything, the expulsion of the Sudetens increased its fear of German revisionism and made it even more dependent on its ally. A close friendship with the two nearby Slav states was also built up. In May 1946 an alliance was concluded with Yugoslavia. A *rapprochement* with the Poles was more difficult. Relations between the two exile governments had been very strained and, after the war, the old dispute over Těšín again erupted. It took heavy pressure from the Soviet Union to freeze it temporarily on pre-Munich lines. However, a Polish alliance was agreed in March 1947; and on most general international questions the three small Slav states found it easy to reach a common line. The promised co-operation with other democratic states also went fairly well. Trade and cultural agreements were reached with most of the smaller west European countries, and on a French approach there was even discussion of a possible treaty linked with the Soviet alliance. Czechoslovak-British relations got off to a bad start with a somewhat high-handed demand for compensation in pounds sterling for nationalised British properties, but they slowly improved. On the other hand, relations with the United States became a little cool. There was some resentment on the Czechoslovak side that the United States supported Hungary, an ex-enemy state, in its stand against the expulsion of the Magyars from Czechoslovakia, while on the American side there was disgruntlement at Czechoslovakia's implementation of a socialist policy. The mutual disenchantment was unfortunate but not necessarily lasting. On the whole, the National Front government did its best to steer a middle course and had some success. In theory there was nothing to prevent it going on from compromise to compromise and development to development, indefinitely.

The Communist Takeover

On the other hand, the internal situation showed many signs of impending division. Constitution-making was proving difficult. In 1946 one set of elections had produced a measure of polarisation; the next was due to be held in 1948. At some stage there would have to be a decision about elections to the national committees. Czech-Slovak relations were very delicately balanced. There were too many organisations and individuals, not necessarily waiting, but certainly willing, to exploit a changing situation. Economic progress was creditable, but hardly miraculous; and the failure of the harvest in 1947 opened the way for all sorts of dissatisfactions and recriminations. Nationalisation and land reform, tools of egalitarianism, were just as much the source of bitter rivalry over patronage. In short, there were numerous ingredients of controversy; everything would depend on whether something would provoke it. Something did; and it came from outside.

As Beneš had made clear and as Gottwald knew all too well, the National Front government and the Košice programme depended for their survival, or inescapability, on continuing East-West cooperation. There is much debate as to who started the Cold War, when, and why. But for Czechoslovakia the crucial point was the growing American-Soviet breach in 1947. The declaration of the Truman doctrine in March; the establishment of the Cominform in September; the breakdown of the Moscow talks on Germany in December; these were the signposts on the road to a rupture. Some way along that road, in July 1947, Czechoslovakia had to choose to be on the Soviet side when the break came. Whatever the United States' intentions may have been in launching the Marshall Plan, the Soviet Union certainly interpreted it as a plot to use American plenty to dominate Europe. That meant specifically western Europe, probably eastern Europe, and on the face of it even Russia. Moscow was anxious even to conceal its own statistics from Washington and had not the slightest intention of abandoning any of its economic sovereignty. From Prague the view was different. Czechoslovakia had no secrets and not very much more sovereignty. In relative economic terms it was probably better off than the Soviet Union; but it was not self-sufficient and depended on aid and trade. Aid could make good the damage of a decade, could develop light industry in the Czech Lands and both kinds of industry in Slovakia, and could revolutionise agricultural production; expanding trade would maintain the new momentum. The Czechoslovak government was not made up of blinkered bolsheviks; some even of its Communist members had experience of the outside world and did not condemn the Americans out of hand. So on 7 July it accepted the invitation to send representatives to discussions in Paris where the details were to be settled. But three days later, on Soviet insistence, it declined.

An intelligent Soviet government might have played things differently. It might have allowed Czechoslovakia to accept American aid and then have claimed the credit itself. But Stalin was better known for cunning than shrewdness; and quite apart from his obvious power mania, he was afraid to sanction anything that might tempt Czechoslovakia away from its Soviet alliance. Moreover, in agreeing to a National Front government in 1945, he had gone as far in pursuit of communist objectives as the tactical situation would allow. The situation was now different. The Czechoslovak Communists were an established political force, with prestige and power. They were therefore ready to go further along the Soviet-style road to a communist state by displacing the bourgeoisie. There was, in addition, the danger that, if they did not, the bourgeoisie would displace them. Stalin was as aware of internal Czechoslovak tension as he was chary of American economic intervention; in the few months before the Marshall Plan was announced there was a noticeable drop in Czechoslovak trade with the East and a corresponding rise in its trade with the West. To Stalin it obviously appeared sinister. He turned down the Marshall offer himself; but if he was to save Czechoslovakia from American imperialism, let alone advance the position of the Czechoslovak Communists, then he must force the Czechoslovaks to reject the proposition. A government delegation, led by Gottwald, was in Moscow on 9 July to discuss the possible French treaty and to hold trade talks. Stalin first saw Gottwald; he then informed the whole delegation that Czechoslovakia must reverse its decision to participate in the Marshall Plan negotiations or it would be regarded as having committed an act hostile to the Soviet Union.

Retrospectively, there is no doubt about the seriousness of the decision to withdraw from the Marshall Plan. It is less certain whether the seriousness was appreciated at the time. There was considerable public disappointment; on the other hand, it appeared to be just one in a series of events. At government level, however, there was no doubt about Stalin's meaning. As it was spelled out in Gottwald's urgent report to Prague, it amounted to an ultimatum. Gottwald himself recommended acceptance; Masaryk and the two other non-communist ministers on the delegation reluctantly agreed. After an extended discussion, their colleagues back in Prague agreed, unanimously but not without argument. Naturally it was easier for the Communists to accept the directive than for the others. They had always looked to Moscow; and the Soviet communists were their ideological blood-brothers. Yet it must have been eery even for them to receive an overnight ultimatum reminiscent of the notorious Anglo-French ultimatum of September 1938. Since 1945 they had spoken frequently about a Czechoslovak road to socialism, and most of them had really come to believe in it. They would obviously have to draw heavily on Soviet experience; in the end, they would have to dominate Czechoslovakia, just as the whole communist world would have to overcome the West. But, in the meantime, they saw no reason why they should not take aid from the West, or trade with it, just as they worked along with non-communist parties in Czechoslovakia. Stalin seemed to be challenging their separate path, and it came as something of a shock. It was the non-communist ministers, however, who were least willing to accept. Stalin's action brought to a head all their doubts about establishing the National Front government and embarking on the Košice programme. Alternatively, it presaged the demise of compromise, an end to East-West co-operation and middle-of-the-road socialism. Nevertheless, they accepted the ultimatum. Indeed, they were probably more cross later, when they realised the full implication, than they were at the time. Later, they blamed Beneš who, they said, was too ill to give them a lead. What his state of health was is not clear. But the non-communist ministers knew as well as he did that the risk was there from 1945. And they would have been at one with him in his view that Czechoslovakia was not only between East and West but between

Russia and Germany, so that, whatever else happened, Czechoslovakia must retain the protective Soviet alliance against Germany. In any case, there was always hope that things would improve.

Whether or not the Czechoslovak politicians realised the full significance of what had happened, their reaction to it gave it even more importance. It was bad enough that Stalin had been able to dictate Czechoslovak foreign policy. It was worse that there were some on both sides of the government coalition who read the signs to imply that the time had come for a showdown. In delivering his ultimatum, Stalin suggested a face-saving formula, the new situation arising from the non-participation of Czechoslovakia's east European neighbours. But the establishment of the Cominform in September showed quite unmistakably that there was to be a much tighter Soviet rein in eastern Europe. To sweeten his ultimatum, Stalin also authorised a trade treaty that was signed a few days later. In September, and again in November, he ordered grain to be sent to offset the bad harvest. But when the trade treaty was negotiated in detail in December, it became clear that over the next five years Russia was to become Czechoslovakia's biggest trading-partner. The Marshall Plan fiasco convinced some extremists on both sides that the time had come, in their own interest, to put an end to the coalition. Everything that happened subsequently strengthened their conviction, and they began to work towards a breach. The feeling also spread. The elections were due in April 1948. The Communist Party had done well in the previous ones, partly on the strength of the post-war recovery. According to opinion polls, however, they were now declining in popularity. As the biggest influence in the National Front government, they naturally suffered for the deterioration in East-West relations and, more particularly, for the disastrous harvest. As they interpreted their own special road to socialism, they could come to power by the electoral process, but certainly not fall from it. They therefore began to place more reliance on non-parliamentary techniques of government. Conversely, their opponents looked to the coming elections with increasing fervour and at the same time jumped to the meticulous defence of the parliamentary system.

From July 1947 onwards the political tension mounted steadily. When it became apparent towards the end of August, for example, that it would be necessary to subsidise the peasantry to save them from financial ruin and to rescue agriculture from economic stagnation, the Communists proposed a special contribution from the propertied, which they cleverly called a millionaires' tax. Their calculation as to who were millionaires went so low in terms of property and income as to threaten the whole spirit of Košice, and their scheme would not have netted the money they claimed it would. In September it was defeated in the cabinet. The Communists thereupon launched a campaign against all the non-communist ministers who had turned down their plan, bitterly attacking them for defending millionaires. In so doing, they secured the crucial support of the Social Democrats who were swayed by the persuasiveness of Fierlinger. But their breach of confidence forced the uncharacteristic public intervention of Jan Masaryk, and they lost as much as they gained. Also in September bombs, later traced to Communist sources, were sent through the post to Masaryk, Drtina, and Zenkl. None of them was hurt; but though he was minister of justice, Drtina was thwarted by Nosek's police at every juncture as he tried to bring the culprits to trial. Yet once more the Communists scarcely profited. Terrorism was alien to Czechoslovakia, and the National Socialists in particular were able to pose as the champions of non-violent parliamentarianism.

The Communists then turned their attention to Slovakia. Since the political settlement in June 1945 relations between Prague and Bratislava had been occasionally good, but frequently uneasy. The two-year plan had provided for a much higher growth-rate for Slovakia than for the Czech Lands. The aim was to make the Slovak level of economic activity comparable with the Czech in both industry and agriculture. Machinery was transferred and capital pumped in; particular emphasis was put on the exploitation of hydro-electric power and raw materials like iron and timber and on the development of transport. Progress was already obvious by the autumn of 1947. There were some well-founded complaints, however. Slovakia was short of skilled labour; and until more could be trained, the deficiency was made good by importing Czech specialists—an old sore. By contrast, the Czechs were short of unskilled labour and were more than delighted to draw Slovaks away from their homes. There were also mixed feelings on the whole question of industrialisation. The Communist Party and the Catholic clergy held opposing views on the virtue of transferring the mass of peasants from the godliness of the countryside to the worldliness of growing industrial cities. Equally, the Communist Party and the Slovak Democratic Party adopted different viewpoints on the desirability of financing almost all the new Slovak projects with public money. In the early part of 1947 there had also been tension over the conviction and execution of Father Tiso. There were enough Slovaks around who mourned some of the better aspects of the Tiso regime, or who simply disliked the regime that had followed it, for there to be a campaign for the exercise of mercy. To many others it looked strangely like Prague's revenge. The Slovak Democrats found themselves in a serious dilemma; they had fought against Tiso, but they were becoming disenchanted with Prague. When the cabinet discussed the clemency issue in April, they, along with the Populists, formed the small minority in favour of mercy. They therefore exposed themselves to public allegations of protecting traitors. The subsequent attempt of the Slovak National Council with its Democrat majority to dismiss the judge who had tried Tiso led to equally damning allegations of attempting to destroy the principle of judicial independence. Matters came to a head in the autumn.

Dissidents from the Ukraine and Poland had been passing through Slovakia on their way to west Germany for some time. Their mere presence incited some of the local population to acts of defiance, and occasionally they themselves joined in. This was something that annoyed most Czechs and many Slovaks, and the Communists seized their opportunity. From the middle of September the police and the army began making arrests. They also discovered an extensive network of spies in contact with Slovaks abroad who had served the Tiso regime. Ján Ursíny, chairman of the Slovak Democrats and a vice-premier in the government, seemed to be involved and resigned. Two Democratic secretary-generals proved to be directly involved, and proceedings were instituted against them. Although they had cabinet support, the Communists opted to make an extra-constitutional matter of it all. Trade unionists and ex-partisans throughout Slovakia were assembled for mass meetings to demand the expulsion of the Democrats from the Slovak board of commissioners. A meeting was summoned of the Slovak parties in the National Front and attended by representatives of workers, peasants, and freedom fighters; the Slovak Democratic Party stayed away, but the meeting still demanded a reorganisation of the commissioners. The same manoeuvre was attempted in Prague, but all the non-communist parties absented themselves and the whole thing failed. Undaunted, however, the Communist members of the board of commissioners resigned and Husák, its chairman, declared it dissolved. As reconstituted by the National Front government in mid-November, the board represented both victory and defeat for the Communists. The Slovak Democrats lost their majority, but the Communists did not inherit it. The balance was held by the Freedom and Labour parties. The Communists' tactics had therefore profited them up to a point. But the non-communists took comfort from a system of government that was tough and resilient enough to blunt the determined assault that had been made on it. The fight was on.

In one sense, the Slovak Democrats were a powerful obstacle to Communist ambitions. They were a popular party with an entrenched position. In another sense, they were extremely weak. They had come together at the end of the war, an alliance of patriotic ex-Agrarians and enlightened Catholics, their main bond the national struggle against Germany. After the war that bond weakened; and their failure to strengthen their autonomy tended to reactivate their former differences. While one group behaved responsibly, another smaller one flirted with subversion and handed the Communists most of the chances they wanted. From all this the non-communist parties generally learned that unity was essential if they were not to be outmanoeuvred as well as outvoted. It was such unity, exercised in the cabinet, that prevented the Communists winning completely in the matter of the Slovak board of commissioners. Similarly, it was in part the need for such unity that drove the Social Democratic congress in Brno in mid-November to elect as chairman, not Fierlinger, the candidate of the extreme left, but the moderate Bohumil Laušman. Yet if the non-communists could learn, so could the Communists. And what they saw was that they might not be able to rely for the attainment of full power on parliamentary means; they must resort as well to guile and to pressure-groups. Several Czechs were arrested on trumped-up charges of espionage for the Americans; a campaign was begun for the inclusion of non-political organisations in the National Front. 1948 opened with the Communists seeking to discredit and undermine their opponents, and the non-communists trying to pull themselves together in preparation for the elections.

A crucial point was the date of the elections. The Communists wanted to leave them to the last possible moment, which was in May. They claimed to be confident of winning a majority, so that this time they would form the largest single party. Yet there were several predictions to the contrary, and they may well have been anxious to play for time. They were also eager to see the task of constitution-building completed so as to be able to take the right kind of package to the country, first to win power and then to use it as they wanted. The constituent assembly had certainly been given the assignment, but the parties could not agree on a number of big issues of central and local government and of social and economic policy. The Communists may well have anticipated that with a little extra time they could bring the others round to their viewpoint by force of argument or with the aid of pressure-groups. The majority of the non-communists, however, took the opposite view. They wanted the elections in April. They saw their own popularity at its height and they wished to capitalise on it while they could.

They were also afraid that the new constitution might be to their disadvantage, and they were convinced it would be against the wishes of most of the public. They therefore felt it in their own interest and that of the Czechoslovak people to go to the polls before the die was cast. A meeting of the National Front on 5 February could not agree on a date, and the two sides became more divided and resentful than ever. The debate turned to policies on agriculture and industry, which had hitherto been matters of agreement. The Communists wished to make the confiscation of land over 50 hectares, permissible under the July 1947 law, a matter of compulsion, and to prevent anyone owning land he did not personally farm. They were also anxious to extend nationalisation to the whole of industry and commerce; indeed, the minister of internal trade had already taken steps aimed at nationalising the wholesale textile trade and the Communists now demanded the nationalisation of all enterprises with over fifty employees. The attitude of the Social Democrats was somewhat ambivalent, but the majority of the non-communists opposed these extensions of the levelling-down process. The division and the resentment were now so obvious that the non-communists hit back with a resolution calling for a special committee of the cabinet to investigate the police, a resolution that the National Front carried. Although no election date had been fixed, the electioneering had begun; and a trial of strength had been announced.

The press became thick with charges of capitalist exploitation and counter-charges of communist subversion. In the cabinet five days later a watershed was reached. Václav Majer, on the right of the Social Democratic Party, introduced a scheme to give pay rises to government servants on a percentage basis. Zápotocký had prepared an alternative on behalf of the trade union movement and suggested a flat-rate settlement; he was allowed to put his case to the meeting. There was inevitably a confrontation on the issue of which income group the National Front government ought to help. When it came to the vote, the non-communist proposal won. The Communists immediately launched a public attack on their reactionary opponents. Zápotocký announced a special congress of trade union and factory council representatives for 22 February. There was then an impressive build-up of propaganda praising the role of the two groups as guardians of the workers' cause coming together to present their justified demands to the government and, if necessary, to fight for them. Preparatory meetings were held throughout the country to elect representatives to the congress, and they were employed both to escalate demand and to increase militancy. Communist members of the agricultural committee of the National Assembly were also outvoted on the question of further land reform at a meeting on 12 February. So Julius Ďuriš, the Communist minister of agriculture, organised a congress of regional farmers' commissions, mostly comprising poor peasants, for 29 February with a similar purpose to that of Zápotocký. When the Communists were outvoted in the constitutional bodies of the parliamentary machine, they took the battle elsewhere and organised a better machine of their own. Conversely, as the non-communists sensed their voting strength within the parliamentary machine, they clearly decided to exploit it to defend the *status quo*.

However, in such a situation, force might be crucial. Each side relied on what it averred to be the popular will; but a decision as to which expression of the popular will should triumph might well depend on access to arms. There were dark rumours about on both sides. It was this that made the police issue vital when it reached the cabinet on 13 February. The National Socialists accused Nosek of interfering with the normal course of justice and of packing the police. In particular, they accused him of having just substituted eight Communist for eight senior non-communist officers in the Prague region. Nosek was absent, but a resolution ordering him to rescind his action was carried against all but the Communist votes. He was to report his compliance with the order on 17 February. If he did carry it out, whatever thought his party might have entertained of gaining control of the police and thereby backing up their pressure-groups would have to be set aside at least for the time being. Conversely, if he did not comply, his party might be in a position to dominate Czechoslovak politics from the streets. It was a point of make or break. The Communists therefore decided that Nosek should refuse to obey the order. They were ready to make their challenge. Before they learned this, the leading National Socialist ministers began to plan their own challenge. If the Communists succeeded in mastering the police, they could exploit their congresses of workers and peasants to prevent or doctor the elections, and there would be no *status quo* to defend. It was against the principle they were seeking to assert to try to use extra-parliamentary methods. They therefore decided to force a governmental crisis that would precipitate elections. The police issue was not only an obvious basis for a crisis; it was immediate and inescapable.

The cabinet meeting of 17 February produced the inevitable deadlock. Nosek was still indisposed; the Communists would not retract. For their part, the non-communists demanded that cabinet resolutions be upheld and refused to do any other business. The meeting was thereupon adjourned to 20 February. The

Communist Party immediately issued an attack on the others for trying to provoke a crisis that would destroy the National Front government, put a government of officials in its place, and so restore the worst evils of the pre-war years. It also prophesied a reformed National Front under Gottwald and called on the meetings of workers and peasants to play their new role in defending the revolution and constructing people's democracy. On the other side, the National Socialists finally decided that they would resign, if need be, to stop the Communists and force an election, and they set to persuading the other ministers to resign with them. Gottwald saw Beneš on 17 February; Zenkl and Ripka saw him the following day; both sides later claimed his support. Thus resolved and reinforced, Communists and National Socialists both refused to budge on 20 February, and twelve non-communist ministers submitted their resignations to Beneš before the day was out.

To be successful, resignation must come from strength, not weakness. Up to a point there was little else those who resigned could do. If they were hoping to secure a parliamentary end, they had to use parliamentary means; and they lacked the expertise to win support on the streets even if they had attempted to do so. Yet, their very lack of alternative was an indication of their weakness. On the other hand, they made at least one fatal mistake: they failed to ensure a majority resignation. The National Socialists, the Populists, and the Slovak Democrats together comprised a slight minority of government ministers, twelve out of the now twenty-six. They apparently endeavoured to bring the Social Democrats with them; but they did not try hard enough, assuming that unity on the police question would automatically mean solidarity on resignation. Majer teetered on the edge; but Fierlinger was almost more Communist now than the Communists themselves, so that there were no Socialist resignations. The twelve also failed to win the backing of Masaryk or Svoboda; in fact, they appear hardly to have tried, despite the prestige of Masaryk's name and the significance of Svoboda's position as defence minister. Understandable, even unavoidable, their action was ill-prepared and disastrous.

In addition, once they had resigned, the twelve non-communists did little or nothing to press their case. They engaged in a number of public and private meetings and protests, but mostly they just waited for victory to arrive. They assumed that the public, the Social Democrats, and Beneš would all support them, and that there would then have to be an election in which they would greatly increase their majority. They did not wish to eliminate the Communists, they merely wanted to reduce their power and restore their respect for political compromise and parliamentary procedure. Oddly enough, the Communists did not really want to eliminate their opponents either; they were simply anxious to secure a commanding position for themselves to protect and develop the changes of the past few years. They prepared their challenge, partly as a counter-challenge, and partly as a means of restraining and restricting the non-communists. However, once they reached their point of decision, they swung vigorously into action and, as it happened, irreversibly into a sudden position of total victory. In face of the inactivity, even ineptitude, of their opponents it was not difficult; but their political tactics made it almost inevitable.

In one sense the Communist ministers were actually surprised at their colleagues' resignation. They had been preparing extra-parliamentary tactics when suddenly, through a minority resignation, they were presented with a possible parliamentary means of obtaining their objective. Husák, chairman of the Slovak commissioners, showed what could be done when, on 21 February, he declared the non-communists' posts vacant and, two days later, simply appointed Communists to fill them. The final decision in Prague, however, rested not with Gottwald, but with Beneš. For the time being, therefore, the Communists pressed on with their marshalling of the proletariat. On the morning of 21 February, for example, Gottwald addressed a mass meeting of sympathisers in the Old Town Square in Prague, calling for the formation throughout the country of action committees of the National Front made up of representatives of all parties and organisations concerned to preserve its original spirit. On the evening of 23 February a select meeting was held in the nearby City Hall to establish a preparatory committee for the central action committee of the revitalised National Front, with Zápotocký as its chairman; and great efforts were made to add a few dissidents from other parties to the solid phalanx of Communists. Finally, on 25 February, the central action committee came into being, dominated by Communists in and out of the Assembly, and claiming to represent the public will. Then again, the prearranged congress of trade union and factory council representatives on 22 February was turned into a vast demonstration in support of Communist social and economic demands and in favour of the immediate formation of a new government without the resigned ministers. To underline the point, a one-hour general strike was called for 24 February; and its effectiveness left no doubt concerning the mushrooming political power of the Communist-organised working class. Indeed, it was to another mass demonstration called to Václav Square on the afternoon of 25 February that Gottwald finally announced victory.

The police, however, played the biassed part that had been marked out for them. But a more important role was played by another of the extra-parliamentary forces intended to refashion politics to the Communists' satisfaction. The factory militia, or works guards, were put on alert as early as 17 February and reinforced with so-called watch patrols. On 20 February they were again enlarged and transformed into what were termed emergency units, whose task was not only to take command of all key points in the factories but also to be ready to intervene in the towns at large. Finally, on 21 February they were reorganised into a people's militia under the direct, undisguised command of the Communist Party. Two days later, their supply of arms was supplemented from the armaments works in Brno; and although their first street patrols were unarmed, by 25 February they had about 7,000 men under arms in strategic points in Prague. If the twelve ministers' resignation did not produce a revolutionary change by parliamentary means, the Communists were ready to force it from the streets.

In the last resort, there was no doubt about Communist power. There was equally no doubt about the non-communists' lack of it. It was also true that many Communists became intoxicated with their growing sense of victory and demanded a sweeping revolutionary settlement. But Gottwald for one never lost sight of the possibility of a legal solution to the crisis. He briefed his agents and harangued his mobs; but he negotiated assiduously to isolate the non-communists. He secured a promise of participation in a new government from Alois Neuman, a National Socialist deputy, and another from Father Josef Plojhar, a Populist. With a mixture of blandishments, promises, and socialist sentimentality he widened the breach between the Social Democrats and the others to the point where, on the night of 24-25 February, Laušman took Fierlinger's standpoint and led most of his colleagues across to the Communist camp in demanding that Beneš accept the resignations and authorise a new government. There were other prerequisites for a constitutional outcome. The army should remain neutral and therefore offer no challenge to Communist para-military forces. Masaryk should stand aside and thereby keep the glamour of his father's name from the non-communist cause. Gottwald was accordingly most careful not to undermine the non-party position of either Svoboda or Masaryk, and by 25 February all the signs were that he had been successful. At that point, everything turned on Beneš.

The President was almost sixty-four. He had held political office of various kinds for half his years. He had worked intensely all his adult life and had known as much tragedy as triumph. He was ageing, tiring, and far from well. Although his prestige was immense, his role in public life had declined since the end of the war. He no longer exercised a conspicuous influence in making policy. On the other hand, he was constantly consulted and extremely powerful, and he believed in his residual responsibility for Czechoslovakia's development. He was also clear in his mind and strong in his principles. He was therefore ready and able to play a decisive part in February 1948. Both sides alternately claimed and condemned him, then and subsequently. For his part, he was obviously unhappy with the course events had taken since the Marshall Plan fiasco. He was equally unhappy at the attitudes assumed by both sides in the February crisis. He favoured unity and decried confrontation. He was desperately anxious to preserve compromise. In so far as he opposed the non-communists by regretting their resignation, it was from the same point of view. The evidence is conflicting, but it does appear as if in the first few days of the crisis he counselled Gottwald against forcing him to accept the resignations and tried to arrange a compromise with him. This, however, quickly became impossible. The Communists would not withdraw their demand for his acceptance of the resignations and the twelve non-communist ministers persisted in their minority act. In the end, as a firm believer in parliamentary democracy, he clearly felt he had no alternative but to accede to the resignations and to ask Gottwald to form a new government. A majority had stayed in office; the will of the majority had to prevail. The new government also contained representatives of all three parties whose ministers had resigned. As Beneš handled it, the February revolution was a constitutional act.

One side in the dispute has since condemned him for yielding to conspiracy and mob violence. The other side has seen his action as recognition of the progressive force of the Communist Party at the head of the popular masses. At the time, he was probably aware that up to a point he was actually doing both things. His dilemma was that he had reason to resist Communist demands, and to accept them. He must have discerned the suspect breadth of representation in the new government. On the other hand, Masaryk, Svoboda, and the majority of the Social Democrats had not resigned from the previous government, and the twelve who did were not a broad enough cross-section to support. At least Beneš preserved the precious concept of constitutional propriety, which neither side in the dispute really liked. However, it can perfectly well be argued that he had no alternative but to accept the *force majeure* represented by the Communist Party. The Communist-controlled people's militia and the Communist-dominated police force could only have been overawed by the army. Svoboda was non-communist, but pro-Russian; the soldiers were apolitical, but if anything, more left-wing than right. At best, the army would have been a doubtful instrument against Communist forces. But that was not the real point. In agreeing to Munich, one of the main considerations in Beneš's mind had been the need to avoid civil war. His policy since then had been dedicated to the same end. In February 1948 the population was split. To resort to force would have been to provoke a terrible bloodbath, in Beneš's view the worst possible outcome of the crisis. A peaceful solution might at least make it possible eventually to reach a compromise settlement.

It can also be argued that, in asking Gottwald to form a new government, Beneš was surrendering to Soviet domination. Valerian Zorin, Soviet deputy foreign minister, turned up in Prague on 19 February, ostensibly to supervise deliveries of grain. He let it be known to a number of waverers and, indirectly, to Beneš that Moscow wholeheartedly supported Gottwald; it was a gentle reminder of Russia's military might, virtually surrounding Czechoslovakia. On the other hand, Lawrence Steinhardt, the American ambassador to Czechoslovakia, also flew into Prague on 19 February, allegedly with an offer of financial assistance. Communist propagandists made much of this American intervention. Yet what it really proved was that there was little else the United States government was able to do. The Cold War had so far advanced that Russia could lay claim to Czechoslovakia, and America could only make vain gestures. Beneš could not really go against Russian wishes. But he seems to have viewed it in a rather more refined way. At one extreme, he wanted to avoid Soviet military intervention and, at the other, exposure to a revived Germany. In between, he wanted to do nothing to worsen the Cold War since, as he saw it, Czechoslovakia would be the main sufferer. All his hopes had been based on continuing East-West co-operation. He had to go along with Russia at this stage so that Czechoslovakia would not provide it with a pretext for putting an end to that co-operation and so to Czechoslovakia. At Munich he had accepted one diktat to save his country; in February 1948 he accepted another. Perhaps it might escape the worst excesses of communism. But his hope was to prove vain.

CHAPTER 13

Communist Czechoslovakia

The Aftermath of February 1948

FEBRUARY 1948 meant virtually the end of the Košice compromise. Some leaders, like Beneš, still nurtured faint hopes. Others, like Ripka, could not afford to, and fled abroad. Still others, like Šrámek, were unable to, since they were arrested and imprisoned. At least one, Jan Masaryk, committed suicide. He could apparently see no alternative. Neither side had been in the right; no place remained for the moderate. He could only use his name and his life to make a gesture. In the end, even Beneš lost hope. With the Berlin blockade, East-West suspicion changed to downright hostility. The new constitution of May 1948 satisfied him in its concern for social and economic welfare, but contravened his concepts of parliamentary democracy and of public and civil rights. Signalling his disapproval by refusing to sign it, he gave up the presidency in June and died in September. A whole age had come to an end, but so had a particular period. Three years had been spent constructing a moderate socialist society, combining the advantages of public ownership and private liberty. But internationally, Czechoslovakia had been drawn too much in the Soviet direction; and internally, the right had become nervous and the left impatient. Under Soviet control, the left was to have it all its own way until the vast upheaval of the 1960s.

In one sense, Gottwald had achieved his stated aim of a Czechoslovak road to socialism. He had established the dictatorship of the proletariat by constitutional means, and he emphasised the fact. On 23 February, for example, he had secured a postponement of the normal Assembly meeting, but on 25 February an action committee distributed a declaration of support for his government and policy to 229 of the 300 deputies and got 223 signatures. The new constitution did not immediately convert Czechoslovakia to the standard Soviet pattern. For one thing, the President did not become a nonentity in the normal east European fashion, but retained the power and prestige of his predecessors. He was elected by the Assembly for a period of seven years, but he could dissolve it as well as adjourn it; and he appointed the government. The prime minister also retained power. And it was significant that Beneš's successor as President was Gottwald himself, and that Gottwald's successor as prime minister was Zápotocký. The constitution also enshrined principles from the past, such as that no one should be withheld from his lawful judge and that everyone had an inviolable right to his personal property. On the surface at least, the new people's democratic republic continued something of the old system and honoured some of the old principles.

Gottwald could also claim to have established a more genuinely socialist society. The public ownership of industry was quickly extended to all enterprises with over fifty employees. The private sector was reduced to not much more than 5 percent of the total. Wholesale and foreign trade was completely nationalised; and more than half the country's retail trade was taken over. At the same time, the constitution specifically guaranteed the private ownership of what were called small and medium enterprises up to a maximum of fifty employees. Land reform was also carried further. What had been permissive became compulsory, namely that no holding dare exceed 50 hectares. It was also made illegal for anyone to possess land he did not farm himself. In this way, possibly another one percent of the land was made available for redistribution. Once again, however, the constitution specifically guaranteed the private ownership of land up to a total of 50 hectares; and at first there was no talk of collectivisation. The number of small individual farmers actually increased in 1949. In sum, the industrial and agricultural changes introduced after February removed the residue of the maligned business and landowning classes but left room still for the small man, above all in farming. Finally, a long-gestated act of April introduced a comprehensive system of national insurance, providing for sickness and disability, old-age and widowhood, on a social instead of the old actuarial principle.

On the other hand, whatever the constitutional means Gottwald used to obtain power, there was no doubt about the force he had been ready to use and now had at his disposal. The people's militia was greatly expanded. There were large-scale purges in the police and the army. The end-product was a loyal security service more than sufficient to overawe any possible resistance. Not that there was much. The resigning ministers had given up without a fight; a conciliatory President was anxious to avoid one. There were no leaders left. The majority of the population were not supporters of the Communists, but that did not automatically make them opponents; they could tolerate the new situation. They had put up with much under the Nazis; and the Communists were neither foreign nor oppressive, at least not yet. Things had simply deteriorated; they had not so far become impossible. In any case, it had been a long hard decade of despair and resistance, of triumph and disillusionment; it surely could not end now in a civil war. There was no power to appeal to. The United Nations could not intervene in an internal imbroglio. The alternative to a Communist dictatorship backed by Russia might even be subservience to a Germany resurrected by the United States. There was little will to resist, or little option but to make the best of a bad job. Those who did speak up were gradually forced to flee abroad or were imprisoned. Even before that, the purges were extended to public life, to industry, and the whole bureaucracy. There were not many with the prestige of the veteran Sychrava who could protest and still be allowed to go abroad with his passport. But his middle-of-the-road newspaper, *Národní osvobození (National Liberation)*, was closed down.

The minority of the population who were Communists or Communist sympathisers were not necessarily bigoted. They believed in the virtue of their cause and rejoiced in its triumph. They saw it as good for Czechoslovakia and for society at large. Certainly the enemies of socialism had to be removed from power, but only to facilitate the construction of socialism. Inevitably there were party members and hangers-on with ambitions to fulfil or personal scores to settle. Inevitably, too, there were doctrinaires with more loyalty to Communist leaders in Moscow than to their colleagues and fellow nationals in Czechoslovakia. In general, however, the February revolution, as it was dubbed, was intended and expected to be for the benefit of Czechoslovakia. That it turned out otherwise was the result of two factors in particular. One was the very ease with which power was won and entrenched. There were few barriers to the dictatorship of the proletariat. There were few restraints on the ambitious, the vindictive, and the doctrinaire. The other was the intensification of the Cold War. The expulsion of Yugoslavia from the Cominform in June 1948, the establishment of Comecon in January 1949, the signing of the North Atlantic Pact in April 1949, and the outbreak of the Korean War in June 1950 were signals for the abandonment of moderation in the communist bloc as a whole and for the subjugation of Czechoslovak interests to those of the Soviet Union and Stalin. Within a few years of February 1948 the Czechoslovak road to socialism, and indeed socialism itself, had been cast aside.

The new constitution was no protection. As in the past, the President and the prime minister might be powerful political influences; but after 1948 both were Communists. As in the post-war years, the National Front provided the government; but it was under the tightest of controls. Of the five non-communist parties, one, the Social Democrats, lost its identity when it was swallowed up by the Communists. Heresy had to be eliminated. The other four were purged by the central and local action committees of the so-called Regenerated National Front and then assigned 61 of the 300 seats on the single ticket for election to the National Assembly in May 1948. They had to be preserved as a symbol of the continuing democratic order and they had their use as a two-way channel of communication; but they were emasculated and reduced to insignificance. The National Front government, like the National Front, regularly backed the policies produced by the Communist Party. Theoretically, the Assembly was the supreme legislative body, with power to appoint and impeach the President and also to question and defeat the government. But the single-ticket system introduced in 1948 ensured that the electors' choice was between the National Front and nothing, since no independent could be found who could muster the necessary one thousand brave signatories to sponsor his candidacy. The National Assembly was therefore the captive of the National Front, which meant of the Communists. In June 1948 it elected Gottwald unanimously to the presidency; and thereafter its every vote was unanimous, its every discussion brief and non-contentious, its every action in absolute support of the decisions and aspirations of the Communist Party.

The first article of the constitution was quite explicit that the people were the sole source of all power in the state. According to the fourth article, the people discharged their power through representative bodies elected by them, controlled by them, and accountable to them. Sovereignty of the people, of course, is difficult to enforce practically in any society. But in post-1948 Czechoslovakia the people at large were virtually disfranchised. Many thousands were literally deprived of the vote by being condemned by action committees for crimes of political hostility or economic disruption. In theory the ballot was secret; but malpractices apart, a great propaganda effort was devoted to encouraging open voting. But the major obstacle to popular control was the single ticket which in general gave the electorate no choice at all —and even forced Communists to vote for non-communists. The election result was determined in advance by decision of the Communist Party as to the make-up of the single ticket. All that remained to be discovered were the statistics of the voting. In 1948 there were still sufficient courageous opponents of the new order to make the statistics interesting. Of 8 million people allowed to vote, a million either voted against the single ticket or spoiled their papers, and half a million abstained. But the 1½ million had no effect on the result. Of the other 6½ million, possibly a majority may have wanted the result that was preordained. The positive vote was also a useful seal of approval for the February revolution and a continuing mandate for the leadership of the Communist Party. But the fact remained that popular sovereignty, like the legislative supremacy of the National Assembly, or the political authority of the much-vaunted National Front, was little more than a useful fiction. Czechoslovakia was now ruled by the Communists.

In some areas, not even the fiction was preserved. The national or people's committees, that had carried out the functions of local government since 1945, were legitimised in the 1948 constitution. But local committees were subordinated to district committees, and district to regional; and the whole structure was subordinated to the ministry of the interior. Constitutionally, all the committees were to lean on the participation and initiative of the people and be subject to their control. But they never had been elected, and they were not elected now; they were simply purged and permitted to operate without popular mandate for another six years. In short, Communist control of local government from above was quite blatant. The constitution was also full of clauses that were capable of abuse. The direction of all education was the competence of the state, which was to ensure that it was in accordance with the results of scientific research but at the same time not inconsistent with the people's democratic order. Broadcasting and television were the exclusive right of the state; if censorship of the press was not permitted, it was made clear that this was not as a rule. Freedom of conscience was guaranteed; but no one could plead his views as grounds for refusing to fulfil the civic duties laid upon him by law. The categories of punishable crime included statements and acts that were a threat to the people's democratic order. The judges were required to abide not only by the laws but by government ordinances, and to interpret them in accordance not only with the constitution but also with the principles of the people's democratic order. Finally, the constitutionality of a law could not be tested in the courts, but only in what was called the praesidium of the Assembly, a committee of the body that first enacted it on behalf of the ruling Communist Party. It was hardly surprising that the praesidium was never requested to exercise this function.

The toughest line the Communists took was with regard to Slovakia. At the end of the war they had exploited the Slovak question to their own obvious advantage, though subsequently, as members of the government, they had been eager to join in reducing Bratislava's autonomy. Through the 1948 constitution they greatly restricted the powers of the Slovak National Council and board of commissioners, confining them to minor economic and social questions and cultural affairs. Enactments of the National Assembly and decisions of the government overrode those of the local bodies. The government could initiate legislation in the Council and ministers could carry their writ into Slovakia over the heads of individual commissioners. The prime minister had the authority to summon and adjourn the Council, and even to dissolve it; he had to sign and interpret Council enactments. The government, not the Council, appointed the commissioners. Finally, the constitution omitted all mention of the 1946 guarantee that the status of Slovakia would not be altered without the agreement of the majority of the Slovak members of the National Assembly. At the party level, too, the Communists vastly reduced Slovak pretensions. In September 1948 the Czechoslovak party absorbed the separate Slovak party and thereafter permitted the Slovaks only a regional organisation with minimal independence. It was one thing to use the Slovaks to help break up the old bourgeois state, but quite another to give them the opportunity to undermine socialism with their nationalist aspirations.

The choice of 9 May for the adoption of the constitution was quite deliberate. It was the third anniversary of the liberation of Prague by the Red Army. Although the new constitution bore traces of its predecessors and was no slavish imitation of the Soviet model, it was nonetheless a pliable instrument for the introduction of Soviet-type socialism to Czechoslovakia. Yet, strangely enough, the local party that was poised ready to use it was not itself a straightforward copy of its Soviet counterpart. Indeed, contrary to Soviet practice, it was a mass party comprising some 2½ million members. Several hundred thousand of these it actually recruited after the February revolution, as if to defy its mentor. Again contrary to Soviet practice, its leading figure at all levels was a chairman who presided, not a secretary who manipulated. This was true at the top, for example, where in 1948 Gottwald stood head and shoulders above Slánský. The Czechoslovak party's base was also different; it was not occupational, the factory or office, but residential, the region or district. The Soviet communist party had long boasted of its inner democracy; but in practice the Czechoslovak party was probably nearer the representative principle, at least in 1948. Finally, despite his Moscow experience, Gottwald was something of a Western-type Communist who in his fifty-second year could not entirely free himself of respect for the principles of the society in which he had grown up. All was not necessarily lost.

When Gottwald assumed command, the Czechoslovak economy was basically sound and on the whole quite promising. The national income for 1948 was 3 percent higher than for 1937, the last normal pre-war year. On a *per capita* basis, allowing for the loss of in particular German population, it was in fact 13 percent higher. Taking 1937 as the base year of 100, the index of industrial production for 1948 stood at 103. From the point of view of future growth, this concealed some useful pointers: the index for machine-tools stood at 125, for consumer goods at 83, and for production in Slovakia as a whole at 196. The emphases were in the right areas. The average growth-rate was also encouraging at 10 percent a year. There were failures, however, and unhappy omens. There was little recovery in the building industry. There was much less industrial unemployment than before the war, but labour had not quite recovered its pre-war level of productivity. The picture in agriculture was gloomy. Climatically, 1948 was a better year than 1947, but production did not rise. The index stood at the same in both years, 74, which compared most unfavourably with the 100 of 1937. On the other hand, there was long-term hope. In the midst of a fundamental reorganisation, agriculture could not really expect to do well. Yet the agricultural labour force was down by a third, whereas productivity was up by an eighth. With the right kind of prescription, agriculture could do as well as industry. It was up to the Communists.

Despite the memories of war and the closeness of revolution, which were politically divisive, Czechoslovak society was more balanced and homogeneous than it had ever been. This emerges from a comparison of census figures. In 1930 some 48 percent of the population of the Czech Lands lived in the towns, and some 26 percent of the population of Slovakia; by 1950 the percentages were 54 and 44 respectively. The percentage of those classed as capitalists dropped by half in both areas, from 6 to 3 in the Czech Lands and from 4 to 2 in Slovakia. Wage differentials narrowed enormously. The most startling change, of course, was ethnic. The percentage of Czechs in the Czech Lands was now 94 as against 68, and of Slovaks in Slovakia 87 as against 68. Czechoslovakia had become overwhelmingly Czech and Slovak. One figure that remained the same concerned age structure. In 1950 as in 1930, despite the impact of war and emigration, some 45 percent of the population as a whole was still within the active age range 20-50. The opportunities facing the Communists were almost remarkable.

The Tragedy of Communism 1948-1960

The period that followed was not without its achievements. Czechoslovak industrial production continued to rise. By the end of the first five-year plan in 1953 it had almost doubled; by the end of the second, in 1960, it had almost doubled again. In a number of industries the rise was even more spectacular. In the chemical, metallurgical, and engineering industries, for example, production was about five or six rather than four times greater in 1960 than it had been in 1948. The building materials sector was not far behind. This represented an important shift in emphasis towards heavy industry, in part designed to cure the lopsided economy of the pre-war years. Engineering, for instance, increased its proportion of industrial production from the 1937 figure of about 17 percent to about 24 percent. The concentration of industry by 1960 was also such—only about 700 enterprises, some 90 percent of them with more than 500 employees each—that the productivity of labour had practically trebled since 1948. Slovak industry, which had been further behind, made the more startling advances. In the twelve-year period overall industrial production increased to more than five times what it had been. The chemical industry went to more than eight, metallurgy and engineering to more than ten. And the electrical industry joined building materials above the average. Productivity more than trebled; and at the end of the period the Slovak share in total Czechoslovak industrial output was about 19 percent compared with about 13 percent at the start. At the same time, urbanisation intensified. By 1960 practically 60 percent of the population in the Czech Lands lived in the towns, while Slovakia had gone rather faster to pass the half-way mark with approximately 52 percent.

What this amounted to was continuing growth and modernisation. A century-old trend, European and Czechoslovak, was allowed to go on unimpeded by war or trade-cycle. It might have gone on under any regime. There have been complicated political and academic arguments as to whether Czechoslovakia's growth-rate was faster or slower than that of various Western countries. Communist politicians and academics were certainly anxious in the 1950s to prove that it was faster. Unfortunately, Communist statistics had more than their fair share of built-in bias. The measure of industrial production was gross and took no account of quality, which was often the subject of fierce criticism. The measure of industrial productivity was annual, not hourly, and neglected the length of the working-week and the bonus of voluntary work for the cause. Nevertheless, the figures remain quite impressive. On the other hand, in one important area, consumer goods, there was slow progress. Output barely trebled between 1948 and 1960. The percentage of manufacture devoted to consumer goods also dropped from its 1937 level of more than 30 to somewhat less than 20, despite some switch of effort in the interval between the first and second five-year plans. The quality of the consumer goods actually produced also invited more criticism than anything else turned out by Czechoslovak industry. Even the most diehard Communist leaders had to admit to a yawning gap between what was with difficulty available to Czechoslovak consumers and what was widely and cheaply on sale in the West.

There were other black areas. Fuel was in short supply, hard coal most of all. Absenteeism was widespread, and industry had to depend regularly on compulsory contributions of voluntary labour. There was an unusually large turnover of manpower. Where planning targets were more important than selling prices, costs of production were high; so was the wear and tear on machinery. And in a planned economy the control of industry had become an industry in itself, employing an unnecessary and wasteful bureaucracy. In fact, by 1960, industry was close to the point of stagnation; three years later, the index of industrial production was actually to fall. However, the big economic failure of the Communist regime was in agriculture. In 1948 it was reasonable to hope for considerable growth. Feudal agriculture had disappeared a century before. Two post-war periods of land reform had broken up the big estates and redistributed the land to the point where no single farmer owned more than 50 hectares. Much of the excess population had drained into industry. A series of co-operatives of various kinds had stepped in to supply small farmers with some of the equipment and services of the big. The Communists in fact accelerated the trends. In February 1949 they established the first so-called unified agricultural co-operatives, designed in the end to collectivise agriculture. They also accelerated the conversion of idle, unassigned, and confiscated lands into so-called state farms. Within a year about 20 percent of all agricultural land was organised in this way, and by 1960 the figure had risen to 90 percent. Of the total, about four-fifths was in unified co-operatives. The Communists also made particular efforts to mechanise agriculture. By 1960 they were adding, for example, 15,000 tractors a year to the available stock of machinery. They were just as concerned to increase the use of artificial fertilisers, and by the same date they had succeeded in doubling the quantity. The move from the countryside continued unabated. Between 1948 and 1960 the number of agricultural workers decreased remarkably from about 2,200,000 to about 1,350,000. The Communists claimed a corresponding rise in productivity. But for all their apparent achievements, they failed miserably. Taking 1936 as the base year of 100, the index of crude agricultural production stood at 73 in 1948; by 1960 it had risen to no more than 99.5. Twelve years of intense Communist effort had failed not only to produce agricultural plenty, but even to restore output to its pre-war level.

Rising industrial and agricultural output is not the only criterion of a government's success, East or West. But in that it reflects on standards of living, it is certainly one that ordinary people use. However, the Communists in Czechoslovakia had confidently promised increased production and accordingly failed by their own criterion. Clearly in agriculture they deserved some sympathy. Their difficulties ranged from climate to problems of reorganisation. And they registered some successes. In animal production they did raise the index above its pre-war level, though in pigs and sheep rather than cattle. Equally, they did raise the index for output as a whole in Slovakia, though that was where farming was more backward and it was easier to make advances. By their own ideological criterion they could also claim a success. Not only had they brought 90 percent of all farmed land within the so-called socialist sector; they had reduced the number of those engaged full-time in the private sector to a mere quarter of a million and had almost eliminated the denigrated kulak or rich peasant class. Yet it was their ideological objectives and their means of achieving them that ruined whatever prospects they had in agriculture.

In their initial legislation and propaganda the Czechoslovak Communists were very careful to talk about co-operatives, not about collectives. The first were in the Czechoslovak tradition, the second carried a sinister Soviet ring. However, although the original title was retained, the Communists were soon following a policy of crude collectivisation on Russian lines. Joining the co-operatives was supposed to be voluntary, and peasants' land to remain their own property. But apart from a fleeting pause in the years 1954-55, the pressure mounted yearly and proprietary rights were forgotten. Propaganda was conducted by local Communists, by officially organised preparatory committees, by factory workers; it was directed at parents and channelled through schoolchildren. For the very poor peasants there was frequently an incentive to join, a share in the profits from other men's land. For the better-off or the reluctant, propaganda gave way to coercion. Quotas for the compulsory delivery of farm produce were fixed at a much higher rate for peasants on their own land or in low-category co-operatives than for those in the full united agricultural co-operatives; and it was only for supplies above the quota that a reasonable price was paid. Those who still held out were forbidden to grow the more rewarding crops, or were unable to obtain their fertilisers, or were forced to sell their machinery to the state. Fiercely discriminatory taxes and social insurance payments ate away at the resources and morale of the remainder. Inevitably, the majority of the peasants joined the collectives with reluctance. Whatever the political rights or wrongs of Communist policy, it certainly had adverse economic effects. Most peasants had supported land reform to benefit their own economic position, to make themselves reasonably prosperous farmers. They not only resented the primitive measures used to force them into the collectives; they disliked the entire new system as almost a reversion to feudalism. By and large, therefore, they were reluctant recruits to the collectives; and although they could achieve miraculous results with their private strips, on the land of their 'lords' they proved almost as unproductive as their forebears. Even more nonsensical, from an economic point of view, was the policy of singling out the kulaks for destruction. They were progressively stripped of their property and their rights and were specifically not allowed to enter the collectives. Yet they were by definition the most successful of the peasants, the ones most likely to raise production if left to continue on their own, or the ones most able to contribute to the know-how of the collectives if coaxed to join. Collectivisation and the destruction of the kulaks condemned the new Communist rulers of Czechoslovakia to agricultural failure.

It was in fact a rather strange policy for the Communists to adopt. During 1917 Lenin had exploited the Russian peasants' land-hunger to win popularity by encouraging individual expropriation on the grand scale; but once in power he had bitterly attacked the principle of private ownership of land. Stalin's collectivisation drive in the 1920s and thirties had been an essential adjunct to the industrialisation of Russia; it was to provide the capital, the labour, the atmosphere. So Gottwald had his models. However, the Czechoslovak revolution of 1948 was totally different from the Russian of 1917; and Gottwald's Czechoslovakia was highly industrialised compared with Stalin's Russia. Gottwald had envisaged a Czechoslovak road to socialism, and collectivisation formed no part of it. Yet he presided over its introduction and bitterest moments. Indeed, despite all the prospects before him in 1948, he presided over one of the saddest periods in Czechoslovak history. And his immediate successors did little better. The absence of an effective opposition and the build-up in the Cold War were obviously the factors permitting and prompting the Communists' rush to extremism. Yet the lengths to which they went, far beyond collectivisation, also stemmed from other factors.

To some extent, it was a matter of filling a vacuum. By the middle of 1948 there was a new government and constitution, a new President and Assembly. With nationalisation, land reform, and comprehensive insurance the Communists' economic and social revolution was complete. They really had no programme left. They had been half-way to their millennium before the February events in any case, and the suddenness and completeness of their success left them unsure where to go next. In such a situation they were open to suggestion and to pressure. Thus the idea of an attack on the Catholic Church was a natural internal suggestion. The mutual hostility of communism and Catholicism was of as long standing in Czechoslovakia as elsewhere. Church lands were confiscated in March 1948; denominational schools were taken over in April. For their part, the bishops declined, first in March and then again in May, either to give an oath of loyalty to the state or to allow priests to stand in the elections. It was a set-piece battle. The Communists struck the popular note of robbing the rich, but were much more concerned to break the ideological hold of the Church over 70 percent of the Czechoslovak people. The Church was anxious to keep out of politics in order to survive and perhaps save something of its lands and schools. The two positions were not incompatible. In June, Gottwald and his cabinet colleagues found no obstacle to attending Mass celebrated by Archbishop Beran in St Vitus Cathedral in Prague. On its side, the Church was already attuned to a considerable degree of state intervention from the inter-war years. But to at least some Communists in search of a policy the chance of victory over Catholicism was too good to miss. And what started out as opportunism ended up as extremism. By June 1949 the archbishops of Prague and Olomouc and all the bishops were interned, and the publication of episcopal letters without prior approval was forbidden. In October of the same year state offices for church affairs were established in Prague and Bratislava with control of almost everything except ritual. The clergy became little more than officials, dependent on the state for their salaries and required to declare their loyalty to it. By April 1950 all Vatican representatives were expelled from Prague and the Catholic Church was effectively cut off from Rome. The bishops refused to take the loyalty oath, but authorised the clergy to do so, and a number did. Those who held out were tried for conspiracy or espionage and imprisoned. Persecution, once started, was difficult to stop. Even the capitulation of the majority of the bishops in March 1951 and the establishment of what was in effect a schismatic church did not wholly put an end to it. They had satisfied their supporters and had broken the most obvious of their opponents, but that was not enough. They enjoyed their power. And last, but not least, they could go on sharpening the class struggle and pandering to their cronies in Warsaw and Budapest and their masters in Moscow.

It was a sad fact that, in their mood of achievement coupled with uncertainty after February 1948, the Communists were particularly vulnerable to pressure from outside. They were sure they had proved their worth but unclear how they could go on doing it. They were over-sensitive to criticism and over-anxious to anticipate it or adjust to it; and the criticism from Poland and Hungary was as strong as from the Soviet Union. Neither of Czechoslovakia's neighbours could tolerate a moderate socialist society on its doorstep when its own communist party was markedly weaker and the task before it much tougher. From their point of view the Czechoslovak revolution had to be pushed further, faster; its class struggle had to be sharpened quickly. From the Soviet Union, however, the pressure was much more severe. Quite apart from the alleged needs of the Cold War, Stalin was once again at his most dictatorial and vitriolic. What was good for the Soviet Union was good for eastern Europe; in both, the class struggle, as an article of faith, had to be pursued with a new ferocity. The kulaks had to be eliminated; the clergy had to be subordinated. Where, as in Czechoslovakia, the Red Army was absent, then the responsibility lay heavily upon the Communist Party. The need to deal with the many Yugoslav heresies after 1948 simply intensified Stalin's determination to impose Soviet-style policies upon the rest of eastern Europe, and particularly upon Czechoslovakia, which had the closest affinities and longest-established links with Yugoslavia. Even if Gottwald had achieved more by the middle of 1948, and even if he had then prepared a blueprint for action on the grand scale, he would still have found himself under severe pressure when he went for an interview with Stalin in September. As it was, he obviously returned determined to strengthen the dictatorship of the proletariat and to intensify the class war. Subsequent internal investigations bore out that it was then that the Communists began infringing even their own laws; and it was certainly then that their search for enemies in their midst started in earnest.

The attack on the kulaks had its counterpart in attacks on tradesmen and shopkeepers who found themselves forced out of business and discriminated against in taxation and social welfare. With certain exceptions, other denominations were not persecuted as much as the Catholic Church, partly because they were less opposed to communism and partly on the principle of dividing and ruling. There was, however, a steady campaign to root out everyone with middle-class background or pretensions from education and the professions. From dismissing teachers and students, officials and lawyers, it was an easy step to mounting trials. In the early days there probably were acts of sabotage, both crude and refined. However, if the class war was to be intensified, it was not at all difficult to extend the definition of anti-state activities and to move up the scale of political importance. In the year following Gottwald's visit to Stalin there were several hundred arrests of members of the still officially allowed non-communist parties; and in June 1950 there was the first mammoth show trial. Of the leading politicians charged, four, including Milada Horáková, the most prominent woman in the National Socialist Party, were condemned to death and executed and nine were sentenced to long terms of imprisonment. Other trials of lesser members of the alleged subversive conspiracy followed in quick succession, and the witch-hunt rapidly spread outside politics. No one was safe, in the end not even the Communist hierarchy.

As was later admitted, most charges were without foundation; evidence was fabricated; and confessions were extorted by various kinds of pressure. At the time, Gottwald and his colleagues may have believed that there were subversive conspiracies, or at least that there might be; the atmosphere both internally and internationally was full of suspicion. The end accordingly justified the means. Many members of the public also seem to have believed that there were deep plots and vast spy-rings. Officially controlled news media constantly told them so; and externally inspired threats explained their domestic failures. As for the means of bringing the guilty to justice, they mostly did not know. They simply called for vengeance. The trials, even as they spread, also sharpened the class struggle. The Communist leadership and rank-and-file united in identifying and eliminating the class enemy. The trials became an end in themselves, a substitute for policy, an alternative to thinking. The cancer was nourished by a combination of mass hysteria and political sterility. And as the trials eliminated alleged opponents, they also mollified supposed friends. It looked better to Stalin and the rest of his east European communist coterie that at last Gottwald was turning on the Czechoslovak bourgeoisie and their variegated following. Yet Stalin wanted more. He wanted tougher and more widespread action.

It was under pressure from dissatisfied Polish and Hungarian colleagues in particular that, in September 1949, Gottwald asked Stalin to send him 'advisers' to assist in rooting out subversion. Once they were in Prague, however, they began acting rather as directors. They organised and commanded a Soviet-style secret police apparatus that sought out victims, forced their confessions, and stage-managed their trials. Czechoslovak efforts in this direction had hitherto been somewhat half-hearted, but they now rapidly gained in momentum. The 'advisers' also extended the range of crimes and included Communists in their purge. In March 1950 Clementis was suddenly dismissed from the office of foreign minister on a charge of bourgeois nationalism. Two months later, Husák was dismissed as chairman of the Slovak board of commissioners, and other Slovaks were also removed from their appointments, all on the same charge. In February 1951 Clementis, Husák, and several others were arrested. In December 1952 Clementis was executed. Bourgeois nationalism was one of the charges against Tito. It rolled easily off the 'advisers'' tongues. It attached itself easily to Slovak leaders discontented with their treatment by the government in Prague and its superiors in Moscow. It was also as good a charge as any to level at a man like Husák who had built up an independent reputation in the 1944 rising and who had taken independent action in the 1948 events. It was an even better charge to level against a man like Clementis who had been expelled from the party in 1939 for his criticisms of the Nazi-Soviet Pact and who had spent much of the war in the West. There were no doubt Czechs, non-communist as well as Communist, who were glad to see the Slovaks kept firmly in their place. There were also Communist leaders who wished to see their own dissidents disciplined. There were others who were anxious to work off old grudges, or were prepared to throw a few of their colleagues to the Moscow wolves to save their own skins. But Stalin and his agents in Prague were not so easily satisfied. They multiplied their fabrications and struck at the heart of the Czechoslovak Communist leadership. When Clementis went to his death, it was for a battery of so-called crimes; and he was in company with ten others from the top echelons of the party. They constituted what was said to be the leadership of an anti-state conspiracy, and they were condemned as 'Trotskyite Titoists, bourgeois nationalist traitors, and enemies of the Czechoslovak Republic and of socialism'. They included four deputy ministers—Karel Šváb (interior), Bedřich Reicin (defence), Otto Fischl (finance), and Rudolf Margolius (foreign trade); two top-ranking officials—Bedřich Geminder (head of the international department of the party secretariat), and Ludvík Frejka (head of the economic department of the President's office); the secretary of the central committee of the party, Josef Frank; and most important and surprising of all, Slánský.

What told against the ten was what told against so many others. Three had spent most of the war in the West. One of them, Otto Šling, had even fought in the Spanish Civil War, which Stalin preferred to forget. Another three had spent the war in concentration camps, away from the purifying influence of Moscow. Most of them had demonstrated their independence—one in the Czechoslovak brigade in the Soviet Union; some may have made enemies— one had done so in the Comintern. What was significantly new was that the majority of them were of Jewish origin, including Slánský. Certainly at the level of leadership the Czechs and Slovaks had not in the past been particularly anti-semitic. But anti-semitism was almost traditional in Russia and may well have seemed to the Soviet mind an emotion that might be whipped up in Czechoslovakia. But apart from that, Soviet foreign policy had taken a distinct anti-Israeli turn; and Stalin himself, who had been haunted by the internationalism of the Jewish mind ever since his struggle with Trotsky in the 1920s, had become obsessed in the fifties with the Jewish menace both inside and outside the Soviet Union. Perhaps it was the fact that Slánský was a Jew that made it easier for Gottwald to connive at his death. It was certainly this that made Stalin pick on him rather than on Gottwald. Two other facts weighed against him: he had less Moscow experience than Gottwald and he was tainted with the Slovak uprising; he was thus not trained in full obedience and had learned some independence. But above all, as a Jewish intellectual, he might be Czechoslovakia's Trotsky and must be removed. Gottwald had demonstrated his obedience in agreeing to reject the Marshall Plan offer. If Czechoslovakia was to be made a faithful satellite, it had to be Slánský and his like who were eliminated.

The eleven who were executed in December 1952 were innocent of the charges against them and were posthumously rehabilitated. On the other hand, they bore their share of responsibility for the circumstances that had led to 1948 and after. They had helped to put Stalin in the position where he could execute them, and a number of them had been party to some of the initial acts of illegality that led to the fake trials. What had been done by the Czechoslovak Communists in the interest of the Czechoslovak working class was in the end seriously damaging to both. The trial at which Slánský was the main accused was the biggest but far from the only one at which Communists were sentenced to death or imprisonment. Many of the prominent Communists of the 1960s were in fact victims of the fifties. And subsequent Communist investigation showed that the largest single social group to suffer from the trials was the industrial working class. However, the period down to the deaths first of Stalin and then of Gottwald in 1953 was one of tragedy for the whole of Czechoslovakia. It was not just the human misery involved in the admitted total of almost two hundred executions; nor the loss to the nation of so much talent. It was not just the wretchedness or misuse of the thousands of prisoners. Whatever enthusiasm there had been for the February revolution evaporated in the atmosphere of suspicion, fear, and hatred bred by a police state. Whatever support there had been for the Czechoslovak model of socialism dwindled steadily as Soviet domination over the Czechoslovak Communists led to one inappropriate Soviet importation after another. There was less and less backing for what was being done; and what was being done was less and less suitable for Czechoslovak conditions, and therefore less and less likely to be popular or successful. If the economy did progress a little, it was almost in the end despite its environment. What was just as bad was that, even with the deaths of Stalin and Gottwald, change was far from easy.

In retrospect, 1953 was a turning-point in international history. It marked at least the beginning of the end of the Cold War. Eisenhower was already President of the United States when Stalin died; and as a token of things to come, an armistice was signed in Korea in midsummer. The same year was a turning-point also in Soviet history. Shortly after Stalin's death his security chief, Lavrenti Beria, was executed; and his triumvirate of successors fired the first shots in the campaign against the cult of personality by their very sharing of power. Both turning-points affected Czechoslovakia directly. International tension had been a convenient pretext for the political trials; and the Soviet secret police had more or less run them. The slow East-West *détente* was obvious even in Prague. Khrushchev specifically informed the Czechoslovak Communist Party about Stalin's uncommunist misdemeanours and advised it to put its own house in order. The 'advisers' were withdrawn and several of them were executed. Yet there was surprisingly little change in Czechoslovakia. At Khrushchev's expressed wish General Svoboda, who had been stripped of all offices, was rehabilitated in 1954. But the trials themselves went on. In the course of 1953 and 1954 many more prominent Communists were sentenced to long terms of imprisonment: Edvard Goldstücker, Jewish diplomat; Marie Švermova, wife of Jan Šverma, dead hero of the Slovak rising and friend of Gottwald and Slánský; Husák, Smrkovský, and other outstanding names. Indeed, it was 1955 before a commission of inquiry was established, a blatantly political committee, its terms of reference confined to a review of sentences. Worse still, it was even presided over by the man who had been minister of the interior since 1953, Rudolf Barák, and it was not allowed to look at the Slánský trial. It reduced a few sentences and set aside some more. Despite the evidence, it evaded the question of who had rigged the trials, at least until it began to blame Slánský as the Czechoslovak Beria. Khrushchev's famous diatribe against Stalin at the twentieth congress of the Soviet communist party in February 1956 produced some improvement. The demand to re-examine the trials spread more widely among party members, and a reassessment took place even of the Slánský trial. But the investigation was really as political as the trials themselves had been and barely scratched the surface. Barák's own report to the central committee of the Communist Party in October 1957 indicated that 6,978 cases had been examined, but that only fifty verdicts had been overturned and twenty-one sentences reduced. Slánský and some others were deemed to have committed lesser crimes but still to have deserved execution. Many of those released still suffered loss of civil rights; and the relatives of those still imprisoned or those who spoke up on their behalf were harassed in various ways. Over the next two or three years there was a trickle of releases, but in April 1960, on the occasion of a partial amnesty, there were still 8,708 political prisoners. Much of the misery persisted, and little or nothing had been done to cleanse the party of the politicians responsible for so many breaches even of socialist legality.

It was tragic that what started out as a Czechoslovak road to socialism and took on one of the worst Soviet features under Soviet pressure went on to retain it because of an unreformed Czechoslovak leadership. Admittedly the Soviet Union itself remained a police state, and the Hungarian rising in 1956 made reform difficult in eastern Europe as a whole. But there was less real change in leadership in Czechoslovakia than anywhere else. In the wake of the worst of the trials the tenth party congress in 1954 produced a number of new faces on the Communist central committee. But the party officials and industrial managers who came on the scene lacked the long-term experience and intellectual independence of those who had been executed or imprisoned. Power had in any case been more and more concentrated in the hands of the politbureau, and even at the eleventh congress in 1958 the new men did not penetrate the inner sanctum. There, apart from a few deaths, natural and otherwise, little or no movement took place. Perhaps if Gottwald had survived to 1956, there would have been a figure to attack and to base a purge on. As it was, his son-in-law, Alexej Čepička, who had risen to be deputy prime minister in 1950, was removed from office in April 1956, to the satisfaction of everyone, but without being a big enough figure to start a purge of the old guard.

Zápotocký bore some responsibility for the trials, enough to make him unwilling to mount a full-scale investigation but not enough to expose him to general condemnation. As a lifelong trade unionist he was an expert at surviving from one difficult situation to another; as the organiser of trade union action in February 1948 he was a skilled political strategist. He also appeared to be a more humane man that Gottwald and showed more of the common touch in dealing with ordinary Czechoslovak people. He managed to survive the workers' riots that followed the prices and currency reform in May 1953. With only minor, non-political concessions he also survived the querulous writers' congress of April 1956 and the first public student demonstrations in May. With no greater difficulty he adjusted back to the familiar hard line dictated by the Soviet intervention in Hungary. Antonín Novotný, Zápotocký's successor as President in November 1957, was also tarred with the trials brush; after Slánský's arrest he had been Gottwald's chief aide in the party and after Gottwald's death he had become secretary to the central committee. A largely colourless party bureaucrat, he had no interest in raking over past history and no predilection for political change; and there was nothing in the post-Hungary situation immediately to impel him towards reform. Like his predecessors, he was still surrounded by a clique of guilty men such as Barák, or Viliám Široký, the Slovak who had displaced Clementis as foreign minister in 1950 and succeeded Zápotocký as prime minister in 1953. With no real change in political leadership it was hardly surprising that there was so little rehabilitation. Much of the blight remained, and so did most of the men who had produced it.

It was asked at the time, and it is still a pertinent question, why there was no revolt in Czechoslovakia in 1956 when there was trouble in both Poland and Hungary. In the late spring there were certainly preliminary rumbles, but no great rebellion followed, aimed at bringing the leadership down and removing the guilty. Partly it was the result of the quality of the leadership; it was hard to mount a revolution against mediocrity. The politbureau might seem to be proceeding over-cautiously, but it had instituted a review of some of the trials. On the economic front it was considering no kind of fundamental change, but it had at least allowed a slight shift of emphasis towards consumer goods and it had slackened the collectivisation campaign, if only temporarily. Partly it was the mood of the people. Even for many of the party faithful there was little glamour left in socialism. Disillusionment with politics in general was widespread and could not be so easily dispelled in the midst of the suspicion and sense of guilt that lingered on after the trials. It was more rewarding, safer, and easier to contemplate other more material things. If the party's policies had been unsuccessful and the political trials wrong, it was still difficult to think through the propaganda that was pushed out at all levels of school, work, and leisure to discover successful alternatives, and still dangerous to criticise. The old and the middle-aged had suffered too much to risk more; the young were too young to know their own minds or to know how to challenge the inner circle of the party. On both counts, therefore, more time was required. The leadership needed time to prove its total bankruptcy. The people needed time for one generation to rediscover its faith and for another to mature and develop its power. 1956 was too early, even before the Hungarian rising; afterwards, there had to be an interval to allow tempers to cool. In any case, revolt in the Hungarian style was contrary to Czechoslovak tradition; and its ruthless suppression proved to the Czechoslovak people how foolish it had been and, at the same time, gave the party old guard a new lease of life. Sychrava, who returned hopefully to welcome 1956 in Prague, found that he could make but little peaceful impact before the situation deteriorated once more.

From the Czechoslovak point of view, as from so many others, 1956 was in fact a real tragedy. The Hungarian débâcle changed the whole east European atmosphere. Concomitantly, the Suez crisis increased East-West tension again and incidentally rekindled east European anti-Zionism. There had been one or two quite promising changes inside Czechoslovakia. In the middle of the year an important concession was made to the Slovaks. Their National Council was once more given the authority to appoint and remove the commissioners, and its chairman regained some of the prerogatives he had lost to the prime minister in Prague in 1948. Neither of these changes meant very much in itself. But along with one or two others (of even less importance)they pointed a way; and had it not been for the sad turn of events by the end of 1956, they might have been the prelude to a wider reform movement. As it was, the official attitude became increasingly reactionary. All talk of reform was suppressed, and a new Communist Party hue and cry went out against revisionism. Renewed collectivisation in agriculture and fresh emphasis on heavy industry were more characteristic of the late 1950s than concern for justice or thoughts of devolution. By 1960 the Czechoslovak economy was basically unsuccessful. The stain of the trials had not been wiped away, and the country was still run by a small party clique. The Czechoslovak people were dispirited. Socialism had been distorted, and there was nothing they could do to restore it; but a new generation was arising that would have to effect a change or explode.

The Reform Movement 1960-1967

In the twelfth year of Communist rule, 1960, Novotný was understandably proud of the achievements of himself and his party. The economy might be stagnating, but there were lots of quotable social statistics. The number of children in nursery schools had more than doubled since 1948; the number of students at universities had gone up by 50 percent. The ratio of doctors to inhabitants had halved; the number of hospital beds had gone up by 50 percent. The number of people in receipt of pensions had increased by a third. Houses were being built at twice the rate of 1948; four times as many people had washing machines, and every sixteenth person was the proud possessor of a television set. Novotný himself had made a remarkable advance. In 1948 he had been no more than influential secretary of the Prague regional committee; in 1953 he had been appointed first secretary of the central committee and, while holding on to that office, he had become President in 1958. He was the first man to combine the top jobs in the party and the state. He and his colleagues had survived much: their own early inexperience and the Soviet-inspired terror; the post-1953 thaw and the post-1956 freeze. They had the blood of the dead on their hands; but they seemed more firmly in power than ever. Indeed, Novotný was more than proud; he was downright aggressive. It was in 1960 that he felt able to introduce a new constitution that established Czechoslovakia officially as the Czechoslovak Socialist Republic and laid the foundations for the expected transition to communism.

There was more than one explanation for the new constitution. The 1948 model had been a mixture of Western democratic and communist ideas, and much of it therefore had been outdated by the practice of the intervening years. So much else was now being done on Soviet lines that it was incongruous not to adapt the constitution as well. The 1960 model inevitably showed fundamental changes. There was no provision for businesses up to fifty employees or landholdings up to 50 hectares. All that was officially allowed was the one-man enterprise, though land was still not nationalised but held in co-operative use. The economic foundation of the state was the socialist economic system, and the entire national economy was to be directed by a plan, promulgated as law. Civil rights were defined as before to include the rights to work, leisure, and medical care; but freedom of expression now had to be consistent with the interests of the working people. Citizens were legally bound to pay heed to the interests of the socialist state, to protect and strengthen socialist ownership as the inviolable foundation of the socialist social order, and also to observe carefully rules of socialist conduct; and it was a function of the courts to ensure that they did. Cultural and educational policy was to be in the spirit of Marxism-Leninism. In fact, the socialist principles and character of the state were writ large in every article of the constitution, and no doubt was now left about who would maintain them. The guiding force was the vanguard of the working class, the Communist Party, specified as a voluntary militant alliance of the most active, politically conscious citizens from the ranks of the workers, farmers, and intelligentsia. In the previous constitution the Communist Party had not even been mentioned; but the new one recognised reality and followed Soviet practice. It also exuded Novotný's confidence: people's democracy had led to the victory of socialism in Czechoslovakia, and everything now had to be directed to creating the conditions for the transition to communism.

Yet, whatever the constitution adumbrated, there were many who saw it as in some measure a sham. That no one would be prosecuted except in cases authorised by law and no one punished except by due process of law cut little ice with those already falsely imprisoned. That the Slovak National Council was now described as the national organ of state power and administration carried little weight with Slovaks who saw that it was palpably unable to do anything worthwhile on its own. On a more general plane, the assertion that the socialist economy made sure of a tremendous development in production and a continuous rise in living standards was a bad joke almost before it was made. The index of industrial production began to rise much less markedly after 1960 and actually declined in 1963. The index of agricultural production levelled off in 1961 and dropped in 1962. From the point of view of the general public this was a serious betrayal. For years they had been promised a higher standard of living. They had learned to sublimate their political discontent in material hopes. They had been encouraged by no less a person than Khrushchev to think that the communist world would soon catch up on Western standards; and despite moments of tension over Berlin and Cuba, they now knew much more about Western standards than before. Yet here were Czechs and Slovaks in the early 1960s entering a period of obvious economic decline. It was no longer enough to blame shortcomings on saboteurs and subversives. The trials were discredited, the failings too great. The young were particularly incredulous and impatient—and particularly numerous. The war and post-war baby boom endowed the 1960s with a teenage and twenty-plus boom. To them the new constitution was not simply a mockery; it was a challenge. Indeed, it might even be said that the constitution did less to prepare the ground for communism than to call socialism into question.

Novotný and his colleagues, in fact, simply did not understand the new society they had helped to fashion. It was one without individual holdings of industrial capital and with few personal savings, one in which little more than 10 percent of the agricultural land was privately farmed. The gap between different incomes had narrowed considerably over twelve years. It was an outwardly socialist society. On the other hand, where the average wage-earner was paid about 15,000 crowns a year, almost a tenth of the total earned less than 10,000 and almost a fifth earned above 20,000. The wage differential between male and female employees had not noticeably diminished; nor had the income differential between employees and pensioners. There were also some surprising individual discrepancies: managers and miners fared very well, doctors, nurses, and textile-workers did comparatively badly. What the top party and security officials earned remained a closely guarded secret, but was reputed to be disproportionately high. There was considerable financial discrimination against politically undesirable pensioners.

Czechoslovak society therefore had residual economic tensions. It was also encountering new social tensions. In twelve years the number of people employed in agriculture and forestry had gone down by a third. Many of them had been absorbed by industry and construction, whose labour force had gone up by a quarter. In both areas of production the ratio of white-collar workers to others had increased noticeably from about 1:6 to about 1:4, many of them highly skilled technical personnel who represented a new pressure-group. There had also been an increase of some 50 percent in the numbers employed in education, cultural activities generally, and the various health services, and of some 200 percent in science and research. They constituted another, similar pressure-group. Educational policy had also had some odd results. The children of the former middle class and of the politically condemned had largely been denied a higher education, and they inevitably formed a small discontented group. The children of co-operative farm workers, who made up less than a tenth of the employed population, got their fair share of higher education. But the children of workers, who made up more than a half of the employed population, received little more than a third of the higher education places, while the children of the technocrats and the intelligentsia took up correspondingly more than their fair share. Consequently there were those young people who felt that socialism had not done well by the workers, and those who had profited from it but were conditioned by their social background and intellectual training to call it seriously in question. Even when students themselves passed into the ranks of the technocrats and the intelligentsia and occasionally lost their ideological edge, they acquired ambition for social standing and economic wellbeing. They were not anti-socialist, but were simply disposed to be critical of Novotný's Soviet-style, unsuccessful socialism. No accumulation of absolute statistics, for example, could hide the fact that Czechoslovakia was producing fewer houses annually, in proportion to its population, than any west European state, and that for the up-and-coming generation it was exceedingly difficult to get something as basic as a home.

To the grudges and disillusionment of the middle-aged had now been added the frustrations and ambitions of the young. In the atmosphere of neo-Stalinism that had persisted since 1956 feelings were bottled up, but they were all the stronger for that. Nowhere were they fiercer than in Slovakia. There it was not simply a question of old scores, of autonomy denied, of Clementis murdered, of Husák still in prison in 1960. By 1960 the Slovaks had gone a quarter to a third of the way towards catching up with the Czechs in industrial and agricultural development. They were already experiencing similar economic and social tensions. On top of that, they still considered themselves disadvantaged in not having caught up further on the Czechs. Their faster rate of development and their speedier rise in population made them more impatient in aspiring to equality. Their residual Catholicism and their unrequited nationalism had made them *a priori* somewhat loth to accept communism as a way forward; but their real hatred now was for the way communism seemed to be used by the Czechs for their own advantage. To have a Slovak as prime minister was no compensation, for Široký was the very man who had stepped into Clementis's shoes, thereby condoning his murder. The Slovaks were anxious to improve their position in the state; and after a dozen years of communism they had at last one accretion of strength. They had a sizeable working class, a much more articulate peasantry, and a large managerial group and intelligentsia of their own. They were set to make or accept a challenge, and they found one in Novotný's totally unyielding constitution.

What Novotný viewed as a blueprint for the future, therefore, many others saw as an indictment of the present. The criticisms of the early 1960s had been foreshadowed in the mid-fifties; they were now proffered with much more confidence. The groups advancing them were more mature and numerous, and had more reason. The economic situation was deteriorating rapidly. The third five-year plan began in January 1961 and was immediately in trouble. Before the end of the year the targets for 1962 were reduced, and by the summer of 1962 the whole plan was cancelled, with no more than the promise of a seven-year plan to start in 1964. The critics also had outside support. In October 1961 the twenty-second congress of the communist party of the Soviet Union gave another push in the direction of de-Stalinisation; and it was obviously impressed upon Novotný that he had to catch up on his fellow leaders in eastern Europe. In fairness to him, it must also be said that those seeking reform found consolation in some aspects of the 1960 constitution. One of its major Marxist tenets was that government, in accordance with the principle of democratic centralism, should be effectively combined with the broad authority and responsibility of lower organs. In theory, therefore, government and reformers could work together. The new constitution also converted the National Assembly from supreme legislative organ to supreme organ of state power, in theory giving it authority over everything, the Communist Party included. There might thus be many roads to reform. Finally, the constitution demoted the President so that he was simply the representative of state power, elected by and accountable to the National Assembly, and without the right to dissolve it or to veto its laws. This meant that the assembly could control the President as well as his party. On the other hand, the old-style presidency was not wholly abandoned; the head of state was not a mere cypher. So there was a relic of pre-communist Czechoslovakia to hearten at least some of those who despaired of the present. However, it must be emphasised that very few, if any, of those who now criticised Novotný wished to go back to the pre-communist period. They might want to resurrect some features of past life more suited to Czechoslovakia; but they were certainly not anti-socialist. They wanted to reform socialism, to make it more humane, prosperous, and alive. And they wished to reform it from within—which meant in the first instance from within the party.

Unfortunately, this proved impossible in the short run, though historians of the long run may one day be able to say that it was successful. The Novotný who imagined in 1960 that Czechoslovakia stood on the threshold of communism was not the person most likely to see the need for reform. The man who would concede little before 1960 and who would then throw down an uncompromising constitution was not the one most likely to welcome his critics. The drama of the years down to 1968 is largely that of reasonable requests unreasonably refused or sensible reforms unduly delayed till, in the end, the situation became uncontrollable.

To abandon the five-year plan was embarrassing—in the wake of the constitution—but planning had already got out of cycle in the mid-1950s. It was also possible to plead special factors such as the drop in trade with China or the delay in various Soviet deliveries. To consider industrial reorganisation was not altogether unprecedented. A limited managerial devolution was accepted in 1958—though it was ineffective. To re-examine agricultural policy was in some measure to extend a review already under way. 1959 had seen the beginning of a campaign to encourage the fusion of small co-operatives into larger ones and to reorganise farming prices. So a thorough study of Czechoslovakia's growth, or lack of it, was not out of the question. It would be difficult; and inferences drawn from it might upset more than the top party brass. But the most difficult, and immediate, task was to get a thoroughgoing review of the trials.

The trouble about going further than before was that it would be impossible to maintain the fiction of Slánský's guilt, that others still ensconced in positions of power would be exposed, that Novotný himself would be deeply implicated, and that there might then be no stopping the overthrow of both policies and people. The fact that the trials had become a symbol made their reversal much more important for the reformers and, equally, much more dangerous for the establishment. At the twelfth congress of the Communist Party held in December 1962, however, it was announced that a commission was already making a detailed investigation. This was a notable advance for the reformers and a significant retreat for Novotný. One of the main reasons for the volte-face was in fact a division within the party hierarchy. It seems that Barák, sensing the new atmosphere and anxious both to protect himself and to advance his career, had been preparing to attack Novotný on the basis of incriminating documents he had collected when responsible for the previous investigation. Novotný discovered the ploy and obviously decided to steal his thunder and make him a scapegoat. It was an opportunity not to be missed, particularly when Barák could with good cause be accused of misappropriation of funds while minister of the interior. Once Barák had been imprisoned in February, the way was open for a commission of inquiry to proceed without putting the responsibility on Novotný. However, what was conceded to the reformers was a point, not the whole match.

This was the tragedy of the situation. The inquiry was not independent; it was entrusted to a special commission of the central committee of the Communist Party, that is, a sub-group of the second most inner sanctum of the body most involved. Its chairman was Drahomír Kolder, only thirty-seven and wholly free of blame for the trials. Its members included Alexander Dubček, four years older but also free of blame. But it had to do everything in agreement with Novotný. It was not allowed to examine the trials as a coherent whole (and of course it paid no attention to the trials of non-communists). One of its prominent members was the man who had prosecuted Slánský; two others had served on the mainly cover-up Barák inquiry of 1955-57. And all the old guard denied both knowledge and responsibility despite the evidence against them. In the end, Novotný stage-managed practically everything. The commission's report, as finally approved in May 1963, put some of the blame on the dead and the disgraced, including Barák. But Novotný saved his own skin by throwing several colleagues to the wolves: in particular, Köhler was removed as secretary to the central committee and Bacílek as first secretary of the Slovak Communist organisation. Most of the victims of the main trials were exonerated, and those who were alive but still in prison were freed. The rehabilitated made an impressive list. But Slánský and four of his group were not posthumously readmitted to the party; it was considered necessary still to be able to smear someone. It also took one of the first Slovak campaigns against Prague, in the press, at meetings of the writers' union and other bodies, and within the party, to persuade Novotný, against his wishes, to rehabilitate Husák, Novomeský, and Clementis in December 1963. Yet although he was compelled to get rid of Široký as prime minister, he nonetheless managed to retain him as a member of the central committee. For the next three years rehabilitations trickled gradually on; so did the trials of officials guilty of injustices. But Novotný evaded responsibility, and the dead Slánský was kept off the party roll. In addition, no effective steps were taken to ensure that the trials would not recur. On the eve of 1968 the stain had still not been completely removed from the Communist Party.

When Novotný told the twelfth congress of the party that a full inquiry was under way, it was to still criticism rather than to seek co-operation. Up to a point he was right in thinking that the rank-and-file were a docile lot, or alternatively that their consciences were as bad as his own. By contrast, when it came to economic matters, they had no guilt-complex; their concern was with success. Here, where there was no question of conscience even for Novotný, he showed singularly little imagination. He sought authorisation for more, not less, centralisation, for the establishment of commissions for development and price determination, and for the institution of pyramids of central commissions in industry and production administrations in agriculture to ensure implementation of government policy at every level. He had too long used the party, like the National Assembly, as an agent for the execution of policy to be able to seek inspiration and initiatives from it. On the other hand, he did announce the setting-up of a committee to consider possible economic reforms. Yet even this was a tactic to quieten critics on the central committee, new men like the forty-three-year-old Professor Ota Šik, head of economics at the Higher Party School since 1953 and increasingly an exponent of devolution in the economy. Šik was a product of the party and anxious to work within it. But Novotný was almost as incapable of seeking and accepting advice from the central committee as from lower down. He would not do anything rash; he would only go so far as to accept a committee.

Šik was only one of the growing economic reform group, the one best placed to exert political pressure. As the group saw things, in broad terms, the Czechoslovak economy had passed its period of crude or extensive development and was entering its period of intensive development. For this, nationalisation was not enough and centralisation could be harmful. It was necessary to introduce some element of marketing, of supply and demand, of cost-accounting and profit-making, of quality against quantity, of devolution of management. Socialist principles were no use without a touch of economic realism—as the disintegration of the five-year plan so eloquently proved. After much discussion, some of this made sense even to Novotný. He needed economic success. If decentralisation were introduced, then responsibility for failure could always be passed down the line. On the other hand, marketing had all the flavour of capitalism; and economic decentralisation could have political consequences that would leave the Communist Party almost powerless. There were also enormous vested interests, from bureaucratic planners who might lose their sinecures to industrial workers who might have to change factories. And there were deep personal factors; Novotný did not like brilliant colleagues, any more than he liked intellectuals and Jews—and unfortunately Šik was all three at once.

In September 1964 the politbureau and the government accepted a new set of economic principles. In theory, they were close to the ideas of the Šik group, and they were timetabled to be introduced in 1965 and to be operative in full by January 1966. In the course of 1965 the functions of several ministries and commissions were redefined to reduce their powers of direction and to leave more decisions to management and the growing operation of economic forces. Also in 1965 a start was made to carving up industry into so-called associations and trusts, vertical and horizontal production groups organised for self-management purposes. Inevitably there were difficulties. It was often just as much of a problem to get managers not to look for instructions as to get ministers not to give them. There was confusion between directive and guidance indices issued by the government, and misunderstanding about the necessity for devolution within the new industrial groups. Four out of five of them were trusts, which were virtual monopolies and made competition difficult. To go from a totally planned to a mixed economy raised particularly tricky questions in relation to wages, investments, and prices. It was not easy to maintain general levels and allow a reasonable degree of freedom to different managements. The reform of wholesale prices, which was central to other changes, was a mammoth task; and in 1966 it was eventually decided to do it in two stages, the first in 1967, the second in 1968. So all in all, reform made some progress, although it was an uphill task.

That it was so uphill was largely due to Novotný. When he accepted the new economic principles in September 1964, he made it clear that he saw them not as a fundamental reform, but as an improved version of the existing system. He himself had not changed, and he would not force others to do so. And the forces of conservatism at all levels were remarkably strong—old-guard politicians and economists who feared for their positions or influence, managers and workers afraid of revelations of their incompetence or laziness. There were other conservative forces in the background. Some of the reformers wanted to apply the new principles to Czechoslovakia's foreign trade. Free competition with the world would be beneficial in introducing foreign technology and raising production standards. Czechoslovakia should cease to lend at a low rate of interest to eastern Europe and the third world, taking payment in raw materials at a disadvantageous price. It should accept credit from the West as a means of access to Western machines and know-how. However, this last was too much even for a few of the reformers. One of them was Oldřich Černík, another of the rising post-war Communists, who became chairman of the state planning commission in 1963 when only forty-two. He was an orthodox balance-of-trade practitioner when it came to exports and imports. With Novotný he approved the expansion of tourism in Czechoslovakia as a hard currency earner, but at the central committee in December 1966 he disapproved of getting into foreign debt. Novotný's disapproval, however, was of getting into Western debt. Gottwald's humiliation over the Marshall Plan offer was engraved on every old guard's memory. With Khrushchev's fall in October 1964, the attitude of the Russians to many things was changing and, loans apart, it was rumoured in 1967 that they were not unhappy to see difficulties arising in Czechoslovakia's commercial talks with Germany and the United States. Novotný had no wish to be in capitalism's debt; but above all, he did not want to fall foul of Moscow. Part of the resistance to economic reform came indirectly from the Soviet Union.

Czechoslovakia's total turnover in foreign trade increased by a half in the period 1960-67; but the proportion with the West grew by a mere 1½ percent to 19½ percent. Šik himself seems to have been keen to go much faster; possibly he was a little impatient, but he was concerned that lack of speed would lead to failure which would put paid to all reform. He was also afraid that the slow progress implied a lack of conviction which would in any case stifle innovation. What was conceivably just as annoying was that, as a result partly of half-measures and partly perhaps of inertia, the Czechoslovak economy was gradually recovering. The index of industrial production, which had fallen to 427 in 1963, was up to 551 by the end of 1967. What the reformers required was either implementation of their whole programme and success, or proof that the whole of it was needed. Novotný seemed to be ensuring them the worst of both worlds.

The reformers also tackled agriculture. Despite the fact that its performance since 1948 had been poorer than that of industry, they tackled it second, largely because of its declining importance in the social product. In 1948 its contribution had been approximately 18 percent; in the 1960s it averaged a mere 10 percent. First things first meant reforming industry. Another reason was the continuing decrease in the number of people employed in farming; from the end of 1960 to the end of 1967 it dropped by practically another 200,000 to 1,170,000. From an economic standpoint the peasants were rationalising themselves, while from a political point of view they represented a diminishing pressure-group. It was also significant that they had no representative body to look after their interests; only the quarter of a million peasants on the state farms were encouraged to join trade unions. Novotný did not want to stimulate those who had been forced into co-operatives—or those still farming privately—to join bodies that might voice their complaints. Nevertheless, the reformers did eventually get round to adapting their industrial principles to agriculture. There was no doubt about the need for reform. After much preparation, Novotný introduced a revised plan for farming early in 1961. Like the new constitution before it, it relied heavily on Soviet practice. Co-operatives were to be amalgamated wherever possible to form large factory-like agricultural enterprises; and in return for handing over their private plots, co-operative farmers were to receive wages and ultimately pensions. But Czechoslovak peasants obviously did not fancy a Russian-style 'agrotown' existence, and although amalgamations reduced the number of co-operatives by a quarter in the period 1961-67, their members still derived a third of their income from private plots. More important, despite an extraordinary success in 1964 when the index of agricultural production rose above the pre-war level for the first time ever, output in the years 1961-65 remained below the 1960 point. By 1966, therefore, the case for reform was overwhelming even for a stubborn Novotný who would have liked properly to socialise the countryside before experimenting with quasi-capitalist notions. A cutback in central planning was announced in June, and a marketing system introduced—though goods still had to be sold to monopolistic state agencies, and little genuine competition resulted. New associations of farms, both state and collective, were formed in 1967. Known as district agricultural organisations, they mirrored their industrial counterparts. By the end of 1967 reform was under way. Yet fear of a farmers' market, the fiercest form of competition there could be, still put a limit on how far Novotný would countenance innovation. Put the clock back in the countryside and socialism would be in jeopardy everywhere else. And oddly enough, what happened in industry happened in agriculture. In 1966 the production index rose above its previous record, and in 1967 it rose even further, a tantalising situation which left the reformers arguing that more reform would work better and their opponents that none was necessary.

Slovak pressure had been important in securing a review of the trials and in carrying it much further than Novotný had intended. Slovak pressure was again important in the quest for economic reform. The man who replaced Široký as prime minister in December 1963 was another Slovak, but one of an entirely different stamp. Jozef Lenárt was one of the young middle-aged who had won his spurs in the Slovak rising and then come to prominence in the later 1950s. Forty years of age in 1963, he was a pragmatist rather than an innate reformer, but he was too radical by 1963 to be Novotný's choice. His experience, including a period working as a young man in the Bat'a concern, taught him a good deal of commonsense economics; and it was this that he applied after 1963. As prime minister he was responsible for much of the work of implementing Šik's proposals, but his support was also crucial at meetings of the central committee of the party. In contrast to Černík, for example, he argued in favour of seeking foreign credit. Dubček also became an advocate of economic change. His background and outlook were somewhat akin to those of Lenárt, but he found himself much more taken up with party work and with matters affecting Slovakia directly. He succeeded Bacílek as Slovak Communist organisation secretary in May 1963, against Novotný's wishes, but he was still relatively middle-of-the-road and mainly concerned with Slovak affairs. By 1966, however, Novotný's hostility, Šik's advocacy, and Slovakia's needs had made of him, too, a supporter of economic decentralisation and competition. In this he mirrored, in particular, the Slovak view that economically it was always the Czechs who benefited. The Slovak record in industry since 1960 was superior to the Czech. In the bad year, 1963, there was actually a fractional rise in the Slovak index of industrial production, and over the period from the end of 1960 to the end of 1967 there was as much as an 80 percent rise. In agriculture the Slovak record was slightly better than the Czech. Looking at these figures, Prague tended to point to the advantages for the Slovaks of the Czech connection. But the Slovaks, including Dubček, saw it the other way round. Slovakia started from such a poor base that its output indices ought to be rising even faster. When Slovakia did well but the Czech Lands did not, everyone had to suffer, including the unfortunate Slovaks. Despite Slovakia's common frontier with Russia, raw materials from there still crossed its territory to be processed in Czech factories and then returned. Almost twice as many Slovaks went to the Czech Lands in search of work as vice versa. Even after the introduction of the first reforms all the new organisations were still in Prague. What was needed was large-scale devolution, even a separate plan and administrative group for Slovakia. By 1967, when the argument over economic reform in Czechoslovakia as a whole came near the point of confrontation, the Slovak viewpoint, as pressed by Dubček, had become an inflammatory constituent.

As the Czechs and Slovaks together, and the Slovaks separately, sought redress of wrongs done in the 1950s, or reform of the economy in the sixties, they increasingly came up against the need for political change. The removal of a number of individuals was not enough. Others would have to be deposed; but what was most required was a change in the system. Dismantling the trials produced a series of laws between 1963 and 1967 that improved the investigation and court procedures and aligned them with the principles of the 1960 constitution. Many held that the new laws did not go far enough and that the 1960 principles required major amendment. However, no matter what set of rules was in force, the question still remained how their implementation could be guaranteed. This was a political question that raised not only the future of Novotný but also the relationship of the Communist Party to the whole constitutional system. The gradual introduction of economic reform both posed political questions and suggested answers. Thus a case could be made out for devolving political decisions to match economic ones and for exposing Communist politicians to the stimulus of competition and the criterion of efficiency. As for the Slovaks, they could hardly say a word without reminding themselves and the country at large that under the 1960 constitution they were barely entitled to. If they were to have more than grudging tolerance, then a fundamental political change was vastly overdue.

Whatever else Novotný was, he was a political animal. He had come up through the party machine and had made himself head both of it and of the state machine. He was not anxious to lose either post, and he was equally disinclined to weaken the control of the party over the state. As the internal party debate intensified during the 1960s he maintained his position, if not his authority, by slowly conceding points and sacrificing colleagues, a process that spread outwards to state matters. His agreement to reconsider the false condemnation of Communists led on to his retreat from planning and his partial reorganisation of central government. It was the same in other areas. The 1962 party congress agreed to several important reforming measures, but the delegates themselves took little real part in the decision-making. By contrast, the thirteenth congress in June 1966 itself moved the party towards the reformers' position, and it was also allowed to revise the party statutes in such a way as to emphasise the democratic as well as to underscore the centralism in the official view of discipline. Greater initiative was permitted to individual members; and more regularity of meetings and turnover of members was stipulated for a variety of committees. The process of conceding a little democracy to the party was obviously a slow one; but in the midst of it a similar concession had to be made to the people at large. In May 1964 Novotný accepted that the National Assembly should in future carry out its constitutional function as the supreme organ of state power. It was to meet regularly, often and for longer periods; it was to debate legislation and question ministers; its committees were to examine regulations and to interrogate officials; it was to cultivate public interest in its work. Laws of 1964 and 1967 even experimented with electoral reform. Electors were given the opportunity of expressing their opinion of possible candidates and then of voting from lists with rather more than the required number of actual contenders. But this was not a major reform. There was no guarantee that electors' views, if expressed, would be heeded in selecting the ultimate lists; and they were not taken into account in determining the order of candidates that more or less decided who would be elected. There was no question of Novotný allowing the composition of the National Assembly to be settled other than by the party. He made a token concession to the public, a minor adjustment to past practice. Equally, the implementation of part of the 1960 constitution concerning the National Assembly was not a major reform. It was the belated recognition in practice of existing theoretical rights. The grant of a greater degree of financial self-sufficiency and political autonomy to national committees at all levels was also both a concession and the honouring of an obligation, but not a basic change in the system. The party remained supreme in the state, and Novotný in both.

The same was true of Slovakia. In May 1964 Novotný accepted the need to restore some semblance of power to the Slovak National Council and therefore authorised legislation granting it rights in the preparation and implementation of economic plans. This also appeared to give it control over the national committees in Slovakia. From then on it met more frequently and debated more robustly. But it remained subject to the National Assembly in Prague in all important questions; and its power over the national committees was largely cancelled out by the parallel process of devolution towards them. The commissioners, who had lost their right to sit together as a board in 1960, now had it restored and had their number doubled. Their views were more often taken into account by the appropriate ministers in Prague and they ceased to be powerless officials. Nonetheless, their authority was not spelled out and they remained in theory and practice responsible to the central government. Novotný yielded little of his own or the party's position.

Grudging progress towards a halfway house did not satisfy the reformers, least of all the Slovaks. In the autumn of 1966 Novotný yielded another point. He agreed that the party should set up and the state fund a committee of the Institute of State and Law to make a long-term study of politics under socialism. In one sense, this was a remarkable concession. It recognised that the class struggle was no longer the main driving force in society, that a new and complex social structure required a fundamentally different political system. The terms of reference for the committee envisaged that it would examine a variety of systems other than socialist and that it would seek means of ensuring the participation in decision-making of all reasonable interest groups and of guaranteeing the democratic formulation of policy. It was free to scrutinise public opinion and to consider topics such as workers' management. Its chairman was Zdeněk Mlynář, a young lawyer of thirty-six, and its membership ran to a variety of Communist academics, including economists, sociologists, and historians. It was to make the first of a series of reports in 1968 or 1969, and one way and another it promised a thoroughgoing look at Czechoslovak politics and the possibility at last of fundamental change. In another sense, however, the setting-up of a further committee was a delaying tactic. The party intelligentsia could go on studying systems and proposing research while Novotný and the old guard went on manipulating the existing system. What the reformers saw as a possible breakthrough, Novotný viewed as a diversion.

It was this difference of approach that produced the tension of 1967. Novotný's delaying tactics eventually exasperated the reformers, particularly since they steadily raised their own expectations. The force behind this was above all the new Czechoslovak intelligentsia. Šik typified one group, part intellectual as he was and part politician, but there were others. Mlynář was an example of the large and varied group of academics with occasional political connections and an intensifying political interest. During the 1960s their research and writing led them inexorably from criticism to condemnation. Initially they fed on the revelations of the rehabilitation commissions, but they went on to compare the theory and practice of Czechoslovak society and politics and to contrast them vividly with much of the rest of the world. They reassessed. Thus Pavel Machonin largely converted the Institute of Marxism-Leninism into an institute of sociological studies and cast aside the class analysis of Czechoslovak society in favour of differentiation of groups by work done. They questioned. Thus Michal Suchý, a Czech philosopher, asked why there was no genuine right to criticise. His Slovak counterpart, Julius Strinka, went on to ask why there was no institutionalised criticism or official opposition. Another Slovak, Michal Lakatos, a legal scholar, queried the lack of widespread participation through genuine elections. Together, and with many others, they were beginning in fact to question the leading role of the party in society, and even to attack it. By implication, Mlynář's committee was to put the party on trial.

But the intelligentsia who pushed furthest were another group, the writers. Since the mid-1950s they had been pressing at the limits of the possible, testing the censors and airing ideas that to others would have been unthinkable. It was the traditional role of the poets, the story-tellers, and the critics; it was the new role thrust on them by a monolithic communist society. At the so-called second writers' congress in 1956 Jaroslav Seifert, the working-class poet who had first made a name for himself between the wars, had called on his colleagues, in the wake of Khrushchev's denunciation of Stalin, to act as the conscience of the nation. This was not a political battle-cry; it was an appeal to cast aside the propagandistic role of the Stalinist years and to evaluate society in the name of truthfulness and humanity. He had been joined by Ladislav Mňačko, a young Slovak novelist, and others weary of the sycophancy and hagiography of the Gottwald era. But under political attack in the late 1950s, they had had to keep their thoughts to themselves. However, the situation changed radically in December 1962 with Novotný's announcement at the twelfth party congress that the hated trials were under review. The two writers' journals—*Literární noviny* (*Literary News*) published in Prague and *Kultúrny život (Cultural Life)* published in Bratislava—rapidly developed as pioneers of criticism, challenging the censorship and the ideology behind it at every possible turn. Other journals sprang to life, and occasionally even the dull party newspapers showed signs of daring. In April 1963, for example, the Slovak *Bratislava pravda (Bratislava Truth)* published a poem in honour of Clementis, written by Novomeský, although neither had yet been rehabilitated. Slovaks, indeed, made some of the earliest running. In the same month the Slovak writers' congress took unilateral action by readmitting Novomeský to membership of the writers' union and electing him to its ruling committee; the congress then went on to attack those writers who succumbed to political pressure and the political pressure to which they were exposed. The third congress of Czechoslovak writers the following month took a line similarly critical of Novotný's policies and called for freedom to travel and to publish. In the same month Goldstücker, released in 1955 and professor of German literature at Prague since 1956, caused a minor storm throughout eastern Europe by running a conference to restore Franz Kafka to his former place in literature. From then on the writers were inextricably involved in political issues, though seldom in politics as such. There was a series of breakthroughs. In 1963 Josef Skvorecký's *The Cowards,* confiscated in 1958 for its lack of respect for the liberation of Czechoslovakia in 1945, was allowed to go to print. So was Mňačko's *Belated Reports,* long vetoed for its sketches of injustice under Stalinism. In 1965 the Czech dramatist Václav Havel succeeded in producing *The Memorandum,* a bitter satire on socialism and bureaucracy. In 1966 the Czechoslovak writers' union sent a delegation to Moscow to protest about the trial of Sinyavsky and Daniel, dissident Soviet writers; and in the same year the Czech novelist Ludvík Vaculík published *The*

Axe, essentially a personal testament to the shortcomings of Czechoslovak communism. However, it was the following year before his fellow novelist Milan Kundera could publish a similar work, *The Joke,* completed in 1965. Nevertheless, between the third and fourth writers' congresses, that is between 1963 and 1967, the literary intelligentsia pushed the party into granting them even greater freedom to make what were fundamentally political criticisms.

They did not have it all their own way. One of the younger old guard, Jiří Hendrych, just on fifty in 1963, was appointed chairman of the ideological commission of the central committee in 1965. On Novotný's behalf he kept up a running battle with the writers' union. Several journals were closed down or their editors replaced. In August 1966 a young Czech author, Jan Beneš, was arrested for writing in a Czech journal based in Paris. About the same time Mňačko was refused permission to publish his latest criticism, *The Taste of Power;* and when he published it in Austria in 1967, the party instituted disciplinary proceedings against him. In October 1966 a new press law was enacted that opened acts of censorship to a challenge in the courts, but it still preserved censorship and made the censors responsible to the ministry of the interior. Early in 1967 the operation of the law became a contentious issue, particularly since more and more of the brilliant but critical products of Czechoslovak film studios were being banned. Yet another issue materialised over the Arab-Israeli war in June, since the official anti-Israeli line smacked of earlier anti-semitism and seemed to champion big neighbours against a progressive small state. The writers felt strongly about being unable to express their views in opposition to the government's, and saw Israel's fate in terms of Czechoslovakia's—past, present, and future. From the point of view of the party, however, foreign policy was nothing to do with the writers, or with the public at large; and there could certainly be no dispute with whatever was the Soviet line on the Middle East. On the eve of the fourth writers' congress tension between the writers and the party old guard was almost at breaking-point.

Hendrych's initial speech on 27 June was predictably hard-line. Kundera's opening address amounted inevitably to an all-out attack on the party's policy towards literature and its continuance of censorship. Others followed in the same vein, but Pavel Kohout, a popular Czech dramatist, turned his invective against its policy towards Israeli independence. On the second day there were some moderate speeches, but the Czech novelist Jan Procházka was one of several to resume the attack. Vaculík, however, went further than anyone else by attacking the party as such, by condemning its leading role as the basis of totalitarianism, and by demanding a new constitution to end its monopoly of power and create a democracy. One of the writers had finally said clearly and publicly what many of the intelligentsia and reformers in general had gradually come to believe that, if the party diehards would not accept far-reaching reforms, then the party itself would have to be demoted and made subject to competition from other groups in a genuinely socialist democracy. There was now open political warfare. Novotný had conceded too little too late and evaded fundamental change. Some of his critics had been pushed to extremes and were striking at the very basis of his power. On the third and last day of the congress Hendrych counter-attacked with a diatribe against Vaculík, while Procházka called again for full freedom of expression. Novotný managed to prevent the major offenders from taking their elected places on the union's praesidium and Procházka from acting as its chairman, but he never succeeded in finding an alternative chairman. In July, Beneš and two others were put on trial, and Beneš was sentenced to five years in prison. In August, Mňačko decamped to Israel and made a public display of his disgust, but he was deprived of Czechoslovak citizenship. At the end of September, Novotný and Hendrych persuaded the central committee to begin proceedings against Procházka, to expel Vaculík and two other dissidents from the party, to transfer *Literární noviny* to the ministry of culture and information, and to close the writers' union publishing house. The sales of *Literární noviny* contracted dramatically; and the Slovak writers, whose unwonted caution in June had been cunningly rewarded with the establishment of their own independent section of the union, came to life again in October through a series of attacks on party policy and the use of *Kultúrny život* as a journal for all the writers, Czech as well as Slovak. As winter came on, neither side would concede an inch.

Many discontents were now pressing together. Justice had neither been fully done for the past, nor secured for the future. The economy was the subject of fierce discussion, the nature of politics a matter of violent public controversy. And the Slovak question surfaced everywhere. Thus, fully rehabilitated but not yet welcomed back as a politician, Husák spoke out in favour of genuine political autonomy for Slovakia. Dubček's interest in economic reform turned increasingly to accelerating the development of Slovakia. One historian, Miloš Gosiorovský, recalled the federal system proposed by the so-called Pittsburgh Agreement in the First World War; another, Ján Mlynárik, wrote enthusiastically about Šmeral's federal ideas after the war; and another, Daniel Rapant, a non-communist, even argued in favour of an ultimately independent Slovakia in a neutral central Europe. The Slovak writers gave succour to their Czech colleagues. And finally, in mid-November, *Bratislava pravda* published an article by Dubček in which he called for a new nationality policy. A full confrontation could not long be avoided.

Behind the complaints of the reformers in general were the feelings of many less vocal Czechs and Slovaks, not least those with education and some ambition. Their frustrations of the early 1960s had been ameliorated a little. But their expectations had not been satisfied and had even increased both with the progress of reform and through growing contact with the West, however vicarious. Yet perhaps the final pressure for genuine change emerged from the attitude and experience of the students. In 1949 a mass Czechoslovak union of youth had been formed to stimulate and direct young people from sixteen to twenty-six years of age. The rights membership conveyed made it almost compulsory. But by 1960 the union included little more than half the age-group, and the proportion declined steadily over the next few years. It was too much to expect one body to embrace such a wide span of years and such a broad range of interests as was presented by young workers and farmers and students; and increasing disillusionment did the rest. That apart, the feeling for a separate student organisation and the tradition of student individuality were both very strong. The year 1956 had proved a false dawn; the customary festival on 1 May frightened the government into a temporary ban that in fact lasted until 1965, and the students felt compelled to withhold their demands. In the 1960s, however, they felt free to advocate reform of the union of youth in such a way as to separate those over eighteen from those under and to divide those over into three sections, one of them the students. They also advocated separate political standing for the union through direct representation on all political bodies such as the National Assembly. The whole party was disturbed about the union; at one extreme, juvenile delinquency was high and increasing, while at the other, Communist enthusiasm was low and decreasing. But the old guard were opposed to the distinctiveness and importance that the students claimed. They attacked proposals put to a students' conference in Prague in December 1965, and exactly a year later they ensured that the main student spokesman, Jiří Mueller, was expelled from the Charles University and from the union and was drafted into the army. In the early part of 1967 the students won some support among workers and intellectuals, but at the union of youth congress in

June they succeeded in doing no more than chipping at the monolithic structure insisted upon by the old guard. During the summer they gathered support from some of the Slovak writers, but the old guard engineered the expulsion of Mueller's successor, Lubomír Holeček, from the university and his drafting, too, into the army. The students' view of Novotný could not really have been worse. But what was more important than the weight of their criticism was the police violence they suddenly encountered. On 31 October students at the Strahov hostel in Prague were complaining about conditions when typically the lights went out. About 1,500 of them started out on a candlelight march to the centre of the city. They were attacked by the police, as later was their hostel, and roughly treated. For the first time, Novotný's reluctance to change had involved him in violent action against his critics; and the damage could not be undone. The students not only demanded a thorough investigation of the affair; they went on loudly to voice their criticisms of the whole regime. And those clamouring for reform avidly used their protests as a means of intensifying the pressure on Novotný. When an apology for the police action was finally published on 15 December, it was already too late to save Novotný.

The movement that eventually produced his removal from power took shape at the meeting of the central committee on 30-31 October. Hendrych introduced a hard-line resolution on the leading role of the party. Dubček, annoyed at the manner and bias of the speech, argued in favour of change in general and to affect the party in particular. Other members split both ways. Novotný replied with an undiplomatic attack on Dubček for propagating nationalism. Novotný had never been at his best in skirmishing with Slovaks; but he was particularly tactless in citing nationalism that had been so abused in persecuting Slovak politicians in the 1950s. The question was immediately raised of Novotný resigning from either his party or his state post, though nothing was agreed before the meeting broke up. This was so far the most serious split within the party, and the two sides began to manoeuvre and argue for position. The November meeting of the central committee was postponed; Novotný tried to replace Dubček and sought Soviet support, while Dubček brought the issue rather more into the open with his article calling for a reform of nationality policy. Brezhnev arrived in Prague on 8 December. He had been invited by Novotný, but he appears to have given him only moderate support. In the last resort, Novotný was essentially Stalin's man. He had bent a little to Khrushchev's liberalism, but preferred his later authoritarianism; in fact, he had complained to Brezhnev at Khrushchev's fall. And such concessions as he had made since 1964 had been encouraged by promptings from Brezhnev. The Soviet leader's interest in Czechoslovakia was in stability, not in one particular individual. Novotný himself was now becoming a threat to stability and was therefore expendable. But too sudden or dramatic a change would also be unsettling. So, in talks with leading Communists, Brezhnev seems to have opted for a partial change, Novotný's removal from office in the party. The central committee met from 19 to 21 December. Novotný withdrew some of his immoderate comments on Dubček and the Slovaks, but otherwise showed no inclination for further reform. It was Šik who exploded, suggesting Novotný's replacement as first secretary and requesting the preparation of a programme for the democratisation of the party. There were some strange alignments: Lenárt apparently sided with Novotný, Hendrych substantially opposed him. Finally, on 21 December, Novotný intimated his resignation.

The issue was not quite settled. There was no outstandingly obvious successor. Hendrych clearly had ambitions, but his repentance came too late. Šik had talent, but he was a specialist and theoretician, not a man of the machine. Dubček's ambition had so far concerned Slovakia. He was an experienced party politician, and he had emerged as a humane but realistic reformer; yet he was only now coming to be known in wider Czechoslovak circles. He was also in the chair at this point of the meeting and perhaps unable to press his own claim. However, either for general or personal reasons, he proposed an adjournment of the issue to 3 January. Despite the opposition of Smrkovský and others, who feared that the interval would offer Novotný the opportunity to create mischief, the delay was agreed. Novotný actually tried to bring part of the army to his rescue. General Jan Šejna was apparently much involved, but he was foiled by reform-minded officers, particularly general Václav Prchlík. The small group appointed to consider a successor had been unable to agree on any one person; so, at the resumed meeting of the central committee on 3 and 4 January, Novotný was able to continue fighting. However, Dubček eventually appeared as the middle-of-the-road candidate whom neither right nor left could reject and whom Novotný would accept as possibly of use to him. After all, Dubček was a Slovak and therefore not necessarily acceptable to the Czechs; and playing off one nationality against another was nothing new in central Europe. On 5 January 1968 Dubček was unanimously elected first secretary of the Czechoslovak Communist Party.

Even so, Novotný's power and influence were not yet dead. He had been forced to give up what in most east European communist states was the more important position. But his two Communist predecessors as political supremo had derived their power, not from the secretaryship, but from the presidency. True enough, matters had been altered slightly by the 1960 constitution; but that also might be reformed to his advantage. During January and February he certainly acted as if he meant at the very least not to retreat. He went around stirring up the natural fears of bureaucrats for reformers and of trade unionists for intellectuals. On 25 February he spoke along with Dubček at the celebrations to mark the twentieth anniversary of the Communist revolution and talked in tones not unlike those of Dubček. His standing was reduced, not destroyed; and nothing was necessarily permanent. Part of the danger stemmed from Dubček's own attitude and position. He was a reformer by experience, not conviction, at least at that stage; and he did not diverge irreversibly from Novotný on anything except the Slovak question. He had also telephoned Brezhnev on 6 January and visited him on 19 January to reassure him that there would be no drastic changes. He had not been the immediate, unanimous choice of his colleagues; and their solidarity behind him was questionable. The situation was therefore one from which Novotný might profit. However, on 25 February of all days, general Šejna defected to the West. Rumours about his attempted intervention on behalf of Novotný and about his supposed corrupt dealings with Novotný's son spread rapidly. On 5 March the party praesidium, under liberal pressure, decided to ask the National Assembly to amend the press law and abolish censorship. Without waiting for the legislation, the press began publishing what it wanted and attacked Novotný and his treacherous, corrupt, and diehard colleagues. In face of a storm of public protest, Novotný had no option but to resign from the presidency. On 22 March the issue was settled at last.

Novotný ultimately had to go because he resisted sensible and necessary change. After he went, reform was bound to come. Unfortunately, the length of his resistance pushed the demand for change to extremes. And the time he actually took to go, and the means he resorted to in his efforts to retain some degree of power, produced a popular mood that pressed reform almost to the point of revolution. Behind him, therefore, he left a situation that would have taxed a host of talented men; but ironically, he commanded a political system that did not encourage brilliance. However, even a group of outstanding statesmen would have found it virtually impossible to contain the pressures within limits that Brezhnev and his Soviet colleagues would have accepted. Two decades of communism had created a series of problems for Czechoslovakia that Russia would not let it solve because of the threat to its own five decades.

CHAPTER 14

Reform and Reaction 1968

THE DEPARTURE OF NOVOTNÝ was in many ways a great opportunity for Czechoslovakia. The man who was the symbol of the 1950s, the obstacle to reform in the sixties, was out of the way at last. The majority of the men now at the top were reformers, and it would therefore be possible to introduce changes in and through the Communist Party. This was what the reformers had always wanted; it was also the only thing the Soviet Union would tolerate. There was no thought of reverting to capitalism, which in any case the Soviet Union would not accept. There was, however, much reflection on 1948. In that year Beneš had refused to sign the new constitution because it threatened the important concepts of parliamentary democracy and civil rights. Experience had since proved him prophetic, and the new liberals were greatly exercised about both questions. In that same year Gottwald had spoken of the Czechoslovak road to socialism, and that was precisely what the reformers wished to resurrect. All this was summed up succinctly in the slogan, socialism with a human face. East-West relations also seemed to be relatively good, and certainly much better than twenty years before. So it was possible that a fresh departure would now be allowed. In addition there was, in one quarter, a good deal of reflection on 1918. It might be feasible for a more advanced Slovak people to gain the measure of dignity and autonomy they had failed to gain fifty years before. Czechoslovakia might emerge a happier place whose prosperity would reflect greater credit on the socialist camp.

A number of Novotný's closest colleagues departed with him; one example was Jan Bartuška who had been prosecutor-general since 1956. Most of the few remaining old-guard leaders were removed from the praesidium on 4 April when the party took on its new look. Yet, within twenty-four hours of Novotný's going on 22 March, the leaders of the Russian and of almost all the east European communist parties were meeting anxiously together in Dresden to lay down limits for the Czechoslovak reform movement that went scarcely beyond Novotný's. Comecon and the Warsaw Pact, the economic and military cornerstones of the Soviet bloc, were sacrosanct. There would be increased vigilance for the aggressive intentions and subversive actions of the imperialist forces. And Czechoslovak internal policy would be based on the decisions of the thirteenth party congress and the leadership of the party itself. Czechoslovakia had an opportunity, but precious little room for manoeuvre.

The great moment had been a long time coming. Yet when it did, it took most of the new men at the centre by surprise; they had very little prepared. There was no plan, no economic, social, and political blueprint. Instead, there were frustrations, ideas, and a number of pressure-groups. Dubček himself was anxious enough to see change, but he was not an original thinker and, for reasons connected with those to the right of him inside and outside the country, he wanted to move slowly. Nevertheless, the central committee of the party was able, on 5 April, to adopt the so-called action programme that gathered into one document the most persistent ideas of the previous few years. Credit was given, where it was thought to be due, to the national liberation and socialist movements. Recognition was also given to achievements since 1948. But strictures were applied to circles in the party responsible for the aberration of the political trials. However, the longer and more important part of a moving document promised resolutions for the proposed fourteenth party congress that would pave the way for a modernised, law-abiding, prosperous, and democratic socialist society. The courts were to be independent of politics; the ministry of the interior was to be controlled by, and the public security service to be subject to, the government and the Assembly; and no undue concentration of power was to be allowed to any minister, or official, or body. Individual industrial enterprises were to be given much more freedom in determining their production to accord with the market; co-operative farmers were to be allowed to organise themselves and to sell direct to both retailers and consumers; economic planning was to take account of short and long-term requirements, was to harmonise all interests—enterprises, consumers, employees, different social and national groups—and was to involve specialist agencies and democratically elected bodies; international trade was to be encouraged on a competitive basis with other areas of the world besides eastern Europe. There was to be a revised constitution and a new political system; the National Assembly was to decide laws and important issues, and all elected bodies were to be responsible to their electors rather than to the Communist Party or the central government; new electoral laws were to be devised and means found for the participation in decision-making of workers and co-operative farmers, of the intelligentsia and social groups of all kinds, and of young as well as old; within the socialist framework the National Front was to be independent and responsible for running the country; there were to be rights of assembly and association, freedom of speech and of the press, and freedom to travel and stay abroad. The whole action programme promised, not a crude breach with the past, but the conjunction of socialism with justice, efficiency, commonsense, and scientific knowledge to provide an improved and improving future.

There was something in it for most people. Non-communist victims of the trials were promised swift and total rehabilitation. The old and the disabled were promised a more equitable pension system and the young an expanded housing programme. Prague and Bratislava in particular were assured of a face-lift. The students were offered a more diversified youth organisation. The group promised most, inevitably, were the Slovaks. The language employed in the action programme and the settlement proposed was a marked improvement even on the Košice programme. The Czechoslovak republic was a joint state of two equal nations in voluntary co-existence; a new constitutional arrangement would be made on socialist federal lines to guarantee both peoples their equality and right to self-determination; the Slovak economy would be developed faster than the Czech, exploiting intensively its natural advantages. In detail, the Slovak National Council would become the local legislative body, a Slovak council of ministers the executive; they would have general oversight of other bodies, such as the national committees, and other activities, such as economic planning; and there would be no possibility of the Czechs outvoting the Slovaks on legal or constitutional questions.

Much of all this was perfectly acceptable to other east European communists. The Union of Soviet Socialist Republics, for example, could not object, at least in theory, to some sort of federalism in Czechoslovakia. On the other hand, there were a number of possible developments that could prove totally unacceptable. The action programme indicated that the new Czech-Slovak relationship would be applied at the party as well as the state level. This was the kind of power split that the Soviet Union had always avoided. In fact, the whole question of the future of the party in Czechoslovakia was obviously one of immense concern. It was no longer a matter of the dictatorship of the proletariat. Modern Czechoslovakia was a classless society, and the party even had to justify its leading role. The action programme envisaged that it would do so by winning voluntary support, not by holding a monopoly of power and issuing directives; that it would have to earn its authority by its activity and its veracity; and that it would operate within the constitutional system in general and the National Front in particular. This also postulated democracy within the party itself through genuine debate, proper elections, and secret ballot. The theory behind this presented no great difficulty to other communists, but the possible practical consequences were frightening. Not only, applying the Czechoslovak programme, might several communist parties lose their political dominance within the state, but within each party several leaders might be voted out. This was not an eventuality that anyone, from Leonid Brezhnev in Moscow to Walter Ulbricht in Berlin, could contemplate with equanimity.

With a risk of this magnitude contained in the action programme, the rest of it was also called in question. Its apparent emphasis on parliamentary sovereignty was altogether too Western in conception. Its wish to put an end to income-levelling and to replace it with payment according to the quantity, quality, and social usefulness of the work done smacked a little of bourgeois differentiation. Freedom to speak, write, and go abroad was an open invitation to Western subversion. Or, to put it another way, the action programme could be a serious challenge to communism as it then was in the Soviet Union and eastern Europe. This was not what Brezhnev had intended when he agreed to Novotný's fall. It was precisely what the Dresden meeting was intended to prevent.

The action programme, however, was a statement of intent. It expressed some reservations; for example, it implied that the party must at least retain a co-ordinating role in politics. In the long run, reaction to it would depend on how it was implemented, and that depended partly on advice coming from Czechoslovakia's allies. But it also depended to an important extent on the attitude of the whole Czechoslovak people. Among the politicians, attitudes were rather mixed. A few of the old-guard leaders still clung to power, notably Antonín Kapek, a candidate member of the party praesidium who was not expelled on 4 April. He and his friends offered a channel for local and foreign opposition to the action programme. The reformers themselves were somewhat divided. Every aspect of the action programme had been the subject of earnest debate for the previous three months. Dubček stood in the middle, long-term Communist, recent reformer. To his right were Lenárt, premier from 1963 to January 1968; Kolder, chairman of the 1962-63 trials review; Vasil Bil'ak, Dubček's successor as secretary of the Slovak

Communist organisation; before that Hendrych's counterpart in Slovakia; Alois Indra, minister of transport from 1963 to 1967 and now secretary of the central committee of the Czechoslovak Communist Party; and Oldřich Švestka, for the past decade editor of *Rudé právo*. All of them were rather reluctant converts to serious reform, possibly men who saw the balance of advantage to lie temporarily with Dubček. Slightly less to the right were others like the Czech Lubomír Štrougal, a deputy premier and the minister of the interior who had succeeded Barák, and Husák, finally back in harness also as a deputy premier. More or less in the centre along with Dubček was Černík, who had become prime minister in succession to Lenárt. To the left was a largish group. It included well-known figures such as Šik, another deputy premier, and the outspoken Smrkovský, now chairman of the National Assembly. It also included less prominent but still powerful figures such as the two Czechs František Kriegel, much-travelled doctor and intermittent politician, now chairman of the National Front, and Čestmír Císař, removed from the ministry of education in 1965 as too liberal an influence and shortly to be chairman of the so-called provisional Czech National Council. It also comprised rising figures such as Mlynář, chairman of the party committee on political reforms; Bohumil Šimon, a candidate member of the party praesidium and chairman of the Prague branch of the party; and Josef Špaček, praesidium member, Brno branch chairman, and Hendrych's successor as head of the party ideological commission. The men supposed to carry through the action programme, therefore, were not united; and some were less than enthusiastic. But the majority were dedicated to its implementation, at least as they understood it. However, they had to respond to pressure from outside, and from the Czechoslovak people.

Popular reaction to the fall of Novotný was remarkably slow. The experience of the last twenty years, not to mention the previous ten, had made the Czechs more than usually cautious; and the Slovaks remained strangely watchful. Certainly Novotný's disappearance was in two stages, the first in midwinter. But it took the abolition of the censorship and the publication of the action programme to convince most people that something had happened and that they could both think and act for themselves. Even so, workers and peasants, especially as organised groups, were in no particular hurry to innovate. Economic conditions for factory workers were markedly better than they had been a few years before, and there were many who feared for their jobs in a possible economic shake-up. The discussion about enterprise councils continued through to the end of June before their function, membership, and relevance to everyday working conditions began to become more obvious. An enforced change of leaders in the trade union movement at the end of March did not automatically transform it from a party propaganda instrument into a free bargaining agent that could argue against enterprise councils or government departments for higher wages or improved benefits. It was almost the end of June before a nationwide trade union conference spelled out the first general statement of a revised role; and even then a number of new unions, emerging from the grass roots to represent individual craft interests, could not win recognition. Improvements in social security did something to win the workers more actively to reform; in the three months following the announcement of the action programme a series of increases in benefits was promised. A new ministry of labour and social welfare was also established to supervise, among other things, the shortening of the working-week and a widening of job opportunities. And possibly most important of all, strikes were permitted, even encouraged so that groups of discontented workers were given a possible means of quick redress for their grievances.

Conditions in the countryside were also better in the spring of 1968 than they had been for a year or two, and the peasants' loyalties were in any case divided by their working separately on state, co-operative, and private farms. The party's agricultural policy after the action programme was also somewhat confused. The state farmers tended therefore to drift away on their own, as did the Slovaks. However, the gradual appreciation of the opportunities the new situation offered encouraged many co-operative farms to band together in organisations for buying and selling and also promoted the growth in the Czech Lands of a farmers' union that embraced peasants on both co-operative and private farms and looked forward to representing them politically on the National Front. The fair treatment meted out to peasants farming their own plots seemed to set the seal on a reforming policy that most peasants could support. By the end of June there was little doubt that a revitalised industrial and agricultural working class had swung behind the reform leaders.

Those who reacted most quickly to the rapid turn of events were the intelligentsia who had helped to shape them. On 24 January, within a few weeks of Dubček's elevation to the party secretaryship, the writers' union, for example, appointed a chairman of their own choosing. They would have preferred the more rebellious Procházka, but they agreed on the more moderate Goldstücker who would have been wholly unacceptable to the Novotný regime; and they went on to make Procházka a vice-chairman. On

1 March, more than three weeks before Novotný's final resignation, they managed to bring out the first number of their new weekly *Literární listy* (*Literary Gazette*), dedicated to the discussion of political as well as literary questions. On 29 March, some days before the action programme was approved, they appointed a commission under Seifert's chairmanship to seek rehabilitation and compensation for imprisoned and disgraced writers; and they entrusted Havel with the setting-up of a circle of non-communist writers to act as a stimulus to their own organisation. They even ventured directly into politics by making specific proposals on a future national assembly. They were therefore poised to take advantage of the post-April situation, and they quickly raised the circulation of *Literární listy* from 100,000 to 300,000. The Slovak writers, who had virtually separated from their Czech colleagues in the summer of 1967 but given them succour over the winter, now drifted further on their own. Yet they, too, were poised to make the most of the spring of 1968 although they fathered a second journal alongside *Kultúrny život—Nové slovo* (*New Word*)—which, under the guidance of Husák and Novomeský, largely concentrated on Slovak national issues. But this was only to make the most of the action programme. For their part, the journalists were a little behind the writers at first but rapidly caught up. Their uncensored reports in March helped to force Novotný's downfall; and in the middle of the month they deposed their own old-guard leaders. Under Stanislav Budín's editorship their journal, *Reportér* (*The Reporter*), became an outspoken advocate of full-blooded reform. And towards the end of June they recast their organisation on strict federal lines to form two separate unions of Czech and Slovak journalists joined by a centre of Czechoslovak journalists to act effectively as their political pressure-group. They thus set an example of federal development as well as campaigning on political questions. By the middle of the year there was hardly a newspaper or journal in Czechoslovakia that did not openly and even enthusiastically support the policies of the action programme. Despite the continuing editorship of Švestka, *Rudé právo* followed the majority line.

In the end, the action programme as the media presented it proved almost irresistible to the Czechoslovak public. As workers or peasants they might have their doubts and fears. But as members of the public they found it hard to resist even just the atmosphere of a liberated press. For years they had been fed stodgy half-truths. Lively critical articles and accurate foreign news items now encouraged faith in the promises of the regime that allowed them. Television played a particularly important role because of the vividness of its reports and the sincerity of its political discussions. Jiří Pelikán, who had directed the state television service since 1963, was himself an active reformer and had been appointed chairman of the Assembly foreign affairs commission in January 1968. So his involvement in expounding the action programme was personal as well as professional and all the more effective. Indeed it was people more than promises or the media that proved convincing. Honest and humane men were a comparatively new experience in public affairs.

There were many Czechs and Slovaks in later middle age who remembered Beneš and the happier moments of Communists such as Gottwald and Zápotocký. But the young had grown up with the cruelty of the 1950s and the hypocrisy of the sixties. The emergence of a character like Svoboda thus seemed to be a guarantee of a genuine new deal. When the National Assembly elected him President in succession to Novotný on 30 March, they recognised the realities of political life. As a hero of the Soviet Union, he was acceptable to Moscow; as a supporter of the 1948 revolution and a temporary victim of the subsequent trials, he represented the most creditable strain of Czechoslovak communism. But over and above that he was a kindly, smiling father figure who spoke in simple direct language about the better road ahead and found no difficulty placing a wreath on Tomáš Masaryk's grave. It was actually the central committee of the party that decided on Svoboda's election by nominating him. The students wanted to nominate Císař, partly on principle, partly because he was nearer to them both in age and in ideals. Many of the intelligentsia are said to have favoured Smrkovský for his sincere convictions and strength of purpose. So the ageing Svoboda had his work cut out to win general acclaim. But his own appeal was in fact helped by that of the two men who had to stand aside for him. As one of a team, Císař carried many young people with him; and Smrkovský's rugged character, patent honesty, and ubiquitous diligence won him widening affection. The reforming politicians as a group won old-fashioned popularity for the men they were.

Dubček won a particular popularity. In the modern context he had more power and standing as first secretary than he would have had as President. The fact that he had not sought his position made him all the more attractive. He had a natural humility and a genuine warmth that endeared him to the majority of his countrymen. He had an attractive wife, he was a good family man, and he had an enviable war record. He was sociable and approachable; and he quite deliberately took the public into his confidence. He would receive a student delegation, reason with newsmen, and make yet another television appearance. To Czechs and Slovaks alike Dubček ultimately was the human face of socialism.

The public steadily warmed to the action programme. Quite apart from the policies and politicians, the whole atmosphere was exciting. There was a great sense of relief from the burdens of the past; people were free to talk without fear of arrest and to make contact with new ideas, inside or outside Czechoslovakia. After all, Prchlík, who had helped to foil Šejna, had become head of the eighth department, the real security centre, in mid-February and he was busy throughout April, May, and June preparing its demise and the transfer of responsibility for security from the party to the Assembly. Josef Pavel, who became minister of the interior in April, had himself been a victim of the trials and immediately set about reducing the ministry's power, restoring proper judicial procedures and removing as many restrictions as possible from the everyday life of ordinary people. Yet, no matter how well the action programme was received, it could not be implemented within a few months. Even in a situation of international harmony and domestic unanimity the necessary legislation would have taken at least a year to pass and several more to act on. But inside two or three months quite a lot of progress was made. Early in April the central committee of the party established a commission under Jan Piller, a middle-of-the-road reformer, to conduct a fundamental review of the main trials of the 1950s. Early in May, Svoboda announced an amnesty for more than 500 political prisoners and almost 100,000 exiles. And towards the end of June the National Assembly passed a judicial rehabilitation law that allowed appeals against all sentences since 1948 and made provision for compensation of victims of injustice and for punishment of those guilty of malpractices. The way was finally open for the cleaning of the Augean stable. On 12 April a new national economic council was created to co-ordinate a slowly decentralising economy; and on 1 July the first enterprise councils came into operation to give workers a substantial share in the running of factories. Care was taken to protect the underdeveloped Slovak economy; but the foundations were already laid for a more open economic system. In the second week of April the Czechoslovak and Slovak National Fronts elected new chairmen who, contrary to previous practice, were separate from the corresponding party chairmen. In the third week of May a government committee on constitutional change settled down to examine the draft of a federation to govern the relations of the Czechs and Slovaks in future. And at the beginning of June it was decided to advance the meeting of the next party congress from October to September. In short, party and state, Czechs and Slovaks were already being separated slightly; and the moment for the complete triumph of the reformers was being brought much nearer. Finally, at the end of June, an amendment to the press law virtually abolished the preliminary censorship of news and views. Writers could still be charged afterwards for what they had published; but they now had plenty of licence to monitor the progress of reform.

Sadly, however, partial implementation of the action programme and growing public support for it increased the suspicion and hostility of the Warsaw Pact powers towards the reform regime. The Dresden meeting on 23 March had not obviated acceptance of the action programme by the Czechoslovak praesidium on 5 April. As the weeks passed, Russian and East German concern at its progress became all too obvious in political speeches and newspaper comments. Dubček, Černík, Smrkovský, and Bil'ak visited Moscow on 4 May. Subsequent versions of what was agreed varied greatly; but the verbal attacks on Czechoslovakia continued unabated. Later in the month rumours of Warsaw Pact manoeuvres on the Polish frontier with Czechoslovakia were confirmed; and on 21 May, following visits to Prague by Alexei Kosygin, the Soviet premier, and Andrei Grechko, the Soviet defence minister, it was announced that Warsaw Pact army signals exercises would be conducted in Poland and Czechoslovakia in June. There was then a brief interlude in the polemics; but despite visits to the Soviet Union by Smrkovský, Štrougal, and other reformers, the attacks on Czechoslovakia resumed. Although the exercises officially terminated at the end of June, the Warsaw troops continued to spin out their stay on Czechoslovak soil. What the Soviet leaders said to Dubček and his colleagues during this period is still not known for sure, but by the beginning of July their intentions were fairly clear: the reforms had to be reversed.

This put the genuine reformers in a serious dilemma. They did not want to displease the Warsaw Pact powers, let alone break with them. At the same time they were wedded to the action programme and determined to defend socialism with a human face. Their parleys with the Soviet leaders and their acceptance of a temporary Warsaw military presence were designed to reassure their partners in the communist bloc. But they never ceased in talks, speeches, and broadcasts to emphasise their belief in the action programme. On the other hand, they themselves joined in criticising the anti-communist ideas and activities of some Czechoslovak groups and individuals. This was an intelligible policy and probably the only one possible. Up to a point it satisfied Moscow, which did not immediately resort to a military solution. But what was interpreted as Dubček's backtracking inevitably annoyed some reformers. The students would not be gainsaid. In the first three months of the year they had won two resounding victories. They had secured the release from the army and return to university life of their former leaders, Mueller and Holeček, and the dismissal of the minister of the interior who bore responsibility for the Strahov affair. They had also effectively broken up the Czechoslovak union of youth, contrary to the wishes of the politicians. In the second three months they continued to press their advantage. In May they established a union of university students for the Czech Lands and another for Slovakia, joining them through a rather nebulous centre; and they went on to campaign on a wide range of issues from individual human rights to student solidarity with the working classes. In June they kept up a barrage of opposition to concessions to Moscow. Some of the writers went further still. On 27 June *Literární listy* published Vaculík's '2,000 words to Workers, Farmers, Scientists, Artists, and Everyone'. It condemned the party of the past that had sold honour for office. It maintained that the reforms had not gone far enough, that just telling the truth was not shaping the new future. In face of possible intervention, aware that words were insufficient, and conscious of a long summer's preoccupation ahead, it called on the Czechoslovak people to take local initiatives to spread the party's action programme by influencing the coming elections to the new central committee, by securing the appointment of good managers in enterprises and the removal of corrupt or inefficient officials in districts, and by monitoring local newspapers, meetings, and security activities. It was a document reminiscent of Vaculík's oratory at the writers' congress just a year before; but, as well as appealing to them, he spoke for many others. The signatories included a wide range of scientists and technocrats, names in the arts (like Jiří Trnka in puppetry), in sport (like Emil Zátopek in athletics), and quite ordinary people like an engineering worker or a sow-breeder. Certainly the document was impatient, but it showed sincere concern for both Dubček's position and Czechoslovakia's future. It was a legitimate protest against external threats and internal conservatism. Ironically, however, it only multiplied Dubček's difficulties, heightening the pressure from his communist neighbours and strengthening Czechoslovakia's own right wing.

Vaculík's article was understandable but perhaps impolitic. Freedom of the press was a heady wine for those not used to it; they were bound to overindulge at first. They also had a serious point to make, as most of the genuine reformers privately confessed. But the whole incident was a gift to the critics and opponents of reform.

Most of the east European press attacked the article as evidence of the strength of anti-communist forces inside Czechoslovakia aiming, with outside assistance, to destroy socialism. There were other gifts. The 1960 constitution had mentioned the Communist Party, but not the other National Front remnants from 1948. They were simply tolerated and allowed to preserve an empty existence. But the new atmosphere gave them an opportunity for a fresh lease of life; indeed, they were variously encouraged to take an active part in the National Front or play the role of an opposition. In the Czech Lands the Socialist Party and the Populist Party changed their leadership, refurbished their journals, and in April, issued new programmes. The one put in a plea for the small entrepreneur and the other for the Christian. Both increased their numbers. Although they both indicated their willingness to work within the National Front, they nevertheless became increasingly scathing in their criticisms of delay in implementing the action programme. There was also a rather less powerful revival of the Freedom and Democratic parties in Slovakia. However, a development that gave more grist to the mill of the reformers' enemies was the attempt to revive the Social Democratic Party. It had been illegally submerged in the Communist Party in 1948, and many of its former members had suffered for their previous independence or continued non-co-operation. In the climate of 1968 it therefore had a right to justice. Those former Socialists, who, like Fierlinger, had helped organise the fusion, opposed a separation bitterly. Others simply thought it unnecessary in the new Communist mood, or unwise in view of the hatred of orthodox Communists for those whom they deemed to be revisionist enemies. In May the praesidium of the Communist Party rejected a clear proposal that the Social Democratic Party be revived, but its supporters continued publicly to campaign for it in June. It was easy for Moscow to point to the growth of revisionism in Czechoslovakia and to warn against the danger of splitting the working class. More damaging still was the emergence of the club of committed non-party people, not a political party, not anti-communist, but mostly young technocrats and teachers who wished to help build socialism without being Communist Party members, and who were anxious in some undefined way to participate in politics. They issued statements from growing meetings in April and May and had quite a large number of active clubs by June. There was a similar, though less well-known, body in Slovakia. It was perfectly natural for some of the several millions who were not Communists to wish to represent or to be represented. However, from an orthodox Communist angle, their existence was a serious danger since potentially they constituted an opposition that could sweep the party right out of power. KAN, as the club was known from its initials, became a favourite target for the diehards at home and abroad.

Other reformist activities produced a hostile reaction for a different reason. When the public prosecutor began an investigation into the circumstances of Jan Masaryk's death twenty years before, he unintentionally added strength to a run of rumours accusing the Soviet government of having organised his murder, an accusation Moscow did not appreciate. Even more upsetting was the so-called K231, a club of former political prisoners started up at the end of March with the new leaders' tacit blessing and deriving its name from the law under which thousands of Czechoslovaks were sentenced for major and minor disagreements with Communist Party rule after 1948. Its objective was commendable, to secure complete rehabilitation and reasonable recompense for every innocent victim. Chaired by Karel Nigrin, one of Beneš's wartime officials in London, its behaviour was correct; it also appears to have kept a tenuous link with the government, and it aimed at reconciliation rather than retribution. On the other hand, it was dealing with upwards of 100,000 cases, some of which proved not to be *bona fide* and caused embarrassment. But the real complaint against it was that it threatened by its very nature to expose many of the guilty who still lived in high places, or at least in comfort, and who were to be identified even in the Soviet Union. Where KAN represented a possible long-term danger to communism, K231 represented an immediate threat to too many individual Communists. The invective against it was all the more bitter, and all the more effective. Communists with a bad conscience could hardly decry party or government investigations, but they could all too easily win support for their condemnation of witch-hunts run by allegedly anti-communist individuals. It was a vicious circle. Attacks on the reform programme made Dubček and his colleagues slow their pace and appeal for internal self-restraint. This in turn encouraged the more impatient or radical advocates of reform to call for greater speed in implementing the action programme or occasionally to take matters into their own hands. The inevitable consequence was further attacks on the action programme and greater justification for mounting them.

The Czechoslovaks had been through a lot in half a century; and in that time, and more, the Czechs in particular had learned to be patient; but it would have been a soulless people indeed that did not throw up a writers' union or a KAN or a K231 after Novotný's fall. In time, the excitement would have passed, politics would have taken on an amended form, and due recompense would have been paid. But from the start there was little or no time or opportunity for excess, or even for experiment. There were some influential men who ought to have paid more attention to the fact. The late spring of 1968 was not the moment for Havel, for example, to argue for a genuine, if loyal, opposition party. Šimon went less far, but far enough in advocating a choice of party programmes as well as of candidates. Mlynář suggested various forms of political pluralism. And at one point Císař even talked of the party giving up its ideological leadership. In the middle of May there was also a move to advance the date for the establishment of a separate Czech Communist Party as a means of promoting the radical cause. All these men represented much that was best in Czechoslovak thought, but arguably they lacked tactical sense. On the other hand, most of them saw the need for restraint as the pressure mounted against reform. In May and June, Mlynář was to be heard arguing in favour of retaining an adequate state security force, and Císař in opposition to parties outside the National Front. Others were more consistent in their hostility to wild ideas. Despite his own sufferings in the past, Smrkovský warned people against becoming obsessed with setting wrongs to right; he also consistently refused to allow the Social Democrats to restore their party. Dubček held to a similar line: he condemned K231; and while he supported party democracy and a more decisive role for a wider range of interests in the National Front, he discounted any serious threat to Communist Party supremacy and rejected an opposition as such, in or out of the National Front. As the polemics against reform intensified, the reform leaders tended quite naturally to band together and avoid provocative extremes. They appealed to others to follow suit. And when they were nevertheless faced with the declaration of '2,000 words', they called a special praesidium meeting to condemn it and thereby, they hoped, undo the damage it had caused.

However, no matter what the reform leaders said, their critics in the Soviet bloc immediately exploited the '2,000 words' against them. They were, it was alleged, failing to guard against imperialist and anti-socialist forces; there was now a serious danger of counter-revolution. But their critics also referred to forces within Czechoslovakia capable of upholding the socialist system. For the progress of reform and, more particularly, the attitude of the Soviet bloc towards it had strengthened the resolve of its opponents inside Czechoslovakia, whether they were completely antagonistic like Kapek or reluctantly co-operative like Indra. Anonymous leaflet and letter attacks on the reformers became more common in May and June; and on 20 June a state-wide militia meeting sent a message to Moscow critical of recent developments in the reform programme. Within the praesidium Indra argued increasingly in favour of a limit being imposed on rehabilitation and on internal party democracy and of security being continued as a function of the party. At the end of June he was one of the main advocates of a condemnation of the '2,000 words'. When Dubček condemned K231 and when he and many of his colleagues condemned the '2,000 words', it was partly with an eye on the internal critics of their action programme. They had others to reckon with as well. Bil'ak was acceptable because he had opposed Novotný, but he had taken his stand for the sake of Slovak autonomy, not political reform. He, too, advocated a limit on rehabilitation; he called for a partial resumption of censorship and attacked television in particular. Politically he was not popular. On the other hand, he represented a degree of national discontent persisting in Slovakia after the acceptance of the action programme. The fact was that although the programme spoke of a need for symmetrical federal development—parallel Czech and Slovak institutions within the one Czechoslovak state—it mentioned only the Slovak institutions, and this seemed to imply the continuation of the *status quo* in which the Slovaks, unlike the Czechs, had their own separate institutions but the Czechs dominated all the national Czechoslovak ones. Czech reformers were often insensitive; Kriegel, for example, made it all too apparent that he did not want Czech institutions, though the Slovaks could do what they wanted. The result was that the Slovaks sometimes backed men like Bil'ak. As a Slovak himself Dubček was very sympathetic to his people's aspirations, but, at least by the late spring, political and social reforms were uppermost in his mind. Yet he had to heed Bil'ak, and so at the end of May he made it clear beyond doubt that the party was as committed to Czech institutions as to Slovak in the federation currently being prepared by the government committee under Husák. And when he came to condemn the '2,000 words' at the end of June, he had Bil'ak in mind as much as Indra; for in collecting signatures for his article Vaculík was insensitive enough to forget to recruit some Slovak reformers, so that it was apparently anti-Slovak as well as allegedly anti-socialist.

As Dubček took a more rigid line, he ostensibly headed off his internal critics on the right, though it has been said that some of them made secret contacts with Soviet leaders. At the same time he upset his critics on the left, though they remained fundamentally loyal to him. But he still failed to satisfy his Russian and east European detractors. There is some debate on why the Warsaw

Pact powers decided to invade Czechoslovakia. There may well have been a long and acrimonious argument. In some ways the Czechoslovak issue was really an east European crisis. Everything was under control in Czechoslovakia. The action programme made sense and was highly popular; it was being implemented neither too slowly nor too quickly; it was being adjusted to meet reasonable pressures; it stood a good chance of making Czechoslovakia a model socialist state. The country was full of Western journalists, many of whom acted less than responsibly by looking for answers to questions that, in a delicate situation, might have been better left unasked. But there was no danger whatsoever of Western subversion. The United States was preoccupied with Vietnam and the Middle East. Western Europe was no match for the Soviet Union and had problems enough with its own Common Market. The new regime was certainly anxious to increase its trade with the West and to win Western credits, but so too was the Soviet Union. The action programme made it clear that the only future for Czechoslovakia was in close military and economic alliance with the Warsaw Pact powers. However, it did emphasise the need for mutual respect among allies and the special importance of Czechoslovakia's position in the centre of Europe. This latter point was taken up in May by Jiří Hajek, the new reform-minded foreign minister, who foresaw Czechoslovakia helping to reduce differences between the two halves of Europe. He did not imply by this that Czechoslovakia would in any way cease to be socialist; and he was too close a student of Munich and had suffered too much from the war to want to leave the Soviet camp. He was simply spelling out the new Czechoslovakia's possible contribution to the European *détente* the Soviet Union was supposedly interested in. Nevertheless, Moscow probably saw it all differently.

If even the more moderate reforming ideas were to drift across to East Germany, Poland, or Russia itself, then serious damage might be done. The Soviet Union had its dissident writers, and there were nationalist stirrings in the Ukrainian Republic. In Poland there were student troubles as the once enlightened rule of Władisław Gomułka turned increasingly sour. East Germany was at risk at a time when West Germany was trying very hard to increase its influence in eastern Europe as a whole—and it had recently been successful in Rumania. The situation in the rest of eastern Europe was not a bit more comforting. Hungary had been quietly liberalising now for several years; and Dubček went to Budapest in the middle of June to sign a new treaty of friendship with János Kádár. Yugoslavia was an old thorn in Russia's side, and Rumania seemed likely to emulate it in striking out, with

Chinese help, for an independent foreign policy. Both Josip Tito and Nicolae Ceausescu had expressed support for Dubček's regime. Only Bulgaria remained doggedly faithful. If the Czechoslovak infection were not stamped out soon, then east European communism might be set back several decades. The Soviet Union's strategic position *vis-à-vis* the United States might also be drastically changed; and its standing in the communist world in comparison with China might fall to a level from which it would never rise. And all this might happen even if the Czechoslovak reformers were sincere in their professions of loyalty and goodwill. Supposing none of this were to happen, it may still have seemed impossible to the Soviet Union to allow Czechoslovakia to imply that its socialism with a human face was somehow or other a better policy for an advanced society than the communism of Lenin, Stalin, and Brezhnev.

It is not at all clear just when Moscow decided on military action. Intervention in Hungary in 1956 had borne a bitter harvest of international hostility and intra-communist division. On this occasion, however, care was taken to prepare the ground on the basis of the Warsaw Pact, so that the Soviet Union could not be charged with acting alone in its own political interest. However, the consequence was that the decision, and its timing, depended to some extent on others than Moscow. East Germany may have been anxious for intervention much earlier than August; in the end, Hungary may have taken some convincing. Yet drastic action was probably implicit from the time of the Dresden meeting in March. Manoeuvres and exercises in May and June were political warnings and military preparations. What no doubt tilted the discussion in favour of actual intervention was the decision by Dubček to accelerate the process of change in the party by calling the fourteenth congress for the autumn of 1968, though it was not due till 1970, and then by advancing it further from October to September. The Dresden communiqué had spoken explicitly of implementing the decisions of the thirteenth congress, and the danger now was not simply of a major shift in policy but also of a complete change in personnel. Brezhnev, Ulbricht, and Gomułka in particular must have balked at the prospect. When they took exception to Vaculík's '2,000 words', it was almost as if they welcomed the opportunity to force a showdown. From the end of June onwards it was a virtually straight run to intervention.

Early in July the Warsaw Pact powers twice invited Dubček to a special meeting, but since some of their troops remained in Czechoslovakia, he declined. How far he suspected their intentions is not known, but he certainly indicated in his replies that he would prefer bilateral negotiations to discuss mutual non-interference and that he would want to include Rumania and Yugoslavia. He did not wish to be boxed in. But the five powers which then met in Warsaw on their own made it clear in a letter they sent on 15 July that they saw Czechoslovakia in imminent danger of a counter-revolution and considered it their right and duty to protect it in the common interest of the international working class. However euphemistically they phrased their missive, it amounted to an ultimatum to Dubček to take back control of the media, to ban all political groups other than the Communist Party, and to bring the Communists themselves to heel, in effect to undo the reforms. It was also a covert appeal to the diehards to come out into the open and work with Moscow and its partners. Dubček apparently made one concession. On the day of the Warsaw meeting Prchlík announced his proposals for transferring state security from the party to the Assembly; he then went on to criticise the structure of the Warsaw Pact and its attempt to interfere in Czechoslovakia's domestic affairs. Ten days later the praesidium accepted his security proposals; but it thereby put him out of a job as head of the eighth department and took no apparent steps to find him a new one. Otherwise Dubček and the praesidium remained firm. Their reply to the Warsaw letter on 18 July was reasonable but determined. They admitted difficulties with the left but emphasised fractiousness on the right; they gave an eloquent account of the reforms, their socialist content, and the urgent need for them; they complained of misunderstandings and misrepresentations in the letter from their Warsaw comrades and elaborated their policy of bilateral talks. They were open and honest, but they would not be cowed.

Brezhnev may at first have taken Dubček's assurances as sincere and have been apprehensive only about the danger of his becoming the prisoner of the more intemperate of his colleagues. But by the middle of July Dubček was firmly and enthusiastically in command of the reform movement and upset at the unwillingness of his Russian and east European friends to accept that the reforms were good for Czechoslovakia and for communism as a whole. The Czechoslovak reply to the Warsaw letter made a direct reference to the principles agreed after the Hungarian events, whereby the relations between communist states were to be based on complete equality, respect for territorial integrity, national independence and sovereignty, and mutual non-interference in internal affairs. Dubček was becoming angry at the bullying tactics and meddling policies of his fellow communists. In this he increasingly reflected the popular mood. The majority of Czechs and Slovaks resented outside interference with a reform programme they regarded both as socialist and as personal to them. The more hostile became the tone of the Russian and east European press and radio, the more determined became the support of the Czech and Slovak populace for reform and, perhaps most of all, for their right to reform. The lingering presence of Warsaw Pact troops on Czechoslovak soil merely intensified the widespread sense of outrage. Speeches by the reform leaders were well received and their pleas for caution were on the whole heeded. Signatures piled up in favour of Dubček and his policies; and barely a murmur was heard from or in favour of his critics on the right. Before the end of July, Brezhnev must have become aware that he was dealing with a Dubček who was at the heart of a very widely supported, pro-reform, anti-interference popular movement.

Brezhnev inevitably refused to accept Czechoslovakia's reply, but at least he took up the bilateral proposal and suggested a Russo-Czechoslovak meeting on Russian soil. Dubček declined to go outside Czechoslovakia, ostensibly because of the continuing failure of Warsaw Pact troops to leave, but conceivably because of distrust of possible Soviet intentions concerning himself. Brezhnev also requested the attendance of the entire party praesidium. Dubček did not like this either, since it would have given the handful of diehards still on the praesidium an opportunity to line up with the Soviet politbureau. Švestka had criticised Dubček's reply to Warsaw in the pages of *Rudé právo,* and both Bil'ak and Kolder had argued against it at the vital praesidium meeting. In fact the mountain came to Mahomet; on 29 July not only Brezhnev and Kosygin came across the frontier to Čierná-nad-Tisou, a little town in Slovakia, but also President Nikolai Podgorny himself and the most important remaining members of the Soviet politbureau. On the other hand, the Czechoslovak party included the diehards. So the meeting represented something of a compromise. It lasted four anxious days and was reputedly quite acrimonious at times. It also resulted in a seeming compromise. The communiqué about it was bland and, according to the Czechoslovak side, there was no secret agreement. But Brezhnev prevailed upon Dubček to impose restrictions on the news media, disband KAN and K231, prevent the emergence of a Social Democratic Party, and remove some reformers to whom the Soviet Union particularly objected. He also got him to agree to a multilateral meeting of the Warsaw Pact powers. Dubček, however, persuaded Brezhnev to stop Soviet press attacks and withdraw the Warsaw Pact troops. He avoided his insistence on Czechoslovak acceptance of the Warsaw letter's demand for the abandonment of reform and the Warsaw letter's principle of a limit on sovereignty. And he agreed to a multilateral meeting on condition that it was held in Czechoslovakia and did not raise the two points last mentioned. In fact, representatives of the Soviet, East German, Polish, Bulgarian, Hungarian, and Czechoslovak parties congregated in Bratislava on 3 August. The communiqué emerging from that meeting also appeared to indicate a compromise. Czechoslovakia was not mentioned, and there was no allusion to a right of intervention. On the other hand, political principles were spelt out in extremely orthodox terms; and the fact remained that Czechoslovakia joined in a declaration that had perhaps too many vague references to friendship and co-operation. Nevertheless, fraternal ties were to be based on respect for sovereignty, national independence, and territorial integrity—and the Warsaw Pact troops left Czechoslovakia.

Dubček and his closest colleagues were not dissatisfied with the outcome of the two much-feared meetings. They had staved off their outside critics; they had not been outmanoeuvred by their own diehards; and they had been ready for some time to impose curbs on the wilder of their own reformers. As they began to prepare the curbs, they encountered a certain degree of suspicion at home, but they managed to allay it and to add to a growing feeling of public relief. Brezhnev must have been less happy. It has been said that he back-pedalled mainly as a result of letters from Tito, Ceausescu, and the common spokesman of eighteen European communist parties which were among those whose support he hoped for at the intended world communist conference in November. He had won no more than token concessions from the Czechoslovak leaders, and he soon learned that they intended to proceed with the essentials of their programme. On 10 August the praesidium published new statutes for discussion and decision at the fourteenth party congress. These provided for the democratisation of what was termed a deeply humanistic party; in particular, they guaranteed the right of a minority to maintain its opinion and recognised the division of the united Czechoslovak Communist Party into national territorial organisations, the Communist Parties of the Czech Lands and of Slovakia, coming together at the centre on a federal basis. It may well have been the announcement of these proposals that finally made Brezhnev decide for intervention, for it was after 10 August that there was apparently a flurry of consultations. On the other hand, if intervention was essentially a matter of time, then the decisions at Čierná-nad-Tisou and Bratislava were irrelevant except in so far as they provided pretexts for the military invasion. Both communiqués were so ambiguous that it was not hard for the Warsaw Pact powers to claim that Dubček had broken his pledged word. The publication of the draft party statutes was the last evidence that was needed to justify an attack. And on this interpretation Brezhnev had played his cards with consummate skill.

In the second week of August tension began to mount inside Czechoslovakia. Tito visited Prague on 9 August and received a heartwarming welcome. But three days later Ulbricht called on Dubček in Karlovy Vary and produced a worried atmosphere. Hostile propaganda against Czechoslovakia was suddenly let loose again on 14 August, though there was compensation the following day in a visit that Ceausescu paid to Prague to conclude a friendship treaty. On 17 August, Kádár came to meet Dubček in Komárno and unsettled the atmosphere once more. In the meantime, the militia were the centre of an unhappy row. There was a public outcry against a group of them who had sent to Moscow a letter attacking Dubček, but the reform leaders felt obliged to defend both their action and their role. In the midst of all this tension the praesidium came together on 20 August to run into its own battle when the diehards submitted a paper on the danger of counter-revolution. But at about 11 p.m., before the debate had been finished, troops of the Warsaw Pact powers crossed Czechoslovakia's frontiers and landed at its airports. By breakfast on 21 August the whole country was under their control, and Dubček, Černík, Smrkovský, Kriegel, Špaček, and others were under arrest. Welcoming the invasion were some of the militia and the majority of the diehards, foremost among them Indra, Bil'ak, Kolder, Švestka, and Kapek. The Dubček regime had worked hard to push through the reform programme, but in the end it was quite suddenly and brutally brought down by the violent reaction of its supposed allies aided by the nostalgic self-interest of a few remnants of the old regime.

CHAPTER 15

Interlude

BY 1968 THE POST—WAR WORLD was inured to peacetime violence and accustomed to the cynicism of the super-powers. Yet the Soviet invasion of Czechoslovakia and the kidnapping of its leaders produced an incredible outburst of international anger. Even the invading forces were affected and were confused or ashamed at the taunt of Nazi that greeted their comradely action. Outraged feelings did not lead to Western intervention, or shame to a Soviet withdrawal. But the emotional reaction to brutality and banditry and to the disturbing parallel with the betrayal and occupation of thirty years before was not less sincere and intense. Less than a decade later, the historian on either side of the divide is still hampered by recollections of the time. The burden of subjectivity is harder than usual to shift; and the problem of reaching conclusions with incomplete evidence and short-term perspective is made no easier. Yet there are some questions that must be asked and some conclusions that can be drawn.

The first question is whether anything could have been done differently to avoid intervention. Some have argued that the Czechoslovak leaders could have proceeded much more quickly from the action programme to the holding of the party congress: a quick and complete change of personnel, followed up with the fast passage of moderate reforms, might have forestalled and reassured the Russians. Yet Dubček probably moved as rapidly as his opponents and his supporters, and the susceptibilities of public opinion, would allow in April, May, and June. Others have argued the contrary, that Dubček should have reduced the pace of change, calmed the people, restrained the intelligentsia and controlled the media, and thus have satisfied the Russians. Yet this was more or less what he was trying to do in June and July; but the public, the writers, the newsmen, and the Russians all had their own idea of what they wanted to do; and in August it was the Russians who could do it. Perhaps somewhere there were hairsbreadth changes on someone's part—and not simply Dubček's—that might have altered things. But in the last resort, Moscow saw the action programme as a threat and would not have been dissuaded from self-preservation by any act of acceleration or deceleration.

The second and associated question is whether the invasion could have been anticipated and action taken accordingly. The Soviet Union had shown both treachery and ruthlessness in Hungary in 1956. In the four or five months before August 1968 it made dreadful accusations against Czechoslovakia and moved its troops in and out. What it failed to utter by way of abuse or threat its Warsaw Pact allies did for it. Dubček and his colleagues may perhaps have been confused or numbed. Dubček himself is alleged to have received direct warnings about what would happen, but too much is hidden in the archives to know for sure. What is certain is that he put a great deal of faith in the Soviet Union; he had been brought up to do so, and he knew it to be more humane in 1968 than it had been in 1956. It it also possible that he was aware of an internal tussle in the Kremlin in which the doves might beat the hawks. Further, he could feel with some pride in the middle of August that he had negotiated Czechoslovakia through some dangerous situations in the past few months and that after Čierná-nad-Tisou and Bratislava nothing could ever be quite so bad again. In the last resort, however, Dubček was a passionate believer in his own cause. He had developed a faith in reform for the good of his own people and of communism as a whole; and he had immense popular backing. In these circumstances the Soviet Union could not possibly think to intervene militarily. In any case, he may well have concluded there was no point in thinking it might, for that would simply mean surrender in advance.

The third question is linked with the second. Since military intervention was not anticipated, there were no preparations made for resisting it. Yet the problem remains why Dubček decided against resistance once the attack had taken place. It is said that Prchlík for one had submitted a defence plan ahead of the invasion; the forces were well-equipped and had a high reputation; and on the morning after the night attack, thousands of Czechoslovaks would have responded to a call to arms. For one thing, however, the invasion was sudden and the occupation of territory quick. For another, Czechoslovakia was virtually indefensible as a small country attacked by four allies across their common frontiers. In fact, it was probably knowledge of this as much as anything else that had persuaded Dubček not to think of the possibility of a Soviet invasion. Once the attack had taken place, conventional resistance was simply out of the question. There was not even the prospect of support from elsewhere. Yugoslavia and

Rumania were sympathetic, but powerless in face of Russia's might and their own difficulties. Opinion in western Europe and the United States was wholeheartedly in favour of Czechoslovakia, but any kind of military involvement would have produced a world war. The West had accepted the assignment of Czechoslovakia to the Soviet bloc long before 1948; and all its thinking in recent years had been devoted to *détente,* not confrontation. Even if, as has been suggested, the United States had known of the attack in advance, it would still have done nothing by way of military assistance. That would merely have been to add substance to the Soviet Union's hollow accusations about imperialist aggression in Czechoslovakia. And the last thing Dubček and his colleagues wanted was Western aid, not just on tactical grounds, but for reasons of principle; they were communists. Nevertheless, there remained the possibility of unconventional, guerilla-type resistance. There were soldiers and civilians who advocated it; the invading forces could have been made to suffer heavily. Yet immediately after the invasion orders went out quite unequivocally that there was to be no armed resistance. For this there were three major reasons. Taking to arms, except as a last resort, was against the Czechoslovak tradition. Dubček did not believe that all was lost; the reform movement had simply entered a new phase. And thirdly, Dubček was aware that, in its extremity, the country was far from united, and, like Beneš before him, he did not wish to provoke what would amount to a civil war.

There was resistance but, with a few exceptions, it was not armed. The demonstrations by students, the general strikes by workers, the slogans, the leaflets, and above all the brilliantly improvised television and radio information services were all part of a most effective passive resistance. In a vague way the aim was to force the troops to go home, but a much more mature and specific objective soon emerged. It was to bring back kidnapped leaders and save something of the reform programme. This was much more in the Czechoslovak tradition than military resistance. Everything that happened was directed to the same end. What was left of the government stayed in session and declared its loyalty to Dubček. Two-thirds of the members of the National Assembly got to the parliamentary buildings and did the same. On 22 August some 1,200 of the roughly 1,500 elected delegates found their way by devious means to a factory in Prague where they held a one-day fourteenth Communist Party congress that swept away the past, approved the new statutes and fresh statements of policy, and elected a reform-minded, pro-Dubček central committee and praesidium—which was exactly what the invasion was supposed to prevent. On the same night Svoboda announced that he intended flying to Moscow to secure the release of his colleagues; and on 23 August he set off with a group of determined men that included Mlynář and Husák. Despite humiliating treatment the kidnapped leaders also kept up their resistance to threats and blandishments. Between 23 and 26 August the Czechoslovak reformers continued the struggle in Moscow. At home the Slovak Communist Party met in Bratislava on 26 August and supported all the actions of the fourteenth congress. And at last on 27 August, Dubček and the others were allowed to return to Prague. This was a victory for reform that fighting would probably not have won.

The triumph was as much a defeat for the diehards. On 22 August the invading high command called for the replacement of the legal government by one headed by those who had welcomed the invasion—and had probably been informed of it in advance. But the Indra-Bil'ak group did not commend themselves to the Czechoslovak populace, and the demand simply had to be dropped. Nevertheless, some of them had to be included, at the Russians' behest, in Svoboda's Moscow team. And they exercised an influence both on the outcome of the Moscow talks and on subsequent Czechoslovak developments. It was no doubt an awareness of their strength, however limited, and of the opinion they represented in Czechoslovakia, as well as of their connection with Russia, that helped to shape Dubček's decision against resistance on the night of 20-21 August. He was probably aware of other divisions of opinion, not least within the leadership. Husák had become a deputy premier in January, though within neither the central committee nor the praesidium. In May he had been put in charge of the committee preparing Czech-Slovak federalisation, a vital assignment, and he had made considerable progress. Legislation was projected for the autumn, and it was likely to satisfy the Slovaks and create a powerful reputation for Husák. In August he was a force to be reckoned with. Both in speeches and in the pages of *Nové slovo* he had made it increasingly clear since the spring that his main interest was in Slovakia in the double sense that national satisfaction for its people had an overriding priority and that Slovakia had gone as far in liberalisation as any socialist society ought to. His position in August was conceivably that, so long as Czechoslovakia was federated, much of the rest of the action programme was negotiable. As a victim of the trials he had supported rehabilitation, but he had warned of the danger of going too far and rehabilitating capitalism, and he had argued for a sense of responsibility, as well as for freedom. He had suffered too much from Stalin to want to accept the dictates of Brezhnev; but this cannot have meant that in August he would have been prepared to fight for what he saw as Czech radicalism when he could negotiate for an autonomous Slovakia and a moderate socialism. And those Slovaks who did not side with Bil'ak might have sided with him. There was little time for thought on the night of the invasion, but Dubček must have realised the danger of dividing Czechoslovakia politically and ethnically by a call to armed resistance.

Dubček returned home saddened, but not beaten. He and his people had saved something from the wreck. He made it clear that he intended to continue with what he now termed the post-January policies, though with inevitable limitations. What all the limitations would be he did not immediately make plain, partly because he clearly wanted to break the news gently, partly because he did not yet know. In due course what he thought would be saving the essence of the action programme became no more than fighting a rearguard action. The pressure to retreat came mainly from Moscow, which was anxious to retrieve the success it almost had in August. Popular resistance at times slowed the retreat, but at others provided a pretext for additional pressure. The diehards ran with Moscow; and Husák stepped in to find a middle way.

The Moscow Protocol, agreed on 26 August, enabled Dubček to go back to Czechoslovakia, but left him little room for manoeuvre. It referred to fraternal ties and the defence of socialism, but it nowhere mentioned respect for sovereignty and integrity. Warsaw Pact troops were to be phased out of the towns and in course of time out of the whole country; but special arrangements were to be made about leaving Russian troops for defence against Germany. In other words Russia had a right to intervene and would retain the troops to do it. Hájek, the foreign minister, who had been on holiday in Yugoslavia, had flown to the Security Council to present the Czechoslovak case against the occupation. The complaint was to be withdrawn since, in the Protocol's view, Czechoslovakia was of no concern whatsoever to the United Nations. Russia intended to deal with Czechoslovakia without even neutral interference. In accordance with the Protocol, the Czechoslovaks were to invalidate the fourteenth party congress, to fortify the party and state apparatus, to remove the more objectionable of the reformers, to eliminate anti-socialist parties, to refortify the ministry of the interior, and to control the media. In short, the Communist Party was to take authoritative command of Czechoslovak society. Dubček was left able to carry on with some social and economic recasting of society; but politics belonged to the Soviet Union—which also demanded that all contacts should be strictly confidential.

Somewhat reluctantly the Moscow Protocol was accepted by the government, the central committee, and the Assembly before the middle of September. From then on its implementation proceeded doggedly. Vasili Kuznetzov, a Soviet deputy foreign minister, settled in Prague to ensure that there was neither delay nor deviation. Dubček, Černík, and Husák went to Moscow at the beginning of October, and Kosygin paid a return visit to Prague in the middle of the same month. Censorship was reintroduced, KAN and K231 were banned, the fourteenth congress was disclaimed, a number of reform leaders were removed from office, and, although other Warsaw Pact forces began drawing out, a treaty was signed allowing the Red Army to remain indefinitely for Czechoslovakia's defence. Dubček participated in all these actions reluctantly; he slowed the pace to the point where the Russians complained; and he still spoke hopefully of the human face of socialism. Smrkovský was more outspoken both with the Russians and with the public; he was also much less optimistic. When about to leave Moscow on 27 August, they and their colleagues had refused to go without Kriegel who, perhaps as a Jew, seemed to attract the Russians' particular animosity. Now in September and October they were unable to save him a second time; he lost his post as chairman of the National Front and his place as a member of the praesidium. Nor could they save Šik or Císař, Hájek or Pelikán, or many others. Despite the objection of the Russians, they managed to oust a number of diehards. Švestka was among those they removed from the praesidium in September, and Mlynář was one of those they brought in. But Mlynář felt constrained to submit his resignation in October; and by then Smrkovský himself was meeting disfavour. Dubček and Smrkovský did their best, but the Russians were masters.

The Czechoslovak public was not informed of the full contents of the Moscow Protocol. After the shock of August some of its old caution had returned, but it still showed disquiet at such news as filtered through. Dubček's reassurances were respectfully listened to, but they carried little weight in face of events. Despite the censorship (which was in fact easier than under the Novotný regime) both writers and journalists managed to publish much that was critical of the Russians, and their unions remained active. In union terms the students had been at odds before August and they could still not settle their differences afterwards; but they did retain the spirit they had shown during the invasion. Tension built up among the public, the newsmen, and the students in November as they awaited what was expected to be a definitive statement of policy by the central committee. The government imposed travel restrictions and banned two journals, including *Reportér*. There were public demonstrations and journalists' meetings; and the students went on strike for almost a week. The upshot was a statement, somewhat general and rather conservative, that complained testily about anti-socialist forces in the period before August and called for a strengthening of the party's leading role in the future. But it was also a statement that upheld some major aspects of the action programme such as continuing rehabilitation and greater public participation in social decision-making. And *Reportér* was allowed to publish again. Popular resistance had to some extent countered Russian pressure.

It scored a further qualified success at the turn of the year. One of the many new phenomena during the invasion had been the close co-operation between the body of students and the workers' unions. After August the trade union movement took on a new lease of life. It became a federal organisation; it approved the establishment of a large number of grass-roots unions; and in general it responded to the anger of the workers. Co-operation between students and workers became commonplace. Trade unions even defended the intelligentsia against censorship. In December a rumour that Smrkovský was about to be removed from all his functions caused widespread popular protest. Many unions complained and the 900,000-strong Czech metal-workers' union threatened to go on strike, as did the students. There was a general call for Smrkovský to be made chairman of the new federal Assembly. At the beginning of January 1969 he was in fact made deputy chairman as well as chairman of the new people's chamber. Protest had once more saved something.

On the other hand, it took emotional appeals from Dubček and Smrkovský himself to prevail upon the protesters to show moderation, or else everything would be lost. What the remaining reformers most feared was a popular demonstration that would get out of hand and give the Russians a pretext to destroy both them and what little was left of the action programme. Russian troops were far too close for people to be irresponsible. On 16 January a young student, Jan Palach, heroically set himself on fire in Václav Square in a symbolic protest reminiscent of the martyrdom of Jan Hus at the hands of his people's enemies. Three days later he died. The whole country was shocked, and so was the outside world. There was a serious danger that letters and demonstrations would provoke a Russian reaction. Svoboda appealed for calm and was joined by the more responsible students. The funeral was almost a national day of mourning, but everything passed off quietly. However, there were some who saw this as the last occasion when

Dubček and the public should be allowed to jeopardise the future of Czechoslovakia.

Among those who were anxious to oust Dubček and silence the public were the diehards who had tried to displace him at the time of the invasion. They helped to organise a series of meetings during the winter that supported the intervention and called for the punishment of the more extreme reformers and the replacement of the still pro-reform government. They were actively assisted by the Soviet government, but among the public they attracted mainly hostility. The effective challenge to Dubček's position came from Husák. It was significant that he had not been arrested on the night of the invasion; but it was equally significant that he had supported the summoning of the fourteenth congress on 22 August and had flown off to Moscow to intercede for those who had been arrested. He had obviously played an important role in the bargaining around the Moscow Protocol; for instance, he had tried to prevent the meeting of the Slovak Communist Party on 26 August and he had become one of the earliest critics of the actions of the fourteenth congress, no doubt as part of the price of getting all the victims home. His subsequent attitude was similarly middle-of-the-road. He had as little as possible to do with the diehards, but he became more and more critical of Dubček and Smrkovský, the interest groups around them, and the popular mood they expressed. He neither favoured the Russians nor strongly opposed the reformers. He had been a cautious moderate before, by choice; he was now a realist, perforce. With the introduction of federalisation in January 1969 he also achieved a useful double in winning standing for himself and at least temporary satisfaction for most of the Slovaks. This meant that he was in a stronger personal political position against a weaker, mainly Czech reform movement. By the time the Palach affair was over, he was ready to displace Dubček and the unrealistic policies that he believed Dubček stood for.

The opportunity that all Dubček's opponents had been looking for came in the spring. On 28 March the Czechoslovak ice-hockey team scored the second of two victories over their Russian opponents in Stockholm. Crowds celebrated all over Czechoslovakia and attacked a number of Soviet buildings and installations. Dubček and Smrkovský condemned the demonstrations. But Grechko arrived in Prague, Husák spoke out against Dubček, and Warsaw Pact manoeuvres were announced. There were writers' and workers' meetings and student strikes, but these only led to several thousand preventive arrests. On 17 April the central committee announced that Husák was to replace Dubček as first secretary of the party and that the praesidium was to be reduced in number to exclude most of the reformers. Smrkovský was excluded and with him Šimon and Špaček. The rearguard action was virtually over.

It took only a little more direct Soviet pressure, a few more muted public protests, and some skilful manoeuvring by Dubček's opponents. At the end of May, Kriegel, Šik, and several others were removed from the central committee; and Kriegel was also expelled from the party. At the end of September Smrkovský was removed from the central committee along with Císař, Mlynář, Špaček, Hájek, and a number of others, and was also replaced as chairman of the people's chamber. Dubček was driven out of the praesidium and forced to give up the chairmanship of the Assembly that he had been given as compensation in April. Černík, who had sailed close to Husák for some time, remained premier. And the purged central committee declared that the Warsaw Pact action in August 1968 had not been aggression or occupation but a defence of socialism. In December 1969, Dubček was appointed ambassador to Turkey, and a month later he joined those of his reforming colleagues who had been pushed out of the central committee. In the same month, January 1970, Černík was demoted from the premiership and removed from the praesidium. In March and April most of those already removed from the party's inner counsels were finally expelled from the party itself; they included both Dubček and Smrkovský. The way was clear for a new twenty-year treaty between Czechoslovakia and the Soviet Union that was signed in Prague in May. In June, Dubček was deprived of his ambassadorship about the same time as Černík submitted his resignation from the government. And the following month Černík too was swept out of the party. By the middle of 1970, therefore, almost the whole reform team was completely without influence on the direction of Czechoslovakia's affairs; Czechoslovakia was inextricably linked with the Soviet Union; and the events of 1968 could be written off, and the action programme replaced with a new policy more in line with orthodox communism as spelt out by the Russians.

* * * * *

As the major reform figures were squeezed out over the period 1969-70, many minor figures were also dismissed from the party, the government, the army, or the Assembly and replaced with people who were more pliant. The screening of party members reduced its numbers from 1,400,000 to 1,100,000. Anyone of consequence who stayed abroad was deprived of his citizenship. In the period 1970-71 the purge was extended beyond formal politics to the central and local bureaucracies, public enterprises, unions of all kinds, the news media, and the universities. In May 1970 the president and six judges of the supreme court were dismissed, and the frequency of trials for anti-state activities began to increase. Accordingly, the delegates who assembled for the new fourteenth party congress in May 1971 were all opposed to reform and aware of the penalties of not being so. They were all equally aware of the limitations imposed on their deliberations and decisions by the Soviet attitude. No one could question Russia's military might or doubt that the dedicated cheering of its Warsaw Pact allies far outweighed the heretical carping of Yugoslavia or Rumania. The right of outside intervention in Czechoslovakia's affairs had first been claimed in the Warsaw letter, and it had since been refined, initially in defence of the August invasion, to be the so-called doctrine of limited sovereignty, or Brezhnev doctrine. In accordance with this, Czechoslovakia had the right to determine its own policies, but not to the detriment of socialism in its own country or elsewhere or of the world socialist movement as a whole. In October 1969 Husák led a large delegation to Moscow to reach agreement with Brezhnev on overwhelmingly the Soviet view of contemporary political and economic questions; and the friendship treaty was signed the following April. Whatever emerged at the fourteenth congress would have to be with the express approval of the Soviet Union.

First and foremost, the congress condemned all that Dubček and the action programme had stood for. Novotný's removal had been necessary, but his successors had neglected Marxism-Leninism, had allowed revisionist and opportunist forces to take over, and had therefore raised the serious danger of a counter-revolution backed by reactionary international imperialism. Fortunately, both the Soviet Union and other socialist friends had responded to the appeals of genuine Czechoslovak Communists and rightly helped to put an end to the threat to the working class everywhere and to socialism in Europe. The congress thanked its friends and its own faithful and went on to approve wholeheartedly everything Husák had done since April 1969 to cleanse the party, to restore its leading role in society, and to consolidate conditions in Czechoslovakia. Finally, it set out the objectives to be achieved by the party in the five years between 1971 and its next congress.

The first one was to strengthen and maintain the party's leading role. This meant, negatively, to prevent the emergence of non-communist political forces and non-orthodox communist factions, to obviate a repetition of 1968. Positively, it meant to indoctrinate rank-and-file members on a continuous basis so that they would remain ideologically sound themselves and provide leadership for others. The second objective was to develop the country's economy in such a way as genuinely to raise the material and cultural standard of living of the Czechoslovak people. Negatively, this implied removing the everyday complaints that instigated the action programme without letting power slip from the party's central planners. Positively, it involved increasing the output of consumer goods and at the same time improving the social services, especially housing, and the whole run of amenities from transport to recreation. Crucially it postulated improved planning and management, better usage of technology and resources, and higher productivity of labour, all of this in close co-ordination with Comecon and aimed at the eventual integration of all the socialist economies. The third objective was to rally all the political forms of the state and all social organisations to the purpose of harmonising the nationalities and aiding the *rapprochement* of the working class, the farmers, and the intelligentsia in the common pursuit of socialism. Negatively, this meant preventing one or other ethnic group from provoking a 1968-type crisis and the different social and occupational groups from demanding a pluralist society on a Western democratic model. Positively it meant reasserting the practice whereby the parliamentary institutions, the national committees, the trade union movement, and the unions of writers, journalists, youth would be used mainly as transmission belts for party policies and government orders and whereby heavy loads of propaganda would be channelled into the education system at every level. The final objective was to strengthen friendship with the Soviet Union and the other Warsaw Pact countries. On one side this was to guard against the alleged 1968 threat of Czechoslovakia leaving the Warsaw Pact; on the other, its declared intention was to promote the world revolution under the guidance of the Soviet Union.

The fifteenth congress met in April 1976 and declared itself well satisfied with the achievements of the intervening five years. From his point of view, Husák has some reason to be content. Some of the former conservatives do now enjoy position: Bil'ak, Indra, Kapek, Lenárt are members of the eleven-man party praesidium. Alongside Husák is Štrougal, who closely emulated his behaviour both before and after the invasion and who is prime minister and a member of the praesidium. Svoboda was re-elected as President in March 1973; but although a man of great courage and fundamentally a reformer, he probably exercised a declining influence on events even before ill-health forced his resignation at the age of seventy-nine in May 1975. It required a constitutional amendment to elect his successor before the completion of his term of office, but the party had no problem in ensuring either that or Husák's election to be President as well as first secretary. It was perhaps ironic that four months after Novotný's death, Husák emulated him in combining the two major political posts in communist Czechoslovakia. On the other hand, Husák (and Štrougal) have never been simple puppets in Russian hands; none of the totally discredited Novotný men have come back; and one or two members of the praesidium are fairly new to high politics. So it would be unfair to impute purely base motives or slavish attitudes to the leaders carrying out the 1971 party programme. Their record is in fact rather mixed.

There is no doubt that, particularly in comparison with 1968, the party leads the country. There are discordant voices abroad, unquiet minds at home. There are high and low officials who follow the old tradition of doing what they are told rather than what they really think, and a great part of the public has retreated into the escapism of material welfare and passing recreation. The promise of 1968 is not forgotten and its fulfilment would meet with wide acclaim. But there is no serious possibility of effective opposition. The party is in command. Yet there have so far been no show trials of the reform leaders in the pre-1968 manner. Most of them have been treated very meanly and, in common with many of the dispossessed intelligentsia, they survive rather than live in somewhat menial jobs. Smrkovský's memory has frequently been reviled since his early death in January 1974; and for complaining about police surveillance and briefly defending his past policies, Dubček has been subjected to press attacks both in Czechoslovakia and in Russia. At a lower level there have been various trials for unauthorised political activities. Obviously, at all levels, there is harassment, and police powers have been greatly increased. Yet the party may be a little more humane now than it was in the period of Gottwald and Novotný. It has learned something from 1968; and some of the credit must be due to Husák and his middle-way colleagues. The fifteenth congress offered to consider the readmission to the party of any who had not been 'active representatives' of the deviations of 1968 and who would now wholeheartedly support the sound policies of 1976.

Enormous effort, however, is being devoted to the education of the Communists themselves. Their loyalty may not be in question, but their effectiveness frequently is. Another lesson of 1968 was the ideological failure of the faithful; they could not understand, or teach, or lead, or remain faithful. Now, party members are nowhere being asked to do more by way of exhortation and leadership than in industry and agriculture. They are initiating and directing a variety of campaigns to increase the productivity of labour, measured both quantitatively and qualitatively, under the umbrella of socialist emulation. They are forming groups to save energy supplies and others to seek means of applying science to factory and farm production. Productivity is in fact said to be increasing; and the indices of industrial and agricultural production, particularly in Slovakia, are also rising. There are more consumer goods available and marked improvements in services. At the fifteenth congress Husák announced both the fulfilment of the 1971-75 five-year plan and the commencement of an equally ambitious 1976-80 plan. It is a major lesson of 1968 that the economy must be successful if the party is to survive in its leading role. And it might be fair to suggest that Husák wants Czechoslovakia to be prosperous, and wants to survive himself.

For the same political reason the economy is being centrally run. Management has an important role to play, but there is no place for market forces or workers' councils. The trade union movement has been reconsolidated, albeit on a federal basis, into eighteen massive state-wide unions. It is consulted about planning and safeguards working conditions, but it does not really participate in decision-making of any major kind. Indeed, its main functions now are to educate workers to higher production and to supplement welfare services. Unions in the cultural field are expected to do a similar job of stimulating writers, journalists, students, and youth in general to greater effort on behalf of policies decided by the party for the good of socialism in Czechoslovakia. The moral of 1968 is that interest groups must not be allowed to run the party, that, on the contrary, they must be employed to win wide support for all its policies. Husák does not intend to be faced with a 1968.

There are other signs of a return to the narrow autocracy of the pre-1968 period. Apart from those aspects of it that have been affected by the laws on federation, the 1960 constitution remains substantially unchanged. The assembly elections of November 1971 were all too reminiscent of the 1950s and sixties: 99.45 percent of the electorate turned out to vote, and 99.8 percent voted for the single list of the National Front. Federation itself was a creature of the reform period, though, as a result of Husák's influence, it inclined to the Soviet model. Czechoslovakia is a federation of two nation-states with equal rights. Its organisation is symmetrical. The federal government is responsible for foreign affairs and security and has certain economic functions. The federal Assembly comprises a chamber of the nations with 75 representatives from each state, and a chamber of the people with 200 representatives divided in accordance with nationality statistics. Constitutional changes affecting the standing of the two states require a majority of two-thirds of the representatives of each in the chamber of the nations. Each state has its separate government and national council. In theory, the system is perfect; it protects the rights of the Slovaks—and of the Czechs. In practice, however, it does not protect the two peoples against the new party autocracy since the party itself has not been federated and economic planning has become essentially the responsibility of the party-dominated federal government.

Nevertheless, the Slovaks cannot complain about their economic fate in recent years. Partly because of 1968, the 1971-75 five-year plan set out to redress the balance in favour of Slovakia, which has received more than its proportionate share of investment and is showing a more rapid rate of development than the Czech Lands. The last man to let the Slovaks have a grievance to use against him is bound to be Husák, who earlier used the same grievance against others. However, there is no question but that it is the party that rules the Slovaks, and not the opposite. Yet a question that does arise is how far the Russians rule the Czechoslovaks. In a sense they obtained in April 1969 what they failed to secure in August 1968, a government in Czechoslovakia to suit their policies and purposes. The reforms have been buried; and Czechoslovakia is now tied to Russia by two-thirds of its foreign trade and its 1970 treaty of friendship. The Czechoslovak leaders show no sign of wanting independence or pursuing different aims in either domestic or foreign policy. Yet they have won considerable economic aid from the Soviet Union to help their consumer industries, and their 1970 treaty is remarkably similar to the previous one dating from 1943 in promising respect for their sovereignty and independence and non-interference in their internal affairs. Czechoslovakia seems to have been left with some room for manoeuvre. This may now have been somewhat enlarged. One of the ostensible reasons for the Soviet invasion was to protect Czechoslovakia against West Germany, and the 1970 treaty with Russia insisted that Munich had been null and void from the start. Czechoslovakia needed the Soviet Union both to defend it and to argue for its rights. However, the entire Soviet bloc then started negotiations with West Germany in order to promote normal diplomatic and trading relations; and Czechoslovakia was permitted to join in. It was July 1974 before the Czechoslovak-German treaty was finally ratified; but it declared Munich null and voil and promised that in future the two states would abstain from force and settle their disputes by peaceful means. The development is significant. The Czechs have spent much of their history struggling with the Germans around them. In 1918 they broke free from the Austro-Germans to join the Slovaks in their own independent state. In 1938-39 Czechoslovakia was destroyed by the Nazis, but reappeared in 1945. However, even then it remained under threat of a revisionist attack, or so it was said. If, therefore, the 1974 treaty lasts—and a further agreement was signed in January 1975—it will mark the end of a vast theme in Czechoslovak history. It will also remove one of the main justifications for the Soviet treaty and the stationing of Soviet troops on Czechoslovak soil. Czechoslovakia may find itself with a little more freedom of action in the future than it anticipated. Things may have changed since 1968, and Husák and his colleagues may be aware of it.

The fact remains that the reformers did not want to take Czechoslovakia out of the Soviet bloc, that the present regime does not want to either, and that so far as can be foreseen it is an unlikely eventuality. There may be some space for semi-independent local policy-making now, and there could be slightly more in future. But reality in Czechoslovakia in the post-Dubček period is the reactionary autocracy of the party machine backed and even driven by the Soviet Union. The machine has its supporters and the regime its compensations. If the economy proves prosperous, the regime's popularity may possibly increase. From its viewpoint the first signs are hopeful. Yet it still has to solve the fundamental problem that brought down the Novotný regime: how to continue to plan intelligently, how to get a bureaucracy to make the best use of scarce resources—materials, fuel, management, labour, machinery—and how to maintain a rate of development comparable with the outside world. All the quotations currently taken from Lenin and all the experiences eagerly copied from Russia may not help. However, even if the economy prospers, the party will yet have its problems.

Prosperity is not everything. The present praesidium itself can have no immunity from divisions of opinion or personal splits; and it may have to face another movement of opinion within the party as a whole not dissimilar from the one that started the last great upheaval. The intellectuals of 1968, or their successors, will go on having ideas. The public at large may not rest content with better houses or shorter working hours. Good government is not necessarily always an acceptable substitute for self-government. The ideas and the experience of 1968 cannot just be forgotten. The Czech-Slovak problem is only partly solved so long as federation remains a rather empty sham. A single Czechoslovak nation cannot be forged from above by the party; it can come only from the habit of Czechs and Slovaks working voluntarily together as equally privileged ethnic partners. Different occupational groups cannot be removed by homogenising propaganda, and their varied interests cannot for long be denied political outlet by some party dictate. In this sense the social problem has been shelved, not solved. It may be that Husák and his colleagues have made a genuine contribution to the solution of the national and social problems in a situation in which the Russians would not allow the more rapid and far-reaching Dubček solutions to proceed. It may be that they will contribute more as conditions change and their own ideas evolve. But however that may be, the situation will not remain static.

1968 was one of the most dramatic periods in Czechoslovak history. The reformers appeared to be grafting together the best of two convergent systems of economic development and social improvement. They seemed to have the opportunity and the talent, and then suddenly were removed. It was their historical tragedy to be at the centre of an international ideological struggle. Now, and not for the first time, the Czechoslovak people are experiencing a period of reaction. Before they can emerge, the Russians may have to change; or perhaps they will find just enough room for independent adjustment. During earlier periods of reaction a new generation always emerged to cope with the post-reaction opportunity. In this connection it is interesting that the largest ten-year segment of the Czechoslovak population at present is the fifteen to twenty-four age group. 1968 was not the end, and what is following is only an interlude.

5 Czechoslovakia: General Map

Czechoslovakia frontier 1919–38
frontier {Slovakia-Ruthenia 1919–38
Czechoslovakia-Russia 1945
"historical" Bohemia-Moravia-Silesia-Slovakia
RAGUE
PRAHA)
MIA
SILESIA
Moravská Ostrava
MORAVIA
Brno
SLOVAKIA
Košice
Užhorod
RUTHENIA
Bratislava
KRAKOW
LWOW
Poland
DUKLA PASS
U.S.S.R.
Těšín
Orava
Žilina
Spiš
Liptovský
Sv.Mikuláš
R.Váh
Poprad
Prešov
R. Hornád
Ružomberok
Krompachy
KOŠICE
Banská
Bystrica
Podbrezová
Rožňava
Užhorod
Čierna
nad Tisou
Zvolen
R. Hron
Banská
Štiavnica
R.Tisa
R.Tisza
BUDAPEST
Romania
ngary

Reading List

(in English, Czech, and Slovak only)

There is no outstanding general history of the Czechs and Slovaks in English. A sensible historical, geographical survey is to be found in:

Wanklyn, H., *Czechoslovakia,* New York, N.Y., 1954.

An ageing but worthy book is:

Seton-Watson, R.W., *History of the Czechs and the Slovaks,* London, 1943;

and a recent but uneven collection of essays is:

Rechcigl, M. (ed.), *Czechoslovakia Past and Present,* 2v., The Hague, 1968.

Two fairly orthodox Czechoslovak Communist surveys, one long, the other a single volume, are:

Macek, J. (*et al.*), *Přehled československých dějin,* 4v., Praha, 1960,

Husa, V., *Dějiny Československa,* Praha, 1961;

and a useful compendium of factual information and a thoughtful set of essays are:

Buchvaldek, M. (*et al.*), *Dějiny Československa v datech,* Praha, 1968,

Graus, F. (*et al.*), *Naše živá i mrtvá minulost,* Praha, 1968.

The coverage of Czechoslovak history since 1848 is uneven, both in English and in Czech and Slovak. The original material is remarkably plentiful (though only some memoirs are listed here). Articles are important and are to be found *particularly* in the following:

Slavonic Review
Slavic Review
Canadian Slavonic Papers
Journal of Central European Affairs
Historica
Studia historica Slovaca
Československý časopis historický
Historický časopis
Revue dějin socialismu

However, the only articles cited below are those in English which are reasonably important or which cover points inadequately or not all dealt with in monographs. For want of suitable alternatives, some of those listed have to be rather partisan. The books mentioned are mostly recent and have been chosen for further study and to represent sometimes radically different points of view.

Economic and Social History

Kučera, M. (*et al.*), *Atlas obyvatelstva ČSSR*, Praha, 1962.

Svetoň, J., *Obyvatel'stvo Slovenska za kapitalizmu*, Bratislava, 1958.

Státní statistický úřad, *Hospodářský a společenský vývoj Československa*, Praha, 1968.

Olšovský, R. (ed.), *Stručný hospodářský vývoj Československa do r. 1955*, Praha, 1969.

Průcha, V. (*et al.*), *Hospodářské dějiny Československa v 19. a 20. století*, Praha, 1974.

Purš, J., 'The Industrial Revolution in the Czech Lands', *Historica*, II.

Purš, J. 'The Situation of the Working Class in the Czech Lands in the Phase of the Expansion and Completion of the Industrial Revolution 1849-1873', *Historica*, VI.

Carter, F.W., 'The Industrial Development of Prague 1800-1850', *Slavonic Review*, April 1973.

Havránek, J., 'Social Classes, Nationality Ratios and Demographic Trends in Prague 1880-1900', *Historica*, XIII.

Reiman, P. (*et al.*), *Otázky vývoje kapitalismu v českých zemích a v Rakousku - Uhersku do r. 1918*, Praha, 1957.

Olšovský, R. (*et al.*), *Přehled hospodářského vývoje Československa v l. 1918-1945*, Praha, 1961.

Basch, A., *The Danube Basin and the German Economic Sphere*, London, 1944.

Lehár, B., 'The Economic Expansion of the Bat'a Concern in Czechoslovakia and Abroad 1929-1938', *Historica*, V.

César, J., *Revoluční hnutí na venkově v českých zemích v letech 1918-1922*, Praha, 1971.

Lacina, V., *Krize československého zemědělství 1928-1934*, Praha, 1974.

Teichova, A., *An Economic Background to Munich*, Cambridge, 1974.

Král, V., *Otázky hospodářského a sociálního vývoje v českých zemích 1938-1945*, Praha, 1957-59.

Bernášek, M., 'Czechoslovak Planning 1945-48', *Soviet Studies*, 1970.

Bernášek, M., 'The Czechoslovak Economic Recession 1962-65', *Soviet Studies*, 1969.

Brada, J.C., 'The Czechoslovak Economic Recession 1962-65: Comment', *Soviet Studies,* 1971.
Holesovsky, V., 'Planning Reforms in Czechoslovakia', *Soviet Studies,* 1968.
Otáhal, M., *Zápas o pozemkovou reformu v ČSR,* Praha, 1963
Anderson, P.E., 'New Directions in Czechoslovak Agricultural Policy under Novotný', *Slavic Review,* 1962.
Kalvoda, J., 'Soviet-style Agricultural Reform in Czechoslovakia', *Journal of Central European Affairs,* 1962-63.
Krejčí, J., *Social Change and Stratification in Postwar Czechoslovakia,* London, 1972.
Machonin, P. (ed.), *Sociální struktura socialistické společnosti,* Praha, 1967.
Kempný, J.(*et al.*), *Development of the Czechoslovak Economy,* Praha, 1974.

To circa 1918
Kann, R.A., *The Multinational Empire: Nationalism and National Reform in the Habsburg Monarchy 1848-1918,* New York, N.Y., 1950.
Krofta, K., *Byli jsme za Rakouska,* Praha, 1936.
Pech, S.Z., *The Czech Revolution of 1848,* Durham, N.C., 1969.
Pech, S.Z., 'Czech Political Parties in 1848', *Canadian Slavonic Papers,* 1973.
Červinka, F., *Český nacionalismus v XIX století,* Praha, 1965.
Havránek, J., 'The Development of Czech Nationalism', *Austrian History Yearbook,* 1967.
Mann, S.E., 'Karel Havlíček: a Slav Pragmatist', *Slavonic Review,* June 1961.
Thomas, T.I.V., 'Karel Havlíček and the Constitutional Question 1849-1851', *Slavonic Review,* October 1974.
Zacek, J.F., *Palacký,* The Hague, 1970.
Jetmarová, M., *František Palacký,* Praha, 1961.
Plaschka, R.G., 'The Political Significance of Frantisek Palacky', *Journal of Contemporary History,* 1973.
Kimball, S.B., 'The Prague "Slav Congress" of 1868', *Journal of Central European Affairs,* 1962-63.
Odložilík, O., 'Russia and Czech National Aspirations', *Journal of Central European Affairs,* 1962-63.
Bradley, J.F.N., 'Czech Nationalism in the Light of French Diplomatic Reports 1867-1914', *Slavonic Review,* December 1963.
Pech, S.Z., 'F.L. Rieger: The Road from Liberalism to Conservatism', *Journal of Central European Affairs,* 1957-58.
Pech, S.Z., 'Passive Resistance of the Czechs 1863-1879', *Slavonic Review,* June 1958.

Winters, S.B., 'The Young Czech Party (1874-1914): An Appraisal', *Slavic Review*, 1969.
Garver, B.M., 'The Reorientation of Czech Politics in the 1890's', *Conférence internationale du 50ᵉ anniversaire de la République Tchècoslovaque - Communications*, Praha, 1968.
Bradley, J. 'Czech Nationalism and Socialism in 1905', *Slavic Review*, 1960.
Bradley, J., 'Czech Pan-Slavism before the First World War', Slavonic *Review*, December 1961.
Polišenský, J. (*et al.*), *Začiatky českej a slovenskej emigrácie do U.S.A.*, Bratislava, 1970.
Čapek, K., *President Masaryk tells his Story*, London, 1934.
Betts, R.R., 'Masaryk's Philosophy of History', *Slavonic Review*, November 1947.
Szporluk, R., 'Masaryk's Idea of Democracy', *Slavonic Review*, December 1962.
Valiani, L., *The End of Austria-Hungary*, London, 1973.
Zeman, Z.A.B., *The Break-up of the Habsburg Empire 1914-1918*, London, 1961.
Hanak, H., *Great Britain and Austria-Hungary during the First World War*, London, 1962.
Pichlík, K., *Zahraniční odboj 1914-1918 bez legend*, Praha, 1968.
Masaryk, T.G., *The Making of a State*, London, 1927.
Seton-Watson, R.W., *Masaryk in England*, Cambridge, 1943.
Unterberger, B.M., 'The Arrest of Alice Masaryk', *Slavic Review*, 1974.
Kozák, J.B., *T.G. Masaryk a vznik Washingtonské deklarace v říjnu 1918*, Praha, 1968.
Beneš, E., *My War Memoirs*, London, 1928.
Kárník, Z., *Habsburk, Masaryk ci Šmeral?*, Praha, 1968.
Bradley, J., *Allied Intervention in Russia 1917-1920*, London, 1968.

To circa 1945

Macartney, C.A. and Palmer, A.W., *Independent Eastern Europe*, London, 1962.
Kerner, R.J. (ed.), *Czechoslovakia*, Berkeley, Calif., 1940.
Olivová, V. and Kvaček, R., *Dějiny Československa od r. 1918 do r. 1945*, Brno, 1967.
Mamatey, V.S., and Luža, R. (eds.), *A History of the Czechoslovak Republic 1918-1948*, Princeton, N.J., 1973.
Perman, D., *The Shaping of the Czechoslovak State*, Leiden, 1962.
Krofta, K., *Z dob naší první republiky*, Praha, 1939.
Olivová, V., *The Doomed Democracy*, London, 1972.
Táborský, E., *Czechoslovak Democracy at Work*, London, 1945.

Táborský, E., 'Local Government in Czechoslovakia 1918-1948', *Slavic Review,* 1951.
Skilling, H.G., 'The Formation of a Communist Party in Czechoslovakia', *Slavic Review,* 1955.
Skilling, H.G., 'The Comintern and Czechoslovak Communism 1921-1929', *Slavic Review,* 1960.
Skilling, H.G., 'Gottwald and the Bolshevisation of the Communist Party of Czechoslovakia 1929-1939', *Slavic Review,* 1961.
Wiskemann, E., *Czechs and Germans,* London, 1938.
César, J. and Černý, B., 'German Irredentist Putsch in the Czech Lands after the First World War', *Historica,* III.
César, J. and Černý, B., 'The Nazi Fifth Column in Czechoslovakia', *Historica,* IV.
César, J. and Černý, B., 'The Policy of the German Activist Parties in Czechoslovakia 1918-1939', *Historica,* VI.
Kvaček, R., *Nad evropou zataženo,* Praha, 1966.
Gajanová, A., *ČSR a středoevropská politika velmocí 1918-1938,* Praha, 1967.
Bruegel, J.W., *Czechoslovakia Before Munich: The German Minority Problem and British Appeasement Policy,* London, 1973.
Mackenzie, C., *Dr. Beneš,* London, 1946.
Wallace, W.V., 'An Appraisal of Edvard Beneš as a Statesman', *Historical Studies,* 1971.
Weinberg, G.L., 'Secret Hitler-Beneš Negotiations in 1936-37', *Journal of Central European Affairs,* 1959-60.
Wallace, W.V., 'The Foreign Policy of President Beneš in the Approach to Munich', *Slavonic Review,* December 1960.
Wallace, W.V., 'The Making of the May Crisis of 1938', *Slavonic Review,* June 1963.
Kvaček, R., *Osudná mise,* Praha, 1958.
Lvová, M., *Mnichov a Edvard Beneš,* Praha, 1968.
Beneš, E., *Mnichovské dny: paměti,* Praha, 1968.
Ripka, H., *Munich: Before and After,* London, 1939.
Král, V., *Politické strany a Mnichov,* Praha, 1961.
Procházka, T., 'The Delimitation of Czechoslovak-German Frontiers after Munich', *Journal of Central European Affairs,* 1961-62.
Lukeš, F., *Podivný mír,* Praha, 1968.
Beneš, E., *Memoirs: From Munich to New War and New Victory,* London, 1954.
Křen, J., *Do emigrace,* Praha, 1963.
Lockhart, R.H.B., *Comes the Reckoning,* London, 1947.
Král, V., 'The Policy of Germanisation enforced in Bohemia and Moravia during the Second World War', *Historica,* II.

Mastny, V., *The Czechs under Nazi Rule,* New York, N.Y., 1971.
Luža, R., *The Transfer of the Sudeten Germans,* London, 1964.
Bareš, G. (*et al.*), *Odboj a revoluce 1938-1945,* Praha, 1965.
Táborský, E., 'Beneš and Stalin - Moscow, 1943 and 1945', *Journal of Central European Affairs,* 1953-54.
Mastny, V., 'The Beneš-Stalin-Molotov Conversations in December 1943: New Documents', *Jahrbücher für Geschichte Östeuropas,* 1972.
Červinková, M., 'Views and Diplomatic Activity of Dr. Edvard Beneš in the Period of Preparation for the Czechoslovak-Soviet Treaty of 1943', *Historica,* XVIII.

Since circa 1945
Fejtö, F., *A History of the People's Democracies,* London, 1971.
Kořalka, J., *Co je národ,* Praha, 1969.
Wallace, W.V., 'Continuity in the Development of Czechoslovakia', *International Affairs,* January 1969.
Zinner, P.E., *Communist Strategy and Tactics in Czechoslovakia 1918-48,* London, 1963.
Korbel, J., *The Communist Subversion of Czechoslovakia 1938-1948,* Princeton, N.J., 1959.
Skilling, H.G., 'Revolution and Continuity in Czechoslovakia 1945-1946', *Journal of Central European Affairs,* 1960-61.
Lacina, V. (ed.), *Československa revoluce v 1. 1944-1948,* Praha, 1966.
Diamond, W., *Czechoslovakia between East and West,* London, 1947.
Kaplan, K., *Znárodnění a socialismus,* Praha, 1968.
Opat, J., *O novou demokracii,* Praha, 1966.
Kaplan, K., 'On the Role of Dr. E. Beneš in February 1948', *Historica,* V.
Belda, J. (*et al.*), *Na rozhraní dvou epoch,* Praha, 1968.
Ripka, H., *Czechoslovakia Enslaved,* London, 1950.
Smutný, J., *Únorový převrat 1948,* London, 1955-57.
Sychrava, L., *Svědectví a úvahy o pražském převratu v únoru 1948,* London, 1952.
Král, V., *Cestou k Únoru,* Praha, 1963.
Táborský, E., *Communism in Czechoslovakia 1948-1960,* Princeton, N.J., 1961.
Skilling, H.G., 'People's Democracy, the Proletarian Dictatorship and the Czechoslovak Path to Socialism', *Slavic Review,* 1951.
Kaplan, K., *Utváření generální linie výstavby socialismu v Československu,* Praha, 1966.
Pelikán, J., *The Czechoslovak Political Trials, 1950-1954,* London, 1971.

Kubát, D., 'Patterns of Leadership in a Communist State: Czechoslovakia 1946-1958', *Journal of Central European Affairs,* 1961-62.
Kalvoda, J., 'Czechoslovakia's Socialist Constitution', *Slavic Review,* 1961.
Holotík, L., *Nemecká otázka a Československo,* Bratislava, 1962.
Brown, A.H., 'Pluralistic Trends in Czechoslovakia', *Soviet Studies,* 1966.
Golan, G., 'Antonin Novotny: the Sources and Nature of his Power', *Canadian Slavonic Papers,* 1972.
Skilling, H.G., 'The Fall of Novotny in Czechoslovakia', *Canadian Slavonic Papers,* 1970.
Golan, G., *The Czechoslovak Reform Movement,* Cambridge, 1971.
Kusin, V.V., *The Intellectual Origins of the Prague Spring,* Cambridge, 1971.
Kusin, V.V., *Political Grouping in the Czechoslovak Reform Movement,* London, 1972.
Hamšik, D., *Writers against Rulers,* London, 1971.
Selucký, R., *Czechoslovakia: The Plan that Failed,* London, 1970.
Jancar, B.W., *Czechoslovakia and the Absolute Monopoly of Power,* New York, N.Y., 1971.
Shawcross, W., *Dubček,* London, 1970.
Schwartz, H., *Prague's 200 Days,* London, 1969.
James, R.R., *The Czechoslovak Crisis 1968,* London, 1969.
Windsor, P. and Roberts, A., *Czechoslovakia 1968,* London, 1969.
Remington, R.A. (ed.), *Winter in Prague,* Cambridge, Mass., 1969.
Pelikán, J., *The Secret Vysočany Congress,* London, 1969.
Tigrid, P., *Why Dubček Fell,* London, 1969.
Golan, G., *Reform Rule in Czechoslovakia,* Cambridge, 1973.
Zartman, I.W., *Czechoslovakia: Intervention and Impact,* New York, N.Y., 1970.
Czerwinski, E.J., and Piekalkiewicz, *The Soviet Invasion of Czechoslovakia: Its Effects on Eastern Europe,* New York, N.Y., 1972.
For fuller reading see Parrish, M., *The 1968 Czechoslovak Crisis: A Bibliography,* Santa Barbara, Calif., 1971.

Slovakia
Mésároš, J. (*et al.*), *Dejiny Slovenska,* Bratislava, 1968.
Seton-Watson, R.W. (ed.), *Slovakia Then and Now,* London, 1931.
Holotík, L., 'Slovak Politics in the 19th century', *Studia historica Slovaca,* V.
Rapant, D., 'Slovak Politics in 1848-1849', *Slavonic Review,* December 1948 and May 1949.
Auty, R., 'Jan Kollár, 1793-1852', *Slavonic Review,* December 1952.

Mésároš, J. (ed.), *Matica slovenská v našich dejinách,* Bratislava, 1963.
Lipták, L., *Slovensko v 20. storočí,* Bratislava, 1968.
Macartney, C.A., *Hungary and her Successors,* London, 1937.
Toma, P.A., 'The Slovak Soviet Republic of 1919', *Slavic Review,* 1958.
Plevza, V., 'The Agrarian Question in Slovakia in the Czechoslovak Republic prior to the Munich Agreement', *Studia historica Slovaca,* II.
Stanek, K., *Zrada a pád,* Praha, 1958.
Kirschbaum, J.M., *Slovakia,* New York, N.Y., 1960.
Jablonický, J., *Slovensko na prelome,* Bratislava, 1965.
Jablonický, J., *Z ilegality do povstania,* Bratislava, 1969.
Holotík, L. (ed.), *Slovenské národné povstanie r. 1944,* Bratislava, 1965.
Toma, P.A., 'Soviet Strategy in the Slovak uprising of 1944', *Journal of Central European Affairs,* 1959-60.
Steiner, E., *The Slovak Dilemma,* Cambridge, 1973.
Grospič, J. (ed.), *Constitutional Foundations of the Czechoslovak Federation,* Praha, 1973.

Index

Index references to individual countries (e.g., Germany or Rumania) are mainly confined to instances involving actions or attitudes affecting Czechoslovakia. Citing of a country in the index may refer to what appears in the text as its government, or people, or capital. There are no references to extensively used names such as Czechoslovakia itself or Austria-Hungary, or to geographical place-names.